# Hockey's Greatest Drills
## for
## Great Practices

**Tom Carroll**

Carroll, Tom
Hockey's Greatest Drills for Great Practices / Tom Carroll
ISBN  0-9719120-0-9

Copyright 2002 by Tom Carroll

All rights reserved. Except for use in a review, the reproduction or utilization of this work in any form by any electronic, mechanical, or other means, now known or hereafter invented, including xerography, photocopying, and recording, and in any information storage and retrieval system, is forbidden without the written permission of the author/publisher.

Photo Credits:
Cover Shot             Bruce Bennett Studios

Text Photos:          Dave Eggen and Dick Carlson
                      Inertia Pro Event Imaging
                      PO Box 91133
                      Sioux Falls, SD 57109-9011
                      www.fallsevents.com

                      United States Hockey League (USHL)

                      Gustavus Adolphus College

                      Mr. Mike Thill

                      Let's Play Hockey

                      Danville Wings

Cindy and Jessica, thank you for your support, guidance, inspiration and motivation. I truly appreciate all of your many sacrifices, understanding and unwavering support.

## Table of Contents

| Chapter | Title and Drill Number | Pages |
|---|---|---|
|  | Acknowledgments | |
|  | Introduction | |
| Chapter 1 | Everyday Skills and Concepts<br>*Drills 1-22* | 1-45 |
| Chapter 2 | Team Drills<br>*Drills 23-50* | 47-103 |
| Chapter 3 | Even Numbered Attacks<br>*Drills 51-69* | 105-143 |
| Chapter 4 | Odd Numbered Attacks<br>*Drills 70-90* | 145-187 |
| Chapter 5 | Special Teams<br>*Drills 91-99* | 189-207 |
| Chapter 6 | Drills for Forwards and Scoring<br>*Drills 100-113* | 209-237 |
| Chapter 7 | Defensemen Specific Drills<br>*Drills 114-128* | 239-269 |
| Chapter 8 | Specialized Goaltender Drills<br>*Drills 129-144* | 271-303 |
| Chapter 9 | Fun and Games<br>*Drills 145-159* | 305-335 |
| Chapter 10 | Sample Practices | 337 |
|  | Drill Locator | |
|  | About the Author | |

# Acknowledgments

I would like to thank all of my many mentors, colleagues, former coaches and former players that have contributed to this book. I would also like to thank the countless teams, coaches and hockey people, who shared their ideas, insights and passion for the game of hockey that inspired this project.

I would lastly like to acknowledge the contribution of Jeffrey G. Nix. Without his technical expertise this project would not have been possible.

# Introduction

Why to we practice? Why are countless hours and literally thousands of dollars spent on practice sessions? Very simply, because individuals possess the capacity to continue their learning and increase their physical and mental development. It is the ability and desire for that improvement that often separates good players from the great and average teams from champions.

As individuals, we practice to improve on the fundamentals of the game of hockey. As a team, we practice to improve team performance.
***Hockey's Greatest Drills for Great Practices*** is designed to provide the instructional tools and the challenges necessary to improve each and every aspect of the game. From individual skill development drills stressing the fundamentals, to team concept drills designed to improve team performance, to position specific drills, it is all here in ***Hockey's Greatest Drills for Great Practices***!

***Hockey's Greatest Drills for Great Practices*** is a compilation of drills used in NHL, NCAA Division 1, US Select Team, Junior, Prep School and youth hockey practices. These drills are proven to develop players and to improve team performance at all levels.

Use the drills and practice methods that the professionals use, ***Hockey's Greatest Drills for Great Practices*** will enable coaches to maximize ice time and to develop players and teams to their highest levels! Keep your practices interesting, challenging and full of enthusiasm. Whether you follow the sample practice suggestions or design your own, ***Hockey's Greatest Drills for Great Practices*** is the ultimate book for all levels of hockey!

Photo courtesy of Mike Thill

# 1

## Everyday Skills and Concepts

This chapter focuses on the fundamentals of the game of hockey. That is, skating, passing and shooting. The drills that follow in this section are designed to be incorporated in everyday practice routines. Each practice should have structured warm-up time to adequately prepare each member of the team to maximize their experience. Teams should take advantage of off ice areas in their facilities to stretch and prepare for the practice session. Arrive in plenty of time to stretch, dress and review practice session goals and objectives in order to maximize the ice session.

This section includes various goaltender warm-up drills, several drills designed to improve skating concepts as well as unique drills designed to improve the passing and shooting skills of your team members. More often, these drills are incorporated in the beginning of practice but be creative, do not limit the skill development portion of your practice to fresh ice and fresh players. After all, games usually are decided late and on poor ice. Prepare your team and team members to perform at high levels when they are both tired and skating on poor ice.

# 1 Chaos

## Emphasis and Objective

Warm-up goalies with a number of shots at different angles.

## Drill Set-Up

- Goalies in net.
- F's and D's in four lines at one end with pucks.
- On 1st whistle, one player from each line takes off and enters the neutral zone with puck. All 4 skate in the neutral zone at full speed, handling the puck and avoiding the other players.
- On the coaches 2nd whistle, the 4 players attack the blue-line positioning themselves for a shot.
- Shots must come from all 4 lanes and in appropriate sequence. Players communicate and stagger their attack.
- On whistle, another group of 4 take off and repeat.

## Key Teaching Points

- Keep feet moving.
- Head up at all times.
- Handle puck in confined area.
- Shoot in stride.
- Shots at 4 varied angles.
- Rebound control.

## Recommended Progressions

- None.

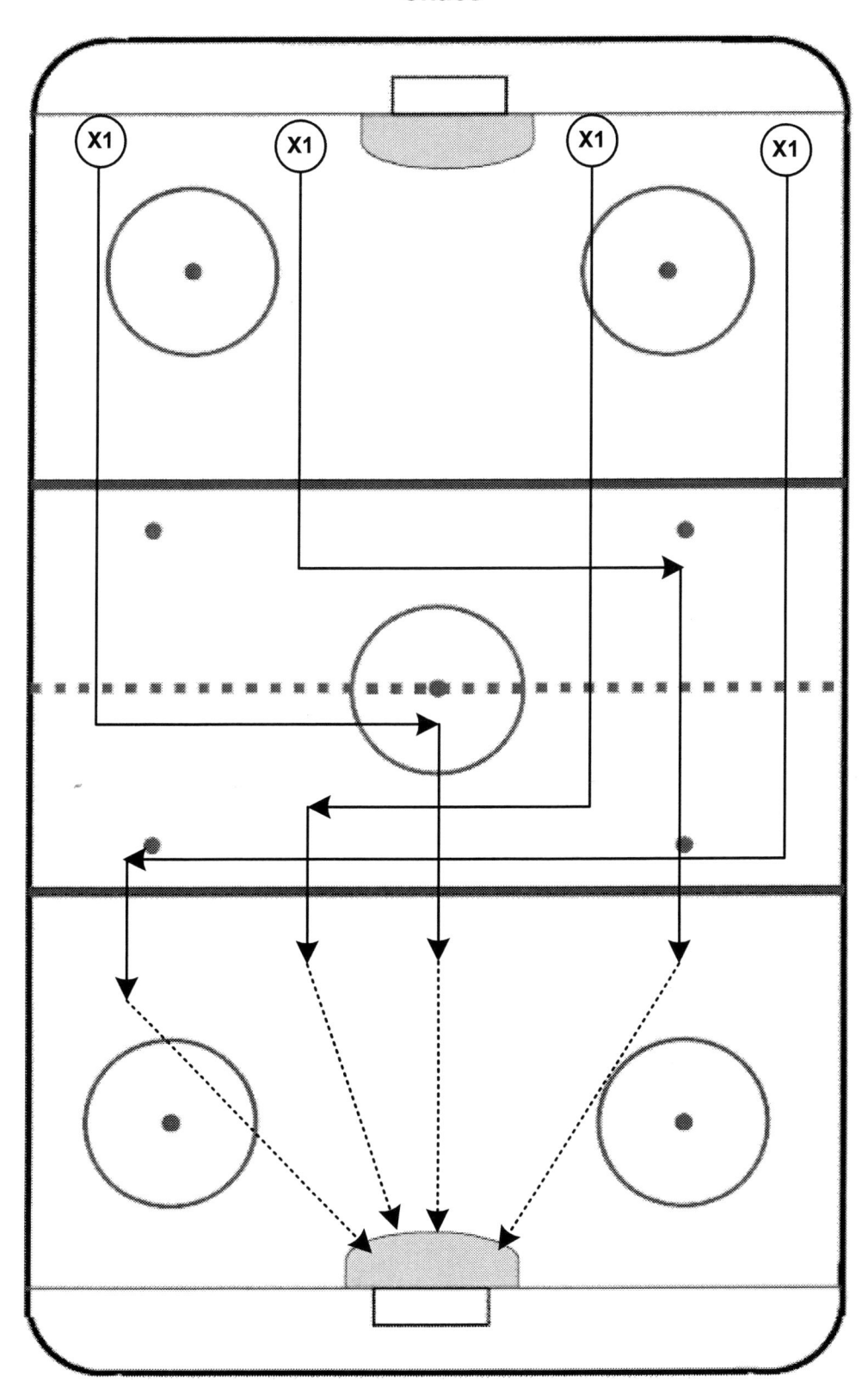

# Chaos

## 2    Quick-Up Shooting

### Emphasis and Objective

Shooting drill emphasizing timing and quick passes.

### Drill Set-Up

* X1 and X2 take off down boards, X1 curls toward the boards at the far neutral zone face-off spot and streaks to the middle ice, X2 receives a pass from X3 and immediately hits a breaking X1 who proceeds to a shot.
* X2, after making the pass, makes a deep curl toward the boards at the neutral zone face-off spot, streaks to the middle and receives a pass from X1 proceeding to a shot.
* On the whistle, X3 and X4 take off and perform a similar action.

### Key Teaching Points

* Emphasize timing.
* Create good passing angles.
* Keep feet moving.
* Handle crisp passes.

### Recommended Progressions

* None.

# Quick-Up Shooting

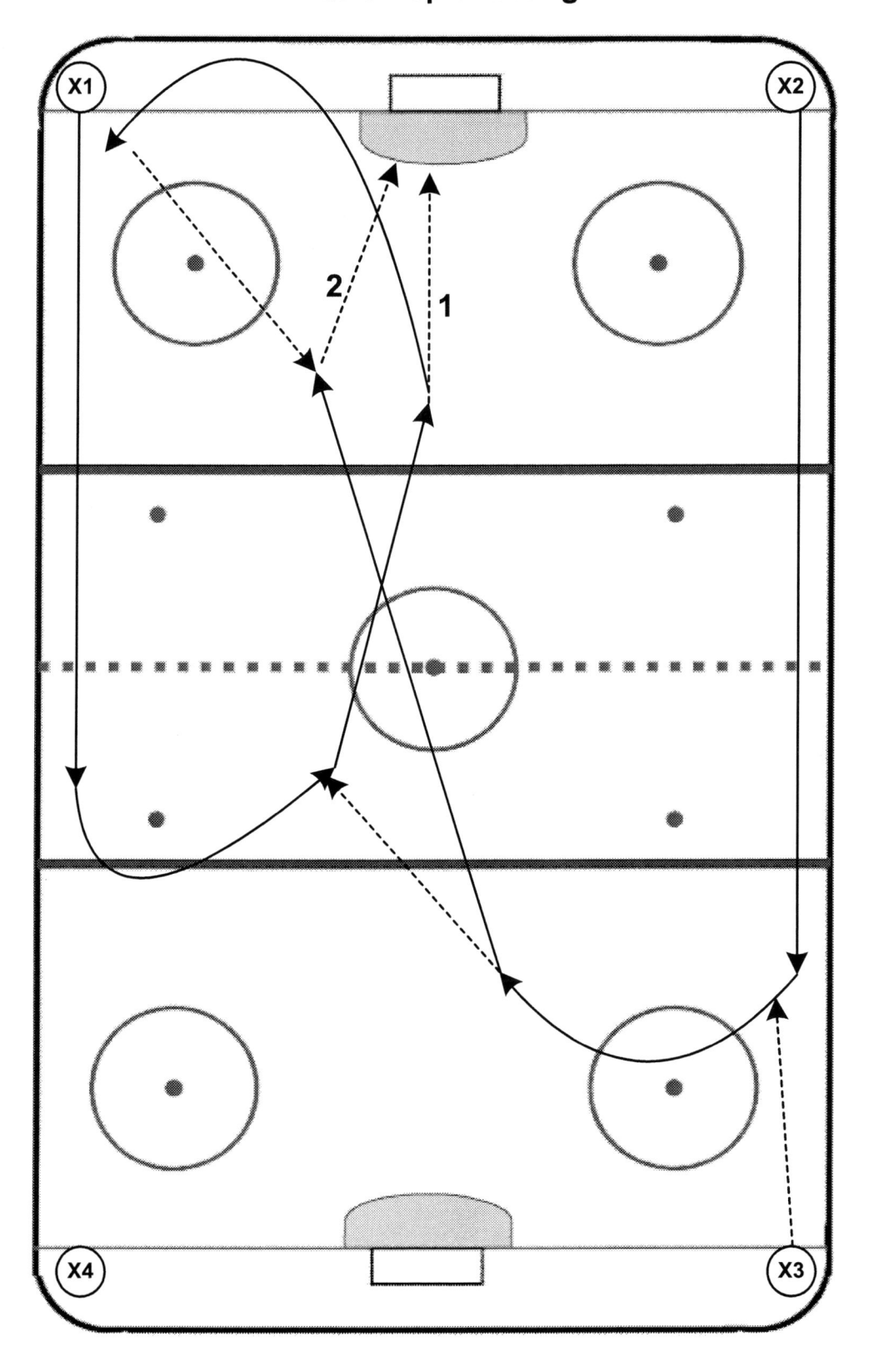

# 3 | Round the Horn 2 v 0

## Emphasis and Objective
Passing and shooting in stride.

## Drill Set-Up
* Players in 4 lines on each blue-line (X1, X2, X3, X4) with pucks.
* X1 passes to X3, X1 follows puck, X3 passes to X4 who joins X1 for a 2 v 0 rush.
* At the same time, X4 passes to X2, X4 follows puck, X2 passes to X1 who joins X4 for a 2 v 0 rush.

## Key Teaching Points
* Make good passes.
* Shots from outside.
* Non shooter drive the net.

## Recommended Progressions
* 2 v 1.

# 2 v 0 Round the Horn

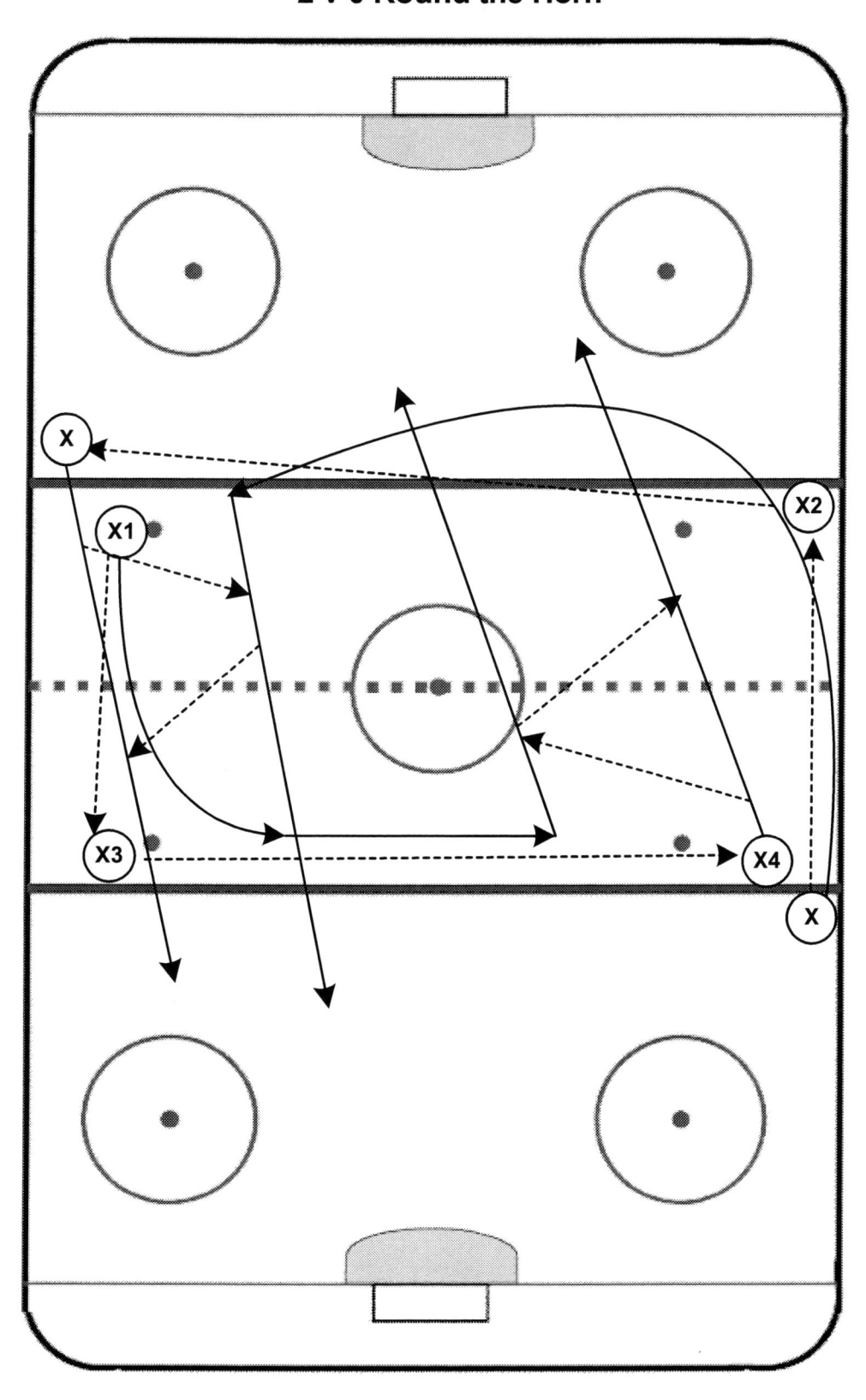

# 4   4 D Pass and Shoot

## Emphasis and Objective

Warm-up drill incorporating passing, receiving and shooting.

## Drill Set-Up

* D in 4 groups, one on each neutral zone face-off dot. F's in 4 groups on each side of blue-line.
* F's and D's in four lines at one end with pucks.
* On 1st whistle, F1 and F3 pass to D1 and D3. Each D pair make 3 D-D passes while F's skate wide behind the D looking for a return pass. Both F's shoot on goal.
* On the coaches 2nd whistle, F's in opposite lines perform a similar action.

## Key Teaching Points

* Good, hard passes.
* Keep feet moving.
* Change speeds of attack.
* Shoot in stride

## Recommended Progressions

* None.

**4D Pass and Shoot**

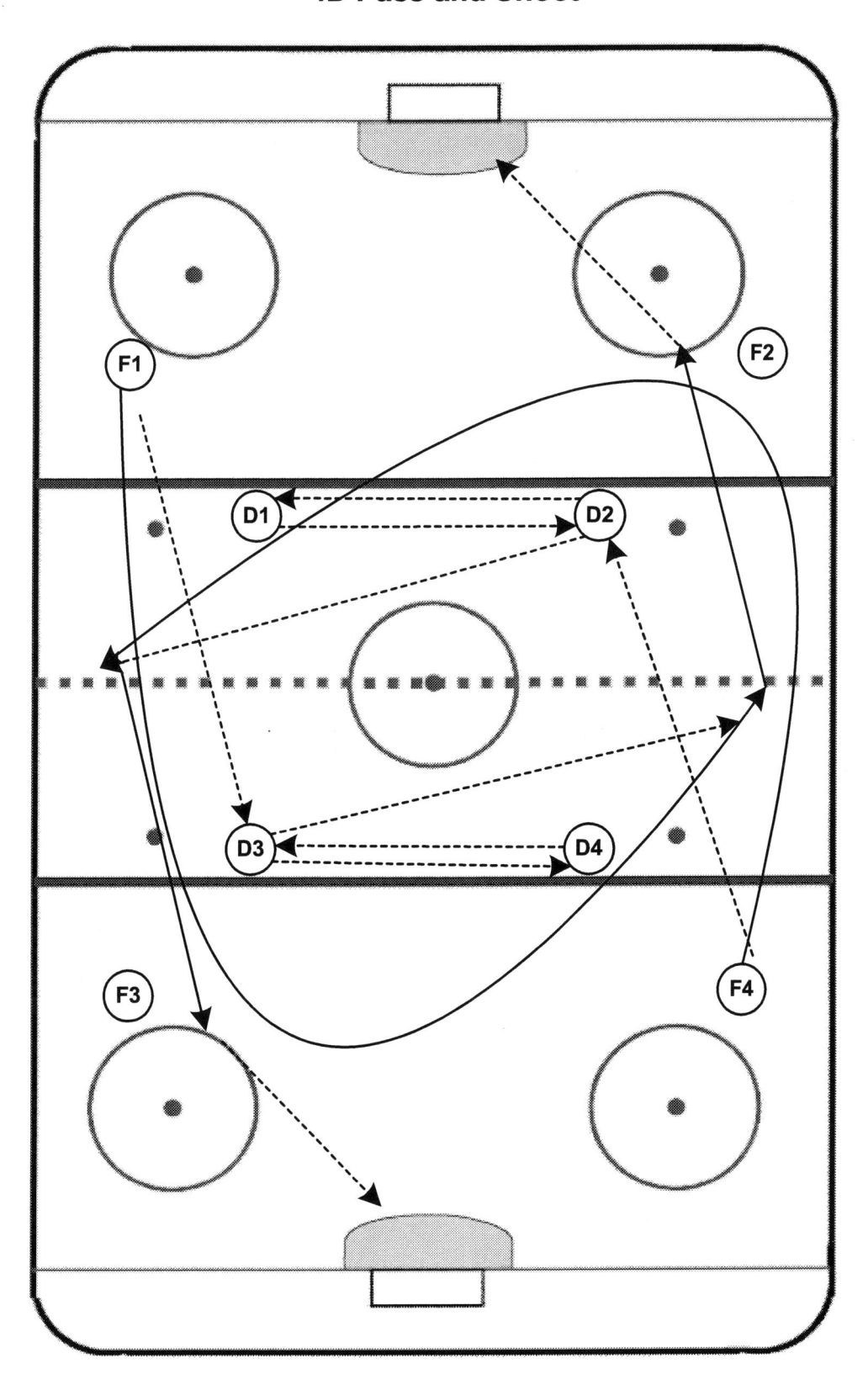

# 5     Double 1 Touch Shooting

## Emphasis and Objective

Work on 1 touch passing and shooting in stride.

## Drill Set-Up

* Players line up at opposite blue-lines with pucks.
* One line at a time.
* X1 and X2 break up the boards, X1 breaks over the far blue-line and passes to X3 while following the pass up the far boards, X2 curls around the center circle.
* X3, 1 touch passes puck to X2 in the center, X2, 1 touches passes to a breaking X1 who proceeds to a shot.
* Switch sides.

## Key Teaching Points

* Keep feet moving.
* Work on timing.
* 1 touch passing.
* Shoot in stride.

## Recommended Progressions

* Have shooters perform different shots from different locations on ice.

# Double 1 - Touch

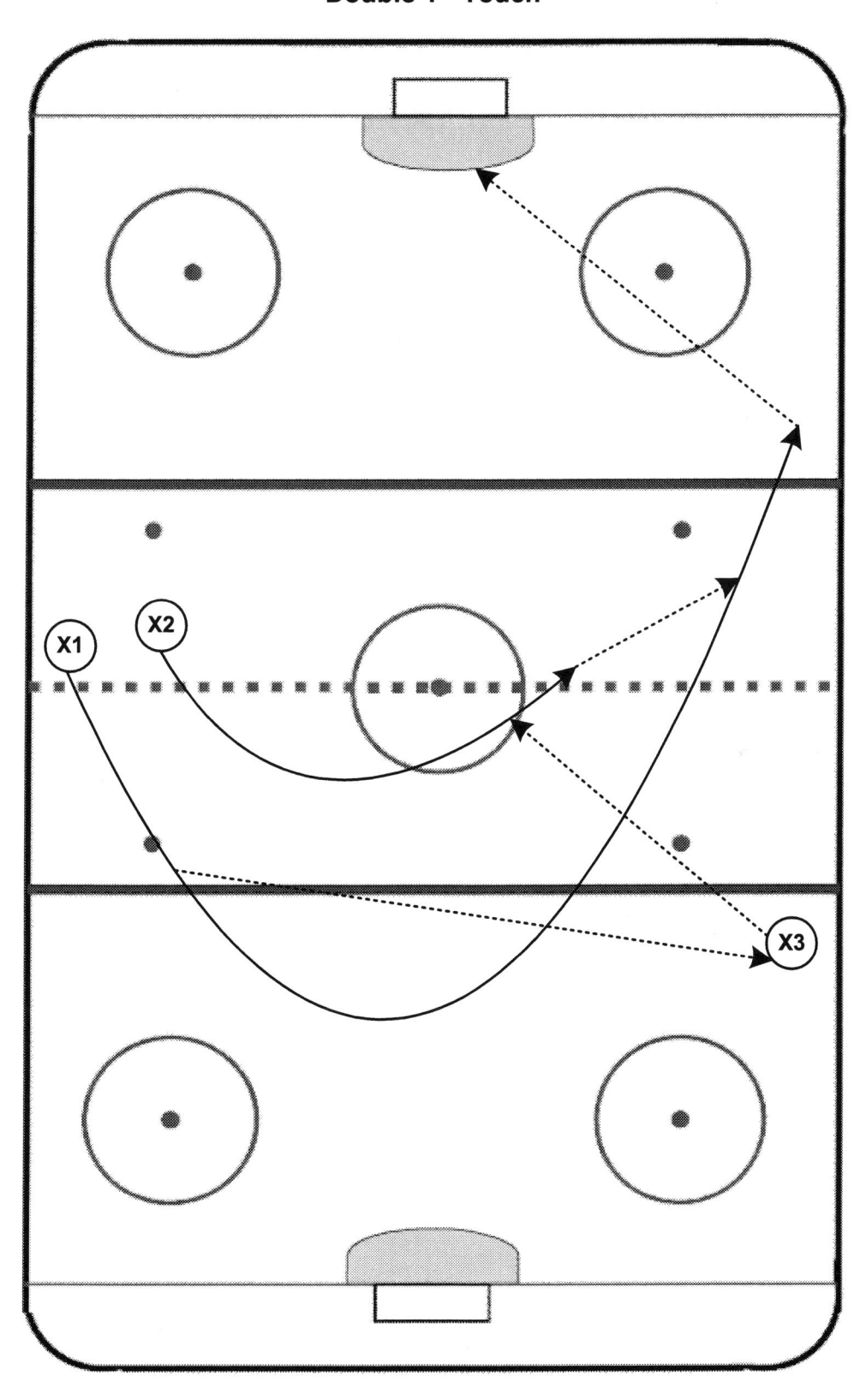

# 6 — 1 v 0, 2 v 0, 3 v 0, 3 Shot Warm-up

## Emphasis and Objective
Warm-up goalies using maximum of players and skills.

## Drill Set-Up
* Players divide into 5 groups, 1 group in each corner and 1 on the red-line.
* X1, on the red-line skates through the neutral zone and fires a shot on net.
* After the shot, he swings to the far corner and partners with X3 and they proceed up the ice for a 2 v 0 followed by a shot from the blue-line.
* After the shot, X1 and X3 swing to the far corner and join X5 for a full ice 3 v 0 rush. Shot is taken inside the blue-line.
* X1 repeats the drill only to swing to the opposite corners.

## Key Teaching Points
* Shots from outside, goalie warm-up.
* Support the puck.
* Good passes.
* Alternate lines.

## Recommended Progressions
* None.

**1 v 0, 2 v 0, 3 v 0, 3 Shots**

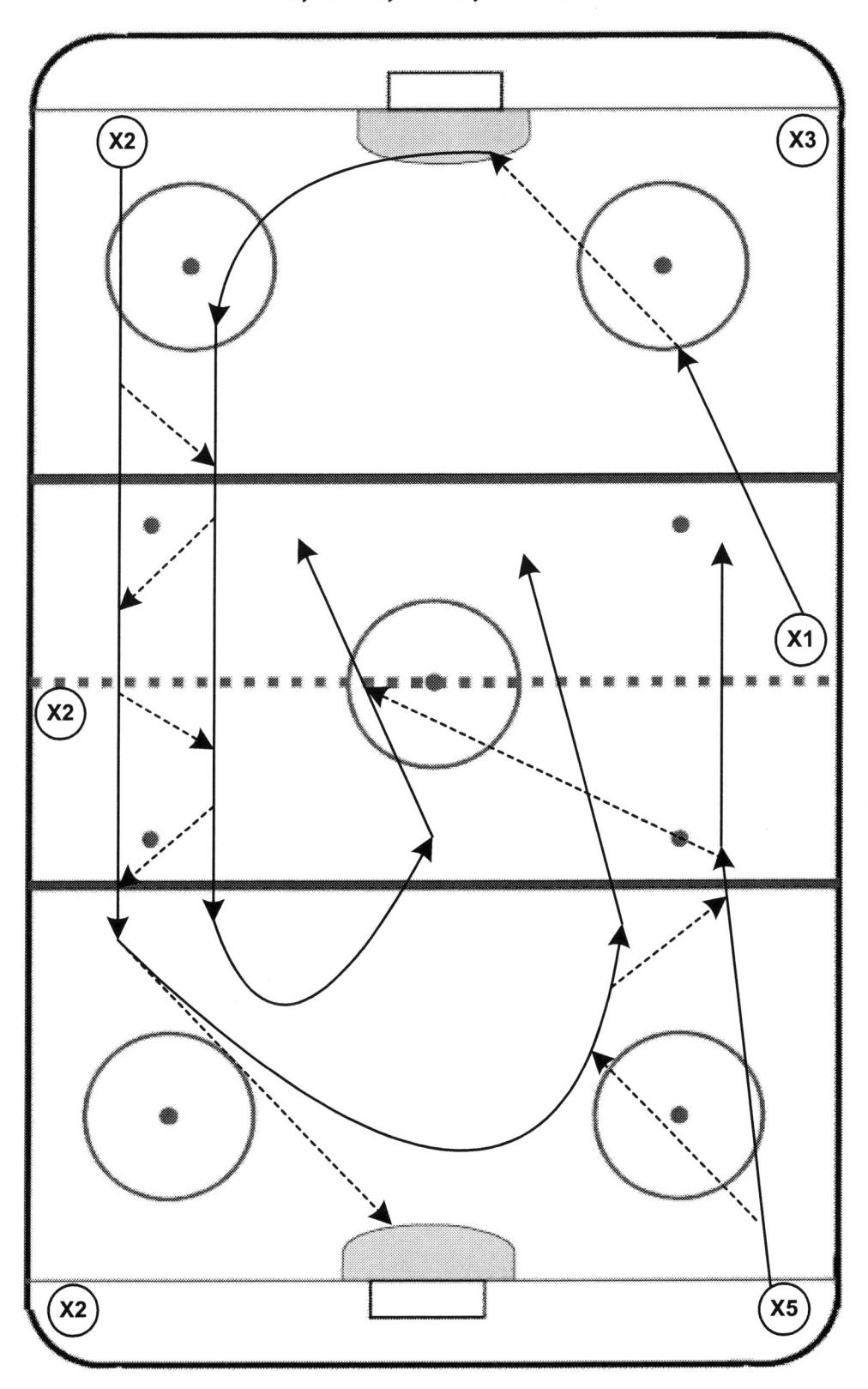

# 7 — The Rocket, D Support to 5 Shots

## Emphasis and Objective
Warm-up goalies, work on support the defense in the neutral zone, point shots and deflections.

## Drill Set-Up
* F's in their forward lines and on, opposite sides on the red-line. D's with their partners, inside the blue-line. Pucks with the F's and in opposite corners.
* 1 group of 3 F's each make a pass to the D, the D pass D to D at a good angle and hit the breaking F's with a pass proceeding to a shot.
* F2 shoots, swings to the corner and picks up 2 pucks, F2 then makes passes to F1 and F3, they shoot and gain position in front of the net. D's follow play up and receive a pass from F2 proceeding to two point shots. F1 and F3 screen and deflect.

## Key Teaching Points
* F's swing deep and time the play to allow for quality passes and shots.
* D present good passing angles.
* Full speed.
* Switch directions.
* Go both ways, one way shown.

## Recommended Progressions
* None.

# The Rocket, D Support to 5 Shots

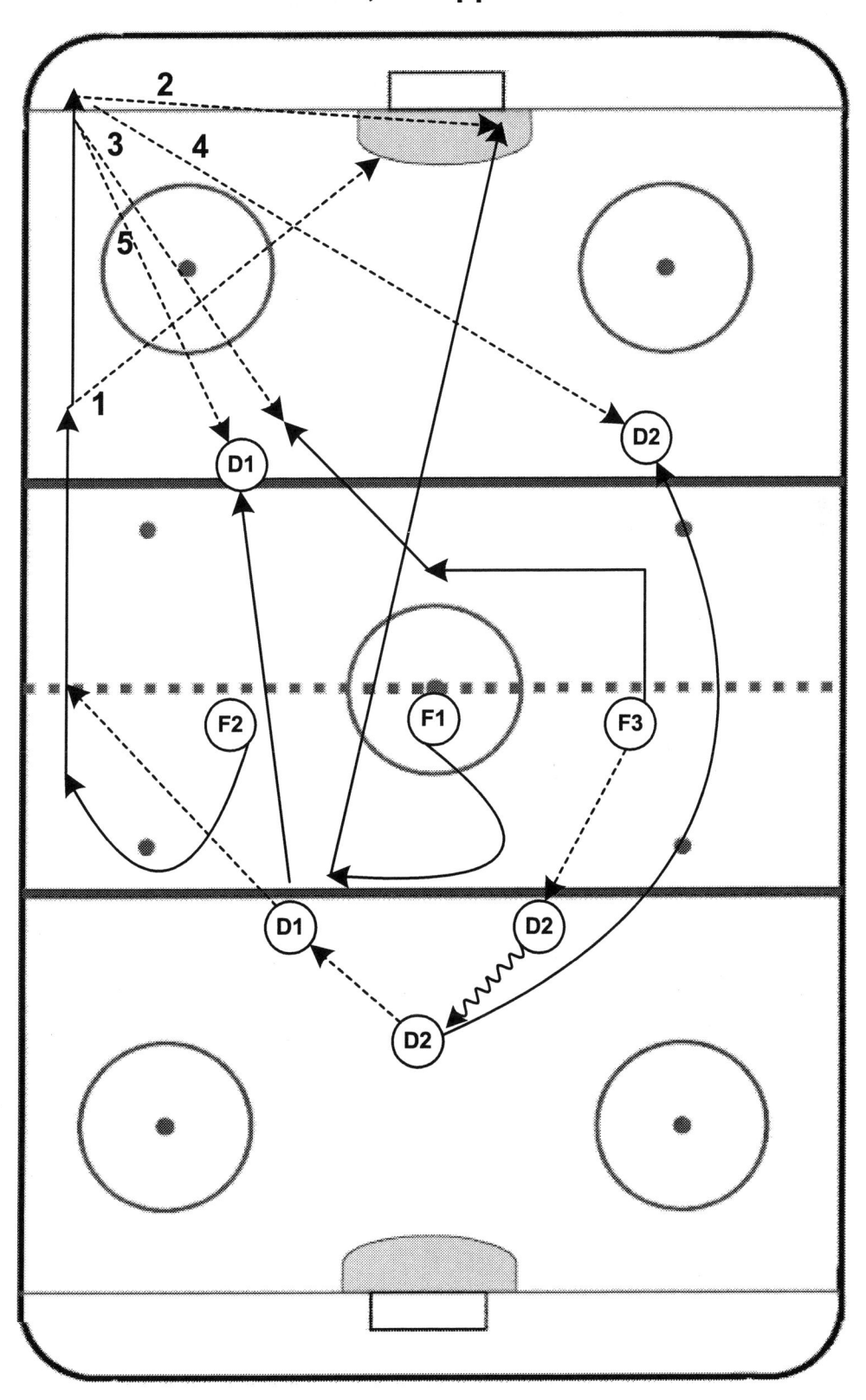

# 8    Bump it Back

## Emphasis and Objective
Warm-up drill with passing and shooting.

## Drill Set-Up
- Players divide in two groups, positioned in opposite corners with pucks.
- Two players (F3, F4) from each line take off and swing at the opposite top of the circles.
- F1 and F2 pass to F3 and F4 who Bump Back the puck to F1 and F2, F3 and F4 proceed up the wall.
- F1 and F2 move to a good passing angle, return a pass to F3 and F4 proceeding to a shot.
- F1 and F2 take off to the far end and repeat the sequence.

## Key Teaching Points
- Good passes.
- Move to good passing angles.
- Shots on net.

## Recommended Progressions
- None.

# Bump it Back

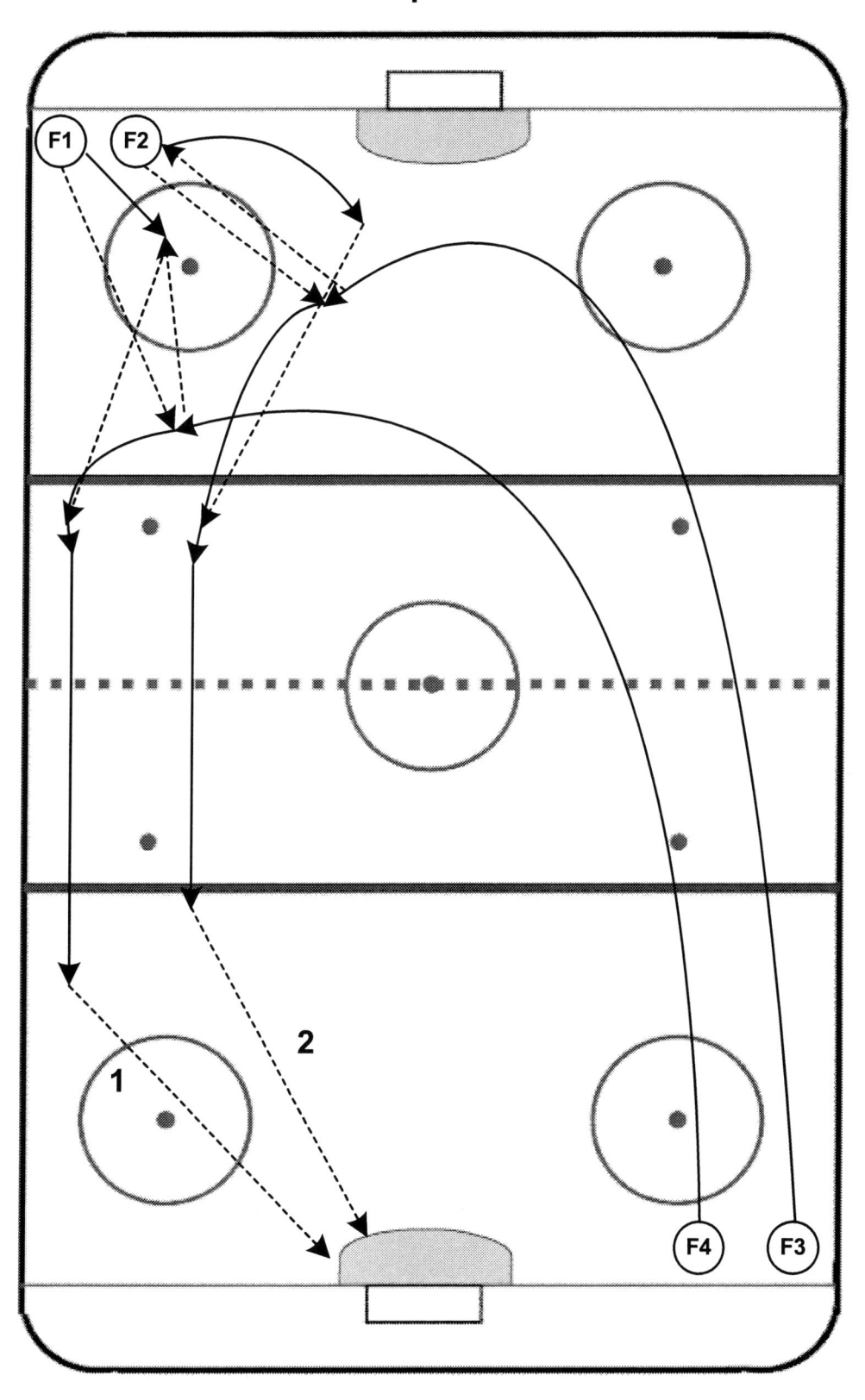

# 9    Long Shot, Short Shot

## Emphasis and Objective
Excellent shooting drill designed to incorporate skating, passing, receiving and shooting.

## Drill Set-Up
- F's at the half boards with pucks, D on the blue-line. Remaining pucks behind goal.
- D1 skates laterally across the blue-line and receives a pass from F1, pivots and shoots and long shot on goal.
- D1, after shooting, skates backwards, pivots to the corner, picks up a puck and passes to F1 who skates in off the wing for a short shot.
- Both ends, switch sides.

## Key Teaching Points
- Handle and move the puck quickly.
- Shots on goal.

## Recommended Progressions
- None.

# Long Shot, Short Shot

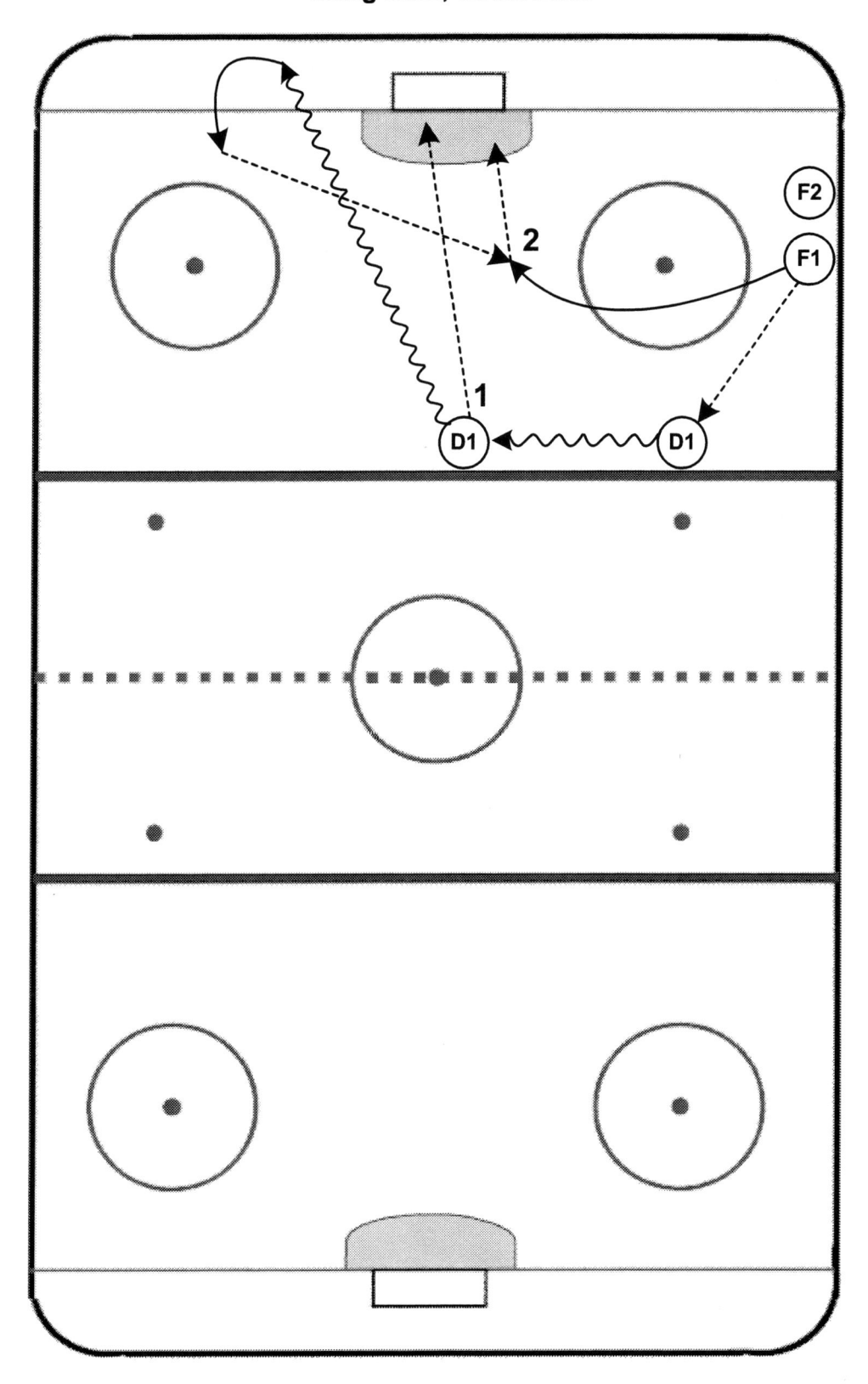

# 10    3 v 0 Return

## Emphasis and Objective

To get all players moving at full speed while making passes through the neutral zone.

## Drill Set-Up

* Players in 3 lines at both ends of ice, pucks at each end.
* On 1st whistle, the 1st group of three take off full speed toward the far end.
* While following their passes through the neutral zone, the player who has the puck at the far blue-line passes to a player in one of the three lines in the attacking end.
* After making the pass, the players regroup and receive a pass from the opposite line. They return to their original end in a similar action.
* Once the regrouping pass is made, that group of 3 three take off toward the opposite end, regroups and returns.

## Key Teaching Points

* Keep feet moving.
* Head up at all times.
* Handle puck at full speed.
* Support the puck and puck carrier.
* Excellent warm-up or conditioning drill
* Use forehand and backhand passes.

## Recommended Progressions

* Insist on one-timing the puck through neutral zone.

# 3 v 0 Return

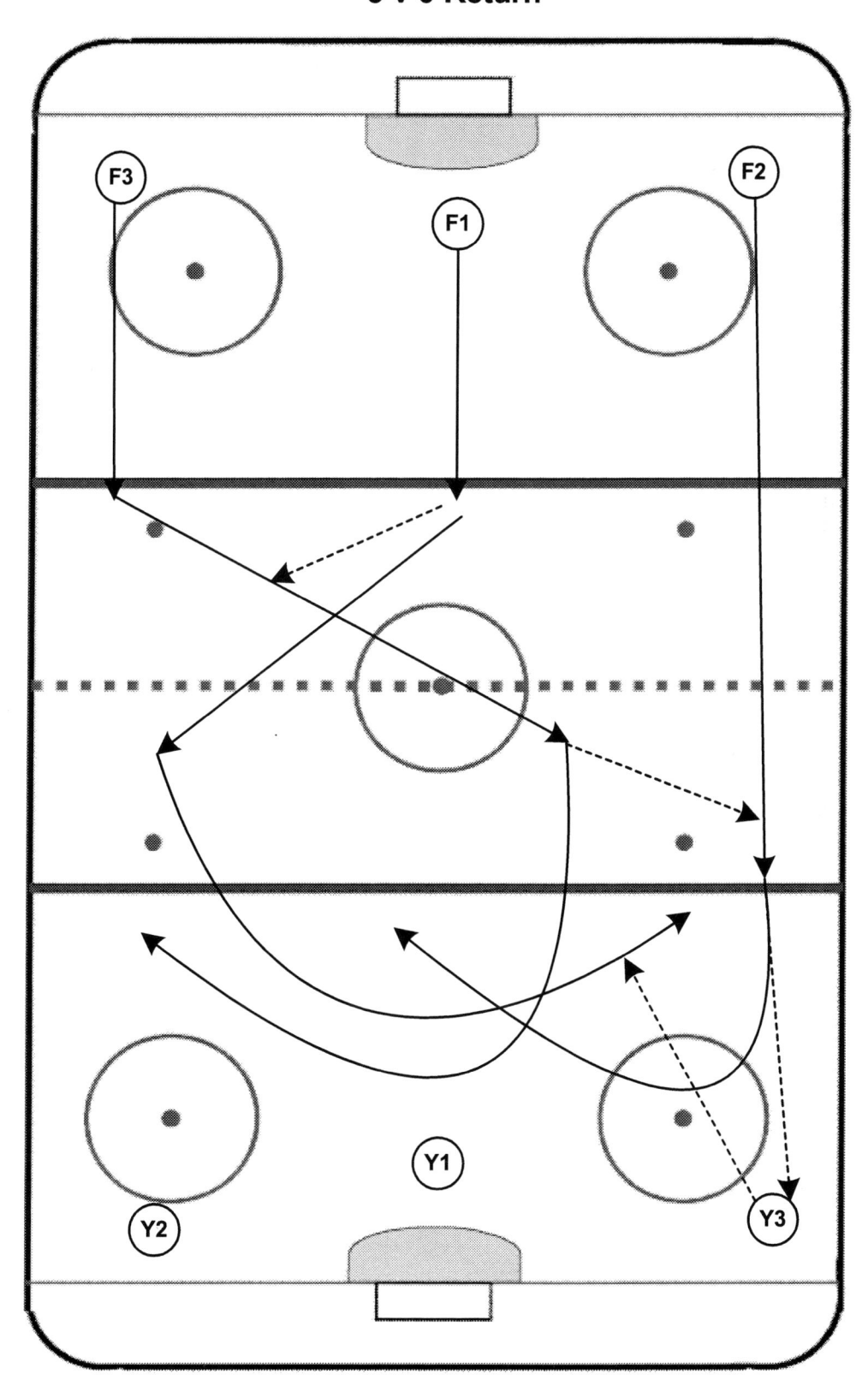

# 11 The Snake

## Emphasis and Objective
Warm up drill for passing and receiving.

## Drill Set-Up
* Players in 2 lines in one end, each with pucks.
* Drill starts with 2 players streaking down the ice passing the puck 15 feet apart.
* When the passing players get to the far blue-line, they curl to the middle and skate back the original direction in the center of the ice.
* Once the players reach the bottom of the in-zone face-off circle, they curl and head back to the far end continuing to make as many passes as possible.

## Key Teaching Points
* Keep feet moving.
* Tape to tape passes.
* Pass receiving.
* Passing in stride

## Recommended Progressions
* Vary distance between skaters.
* 1 skater skate forward, 1 backwards.

# The Snake

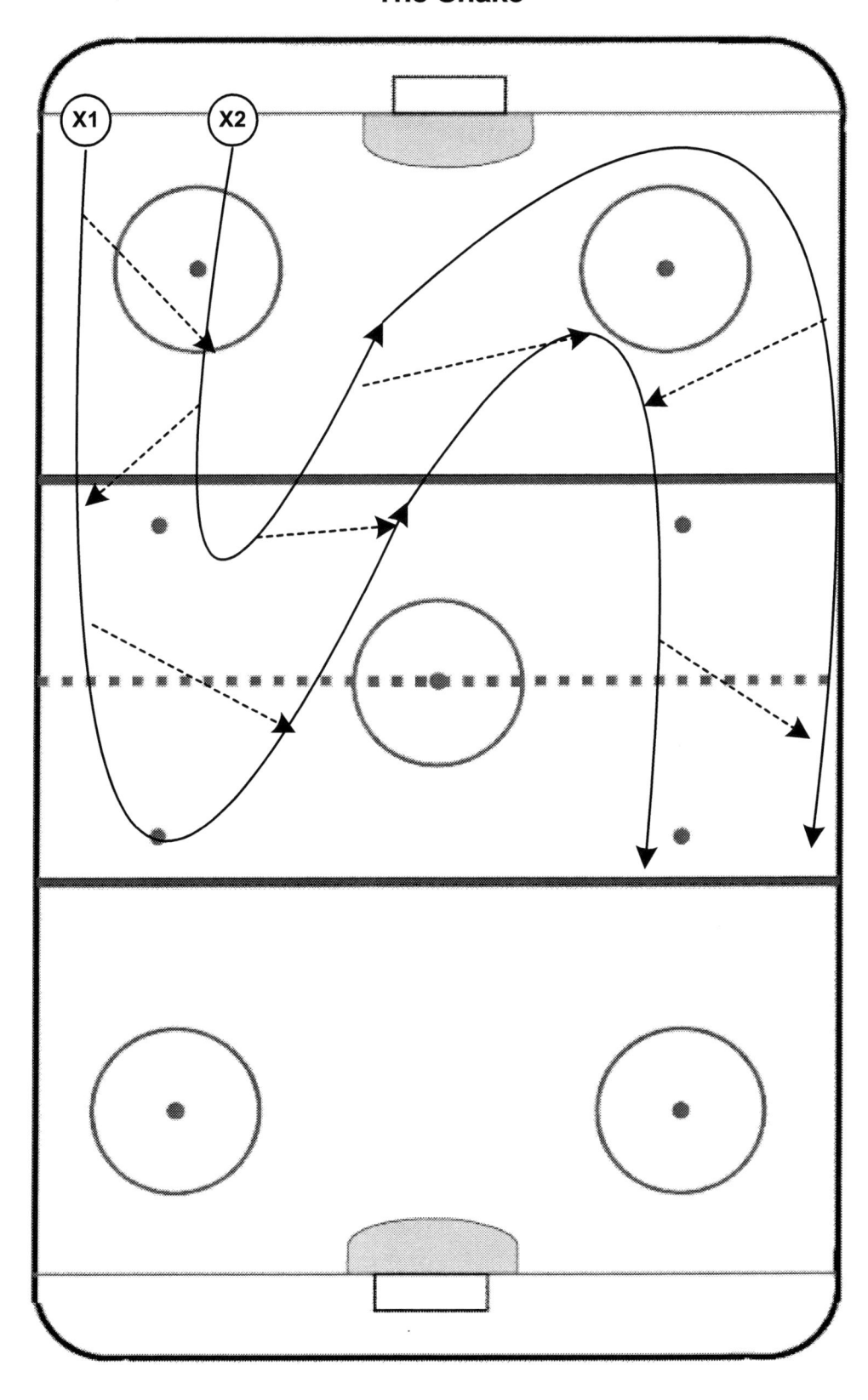

# 12 — 4 Spot Shuttle

## Emphasis and Objective
Improve hands and stress quick feet.

## Drill Set-Up
- 4 lines at each blue-line, each with pucks.
- Each line performs simultaneously.
- Line 1: Accelerate to Red-line and pass.
  Line 2: Forehand and backhand saucer pass over stick.
  Line 3: Skate a figure 8 and pass.
  Line 4: Skate forward to Red-line, backwards to blue-line, forward to Red-line and pass.
- 30 second shifts, be sure to change lines.

## Key Teaching Points
- Keep feet moving at all times.
- Stress soft hands.
- Full speed.

## Recommended Progressions
- None

# 4 Spot Shuttle

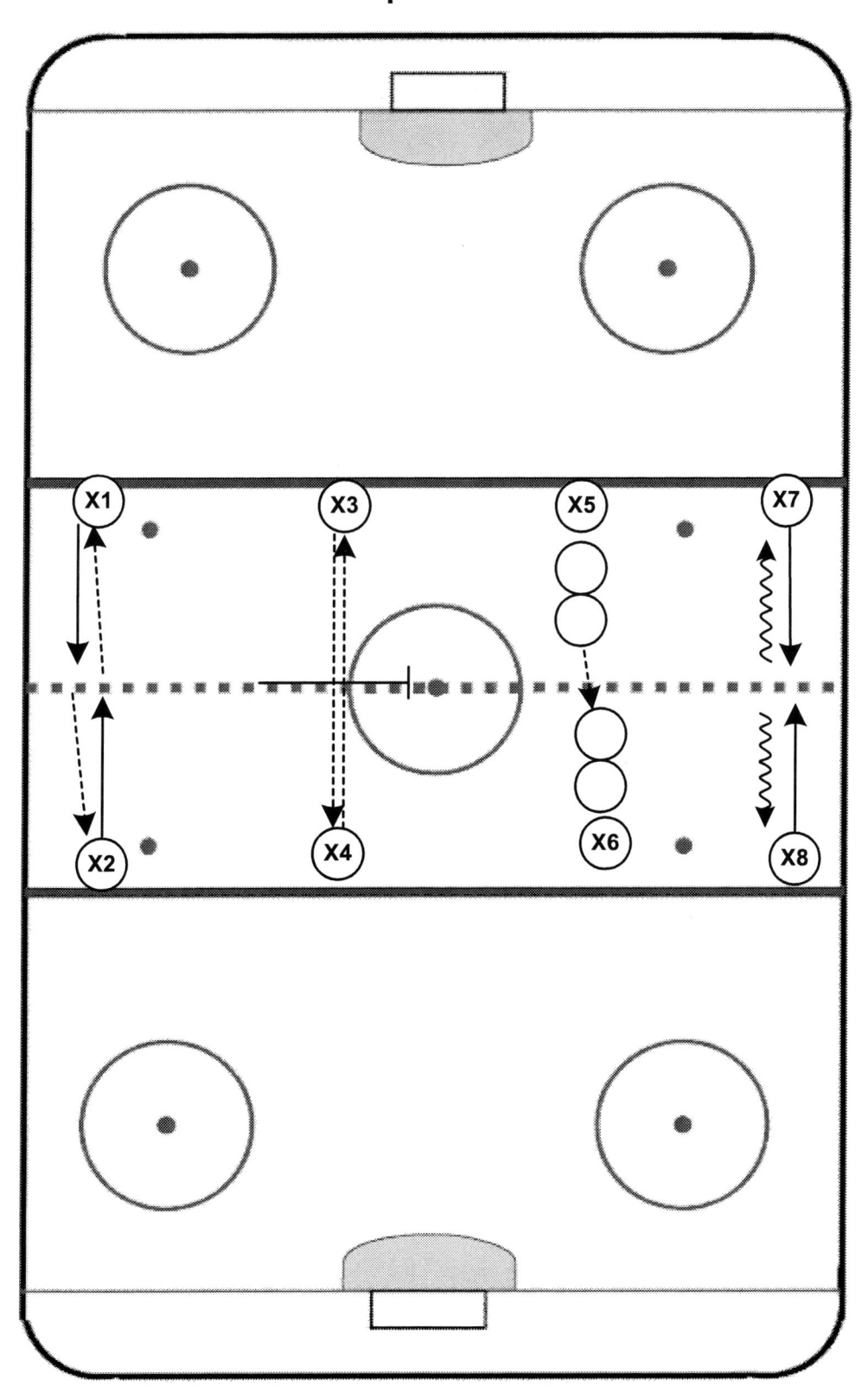

# 13 Cross and Drop

## Emphasis and Objective
Execute 3 skill passes.

## Drill Set-Up
* Players in 4 lines on each blue-line (X1, X2, X3, X4) with pucks.
* X1 and O3 skate just outside the blue-line with a puck, X2 and X4 skate behind X1 and O3, X1 and O3 execute a drop pass.
* X2 and X4, after receiving the drop pass, continue up the wall with the puck, they pass to the next X and X who 1 time passes the puck back for a shot on goal.
* Original X1 and O3 continue their path up the wall, receive and pass from the next X2 and X4 for a shot on goal.

## Key Teaching Points
* Stagger the lines for 2 good, outside shots.
* Head up at all times.
* Work on soft hands for giving and receiving.
* Shots on net.
* Be sure to switch lines.

## Recommended Progressions
* None.

# Cross and Drop

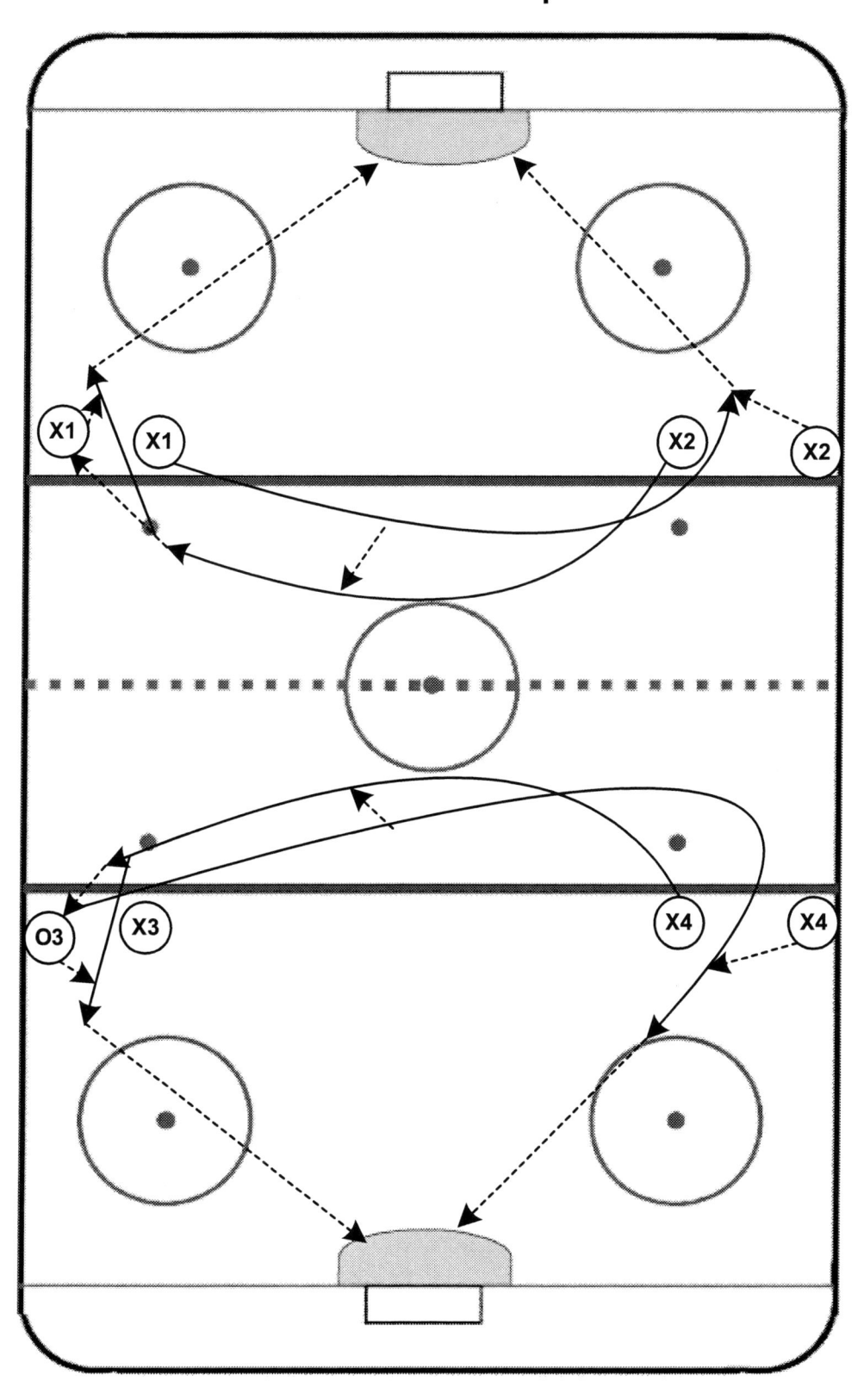

## 14     Laker Delay

### Emphasis and Objective
Work on different types of escapes after entering the offensive zone.

### Drill Set-Up
- Players in two lines at both ends.
- 2 players from each line take of 2 v 0 down their respective sides.
- At the red-line, the player closest to the boards controls the puck and drives down the wall entering the offensive zone.
- The inside players without the puck turn and support the play heading into the zone they originated.
- Puck carriers perform 1 of 2 escapes:
  1. Curl toward the board looking to the slot
  2. Cut to the middle and drop pass.

### Key Teaching Points
- Keep puck moving.
- Support the puck at a good distance.
- Both players attack the net.

### Recommended Progressions
- Be sure to switch sides.

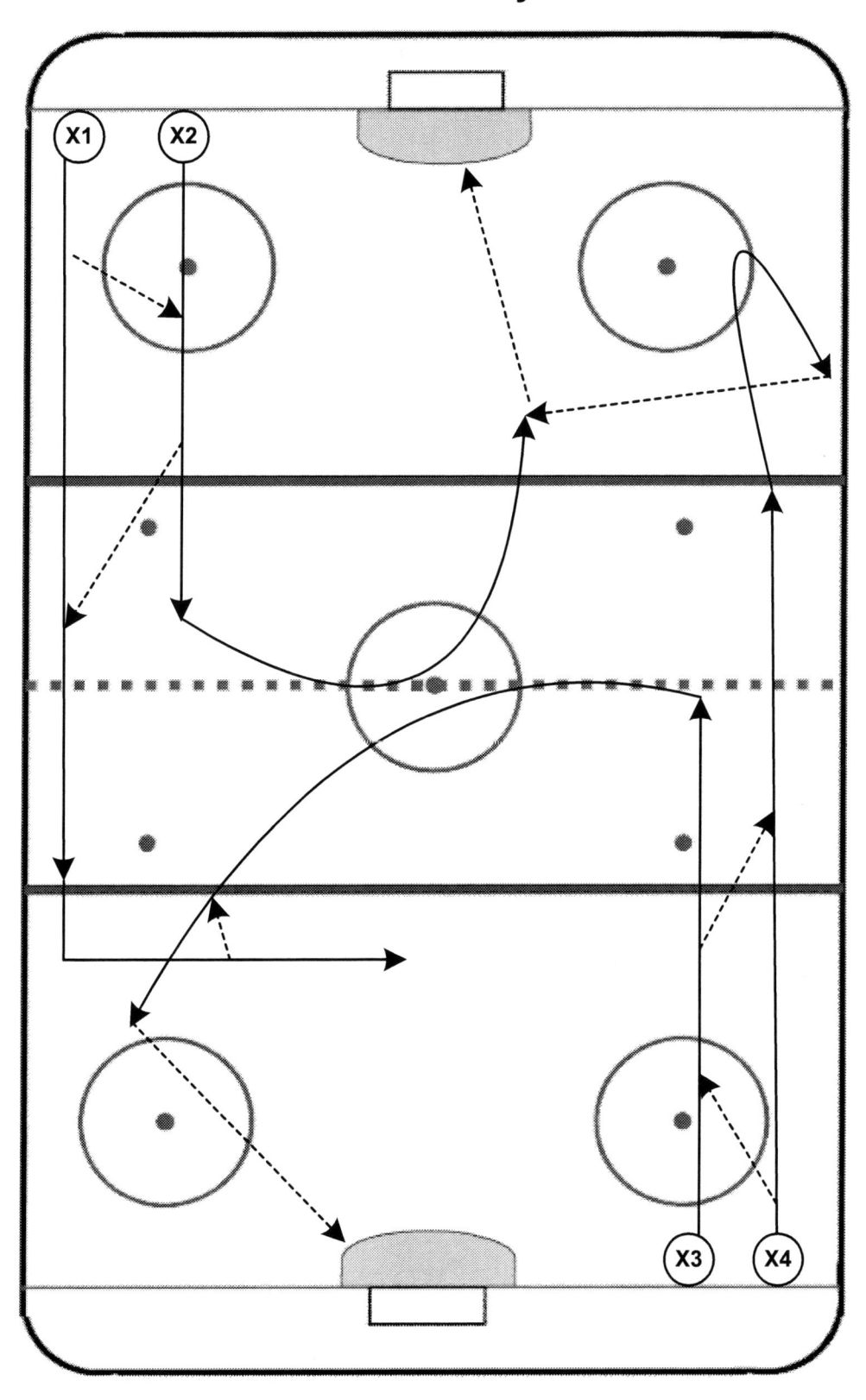

# Laker Delay

# 15 Stretch Pass

## Emphasis and Objective
Work on recognizing the quick stretch pass up the middle to a shot on goal.

## Drill Set-Up
- Players with pucks on all 4 blue-lines.
- 1st player in each opposite line loops around the neutral zone face-off dot and continues on to the far blue where the 2nd player in line hits him with a long stretch pass.
- Shoot from outside, follow the shot to the net.

## Key Teaching Points
- Full speed.
- Timing.
- Positioning to receive pass.

## Recommended Progressions
- None.

# Stretch Pass

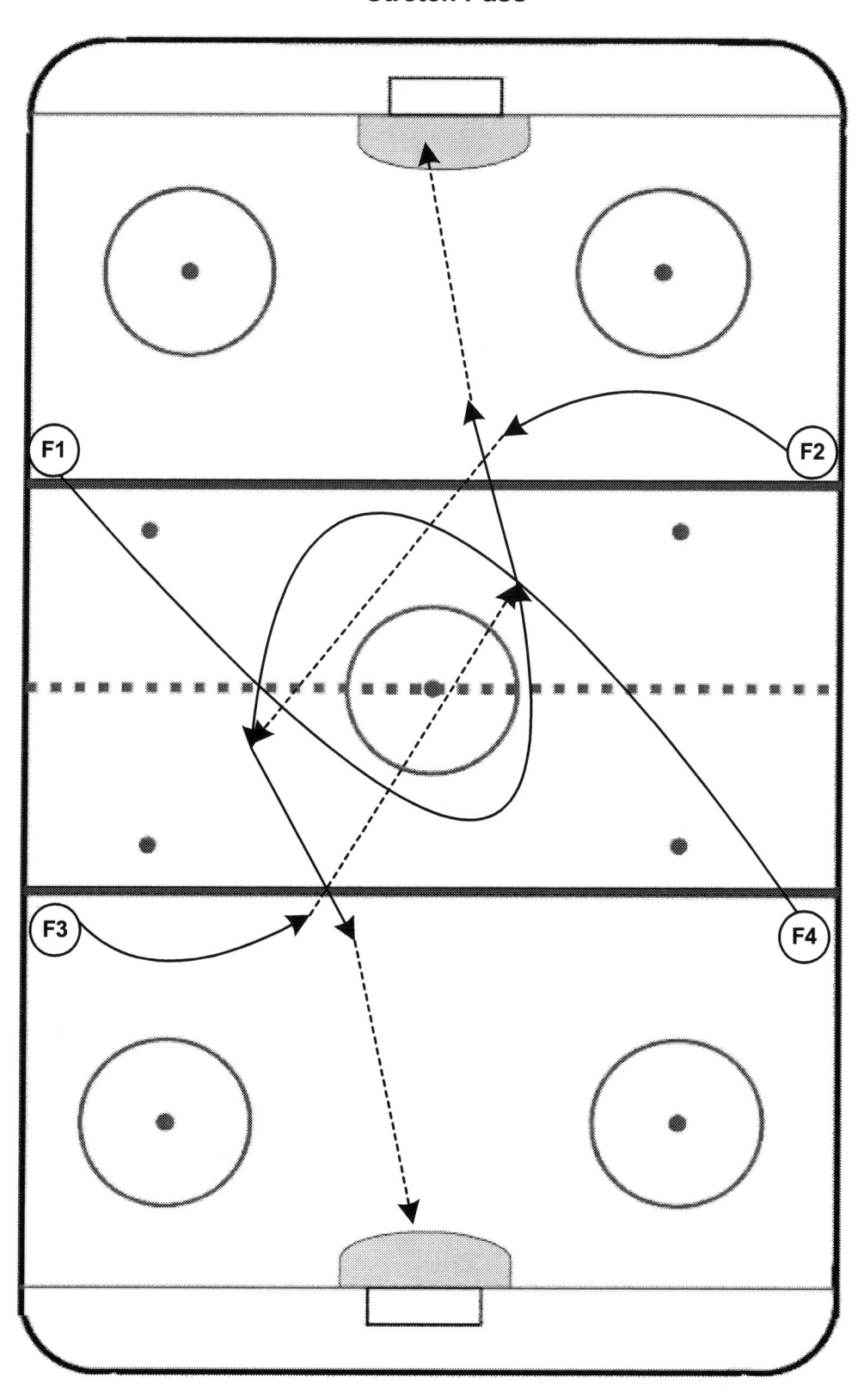

## 16 — Golden Bear: 4 Circle Stickhandling

### Emphasis and Objective
Improve puck handling skills in a confined area.

### Drill Set-Up
* All players in 3 lines at one end of ice with pucks.
* On the 1st whistle, 3 players (Group 1) sprint to the near circle and begin stick handling inside the circle.
* On the 2nd whistle, Group 2 to the near circle, Group 1 to the center circle. Both Group 1 and Group 2 stick handle in the confined area.
* On the 3rd whistle, the Group 3 to the near circle, Group 2 to the center and Group 1 to the far end.
* On the 4th whistle, Group 4 to the near circle, Group 3 to the center, Group 2 to the far end and Group 1 to the opposite far end circle.
* On the 5th whistle, Group 5 to the near circle, Group 4 to the center, Group 3 to the far end, Group 2 to the opposite far end circle and Group 1 sprints full ice to the end of the line.

### Key Teaching Points
* Keep feet moving.
* Head up at all times.
* Handle puck in confined area.
* 1st two groups shown.

### Recommended Progressions
* Vary times in each circle, switch sides.

# Golden Bear 4 Circle Stickhandling

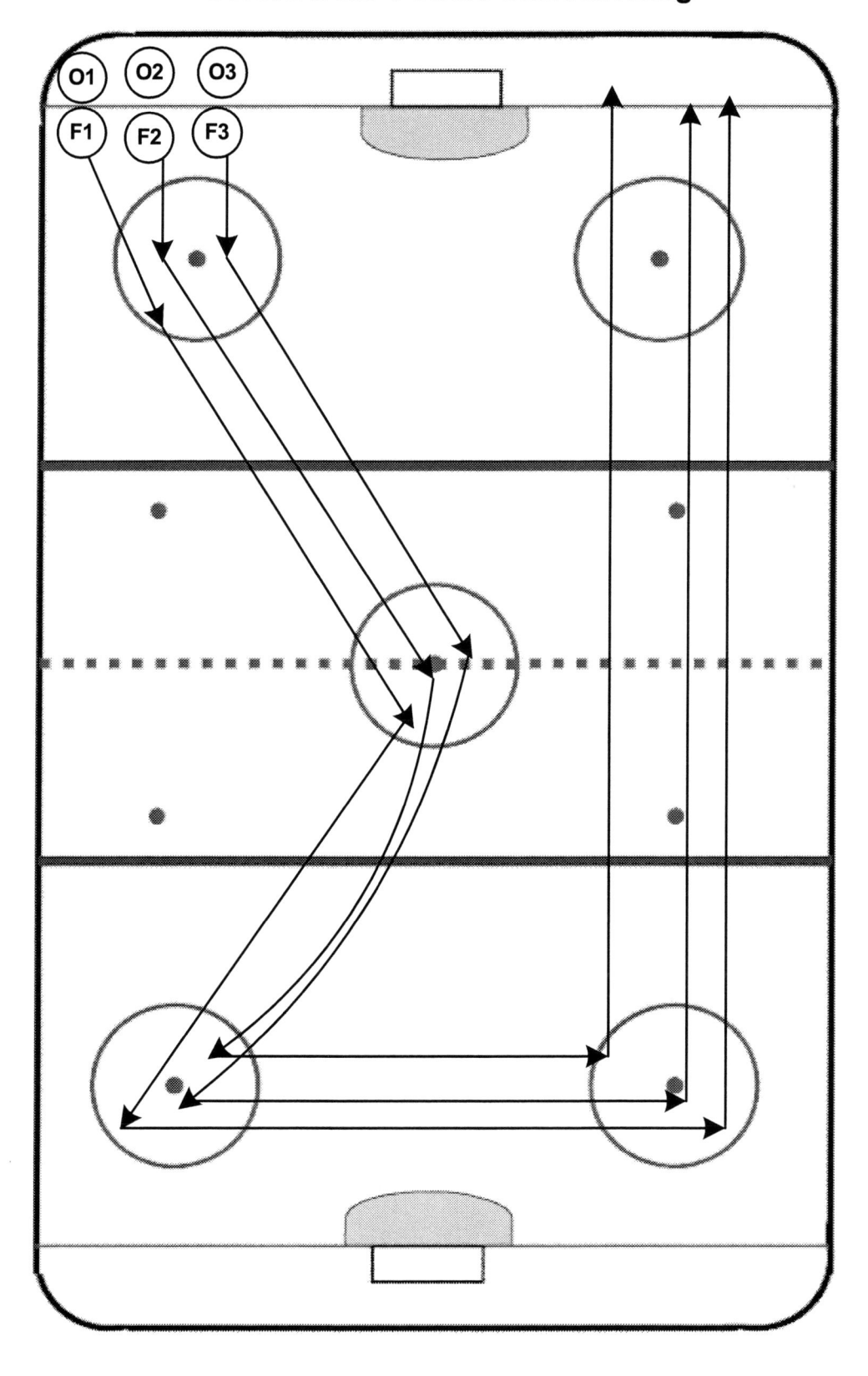

# 17 — 3 zone, Change it Up

## Emphasis and Objective
Work on fundamentals in a competitive environment.

## Drill Set-Up
* All players, with partners, divide up in all 3 zones.
* Zone 1: Players will be partner passing.
  Zone 2: Players will be playing 1 v 1 keep away.
  Zone 3: Players will be stick handling.
* On 1st whistle, Zone 1 goes full speed, Zone 2 and 3 half speed.
* On the 2nd whistle, Zone 2 full speed, Zone 1 and 3 half speed.
* On the 3rd whistle, Zone 3 full speed, Zone 1 and 2 half speed.
* 30-45 second shifts, players switch zones after each rotation.

## Key Teaching Points
* Strong on the puck.
* Compete.
* Work ethic.

## Recommended Progressions
* None.

# 3 Zone Change Up

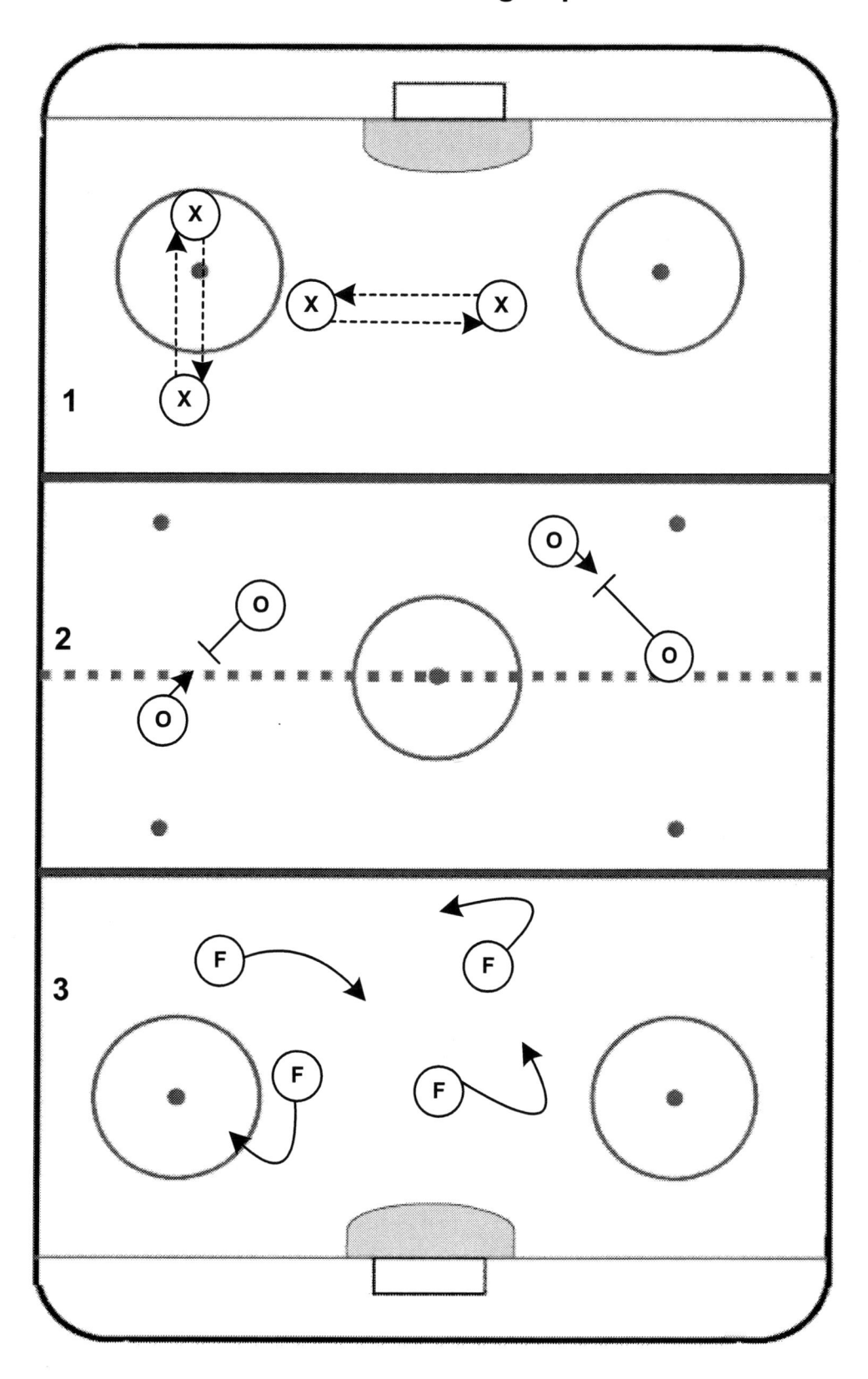

1

2

3

# 18 — Center Pivot

## Emphasis and Objective
Quick transition and puck movement through the neutral zone.

## Drill Set-Up
* C behind net with pucks. Centers at the center of the near blue-line, wingers on the each side on the blue-line.
* On the whistle, Center skates toward the coach, wingers skate back into the zone along the boards.
* C passes to the center, who must pivot and immediately hit a streaking winger.
* The wingers accelerate through the neutral zone moving the puck. Centers follow the play and become the trailer.

## Key Teaching Points
* Handle and move the puck quickly.
* Timing.
* Full speed puck movement.
* Neutral zone puck movement.

## Recommended Progressions
* Add defense for a 3 v 1 or 3 v 2.

# Center Pivot

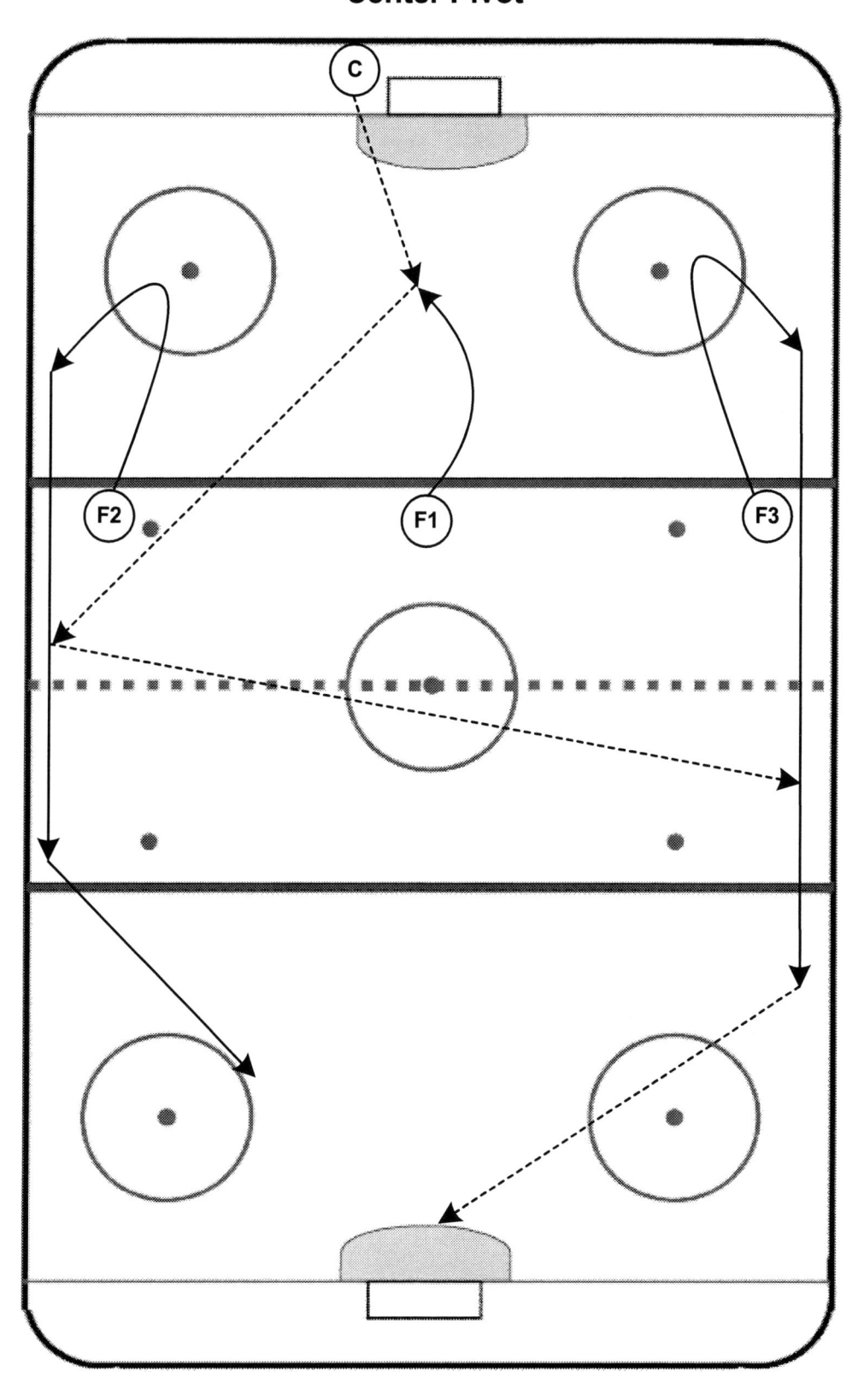

# 19 Jackhammer

## Emphasis and Objective
Improve passing and shooting skills.

## Drill Set-Up
* Players in both ends and in the center as diagrammed.
* X1 breaks down the wall with the puck, X2 skates back toward the defensive zone, X1 passes to X2 who one touch passes back to X1, X2 follows the play up the wall.
* At the far blue-line, X1 curls back to the middle and hits a breaking X2 who proceeds for a shot.
* X2 is now in the center passing with a new breaking X1.

## Key Teaching Points
* Timing.
* One touch passing.
* Full speed puck movement.
* Skill development.

## Recommended Progressions
* None.

# Jackhammer

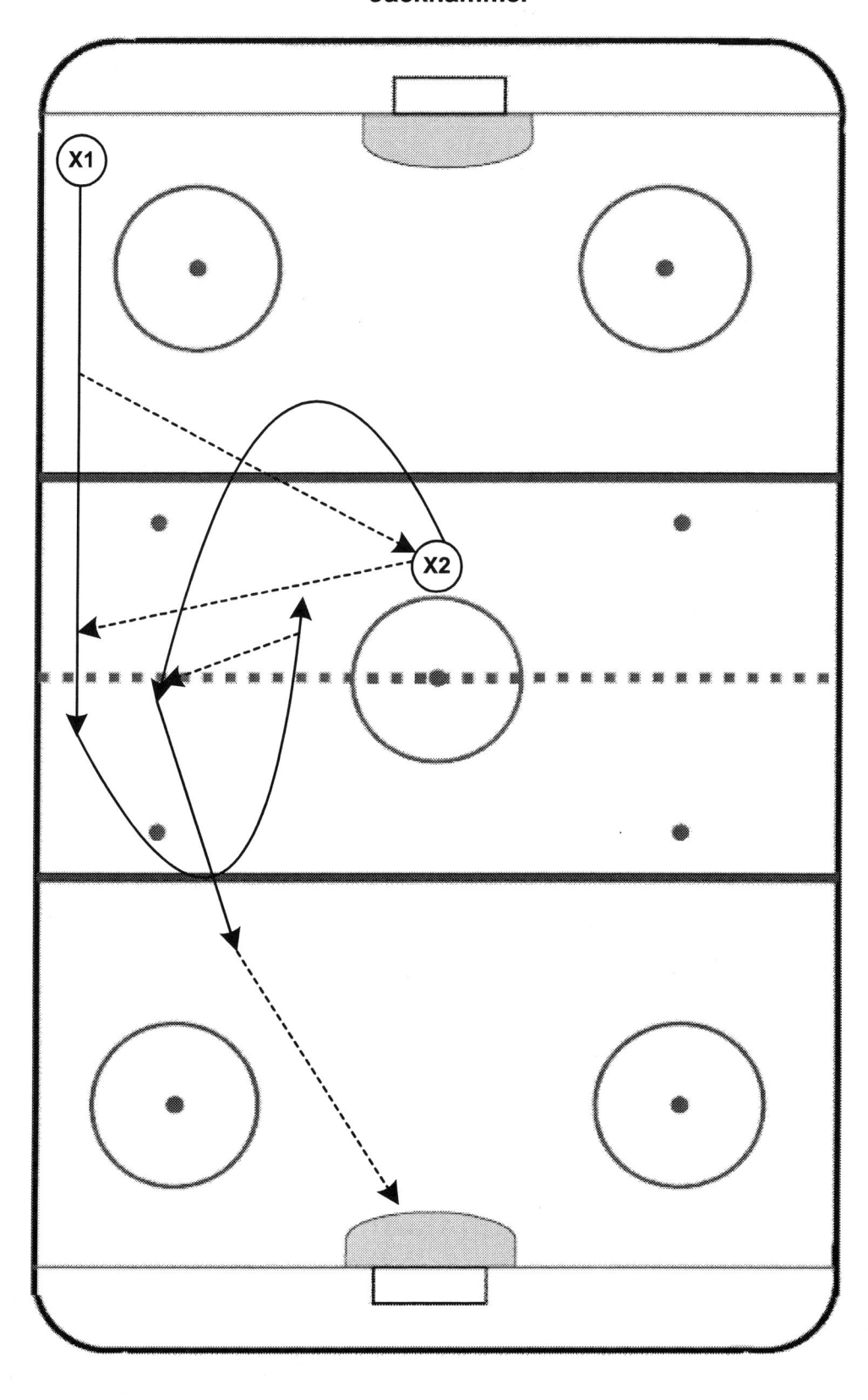

## 20     Challenge Cup

### Emphasis and Objective

    Improve puck support, angles and timing.

### Drill Set-Up

- Players in 4 lines as shown, pucks in corner.
- F1 shoots on goal from slot and proceeds to pick up puck in corner and skates up the wall.
- F2 curls to middle ice looking for a pass from F1. F1 passes to F2 who heads up middle ice while F3 deep curls to the boards looking for a pass from F2.
- F2 passes to F3 who skates down the wall for a shot on goal.
- After shot, F3 proceeds to far corner, picks up a puck and passes to F4 who has curled to middle ice.
- F4 heads up middle ice passing to F5 who has curled to the boards proceeding down the wall for a shot on goal.

### Key Teaching Points

- Full speed.
- Work on good passing angles.
- Work on timing.
- All shots on net.
- Be sure to rotate lines.

### Recommended Progressions

- None

# Challenge Cup

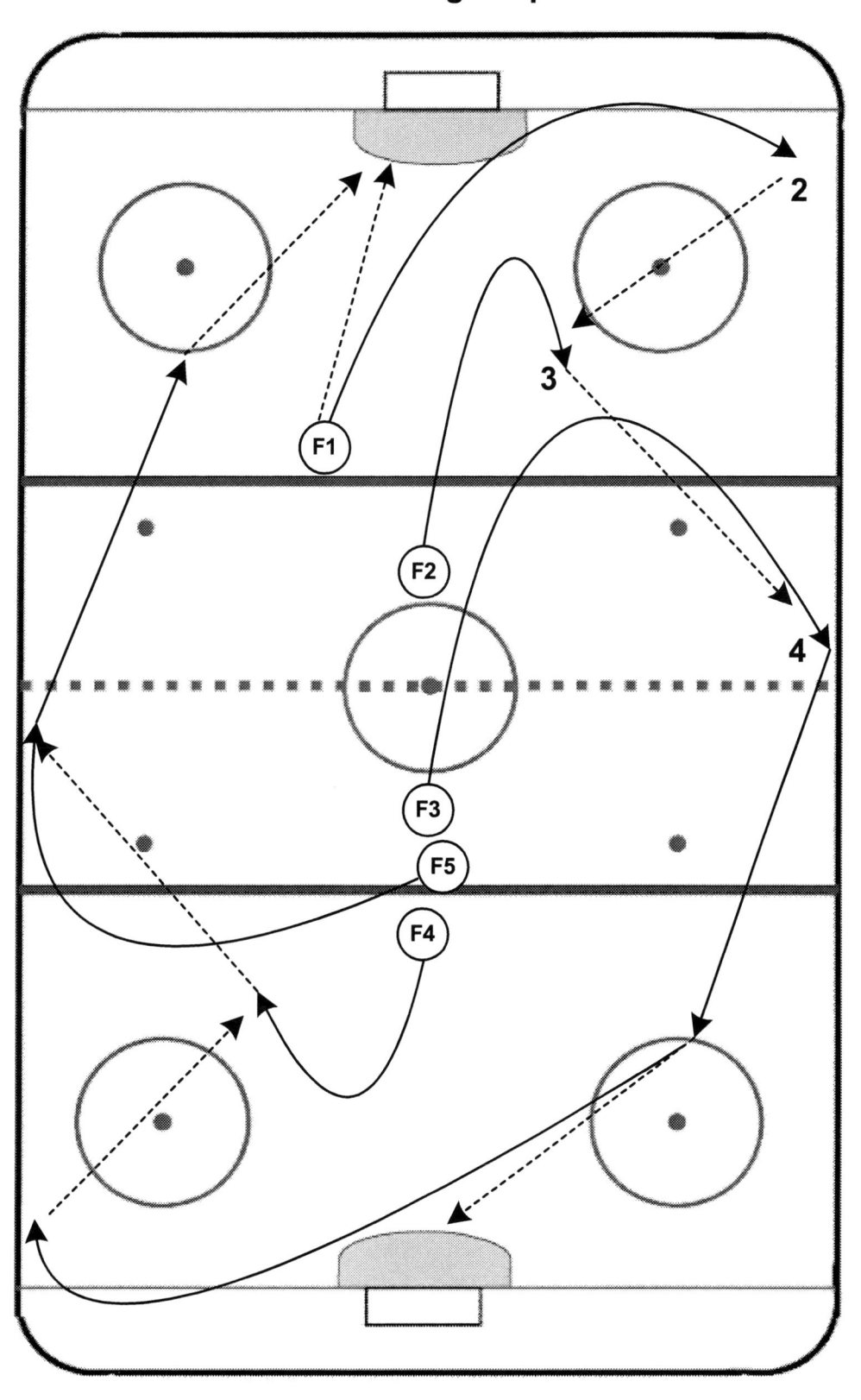

## 21 Continuous Breakouts

### Emphasis and Objective
Work on all breakout options and patterns.

### Drill Set-Up
* Forward lines and defensive pairs in the neutral zone, C with puck.
* Two forward lines up with defensive pairs.
* C dumps pick into one zone, that group of 5 (2 D and 3 F's) breakout and attack the neutral zone. The other group of 5 (2 D and 3 X's) waits in the neutral zone to meet the attack.
* Once each F touches the puck, they dump the puck into the zone and drop off to the bench. 3 Y's and 2 D move from the bench into the neutral zone.
* X's must break the puck out, gain the neutral zone and dump the puck in for the Y's to break out.
* Continuous.

### Key Teaching Points
* Go through all breakout options.
* Make easy, high percentage passes.
* Communication.
* One rotation shown.

### Recommended Progressions
* Remove a forward for 4 v 4 practice.
* Incorporate power play breakouts.

# Continuous Breakouts

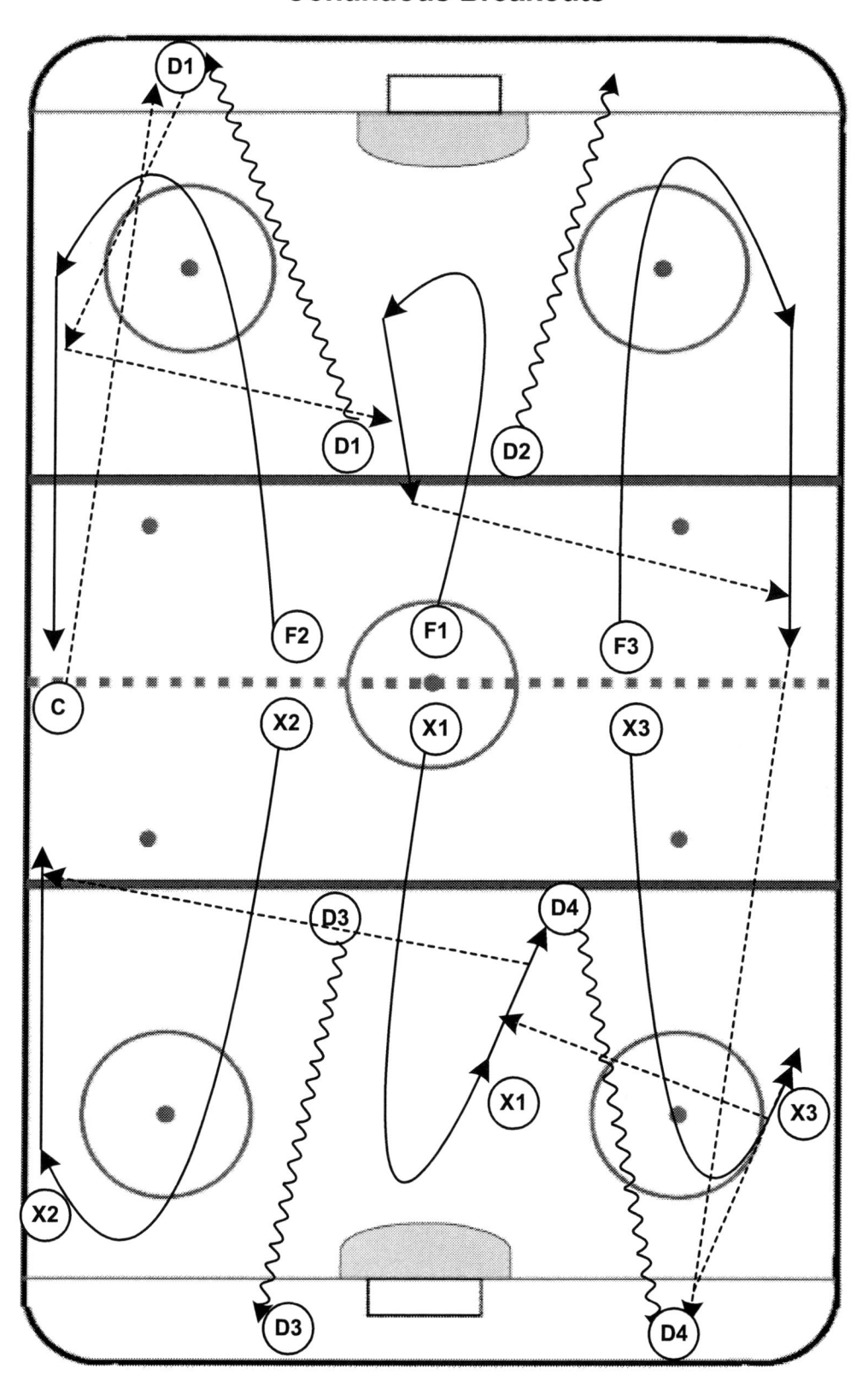

# 22 — 2 v 0, D Support

## Emphasis and Objective

To have forwards support the puck in a neutral zone regroup. Defensemen move feet and make good decisions. Forwards drive the net, goalies control rebounds.

## Drill Set-Up

* F's on both sides of center red-line. D's on blue-line with partners.
* On whistle, F1 passes to D1. D1 begins backwards skating to middle of ice, D2 hinges supporting the puck at a good passing angle.
* F1 and F2 cross deep in neutral zone positioning for an outlet pass.
* D1 to D2. D2 to F1 before red-line.
* F1 to F2. F2 shoots from outside. F1 drives the net for rebound.

## Key Teaching Points

* Continuous.
* Hard passes at good angles.
* Support puck in all zones.
* Shoot in stride.
* Attack blue-line with speed.
* Drive the net with stick on ice.
* Rebound control.

## Recommended Progressions

* 2 v 1 add a defenseman.

# 2 v 0 D-Support

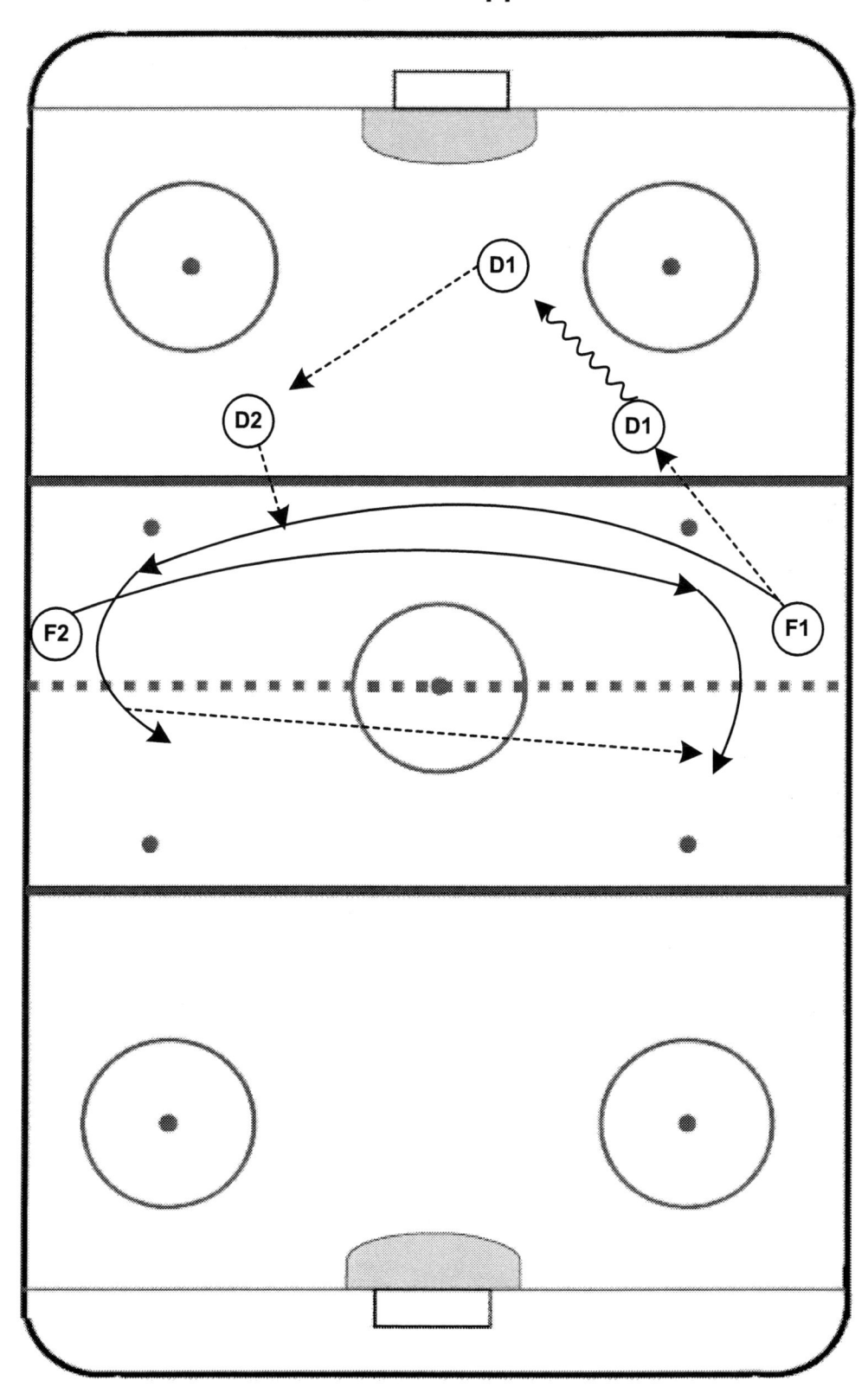

Photo courtesy of Dave Eggen & Dick Carlson of Inertia Pro Event Imaging and The USHL

# 2

## Team Drills

Included in this section are drills to improve transitional play, neutral zone play and various drills to improve breakout skills as well as forechecking and backchecking skills and concepts. These drills are critical components to team performance. While adherence to an individual system of play is also a critical factor in team success, these drills are designed to challenge and develop the necessary skills for the different aspects of team play.

Design your system of play to suit your abilities but use this section to introduce and reinforce the fundamentals and concepts of transition, neutral zone play, breakouts, forechecking and backchecking. At all levels of play, these skills and the ability to perform them at high proficiency will often dictate the success of the team.

# 23 — 3 Counters, 3 v 2

## Emphasis and Objective
Work on different neutral zone counters to a 3 v 2.

## Drill Set-Up
- C with pucks at blue-line, F's in their lines at the red-line, D1, D2 and D3, D4 at each blue-line.
- C dumps puck to side boards, F1, F2 and F3 regroup with D1 and D2.
- On each counter attack and after each F touches the puck, they pass it back to the C who places the puck at a spot in the neutral zone and D1 and D2 repeat the process for counter attacks 2 and 3.
- On the 3rd counter attack and regroup, F's attack D3 and D4 3 v 2.

## Key Teaching Points
- D hinge at good passing angles.
- F's coordinate and stagger the attack.
- D maintain good Gap.
- Support puck through the neutral zone.
- Speed through the neutral zone.
- Create 2 v 1 out of 3 v 2.
- 1st regroup and transition is shown.

## Recommended Progressions
- C can forecheck to provide opposition.

# 3 Counters, 3 v 2

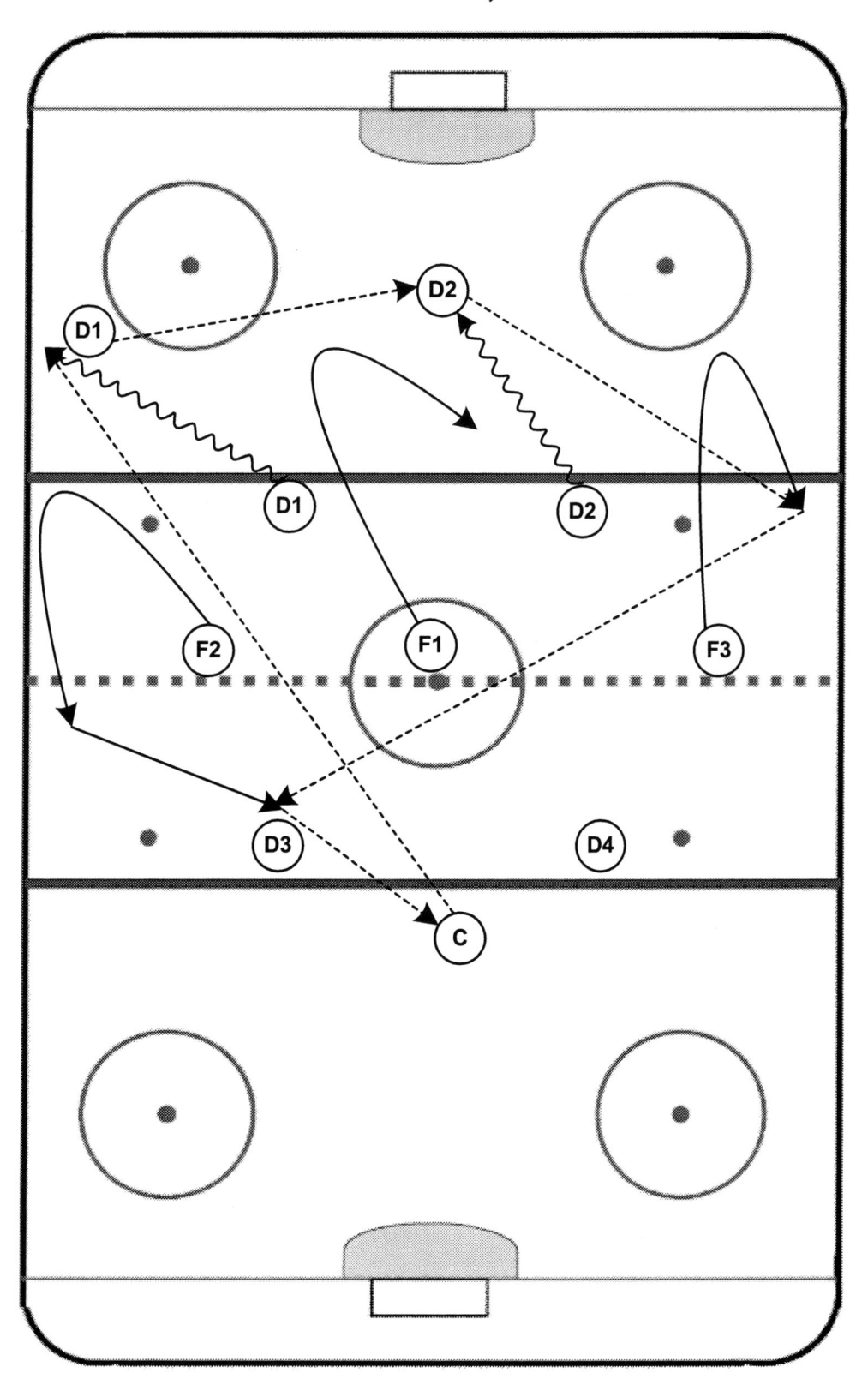

## 24 — 4 v 3 Transition

### Emphasis and Objective
Puck support and transition through the neutral zone, changing offense to defense.

### Drill Set-Up
* F1, F2 and F3 in neutral zone, D1 and D2 behind in support position. X1, X2 and X3 inside blue-line.
* F's regroup with D1 and D2 and attack X's 3 v 3, one of the D's joins the rush to create a 4 v 3 offensive situation.
* Once the X's create the turnover, they pass to the remaining D in the neutral zone, they hustle to the neutral zone, regroup and transition attack against the F's, 4 v 3.

### Key Teaching Points
* Puck support.
* Puck protection.
* Angling and checking.
* Quick transition, offense to defense, defense to offense.

### Recommended Progressions
* None.

# 4 v 3 Transition

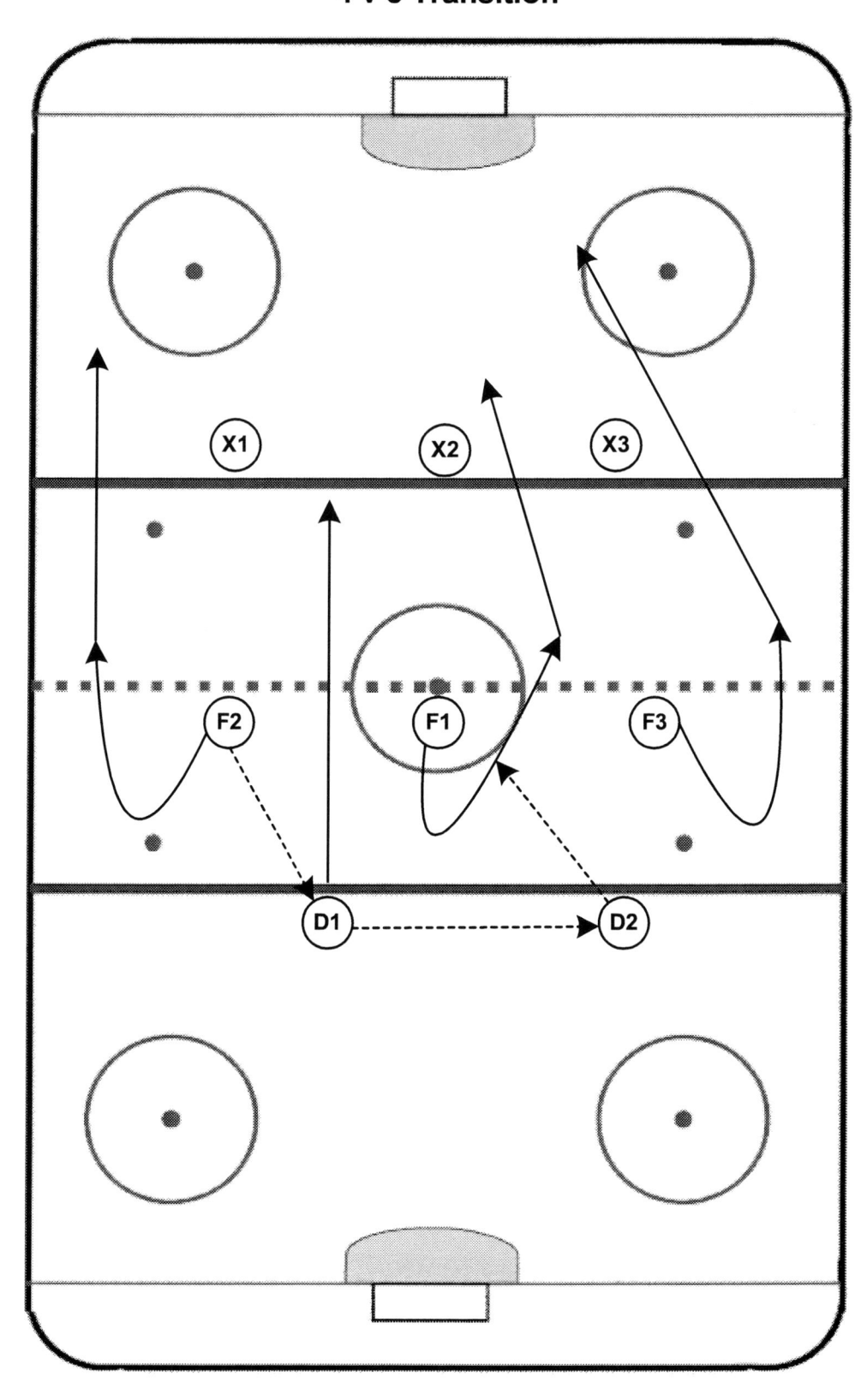

# 25. Raider Transition, 5 v 2 Either Way

## Emphasis and Objective
Full ice situational transition.

## Drill Set-Up
* Players in boxes. Forward line (F1, F2 and F3) at redline, D1 and D2 at one blue-line, D3 and D4 at opposite blue-line. C with pucks.
* C dumps puck into zone for a breakout, F1, F2 and F3 breakout and attack D3 and D4, 5 v 2.
* On 1st whistle, the puck carrier gives the puck to one of the defending D's (D3 or D4). They regroup and transition to a 3 v 2 against the original D (D1 and D2). If no 2nd whistle, play continues to a 5 v 2 in the zone.
* C vary the number of whistles for multiple transitional situations.

## Key Teaching Points
* Do not anticipate whistles.
* Speed through the neutral zone.
* Puck support.
* Width and depth of transition.

## Recommended Progressions
* None.

# Raider Transition, 5 v 2 Either Way

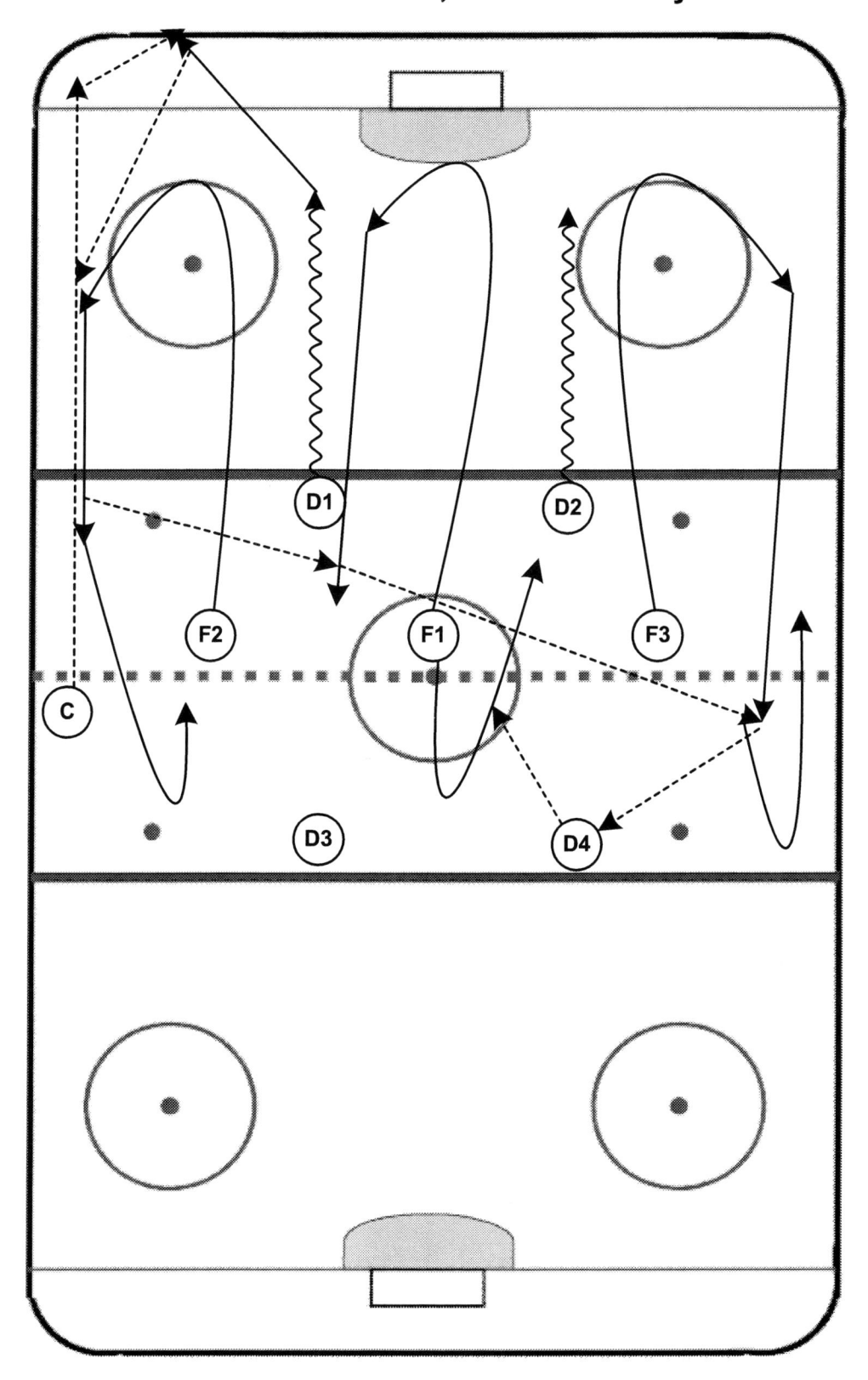

## 26 Grizzly Transition Scoring

### Emphasis and Objective
To work on goal scoring in a variety of situations.

### Drill Set-Up
* Pucks in 4 corners. F's divide into 2 groups, 1 on each side in the neutral zone, D's on each side of red-line.
* D1 backpedals and picks up a puck and hits a curling F1 who attacks D2, 1 v 1. F1 must stay in the zone until a goal is scored.
* D2 defends F1 for 1 shot on net then proceeds to pass to a curling F2 who attacks D3 in the opposite end, 1 v 1.

### Key Teaching Points
* Strong transition passes.
* Goal scoring techniques.
* Read rushes.
* Speed in neutral zone.
* Rebound control

### Recommended Progressions
* 2 v 1, 2 v 2, 3 v 2.

# Grizzly Transition Scoring

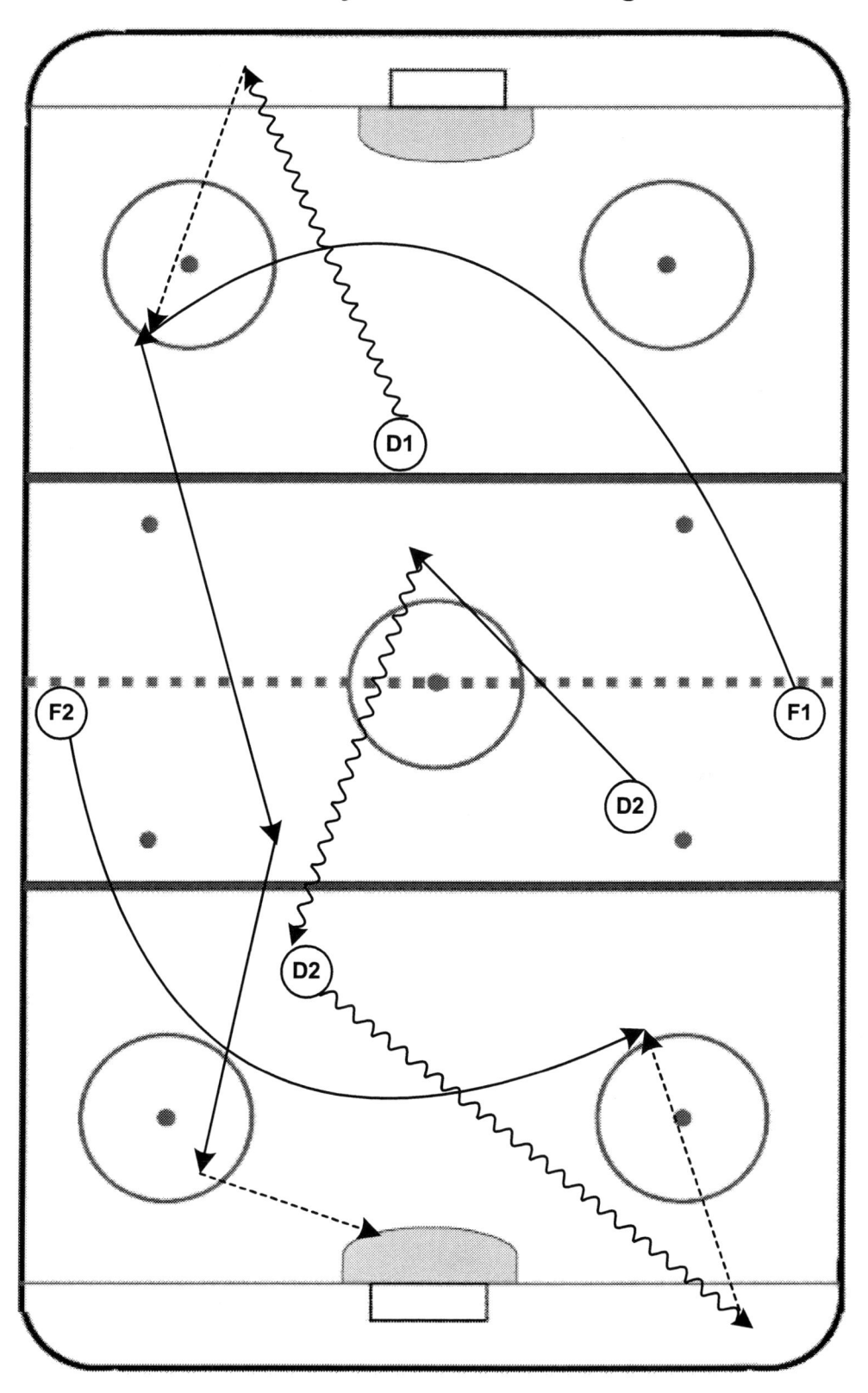

# 27 — 5 v 0, 3 Times

## Emphasis and Objective
Work on breakouts, neutral zone regrouping and scoring.

## Drill Set-Up
* All players in boxes except 3 F's and 2 D's.
* On 1st whistle, C dumps puck in for a breakout play.
* Play proceeds 5 v 0 until goal is scored.
* On the C 2nd whistle, the C places a puck somewhere in the neutral zone and the 3 F's and 2 D's regroup and counter attack 5 v 0 continuing until a goal is scored.
* On the C's 3rd whistle, C places a puck in the neutral zone for another neutral zone regroup and counter attack.
* Once a goal is scored, the next line is up and the drill is repeated.

## Key Teaching Points
* Puck support in all 3 zones.
* Tape to tape passes.
* Movement through neutral zone.
* Neutral zone regrouping patterns.
* Score goals.
* Use defense for point shots/deflections.

## Recommended Progressions
* Add a neutral zone forechecker for the regroups.
* Vary forecheckers on the initial breakout play.
* Dump to goaltenders on regroup for a pass from goaltender.

**5 v 0, 3 Times**

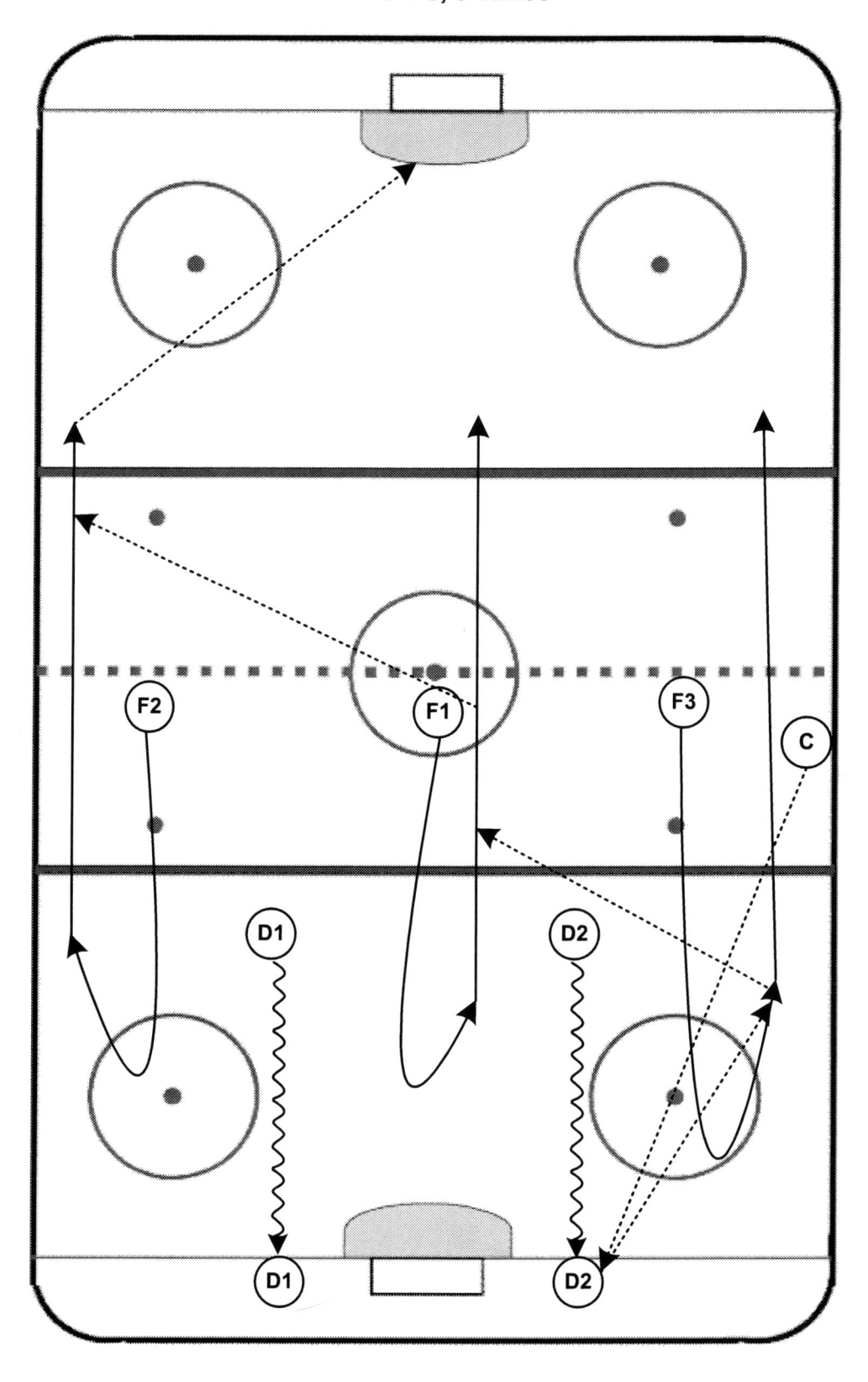

## 28. Half Ice Gap, Name the Situation

### Emphasis and Objective

Maintain good Gap control in a variety of situations.

### Drill Set-Up

* C in front of net on hash marks, D1 and D2 inside blue-line opposite end with pucks. F's in lines at each red-line.
* On the whistle, D's begin drill by passing D to D while retreating into the defensive zone. Regrouping forwards (2 or 3, Name the Situation) support the puck back into the zone and receive a pass from D1 or D2.
* F's attack through the neutral zone with speed, D's follow the play up the ice. At the blue-line, F's pass to C who returns a pass to the F's for an attack. Original D's play the rush maintaining a tight Gap.

### Key Teaching Points

* 2 stick length Gap.
* F's stagger attack at full speed.
* Puck support.
* Force play at blue-line.
* C Names The Situation.

### Recommended Progressions

* 2 v 1, 2 v 2, 3 v 1, 3 v 2.

# Half Ice Gap, Name the Situation

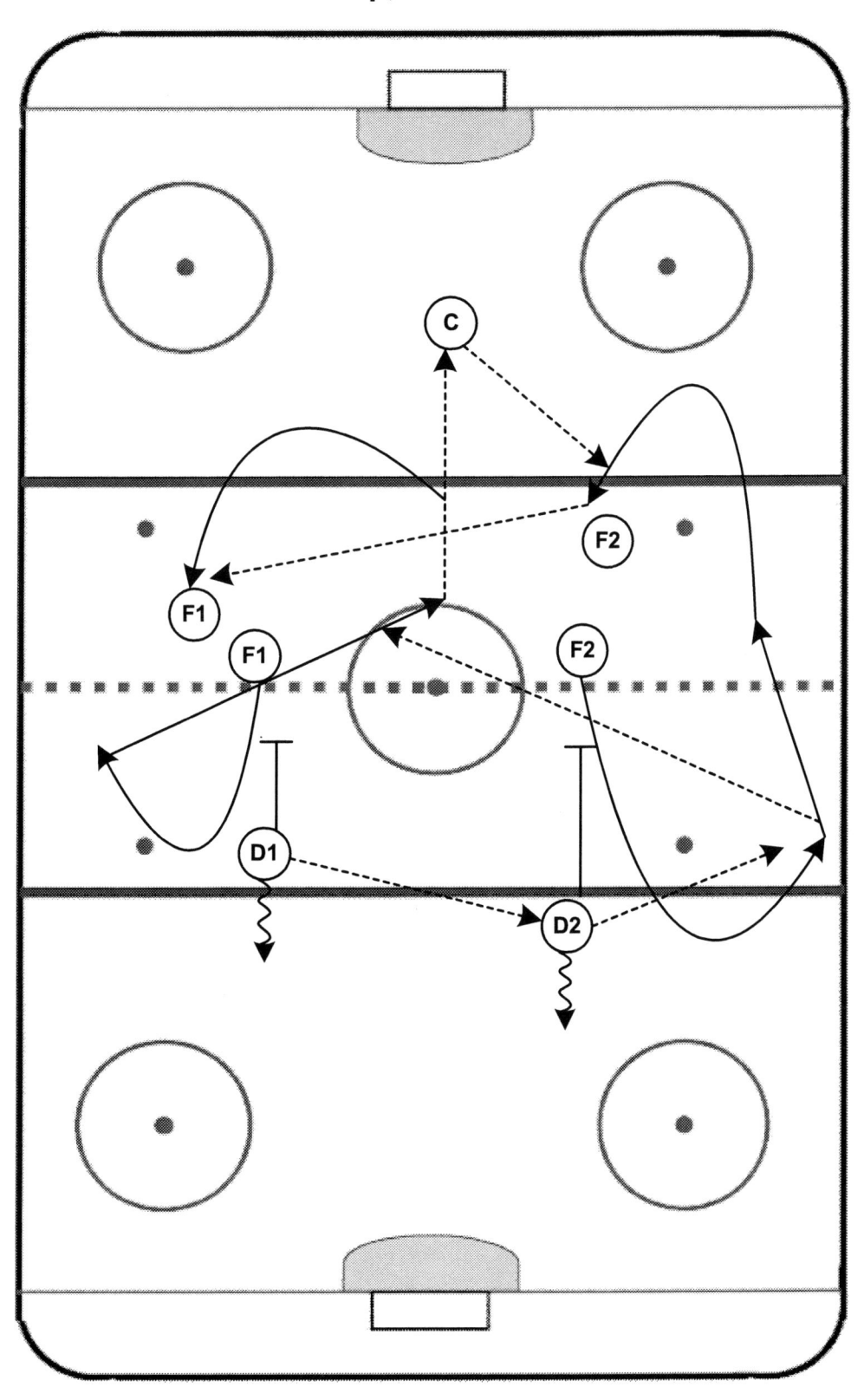

# 29 Czech Breakout and Regroup, 5 v 4 to a 5 v 3

## Emphasis and Objective

Develop breakout skills, reading the forecheck and regroup in the neutral zone.

## Drill Set-Up

* D1, D2 positioned behind the net, F1,F2, F3 in breakout position. X1, X2 in front of the goal prepared to forecheck. D3, D4 on the blue-line preparing to meet the rush.
* On the whistle, D1, D2 and 3 F's breakout against X's and attack D3, D4.
* In the neutral zone, F's pass the puck to D3 or D4 and regroup and attack 1 X and D1, D2 for a 5 v 3.
* Continue play in the zone 5 v 3.

## Key Teaching Points

* Read the forecheck.
* Hard passes.
* Support the puck.
* Good regrouping skills.
* Staggered attack and puck possession.

## Recommended Progressions

* None.

# Czech Breakout and Regroup, 5 v 4 to a 5 v 3

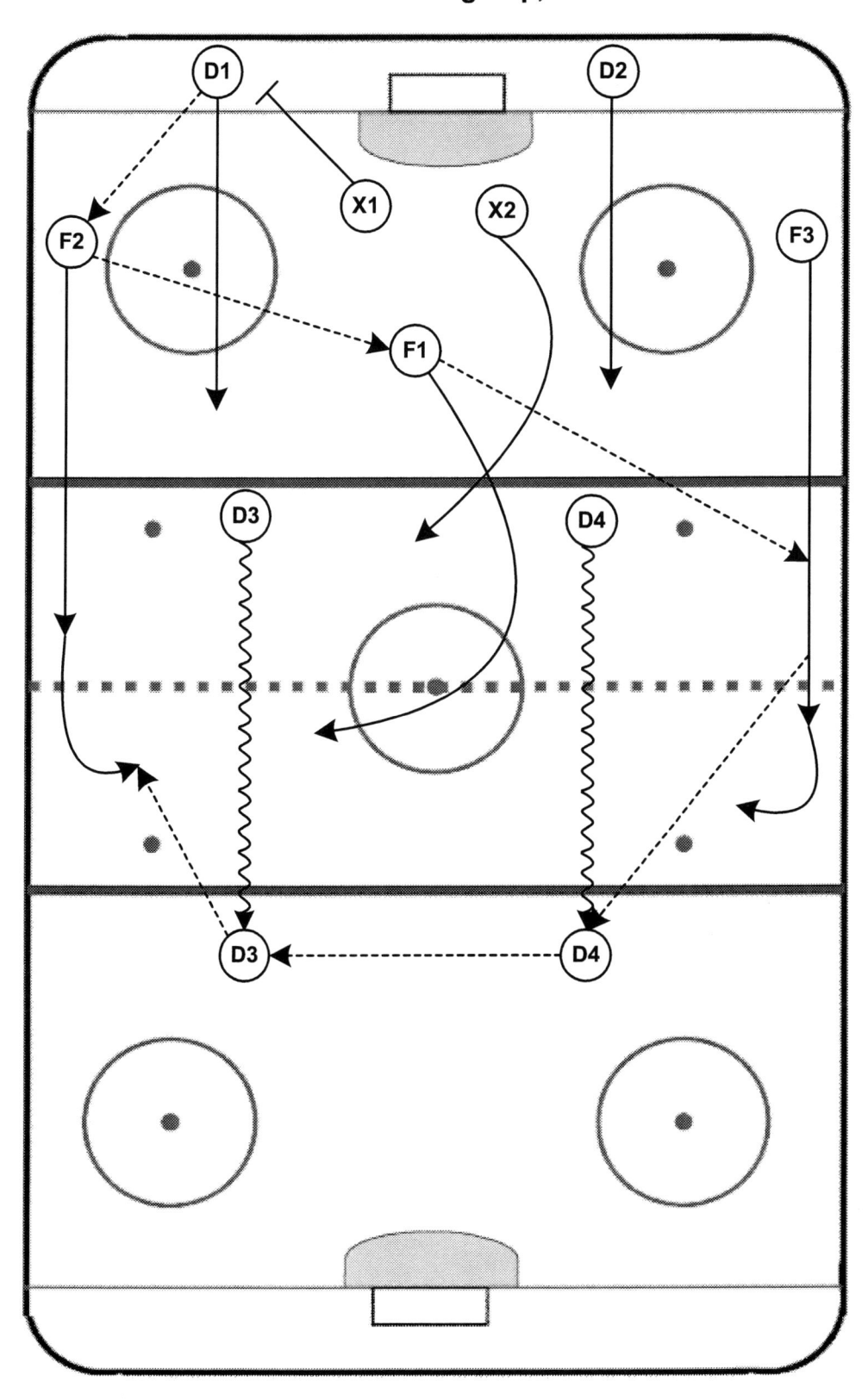

## 30 — Neutral Zone Step-up, 1 v 2

### Emphasis and Objective
Work on reading and forcing the play in neutral ice.

### Drill Set-Up
* 4 D in the neutral zone, F's at the bench.
* On the whistle, F1 regroups with D1 and D2. F1 attacks D3 and D4, 1 v 2.
* D3 and D4 must read the play and force the puck carrier in neutral ice.
* Once puck turns over, F2 regroups with D3 and D4 and attacks D1 and D2, 1 v 2.
* Continuous.

### Key Teaching Points
* Good regroups/counter attacks.
* Head up at all times.
* D must communicate and take good attack angles and support.
* Puck protection.
* Puck support.
* One way shown.

### Recommended Progressions
* 2 v 2.

# Neutral Zone Step-up 1 v 2

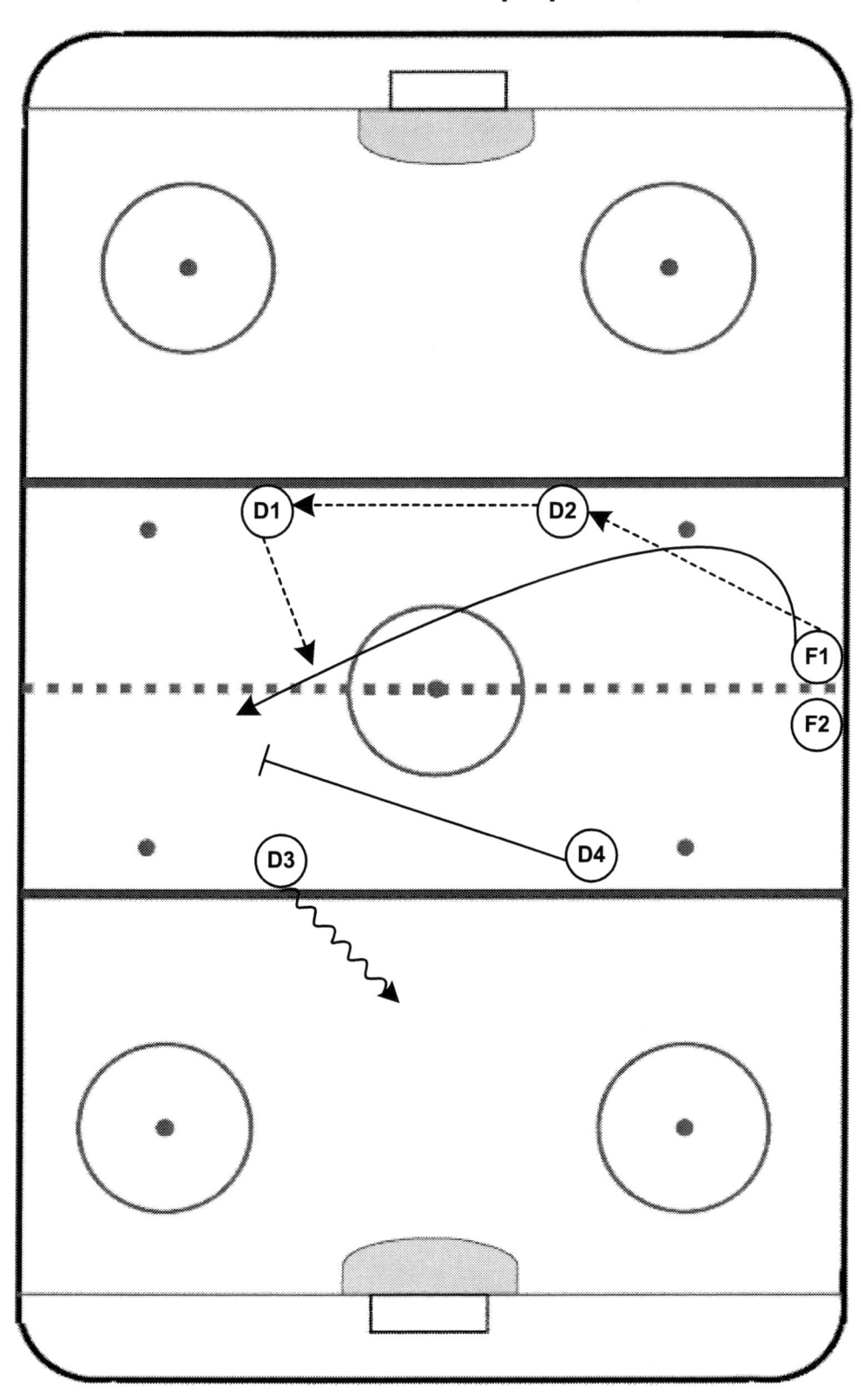

# 31 — 3 v 3, 3 Zone Transition

## Emphasis and Objective

Work on transitioning from defense to offense, offense to defense in all 3 zones.

## Drill Set-Up

* 3 X's and 3 Y's in each zone. Nets moved to the hash marks.
* Pucks with X1, X2 and X3 in defensive zone.
* X1, X2 and X3 must move the puck through the neutral zone via X4, X5 and X6 to X7, X8 and X9 for a scoring opportunity.
* Y's initially defend attempting to transition from defense to offense.

## Key Teaching Points

* Team with puck is on offense, team without, defense.
* Defending team in the neutral zone cannot cross center until the puck enters the zone.
* Puck cannot be passed from defensive zone to offensive zone without first going through the neutral zone players.
* Players must support the puck and move to open areas.

## Recommended Progressions

* Have players switch zones to work on transition in all 3 situations.
* Move attackers and defenders to the side for side board 3 v 2.

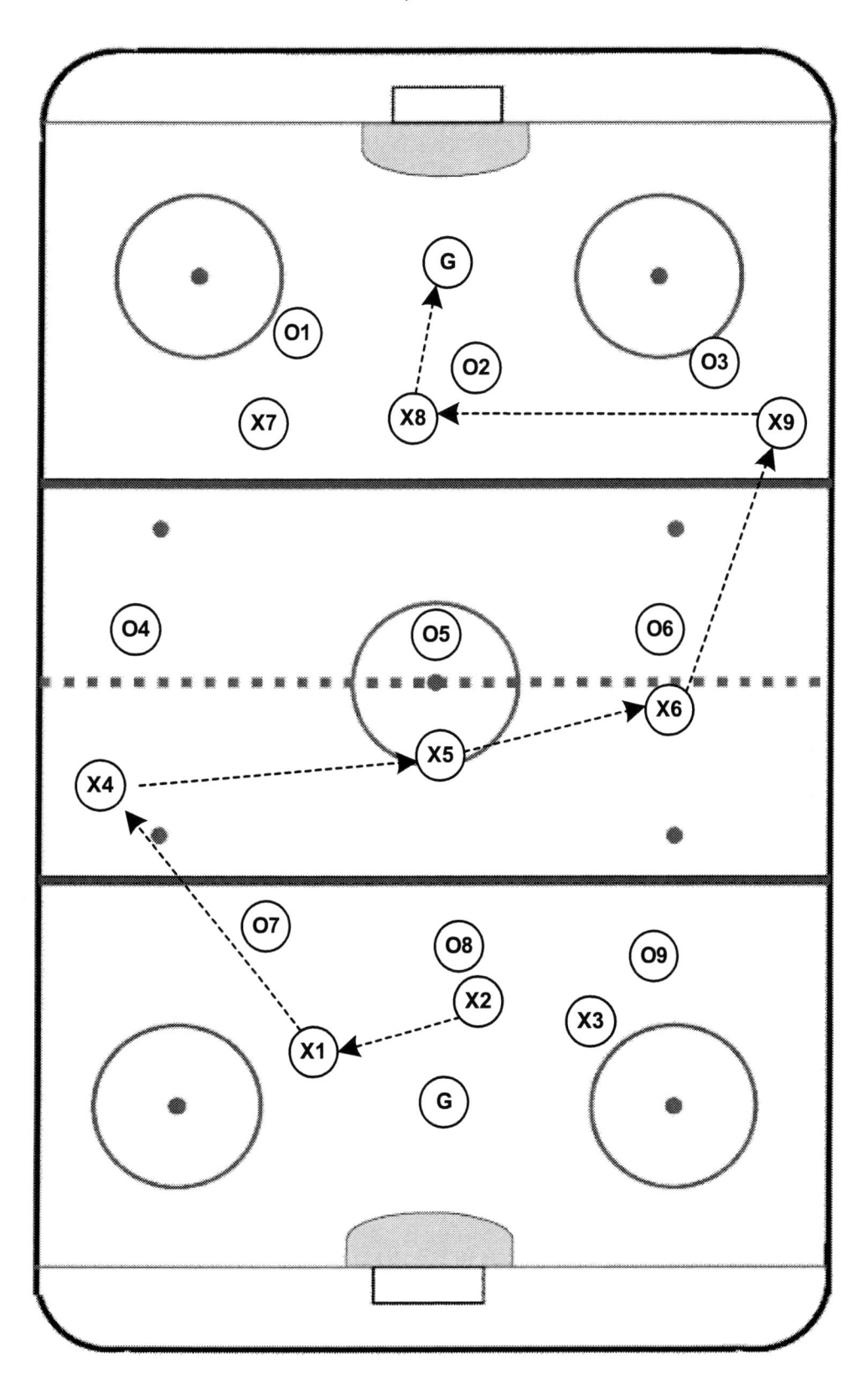

# 3 v 3, 3 Zones

# Bucky: 5 v 2 Twice to a 2 v 1

## Emphasis and Objective

Work on break out and attack skills and flow.

## Drill Set-Up

* 3 F's and D1, D2, in zone in breakout position, D3 and D4 on the blue-line, remaining players at the bench. C's with pucks in the corners.
* On the whistle, C places the puck for a breakout (either a hard rim or a spot placement), D1, D2 and 3 F's breakout and attack D3 and D4.
* On the whistle, C again places a puck for D3 and D4 to breakout the 3 F's against the original D1 and D2.
* On the whistle, D's drop off, C places a puck for 2 F's and they attack the remaining F 2 v 1.
* Next group jumps in and the drill repeats

## Key Teaching Points

* Full speed.
* Handle the puck.
* Staggered attack.
* Go to the net.

## Recommended Progressions

* None.

**Bucky: 5 v 2 Twice to a 2 v 1**

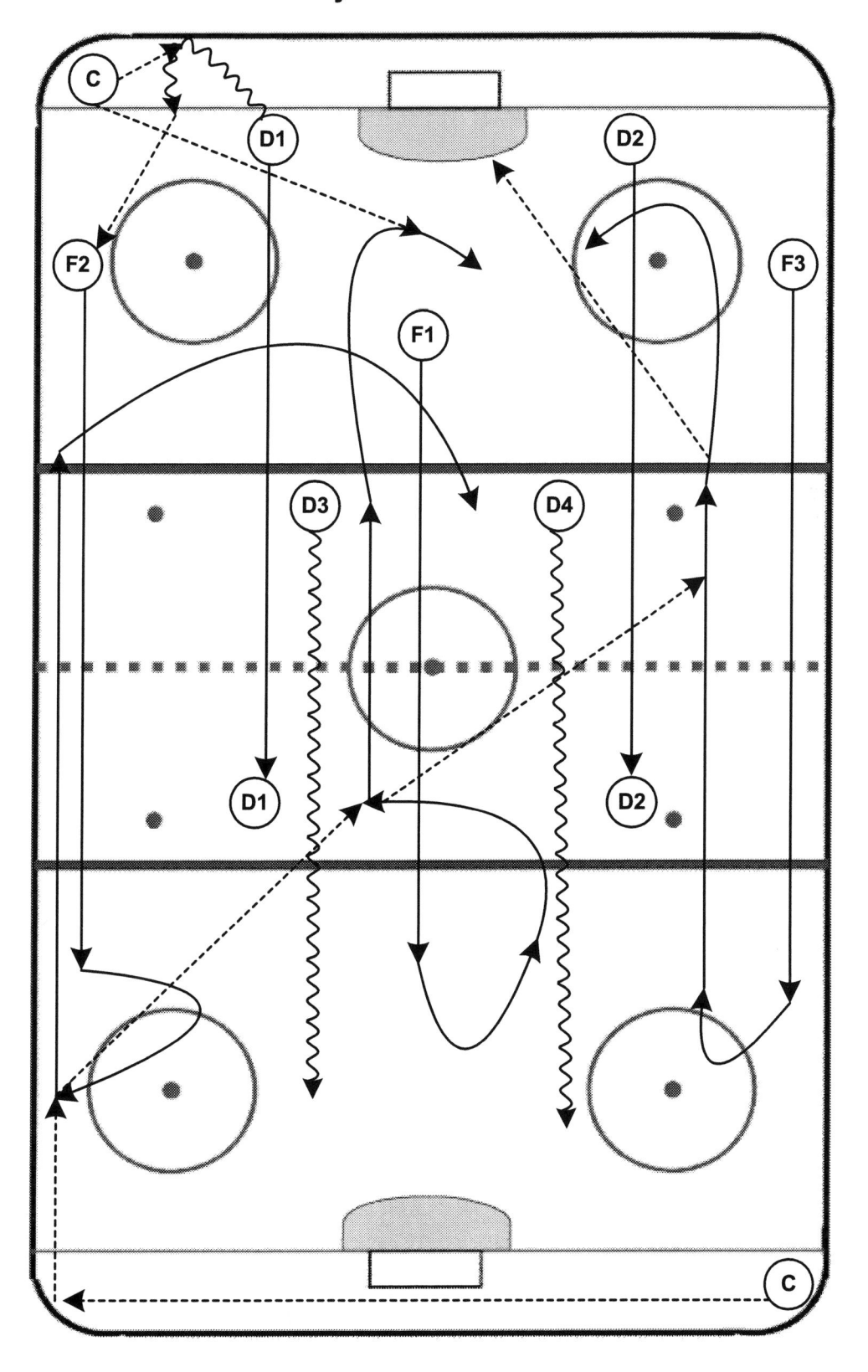

# 33. Continuous Forecheck

## Emphasis and Objective

Work on forechecking systems and breakouts under pressure.

## Drill Set-Up

* Forward lines and defensive pairs in the neutral zone, C with puck.
* Two forward lines up with defensive pairs.
* C dumps pick into one zone, that group of 5 (2 D and 3 F's) breakout and attack the neutral zone. The other group of 5 (2 D and 3 X's) waits in the neutral zone to meet the attack.
* Once each F touches the puck, they dump the puck into the zone and forecheck the 2 D and 3 X's. 3 Y's and 2 D move from the bench into the neutral zone.
* X's must break the puck out against the forecheck, gain the neutral zone, dump the puck in and forecheck Y's.
* Continuous.

## Key Teaching Points

* Read the forecheck.
* Head up at all times.
* Make easy, high percentage passes.
* Hold up forecheckers to give D added time.
* Communication.
* Defensive coverage.

## Recommended Progressions

* None.

# Continuous Forecheck

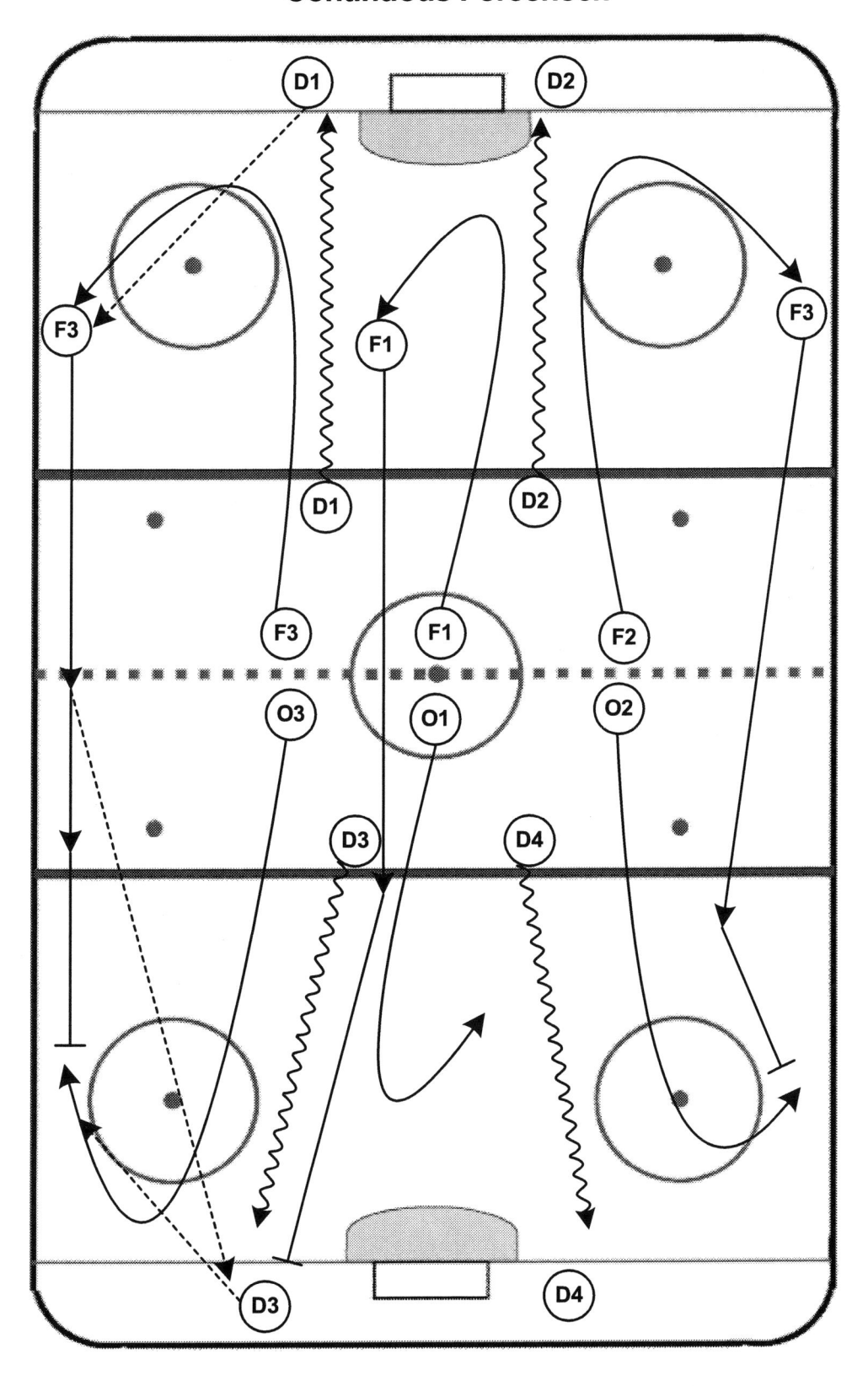

## 34    Defensive Challenge: 3 v 2, 2 v 2, 5 v 5

### Emphasis and Objective

    Work on a variety of attacks and defenses.

### Drill Set-Up

- Players positioned as diagrammed. Remaining players at the bench.
- On the whistle, C dumps puck into the zone, D 1 and D2 and F1, F2 and F3 breakout against X1 and attack D3 and D4, 3 v 2. X1 backchecks all the way into the zone.
- On the 1st whistle, X2 and X3 counter attack against D1 and D2, 2 v 2.
- On the 2nd whistle, D1, D2 and X2, X3 stop and join the original 3 v 2 thus creating a 5 v 5 in zone situation.

### Key Teaching Points

- Read the forecheck.
- Read the rush.
- Maintain good Gap control.
- Stress defensive coverage.
- Puck control and protection.

### Recommended Progressions

- Multiple pucks for extending play.

# Defensive Challenge 3 v 3, 2 v 2, 5 v 5

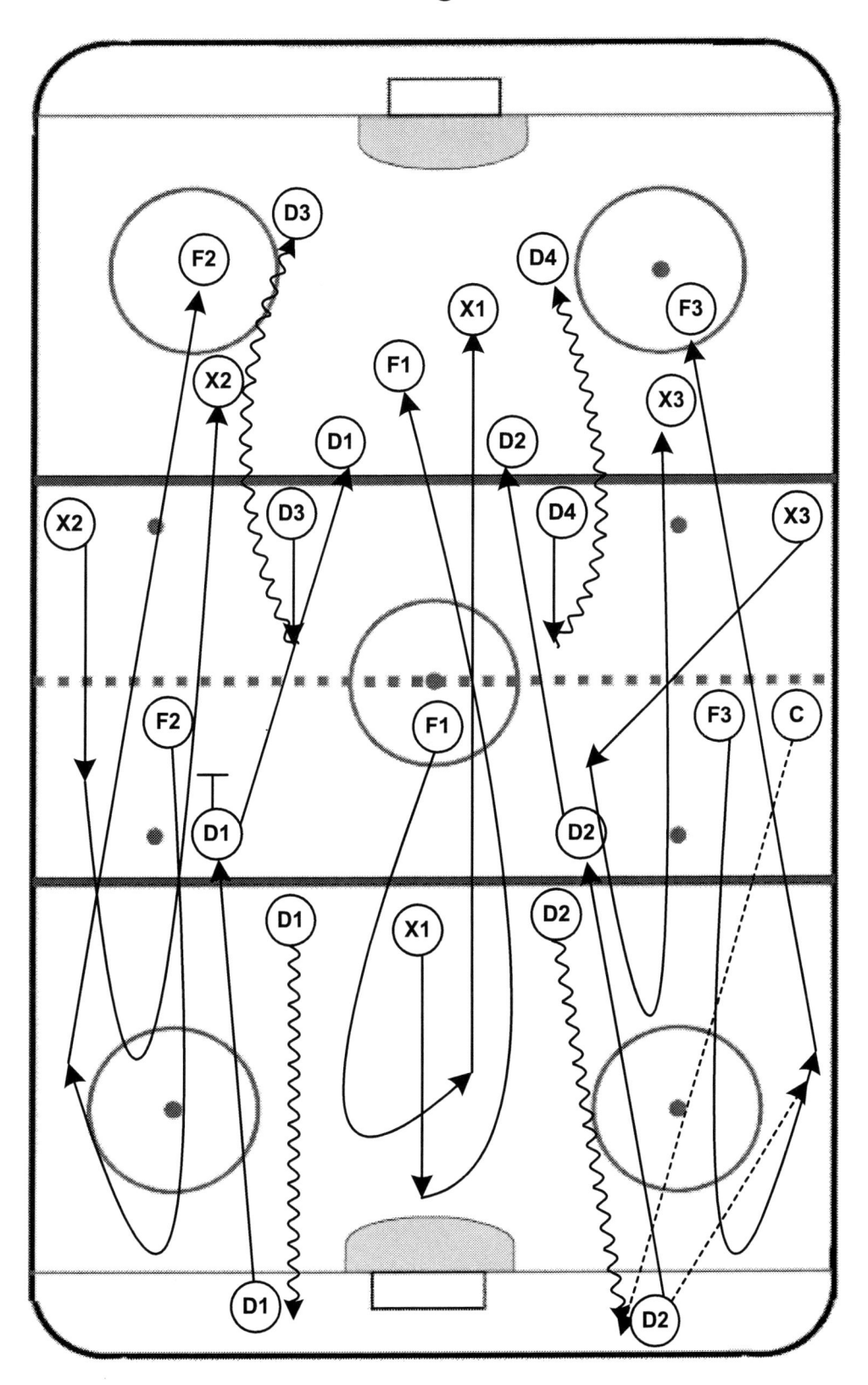

# 35 Jaguar Continuous Attack

## Emphasis and Objective
Full ice situational attack and defend under pressure.

## Drill Set-Up
* Pucks in each corner, players at the benches.
* C dumps a puck into one end, D1, D2 and F1, F2 and F3 breakout against 1 forechecking X1 and D3 and D4. X2, X3 positioned along each board preparing for next sequence, Y1 in the center at the blue-line.
* Full ice attack into the zone 5 v 3.
* On the whistle, F1, F2 and F3 drop out of the way, D3 and D4 retrieve a puck, X2 and X3 enter zone for breakout with D3 and D4, Y1 forechecks making it a 5 v 3 in the other direction. Y2 and Y3 get into position for next sequence.

## Key Teaching Points
* Quick decisions.
* Read the forecheck and backcheck.
* Communication.
* Neutral zone speed puck movement.
* Defense stay up with the play.

## Recommended Progressions
* None.

**Jaguar Continuous Attack**

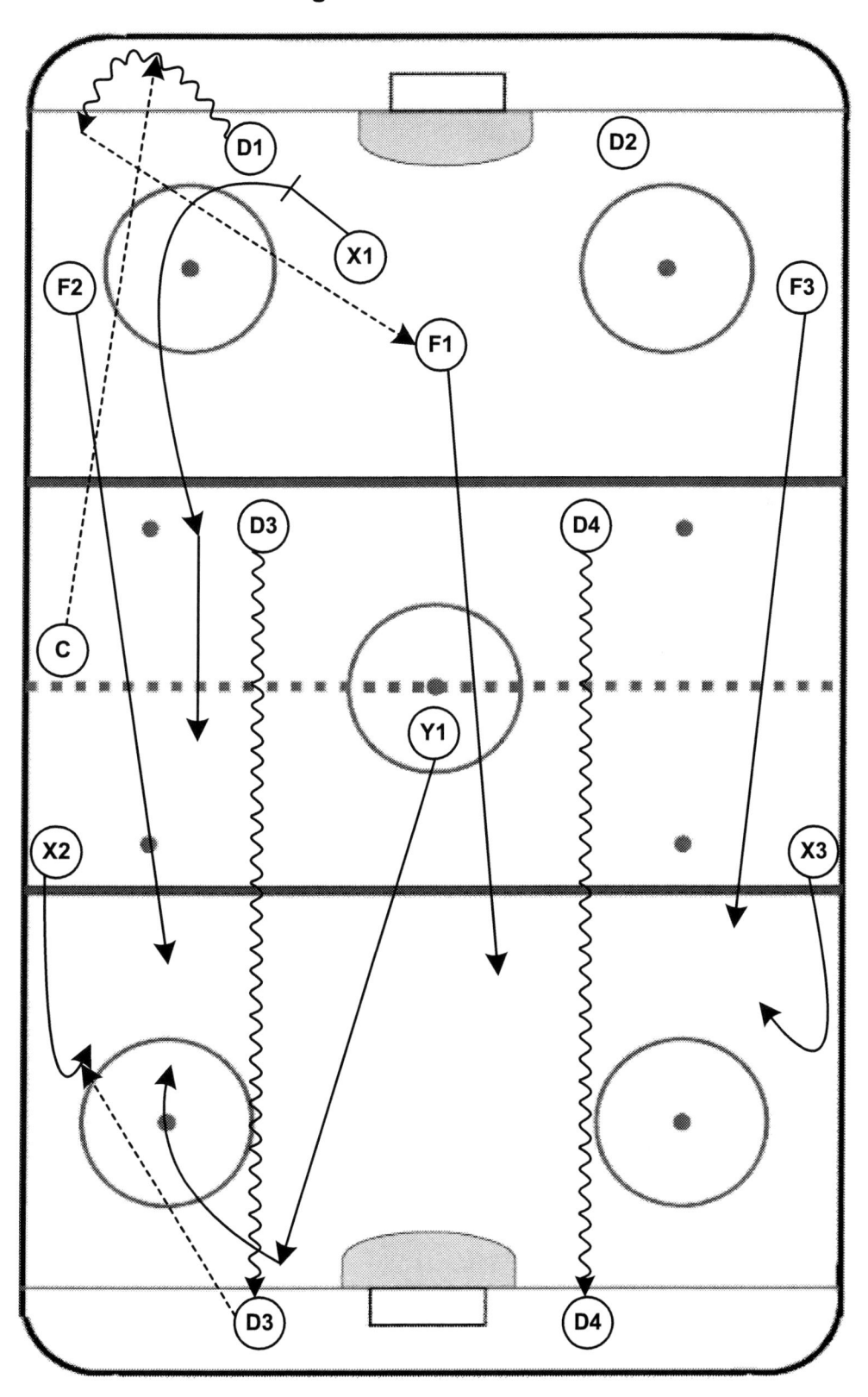

# 36 Seagull Backchecking

## Emphasis and Objective
Develop backchecking skills in a variety of situations.

## Drill Set-Up
- F's in opposite corners with pucks, D's in opposite corners other side.
- On 1st whistle, F1 skates to the blue-line and attacks D1, 1 v 1.
- On the 2nd whistle, F2 attacks D2 at the other end 1 v 1, D1 joins the offensive rush with F2, F1 backchecks to the net.

## Key Teaching Points
- 1 v 1 skills.
- Acceleration.
- Backcheck inside out.
- Communication.
- Backcheck to the net.
- Read the play.

## Recommended Progressions
- None

# Seagull Backcheck

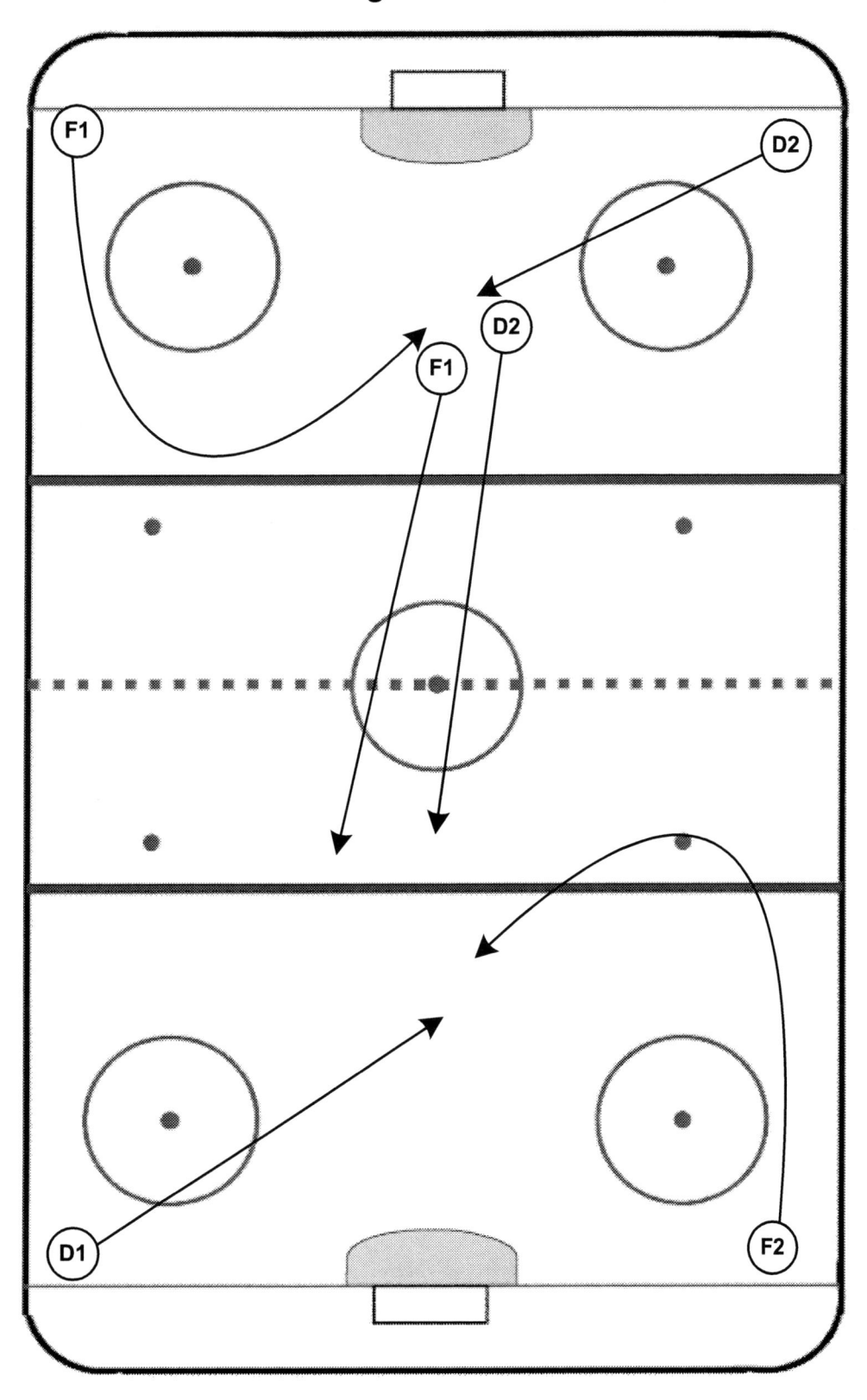

# 37 — Trojan Situational Backcheck

## Emphasis and Objective
Improve play without the puck, recognize backchecking situations.

## Drill Set-Up
* Half the F's in the neutral zone along the wall other half of F's in 3 lines (X1, X2 and X3') behind the goal line. 2 D's at point position. C in corner with pucks.
* 3 neutral zone F's come off the wall and attack 3 v 0. After 1st shot, C passes to point, forwards establish position in front of the net while points shoot.
* On the 1st whistle, coach passes to one of the 3 F's and they attack the opposite end 3 v 2 against D.
* After the pass, C sends any number X's (0-3) to backcheck the play.

## Key Teaching Points
* Scoring.
* Positioning.
* Read the rush.
* Backchecking skills.
* Communication.

## Recommended Progressions
* None.

# Trojan Situational Backcheck

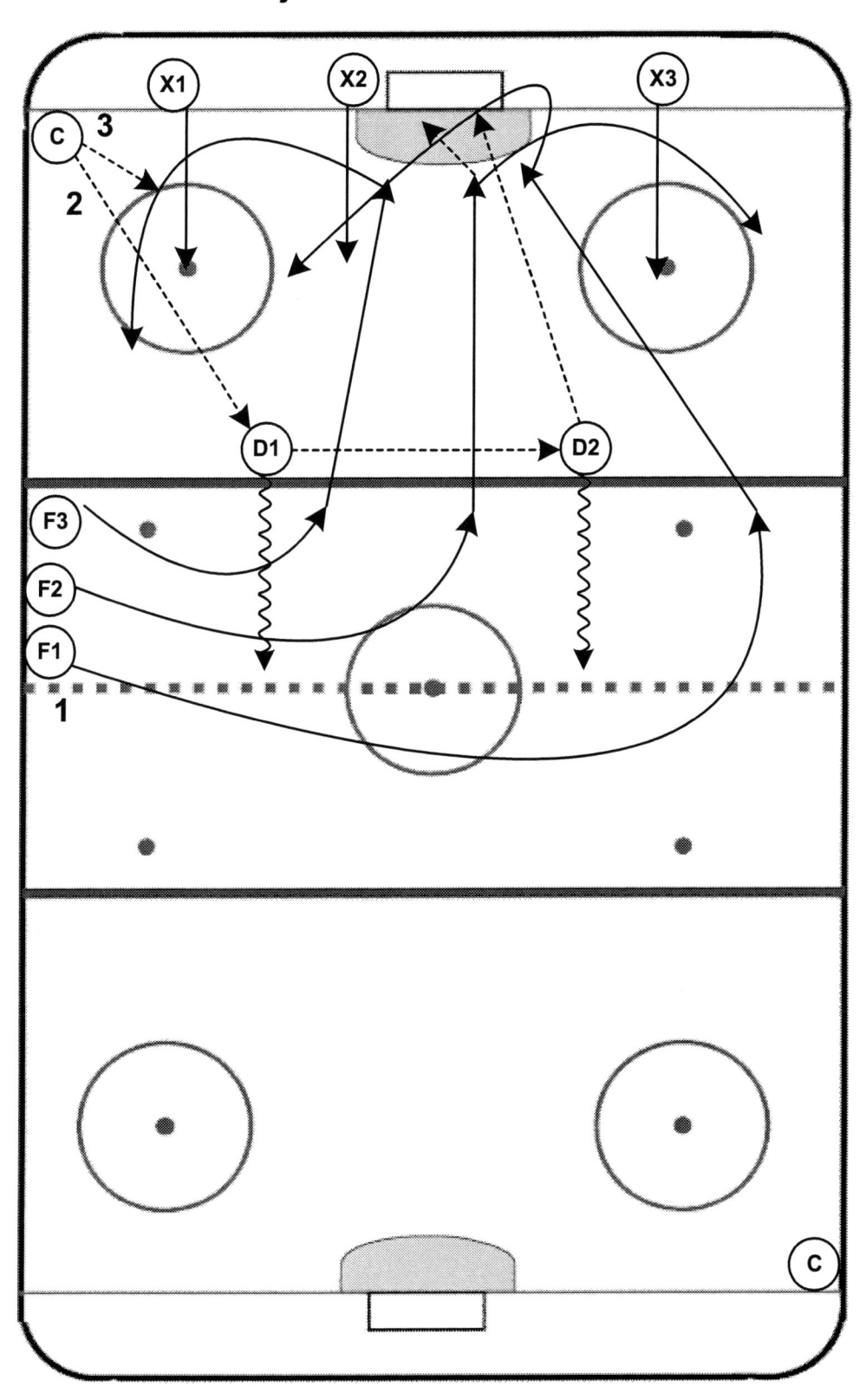

## 38    Backcheck Transition, 5 v 0 - 5 v 5

### Emphasis and Objective

Work on breakouts, backchecking and defensive coverage.

### Drill Set-Up

* C in neutral zone with pucks. D's with partners on blue-line, 2 sets of 3 F's on either side of the red-line.
* C dumps puck into either zone, one group of F's with 2 D's breakout and attack 5 v 0. The non breaking out F's wait for attackers to pass them at the red-line they then follow them into the defensive zone assuming a good breakout position.
* On the whistle, the 2nd group of F's breakout 3 v 2 against the original D, the attacking F's turn and backcheck into the zone. The 2nd group of D joins and follows the play into the zone creating a 5 v 5 situation.
* Play multiple pucks.

### Key Teaching Points

* Go through all breakout patterns.
* Speed through the neutral zone.
* Backcheck inside out.
* Defensive coverage, angling.
* Good conditioning drill.

### Recommended Progressions

* Add a forechecker to the breakout portion.

# Backcheck Transition 5 v 0, 5 v 5

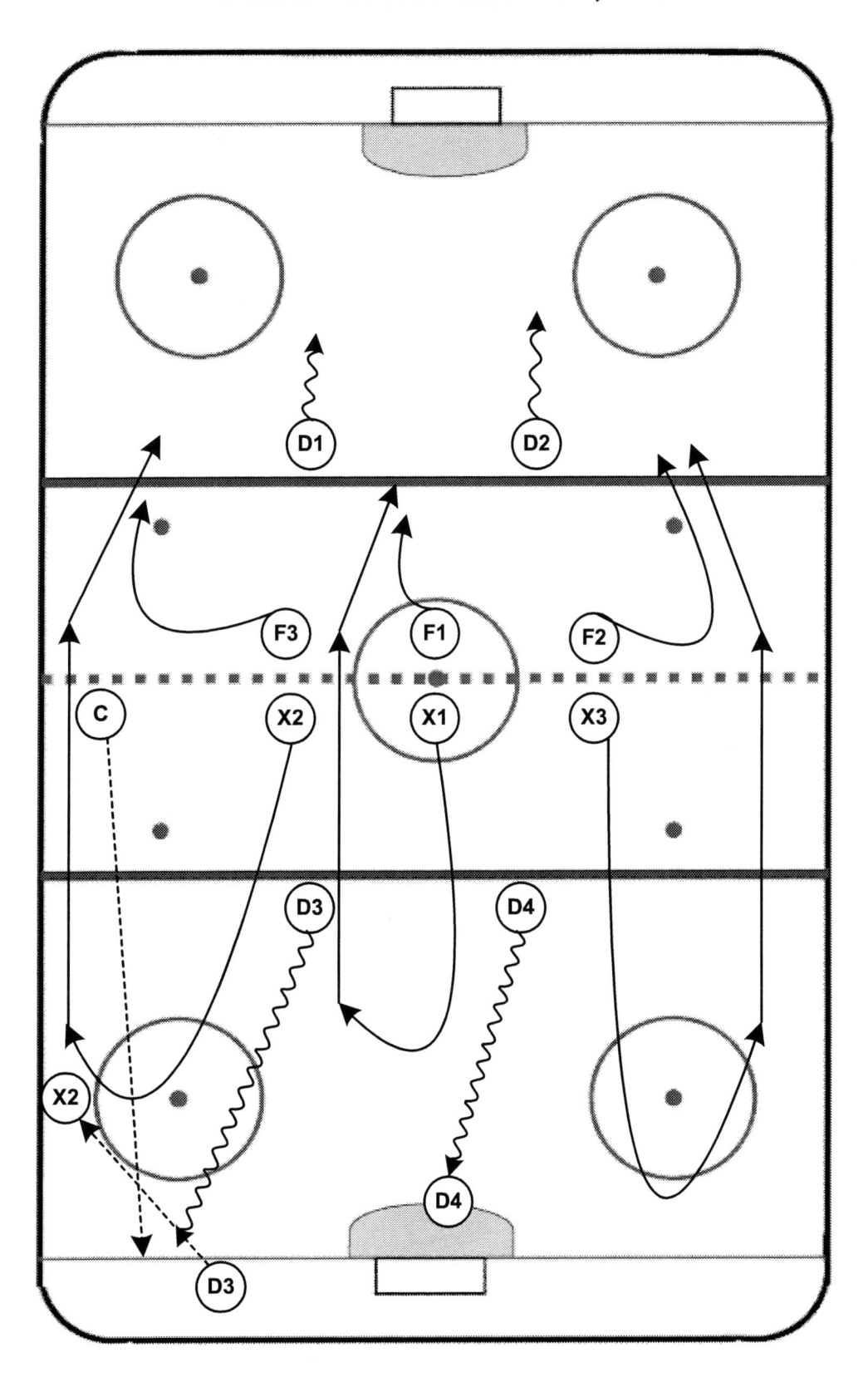

# 39     Sprint: 3 v 2 Backcheck

## Emphasis and Objective

Work on backchecking skills and reading the rush.

## Drill Set-Up

* Players at the bench. 3 F's and 2 D's at the red-line, 1 backchecking X in the corner with pucks.
* On the whistle, 3 F's retreat in a backchecking fashion to the defensive zone, D follow to the blue-line.
* X passes to one of the F's who attack the 2 D 3 v 2. After making the regrouping pass, X must Sprint to backcheck the play making it a 3 v 3.
* Play 3 v 3 in the zone until the whistle.

## Key Teaching Points

* Good breakout position.
* Backcheck a lane, not the puck.
* D read the rush.
* Communication.
* Maintain a proper defensive Gap.
* Puck protection

## Recommended Progressions

* 3 v 1.
* Multiple pucks for longer 3 v 3 play.

# Sprint 3 v 2 Backcheck

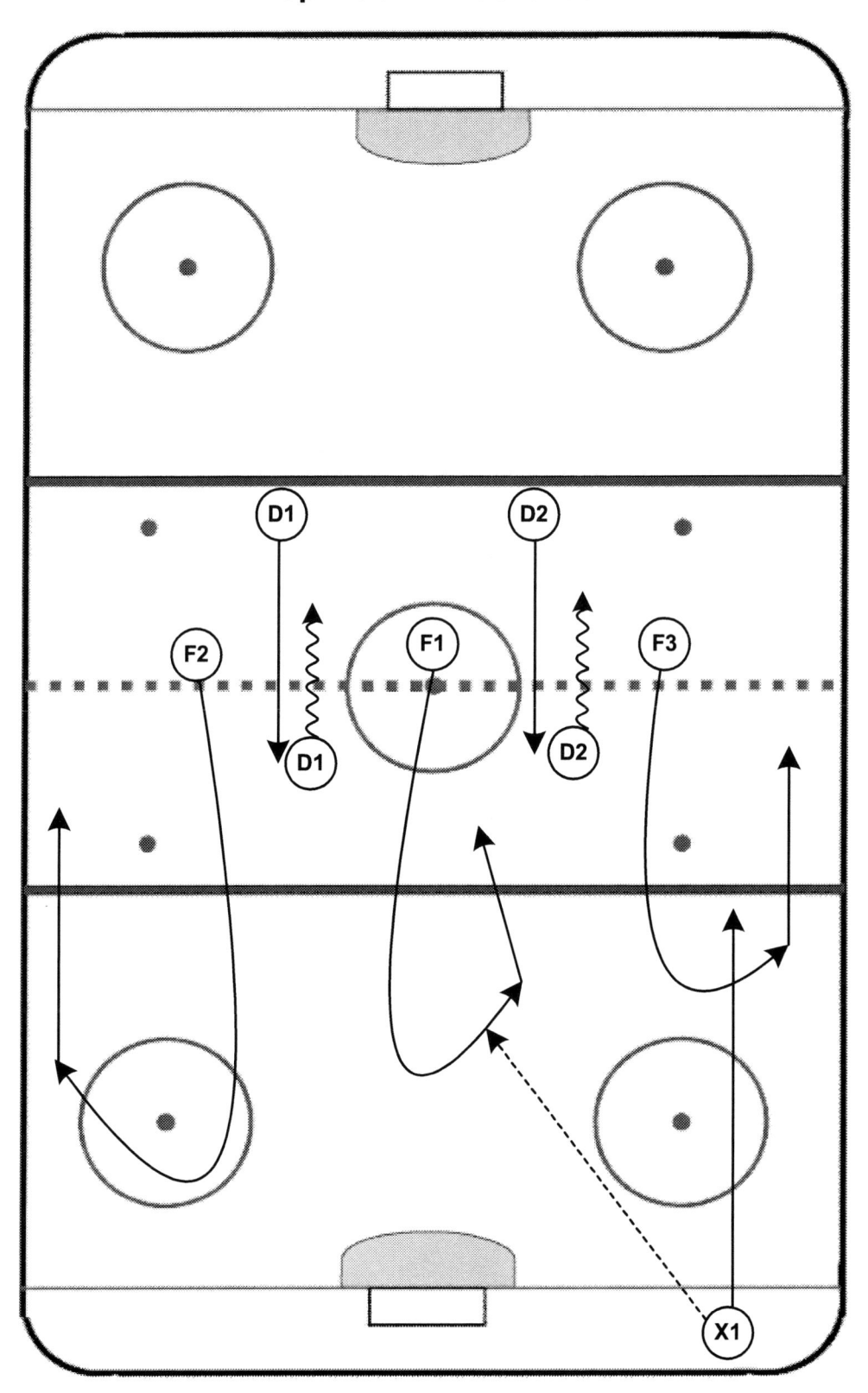

# 40 · Center Backcheck, 2 v 2

## Emphasis and Objective
Work on backchecking skills and shooting under pressure.

## Drill Set-Up
* 2 players at each blue-line (F1 and F2), 2 players (X1 and X2) inside the red-line. One X with puck.
* On the whistle, X1 passes to either F1 or F2, both X1 and X2 backcheck and pressure the both the puck carrier and the supporting player.
* The puck carrier must make a quick decision to pass or shoot.
* Backcheck to the far post and play in zone 2 v 2 until the whistle.

## Key Teaching Points
* Quick decisions.
* Backcheck inside out to the far post.
* Hit the net.
* Shoot in stride.
* Puck protection.
* Rebound control.

## Recommended Progressions
* 3 v 2.

# Center Backcheck, 2 v 2

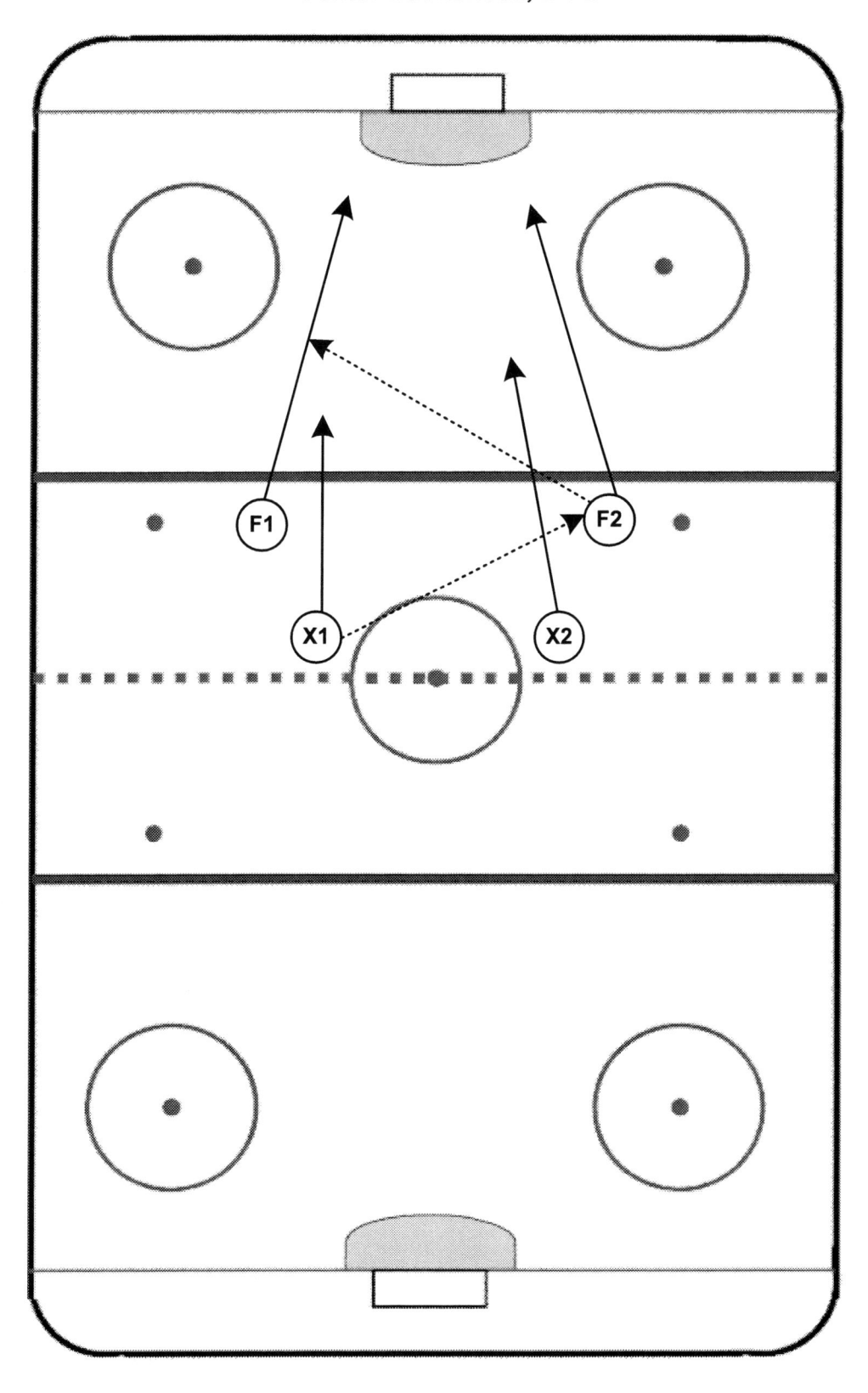

# 41 Funnel Defensive Play

## Emphasis and Objective

Work on play without the puck and recognition of defensive responsibilities.

## Drill Set-Up

* F1, F2, and F3 positioned just outside attacking blue-line with pucks. D1 and D2 in defensive position. F4, F5 and F6 in center circle behind the red-line.
* On the whistle, F1, F2 and F3 attack D1 and D2, 3 v 2. X1, X2 and X3 funnel into the defensive zone for coverage creating a 3 v 5.
* On the 2nd whistle, all players leave zone and attack again.
* X1, X2 and X3 must return to center circle.
* Alternate ends.

## Key Teaching Points

* Communicate.
* Defensive position.
* Attack angles.
* Puck protection and control.
* Transition, defense to offense.

## Recommended Progressions

* Add D3 and D4 for a 5 v 5.

# Funnel Defensive Play

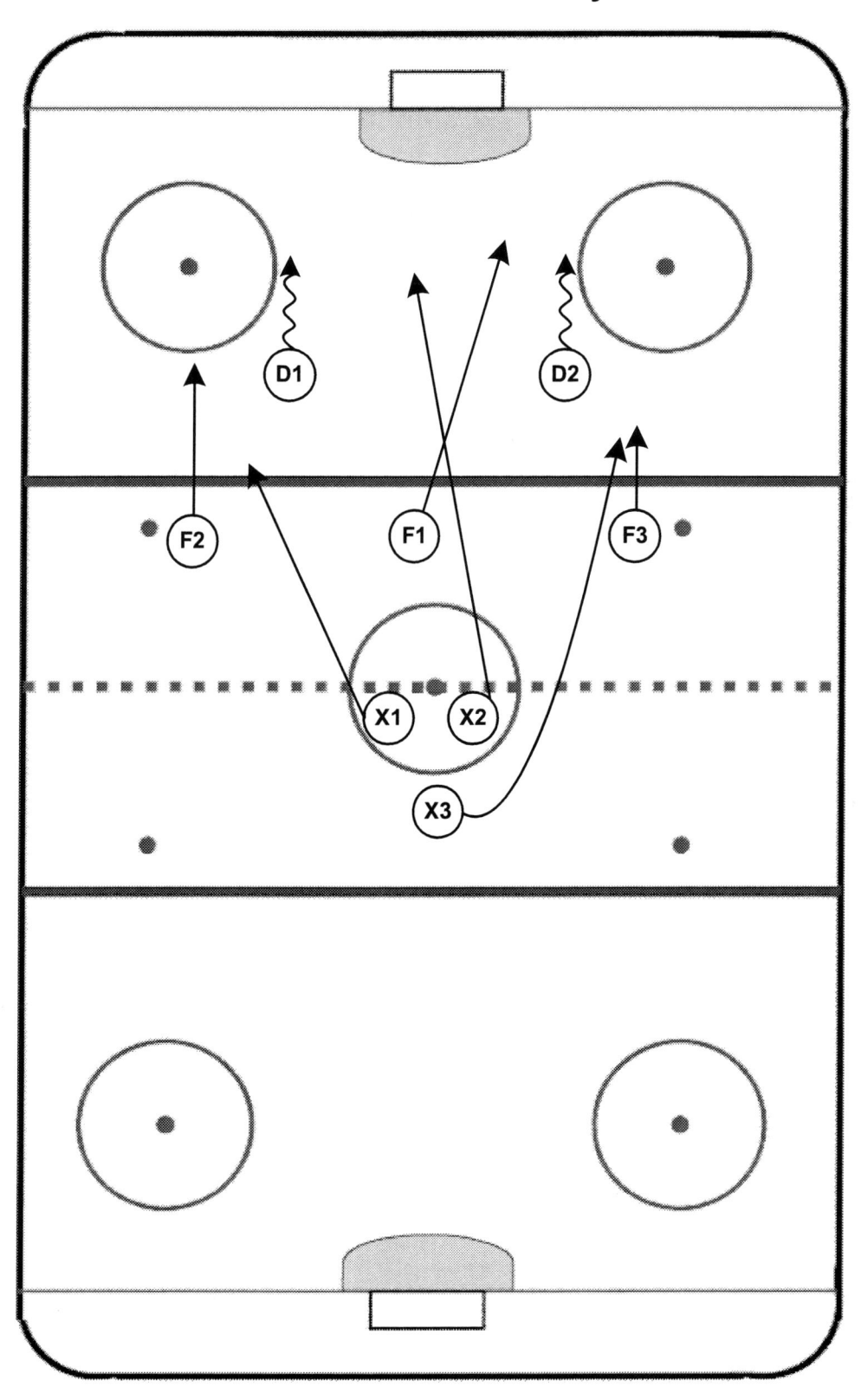

## 42 — Russian D Coverage, 3 v 3 to 5 v 5

### Emphasis and Objective

Defensive zone coverage in a variety of situations.

### Drill Set-Up

* In both offensive zones, 3 offensive forwards (F1, F2 and F3) against 2 defensemen (D1 and D2) and 1 defensive forward (X1). D3 and D4 along with X2 and X3 in neutral zone.
* On 1st whistle, F1, F2 and F3 play 3 v 3 against D1, D2 and X1.
* On the 2nd whistle, D3, D4 and X2 and X3 join play for a 5 v 5.
* 45 second shifts, new puck if defensive team clears.

### Key Teaching Points

* Defensive awareness.
* Angling.
* Positioning.
* Puck support.
* Puck protection.

### Recommended Progressions

* None.

# Russian D Coverage 3 v 3, 5 v 5

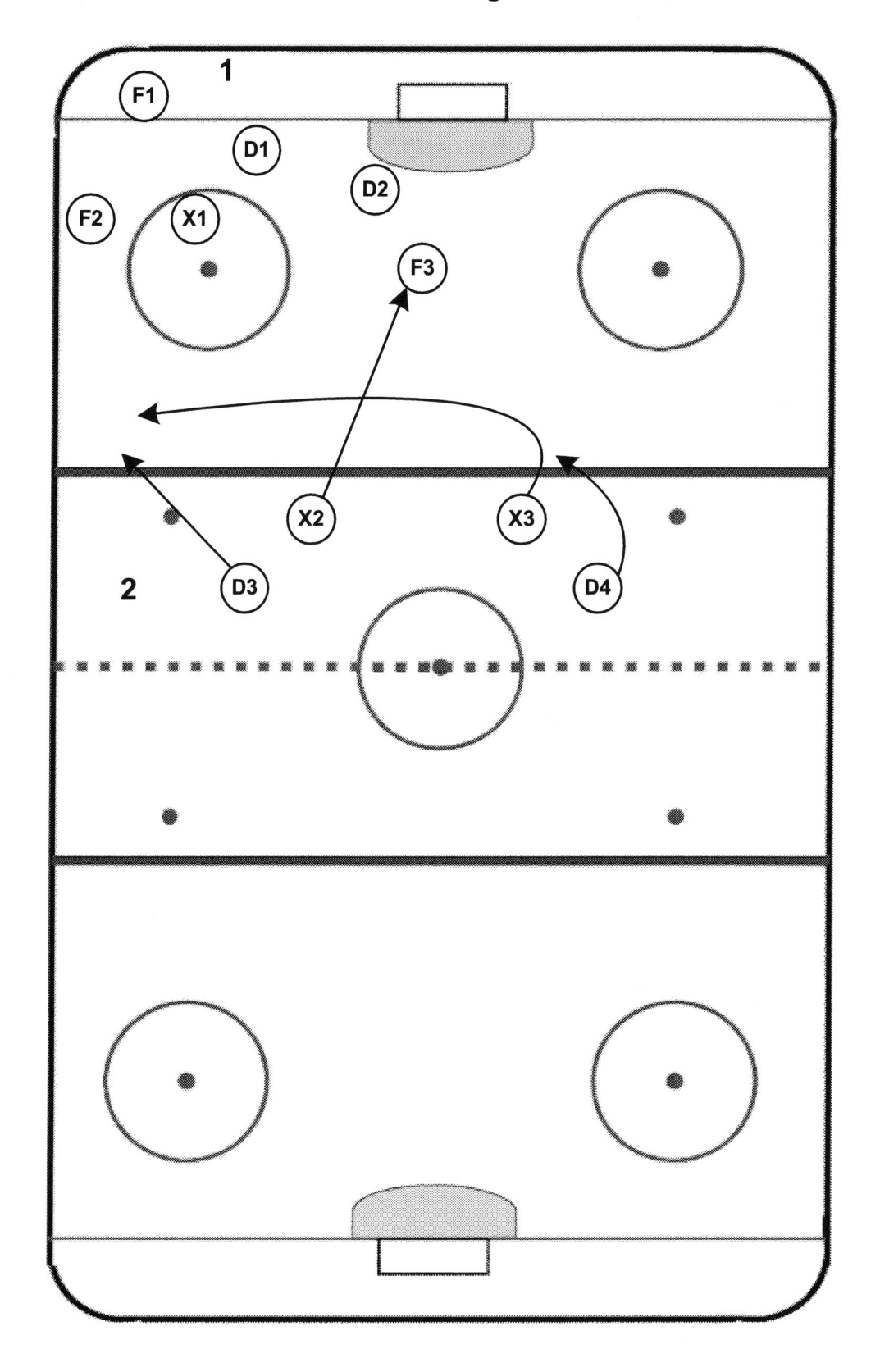

## 43 | Defensive Inzone Coverage, 5 v 5

### Emphasis and Objective
Work on defensive coverage skills, closing on the puck and offensive attacks.

### Drill Set-Up
- 2 groups of 5 in each zone.
- Play begins 5 v 5 with defense playing very passive, on the whistle, full speed 5 v 5 defensive players close on the puck carrier.
- On the next whistle, return to passive play. 30-45 second full speed shifts, alternate offensive and defensive players.

### Key Teaching Points
- Good closing and containment angles.
- Hit and pin, opponent control.
- Fight through checks.
- Picks and screens, puck support.
- Compete.

### Recommended Progressions
- None.

# Defensive Inzone Coverage, 5 v 5

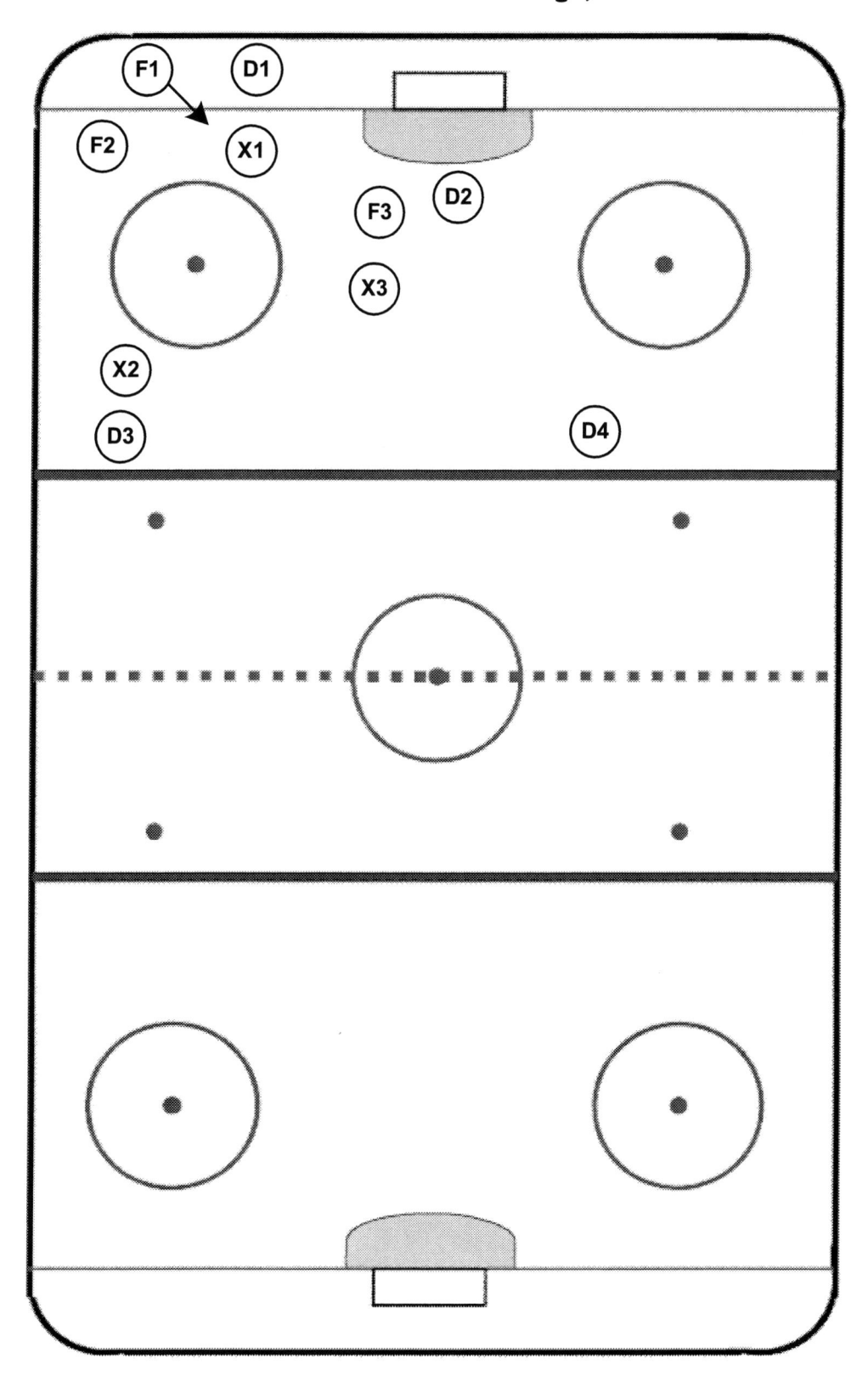

## 44. The Chipper, 1/2 Ice Zone Attack

### Emphasis and Objective

To practice entering the zone by chipping the puck behind the challenging defenseman to a 2 v 1.

### Drill Set-Up

* F's in their lines (C,LW,RW), across the red-line. D1 and D2 facing the F's in a good Gap.
* The center moves the puck to either the LW or RW who is immediately confronted by a D. The LW or RW must chip the puck past the D to a spot on the ice where the Center can retrieve the puck and attack with the LW or RW 2 v 1 against D2.

### Key Teaching Points

* Center must follow pass and support the puck.
* Soft hands to develop effective "chips".
* Opposite winger must stay back in good position.
* D stay between the attackers.
* Make good 2 v 1 decisions.

### Recommended Progressions

* None.

# The Chipper, 1/2 Ice Zone Attack

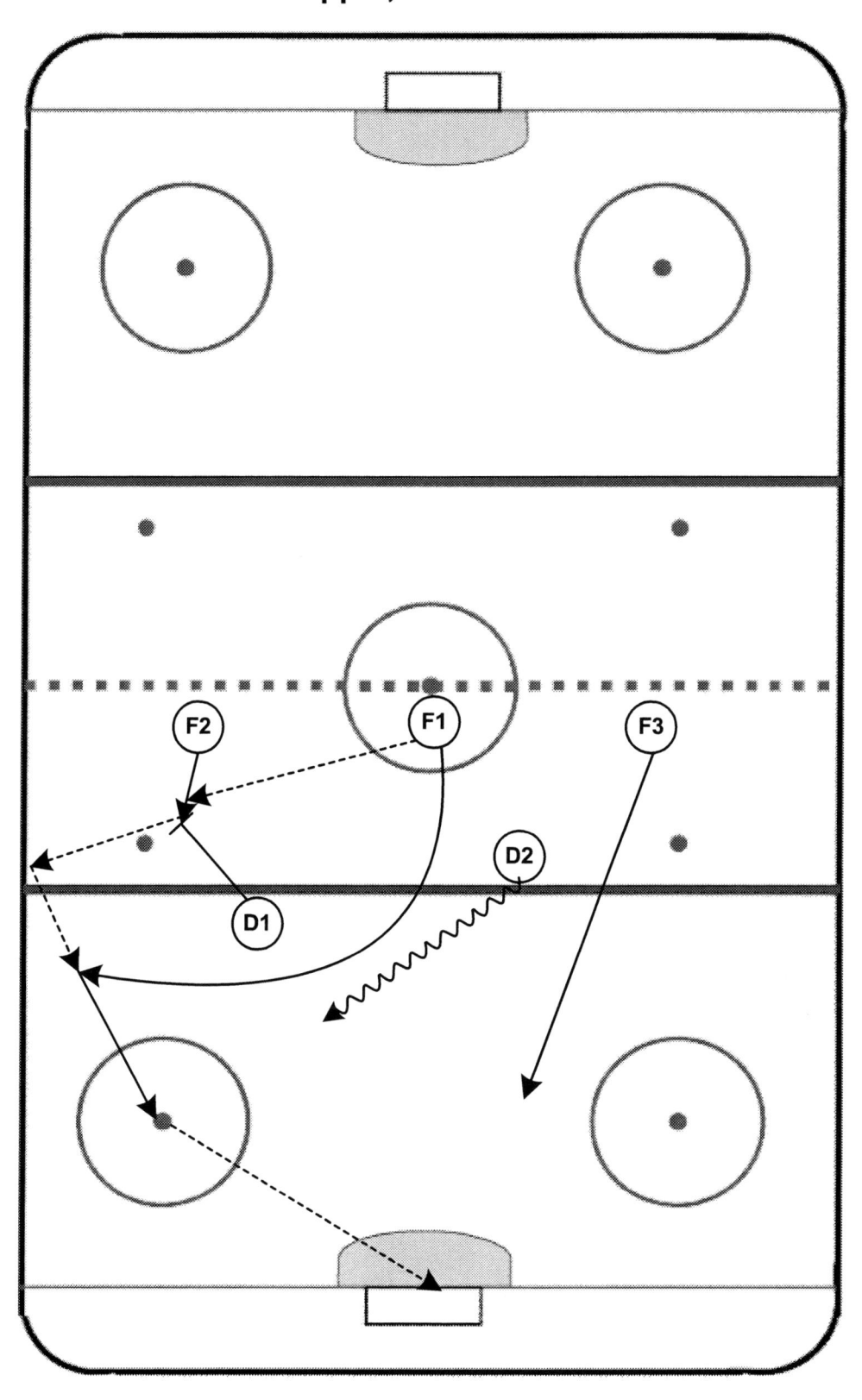

# 45 — 3 v 0, 3/4 Ice

## Emphasis and Objective

Move puck through neutral zone, drive the net.

## Drill Set-Up

* F's in their lines on blue-line with pucks.
* F1 starts with puck and attacks offensive end, making passes through the neutral zone.
* Moving the puck to the outside at the blue-line, the middle F drives to the far post with the far F assuming the high slot.
* Pass or shot comes from the wide F.
* Puck must be taken wide at the attacking blue-line.

## Key Teaching Points

* Full speed.
* Make crisp passes.
* Middle F goes hard to the net.
* Shot on net.
* Anticipate rebound.

## Recommended Progressions

* Have F's compete until they score a goal.
* Add 1 or 2 D for opposition.
* Add 2 attacking D for point shots after initial rush.

# 3 v 0 3/4 Ice

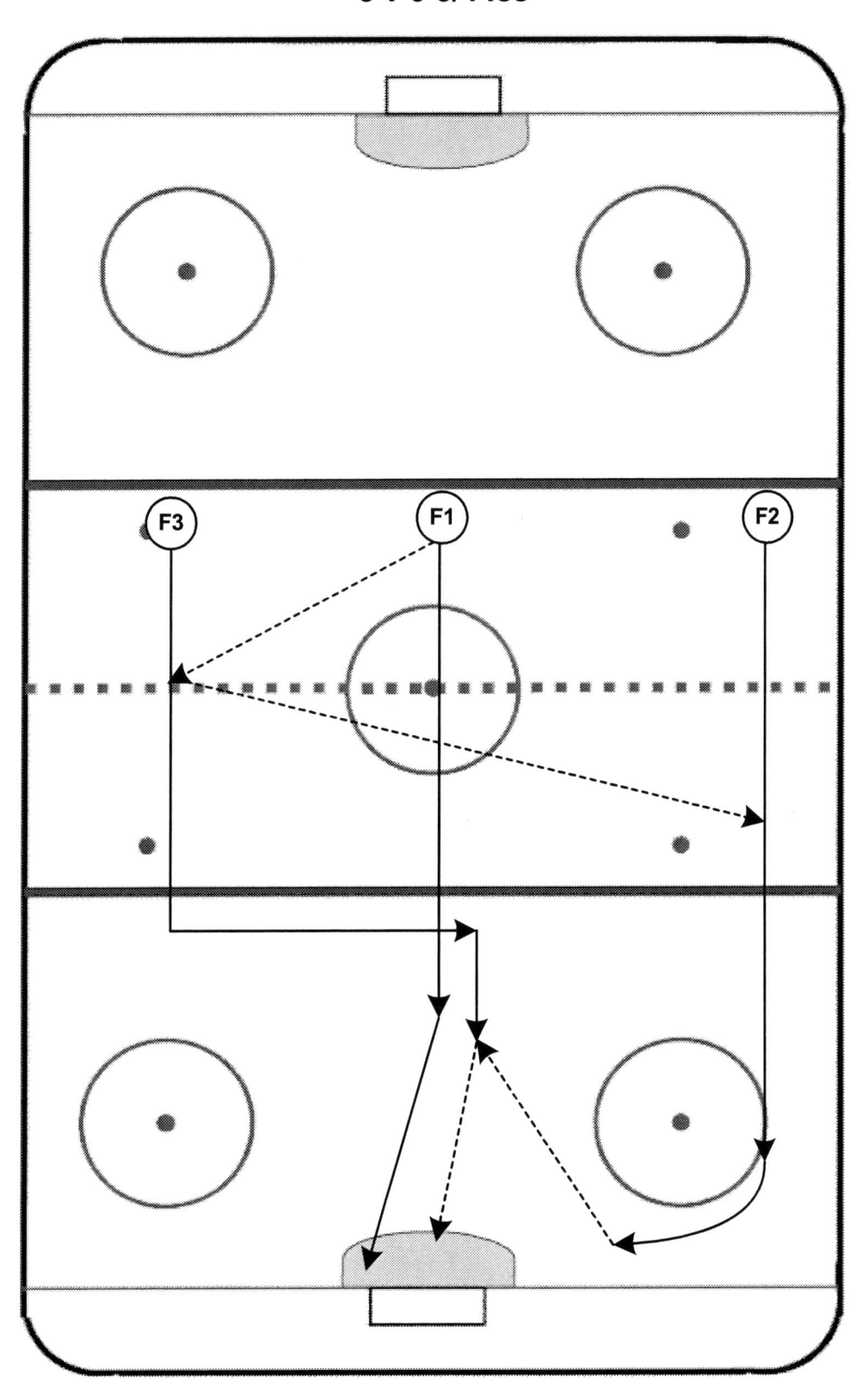

# 46 — 5 v 0, 3 v 2, 2 v 1, 1 v 0

## Emphasis and Objective

Passing and attacks in varied situations.

## Drill Set-Up

* All players in players boxes, 3 F's and 2 D's on ice, pucks in each corner and with the C.
* C dumps puck in, goalie sets up for breakout. 2D and 3 F's break out 5 v 0.
* On 1st whistle, the 3 F's finish their initial attack, receive a pass from the coach and attack the opposite end 3 v 2.
* On the C 2nd whistle, the 2 defending D return to the original blue-line preparing for a rush.
* 2 F's receive a pass from the coach and attack 1 D for a full ice 2 v 1.
* The remaining F grabs a puck from the corner, feeds the remaining D for a point shot/deflection.
* On the 3rd whistle, the last F receives a pass from C and proceeds to 1 v 0 on the goalie.

## Key Teaching Points

* Attack defense and Attack angles.
* Scoring and shooting at all angles.
* Good Gap control.

## Recommended Progressions

* None.

**5 v 0, 3 v 2, 2 v 1, 1 v 0**

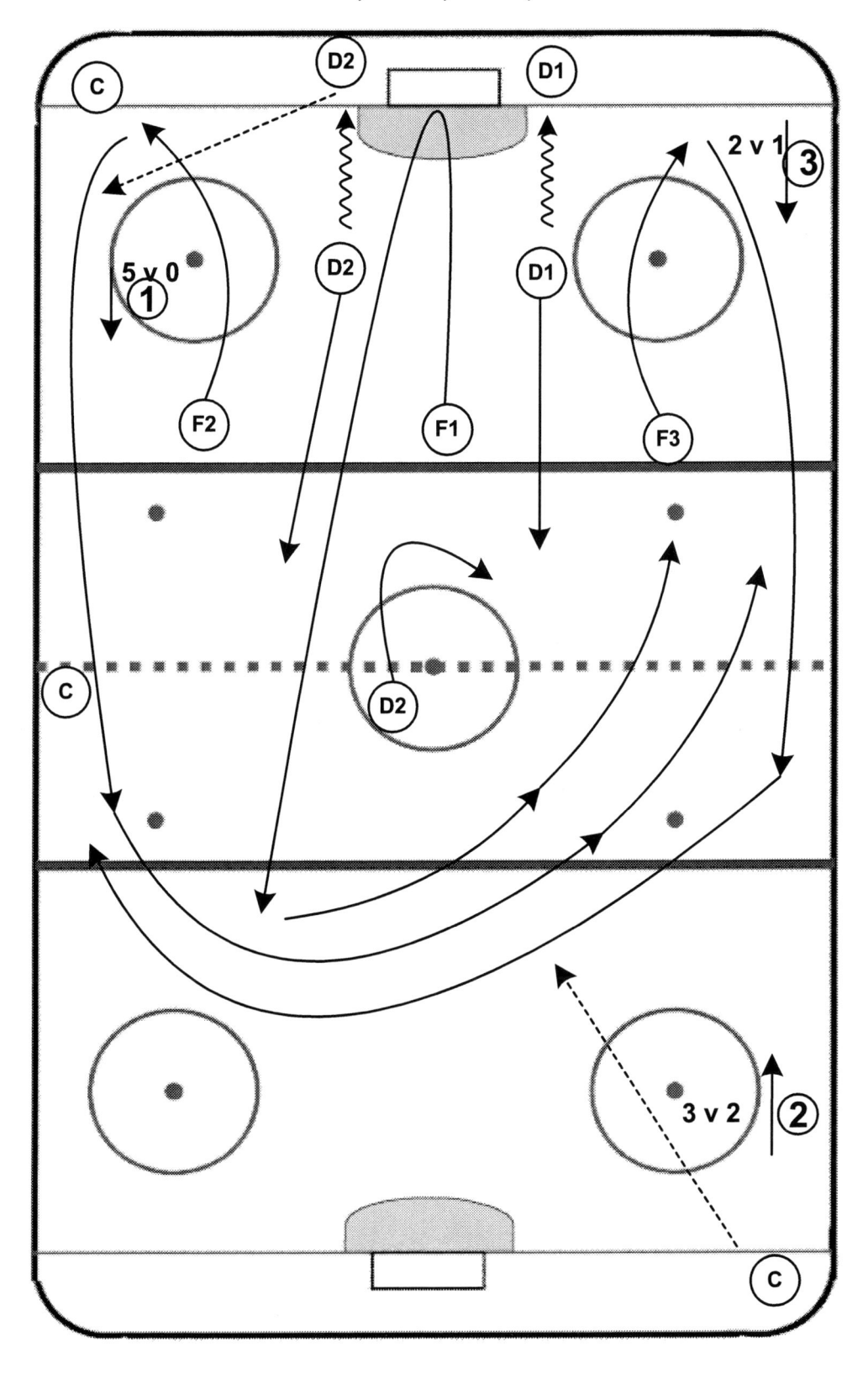

## 47 — Point Shot and Attack: 2 v 2

### Emphasis and Objective
Work on rebounds, tips screens and even numbered situations.

### Drill Set-Up
* Forwards (F) in each corner with pucks. Defensemen on the blue-line.
* F passes to the D who moves across the blue-line, shoots or passes D to D for a shot.
* One F from each line move to the front of the net for screens, tips and rebounds.
* On the whistle, the F's receive a pass from the C and they attack the 2 D for a full ice 2 v 2.

### Key Teaching Points
* Keep feet moving.
* Head up at all times.
* Handle puck in confined area.
* Shoot in stride.
* Shots at 4 varied angles.
* Rebound control.

### Recommended Progressions
* 3 v 2.

# Point Shot & Attack

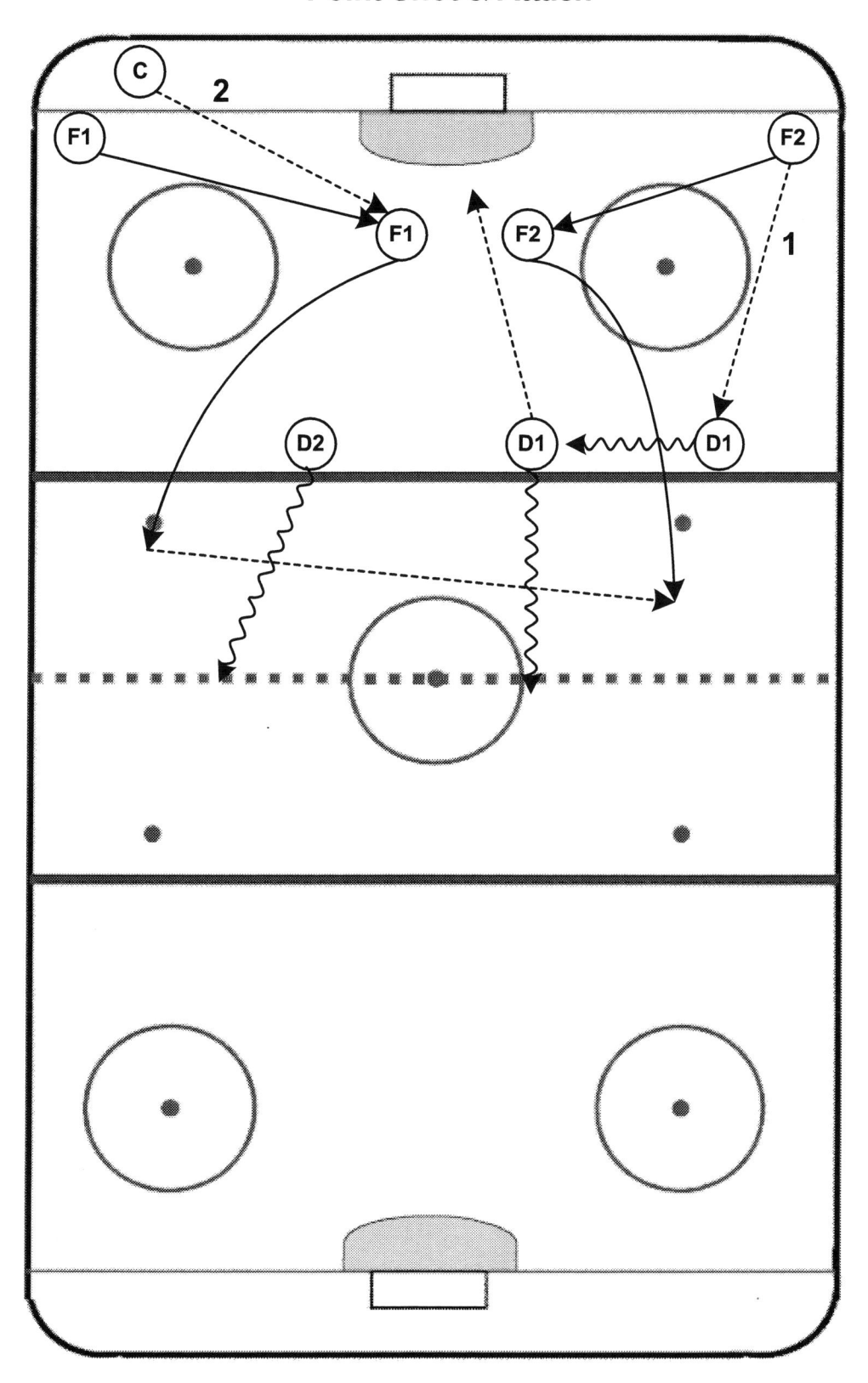

# 48 — 5 v 5, 1/2 Ice Forecheck

## Emphasis and Objective

Situational forecheck drill to improve skills and individual systems.

## Drill Set-Up

* X1, X2 and X3 on offense along with D3 and D4.
* F1, F2 and F3 on defense along with D1 and D2.
* C dumps puck into offensive zone, X's and D3 and D4 forecheck against Y's and D1 and D2.
* X's execute a desired forechecking system attempting to sustain pressure, F's and D1 and D2 attempt to break the puck out of the zone.

## Key Teaching Points

* Finish checks.
* Support the puck.
* Defensive positioning and coverage.
* Pucks must be carried out of zone.

## Recommended Progressions

* None.

# 5 v 5, 1/2 Ice Forecheck

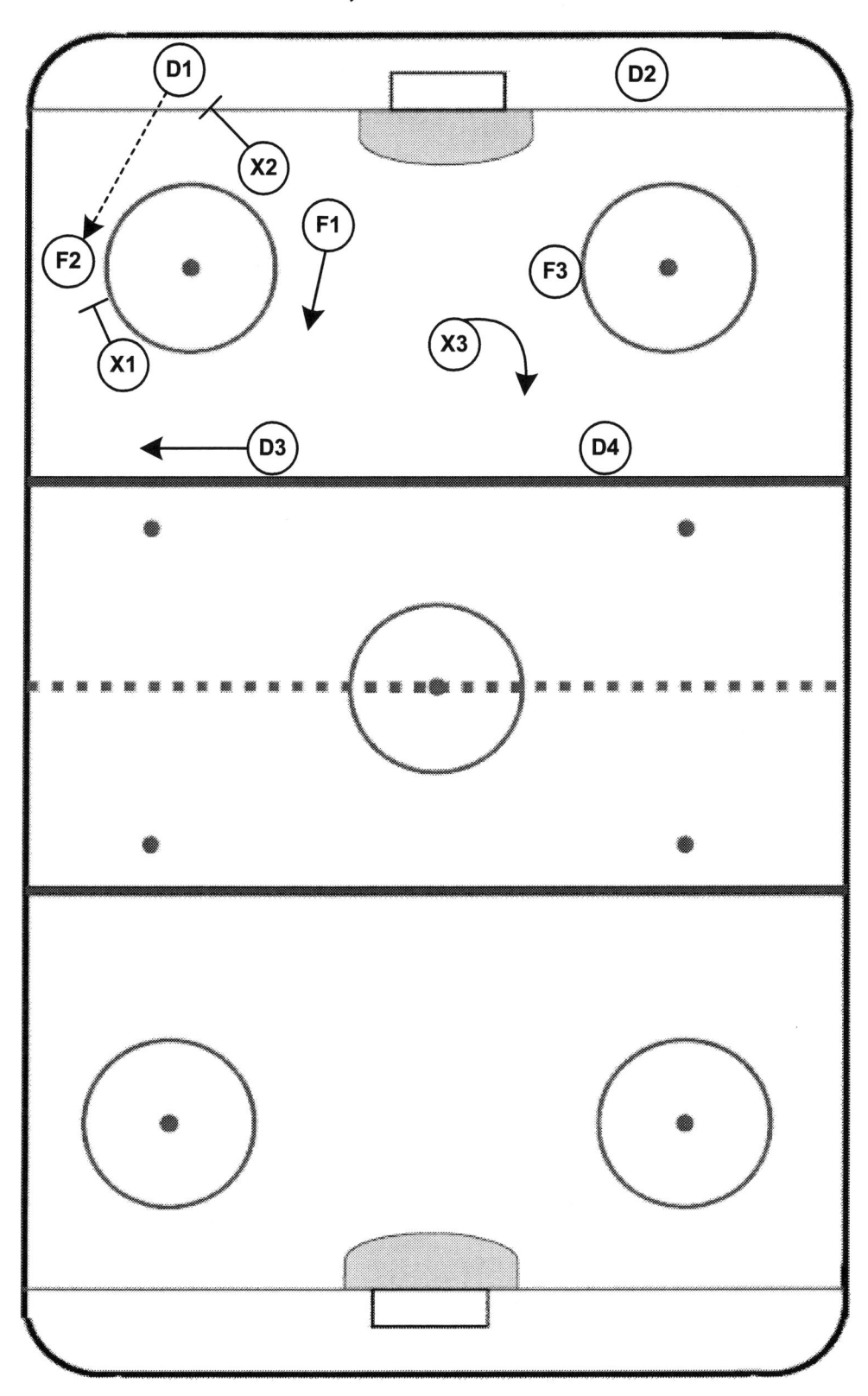

## 49 Forechecking Skill Development

### Emphasis and Objective
Improve pursuit and angling skills of forecheckers.

### Drill Set-Up
* Two forechecking forwards (F1 and F2), positioned in front of goal and on tops of circles.
* D1 in front of the net, X1 in defensive position.
* C dumps puck into corner, D1 pivots and gathers the puck looking to breakout with X1.
* F1 pursues D1, finishes check, F2 reads the play and pursues the puck or contains X1.

### Key Teaching Points
* Take good pursuit angles.
* Sticks in passing lanes.
* Protect the puck.

### Recommended Progressions
* Can add additional players for full forecheck.

# Forechecking Skill Development

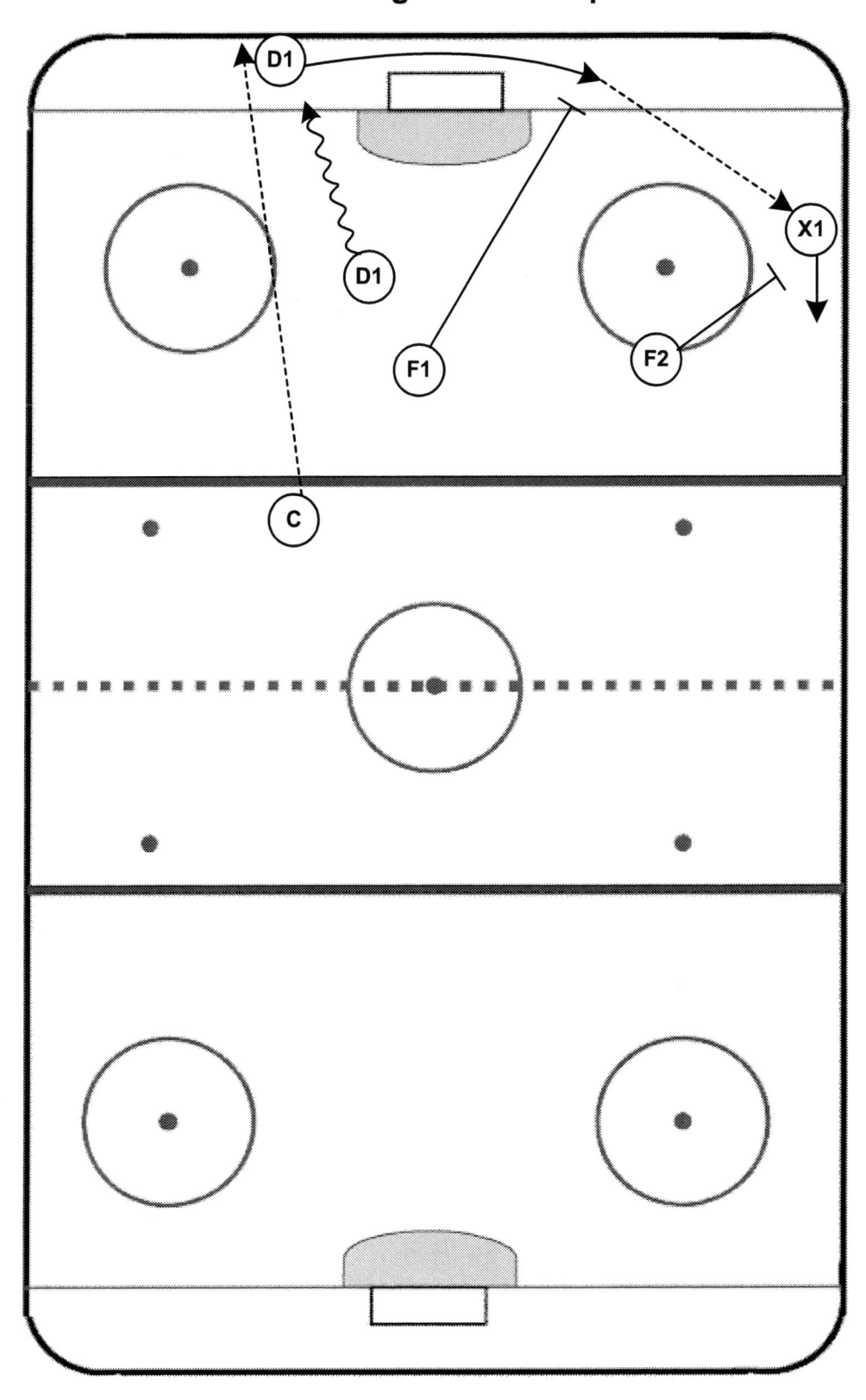

# 50 — Continuous Neutral Zone

## Emphasis and Objective

Work on neutral zone regroups and passing skills.

## Drill Set-Up

* Forward lines and defensive pairs in the neutral zone, C with puck.
* Two forward lines up with defensive pairs.
* C dumps puck behind one set of defense, that group of 5 (2 D and 3 F's) regroup in the neutral zone. The other group of 5 (D3, D4 and 3 X's) wait in the neutral zone.
* After each F touches the puck, they pass the puck to either D3 or D4 who begin to execute a neutral zone attack with the 3 X's.
* Y's move from the bench into the neutral zone.
* X's regroup, each touch the puck and pass to the new set of D who are waiting to counter attack with Y's.
* Continuous.

## Key Teaching Points

* Support the puck.
* Head up at all times.
* Make easy, high percentage passes.
* players must be positioned at good passing angles.
* Communication.

## Recommended Progressions

* None.

# Continuous Neutral Zone

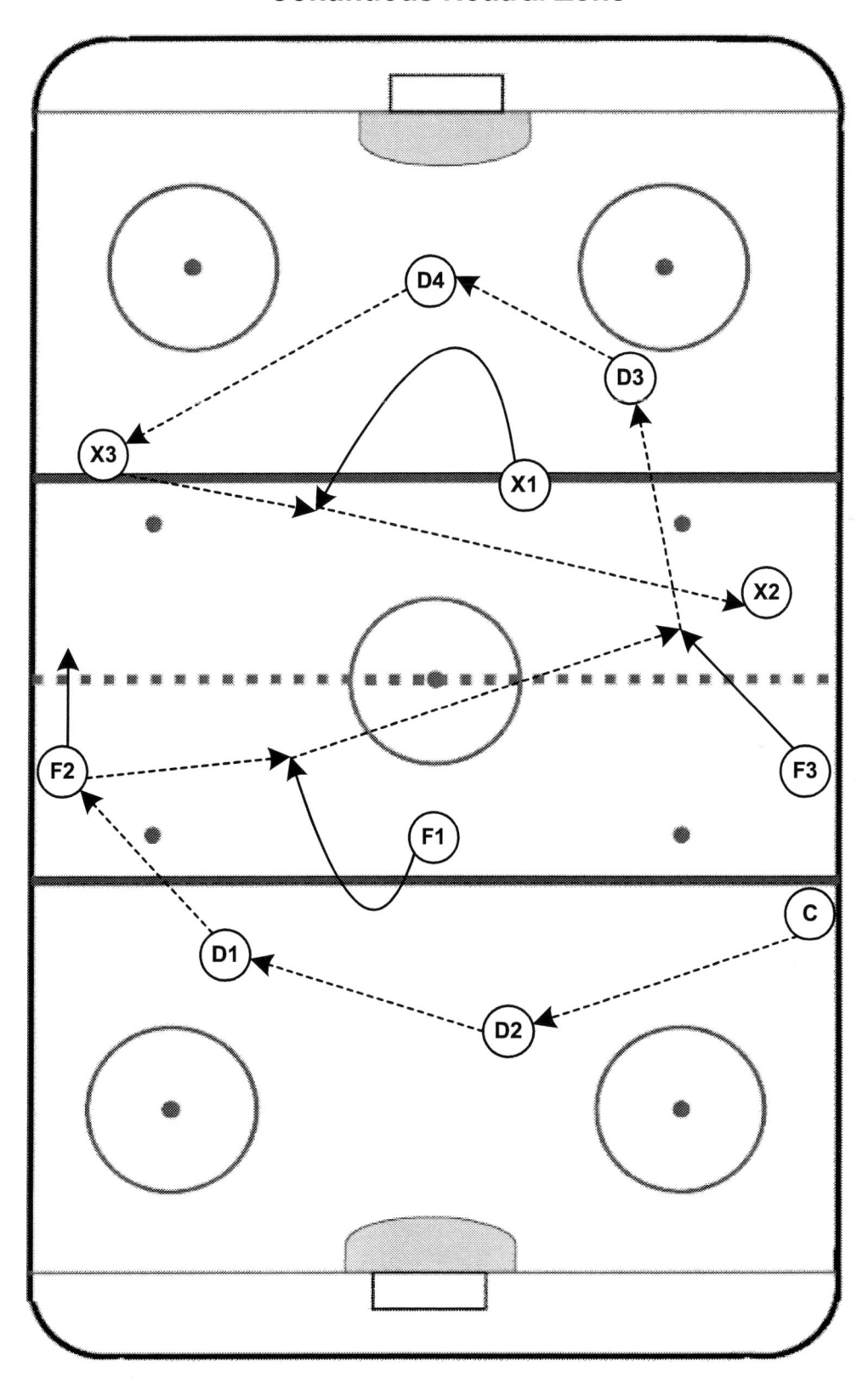

Photo Courtesy of the Danville Wings

# 3

## Even Numbered Attacks

This section provides a number of 1 v 1, 2 v 2 and 3 v 3 drills designed to introduce the concept of even numbered situations and to challenge your participants.

1 v 1 play is a critical skill whether in possession of the puck or pursuing possession. The ability to defend and the ability to out duel or win even numbered confrontations separates players and the success of teams. The 1 v 1 drills progress to 2 v 2 and 3 v 3 in all situations and in all 3 zones.

This section also introduces the term Gap and Gap Control as a way to measure the distance between the puck carrier and the defender. As a guide or rule, a two stick length Gap is ideal as it provides an ideal distance for the defender to challenge the puck carrier while always maintaining a clear view of the entire situation.

Challenge your participants to be good 1 v 1 players. Competition and winning battles is the name of the game!

# 51 — 1 v 1, Close the Gap

## Emphasis and Objective

Work on 1 v 1 skills while keeping a tight, 2 stick length Gap.

## Drill Set-Up

* F's in opposite corners, D in neutral zone.
* On 1st whistle, F's from each end take off and curl for a pass at the opposite end. 2 D's skate with each F, mirroring their actions.
* F's receive a pass and attack 1 v 1.
* On the 2nd whistle, F's change directions while the D's must stop and meet the new attacking F maintaining a tight gap.
* C continues to blow whistle for several directional changes.
* On the double whistle, F's attempt to beat the D 1 v 1.

## Key Teaching Points

* Have D challenge themselves to close Gap.
* Head up at all times.
* Forwards change speeds.
* Finish checks.
* Use D as a screen.

## Recommended Progressions

* None.

# 1 v 1 Close the Gap

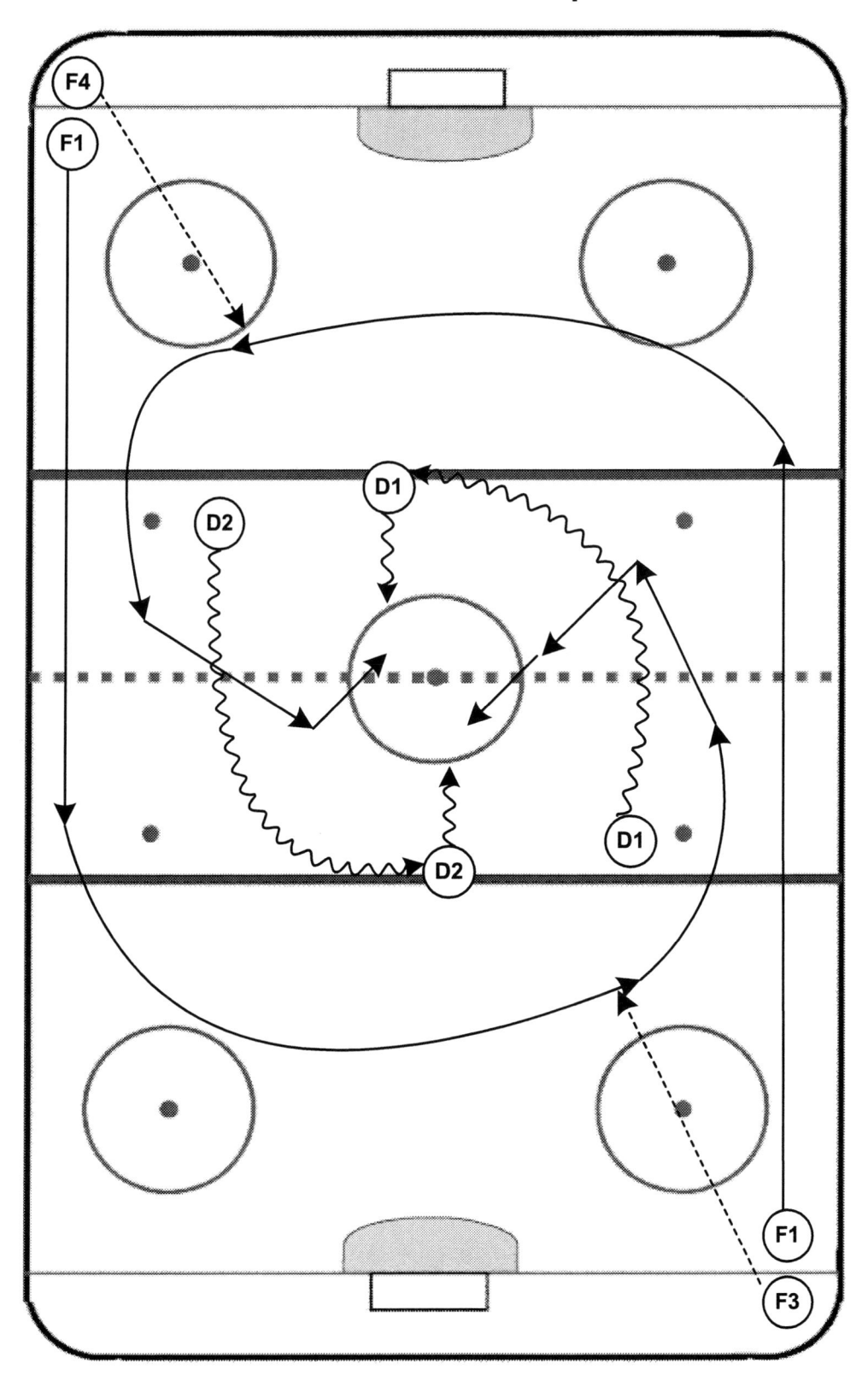

# 1 v 1 Transition

## Emphasis and Objective

Improve passing and receiving and attacking and defending 1 v 1 skills.

## Drill Set-Up

* F's in opposite ends with pucks, D's on the blue-line.
* Both ends simultaneously.
* F's with puck, begin with a 1 touch exchange with backward skating D.
* At the red-line, D with the puck, F curls at a good angle for a transition pass from D.
* F accelerates into zone, curls toward the boards and attacks D who has closed the gap, 1 v 1 into zone.
* Once transition pass is made, the next 2 F's and 2 D's activate.

## Key Teaching Points

* Good passing angles.
* Move feet and close Gap.
* 1 touch passing and receiving.
* Finish checks.

## Recommended Progressions

* None.

# 1 v 1 Transition

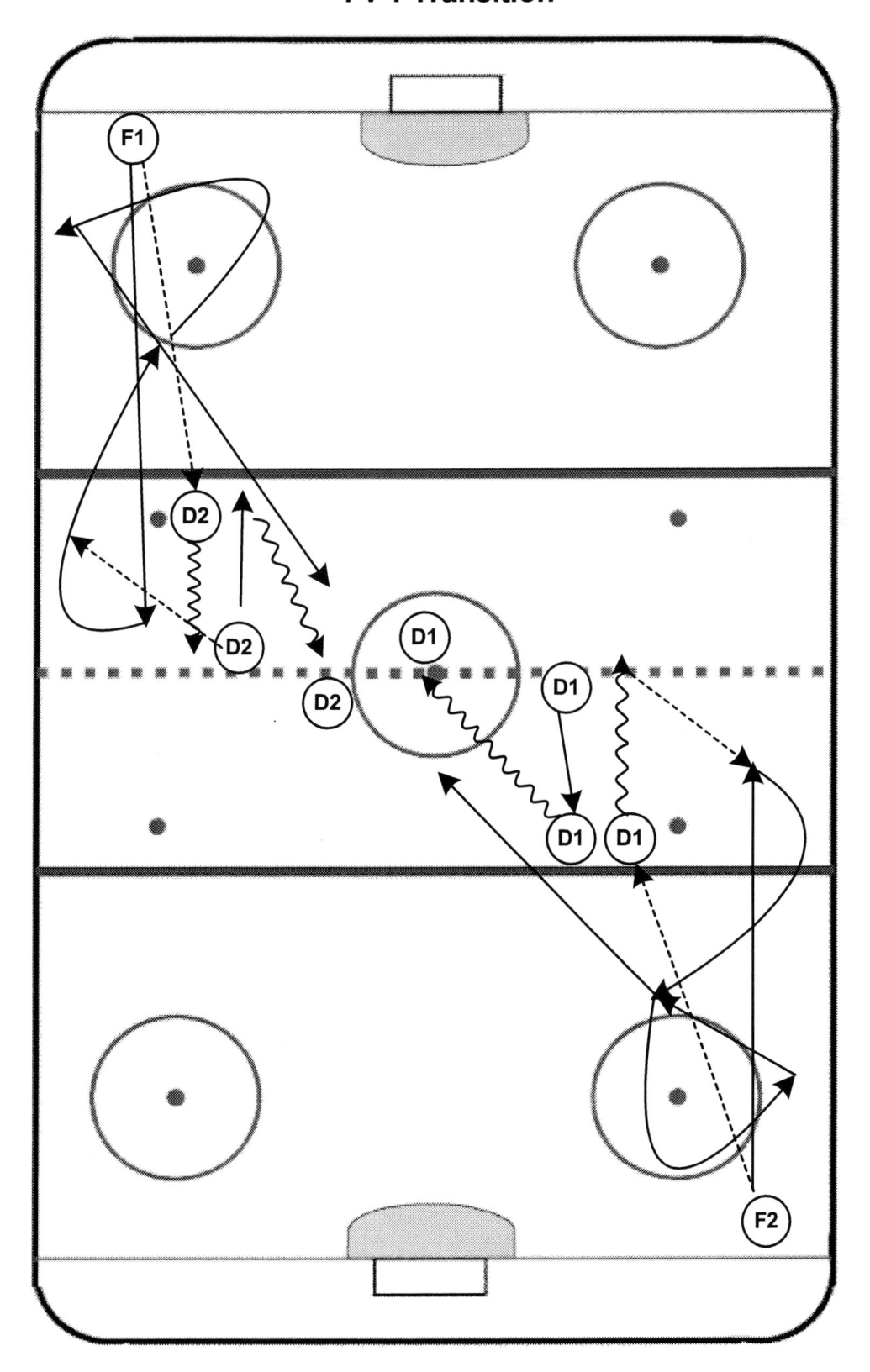

# 53     1 v 1 Oriole Gap

## Emphasis and Objective

Work on Gap control and 1 v 1 skills.

## Drill Set-Up

* C in corner with pucks, F's and D's at hash marks in each end.
* On the whistle, F skates forward down the wall, D1 skates backwards maintaining a 2 stick length Gap.
* At the far blue-line, F curls toward D2 and they exchange 2 passes progressing to a 1 v 1 attack on D1.
* Maintaining a 2 stick length Gap, D1 defends the 1 v 1 into zone, D2 follows play into zone.
* On the whistle, Coach passes to D2 at the point, D1 and F1 battle for positioning in front, D2 shoots.

## Key Teaching Points

* Maintain 2 stick length Gap.
* Pass and receive at good angles.
* Good body position.
* Quick shots
* Be sure passing D moves to proper angle.

## Recommended Progressions

* None.

# 1 v 1 Oriole Gap

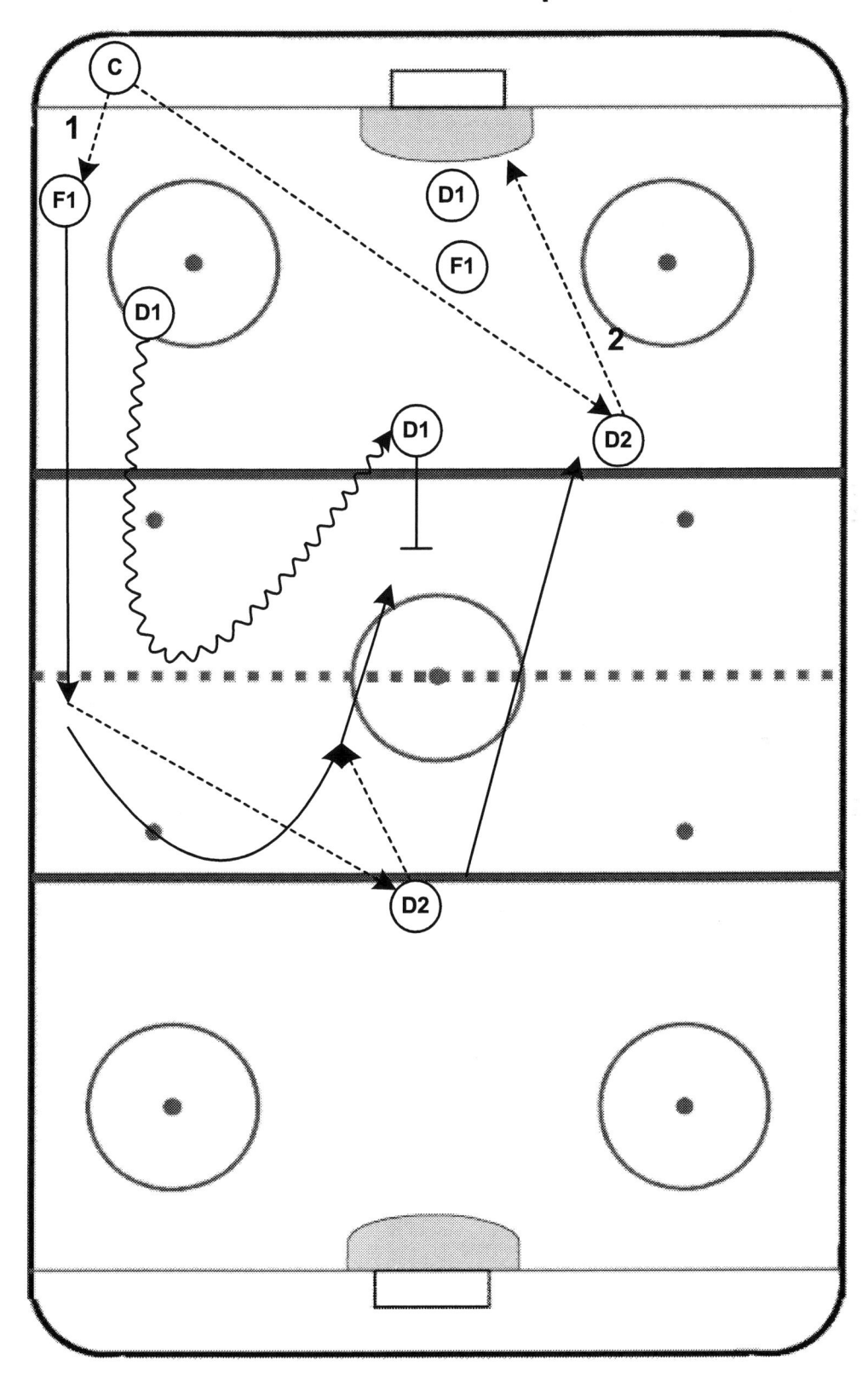

# 54 — Shoot and Rim: 1 v 1

## Emphasis and Objective

Improve shooting, deflecting, handling the rim breakout and 1 v 1 skills.

## Drill Set-Up

* F's in both ends in opposite corners. D on the blue-lines.
* F1 passes to D1, F1 goes to the front of the net to deflect and rebound. D1 handles the pass, and moves to the prime shooting area for a shot.
* The last F in line rims the puck around to the far side where F1 must collect and control the puck proceeding to a 1 v 1 rush against D1.

## Key Teaching Points

* Lateral movement for defense.
* Good, low shot on net.
* Proper positioning.
* Tips and screens.
* 1 v 1 skills.
* Gap control.
* Done at both ends, 1 end is shown.

## Recommended Progressions

* Both ends.
* 2 v 1, 2 v 2, 3 v 1, 3 v 2.

# Shoot and Rim 1 v 1

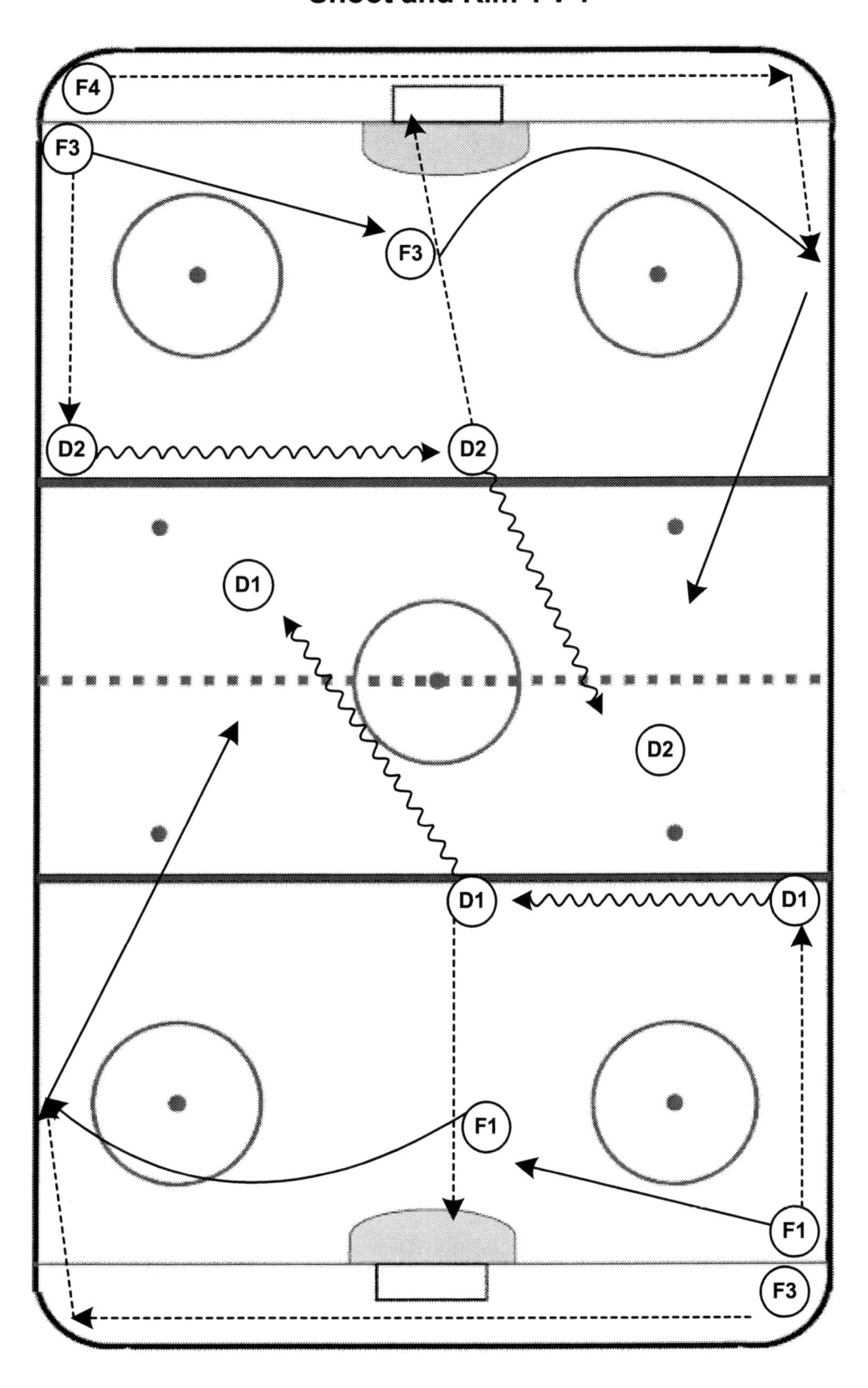

# 55 Wheel House 1 v 1

## Emphasis and Objective
Full ice 1 v 1 drill incorporating breakout skills and Gap control.

## Drill Set-Up
* F1 and F2 and opposite blue-lines with pucks, D1 and D2 positioned at mid-ice.
* At the same time, F1 and F2 dump a puck into the corner, F1 and F2 hustle and get into breakout position at the opposite wall.
* D1 and D2 pivot, gather the puck, breakout with F1 and F2 and proceed up the ice to meet the attacking F for a 1 v 1.
* Both ends, switch sides.

## Key Teaching Points
* Handle and move the puck quickly.
* Maintain 2 stick length Gap control.
* Move feet.
* F's be sure to attack full speed.

## Recommended Progressions
* None.

# Wheel House 1 v 1

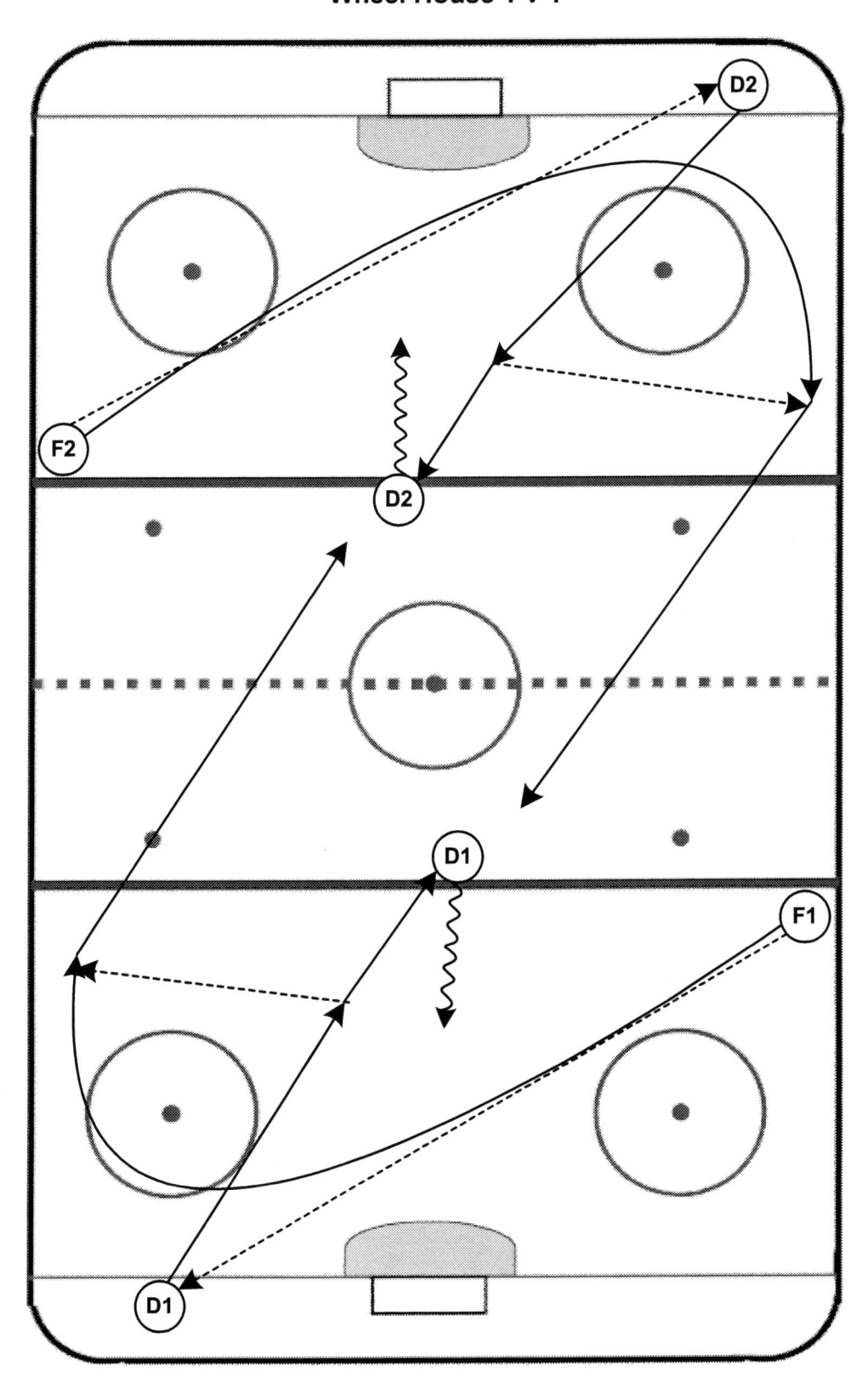

# 56 — Half ice 1 v 1

## Emphasis and Objective
1 v 1 drill to improve foot speed and foot work.

## Drill Set-Up
* F's at opposite blue-lines with pucks, D positioned on the blue-line, inside of F's.
* F1 curls deep into the opposite zone and receives a pass from F2.
* D1, skates with F1, pivots at the far blue-line and meets F1 for a half ice 1 v 1.
* Alternate sides.

## Key Teaching Points
* Move feet.
* Attack with speed.

## Recommended Progressions
* 2 v 1.

# 1/2 Ice 1 v 1

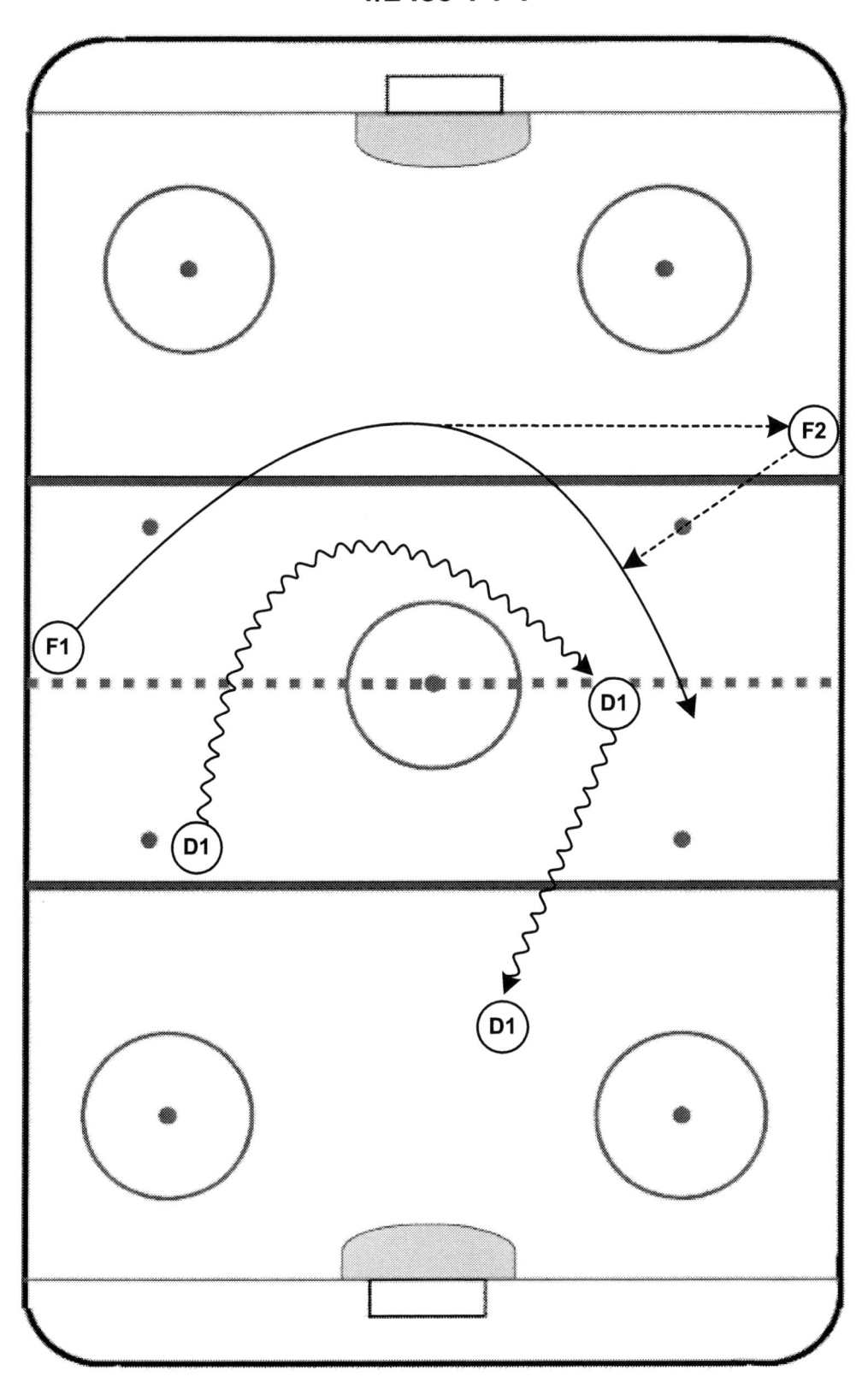

# 57 — 2 v 2 Quick

## Emphasis and Objective

To have players make quick offensive and defensive decisions in varied pressure situations.

## Drill Set-Up

* F's in both ends positioned on the tops of the circles. D's in the neutral zone with partners.
* On 1st whistle, F's begin skating a figure 8 in zone. D's skate red line to blue-line forward and backwards.
* On the C's 2nd whistle, F's attack neutral zone looking for a pass from C. D's react, quickly, close the gap and play the 2 v 2 rush.
* Play continues into the offensive zone until whistle. Whistle signifies the next group of 2 F's to begin figure 8 skating and 2 D's red line to blue-line forward and backwards anticipating the attack.

## Key Teaching Points

* Stagger the offensive attack.
* Attack blue-line with speed.
* Utilize criss-cross at blue-line.
* Puck protection.
* Defensive Gap control.
* 1 v 1 defensive skills/containment.
* Stay onside.
* C varies timing of initial pass.

## Recommended Progressions

* 3 v 2.

# 2 v 2 Quick

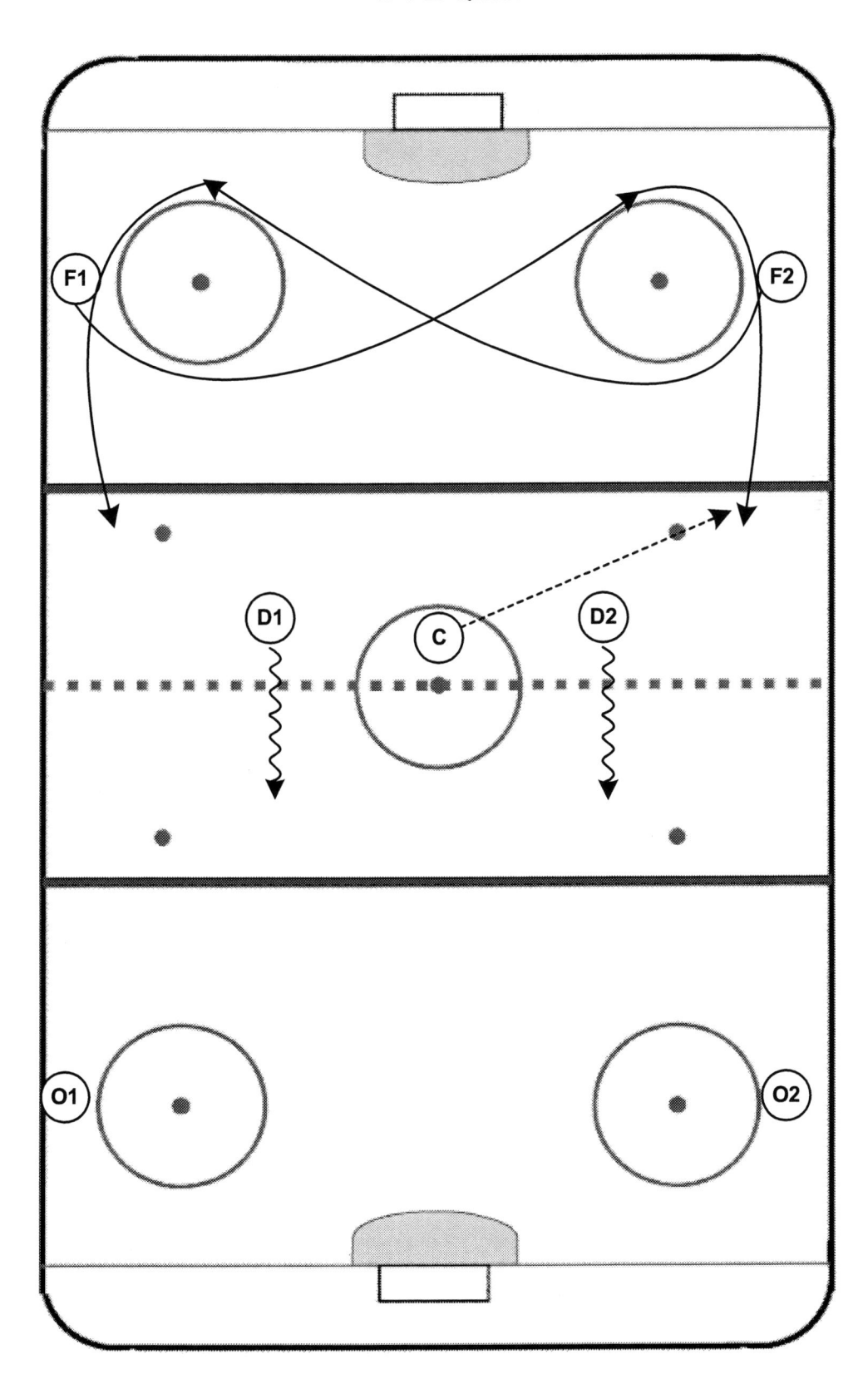

## 58     Badger 2 v 2

### Emphasis and Objective
Neutral zone regrouping and attacks.

### Drill Set-Up
* D's in 4 groups on each side of blue-line. F's in 4 lines at each red-line.
* On the whistle, F1 passes to D1 who skates backwards and passes to a hinging D2.
* On the pass, F1 and F2 regroup and receive a pass from either D1 or D2. F1 and F2 attack D3 and D4 2 v 2.
* After play ends, F3 and F4 start a similar action attacking in the opposite direction.

### Key Teaching Points
* Puck support.
* Good angles for passes.
* Gap control.
* Puck protection.

### Recommended Progressions
* 3 v 1, 3 v 2, 3 v 3.

# Badger 2 v 2

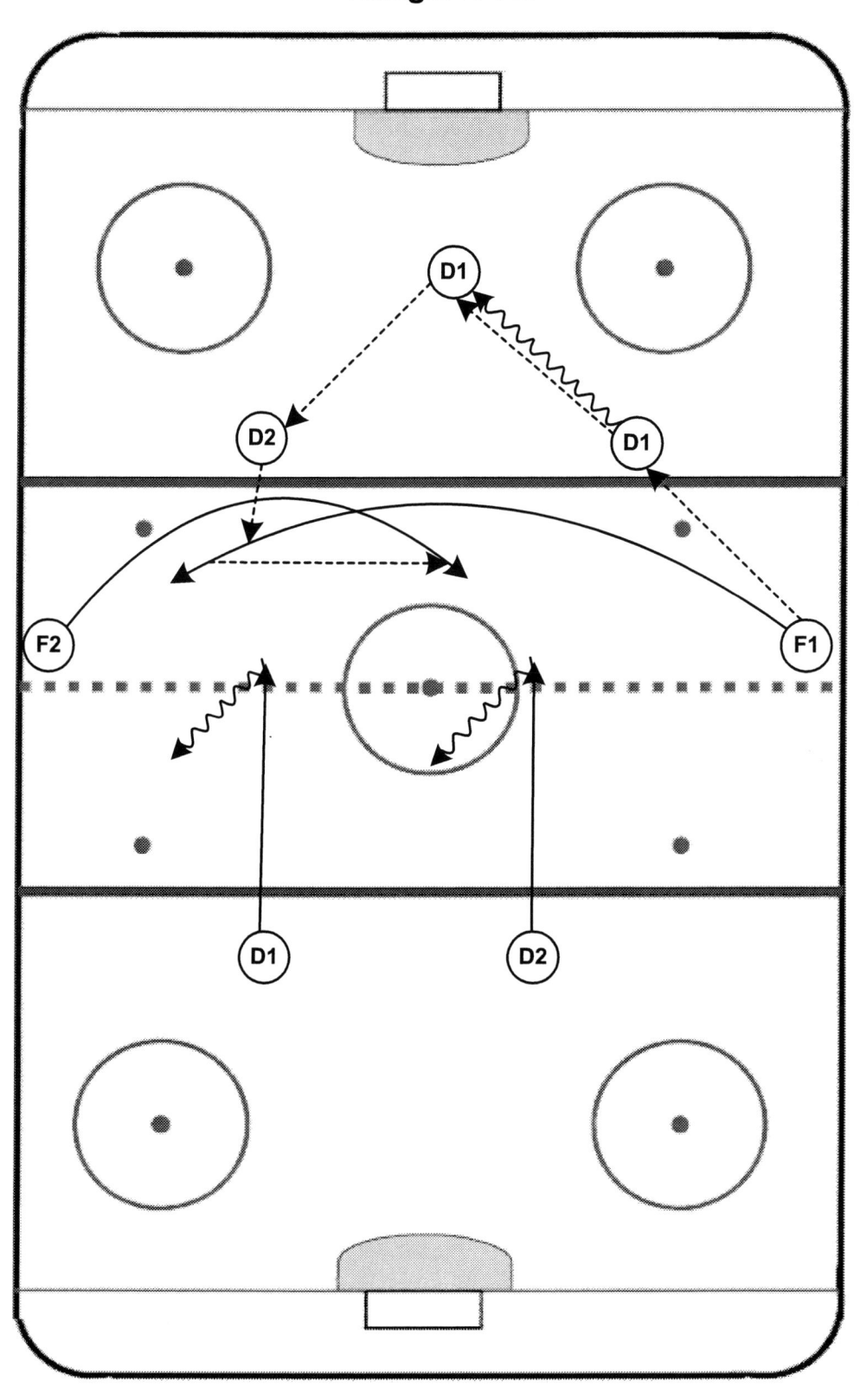

# 59 — 2 v 2, Confined Areas

## Emphasis and Objective
Offensive and defensive skill development in confined areas.

## Drill Set-Up
* Players in each end, half the F's, half the D's.
* 2 F's and 2 D's in a confined area, the remaining players enclose the area.
* C throws a puck into the corner, 2 F's try to score, 2 D's defend. Remaining players keep puck in the confined area.
* 30-45 second shifts.

## Key Teaching Points
* Puck protection.
* Offensive and defensive body positioning.
* Picks and screens.
* Attack and defend the goal.

## Recommended Progressions
* Can be done in a variety of situations: 3 v 2, 3 v 3, 2 v 3.

# 2 v 2 Confined Area

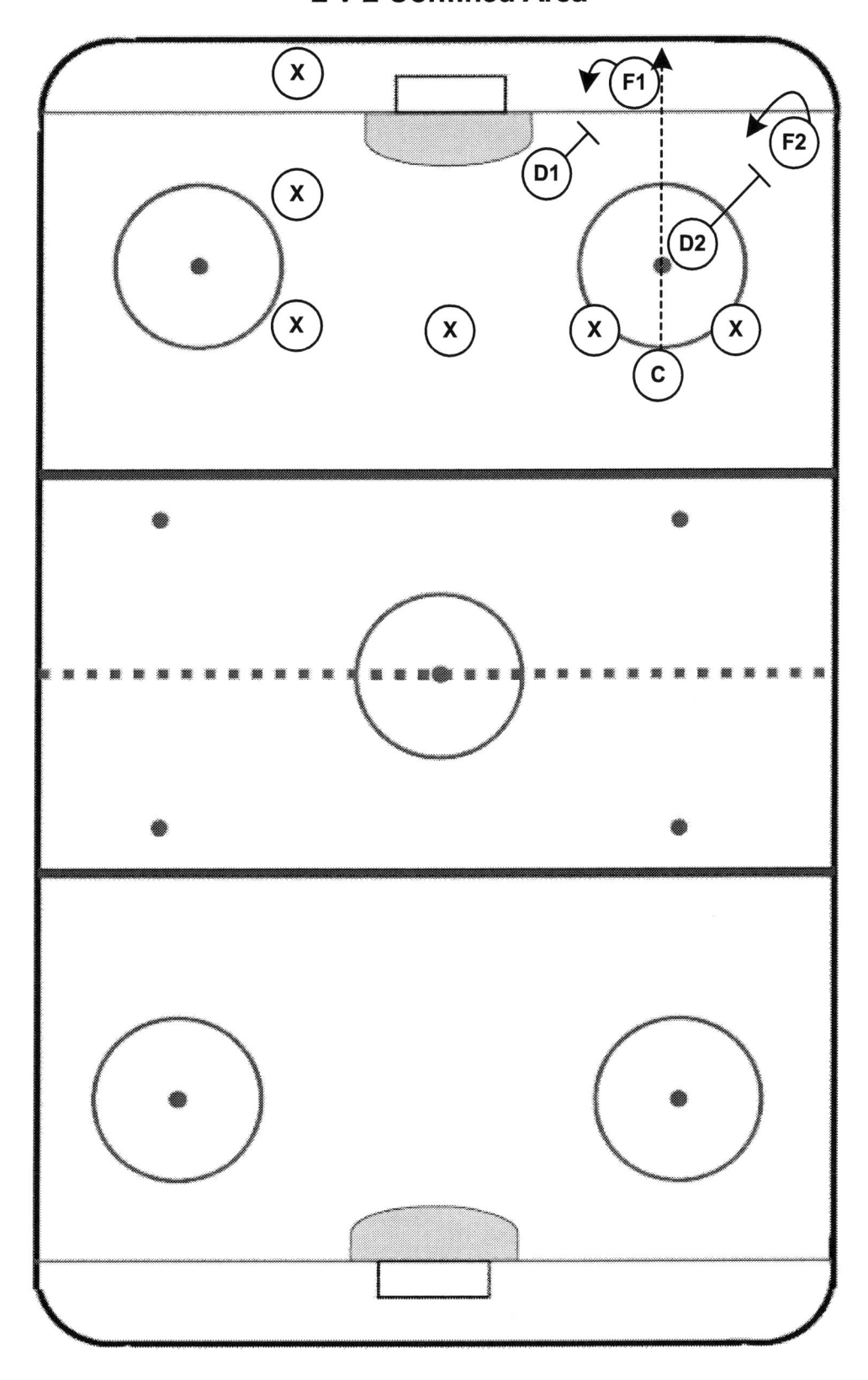

# 60    Deep Wheel, 2 v 2

## Emphasis and Objective

    Improve 2 v 2 attacking and defending skills.

## Drill Set-Up

* F's in each of the four corners with pucks, D's even with the face-off spot, on the goal-line.
* F1 and F2 skate hard to the far end, curl and attacks the zone. D1 and D2 follow the play, pivot and meets the 2 v 2 attack at or near the blue-line.
* Both ends at the same time, alternating sides.

## Key Teaching Points

* Gap control.
* Keep shooters to the outside.
* Finish checks.

## Recommended Progressions

* None.

# Deep Wheel 2 v 2

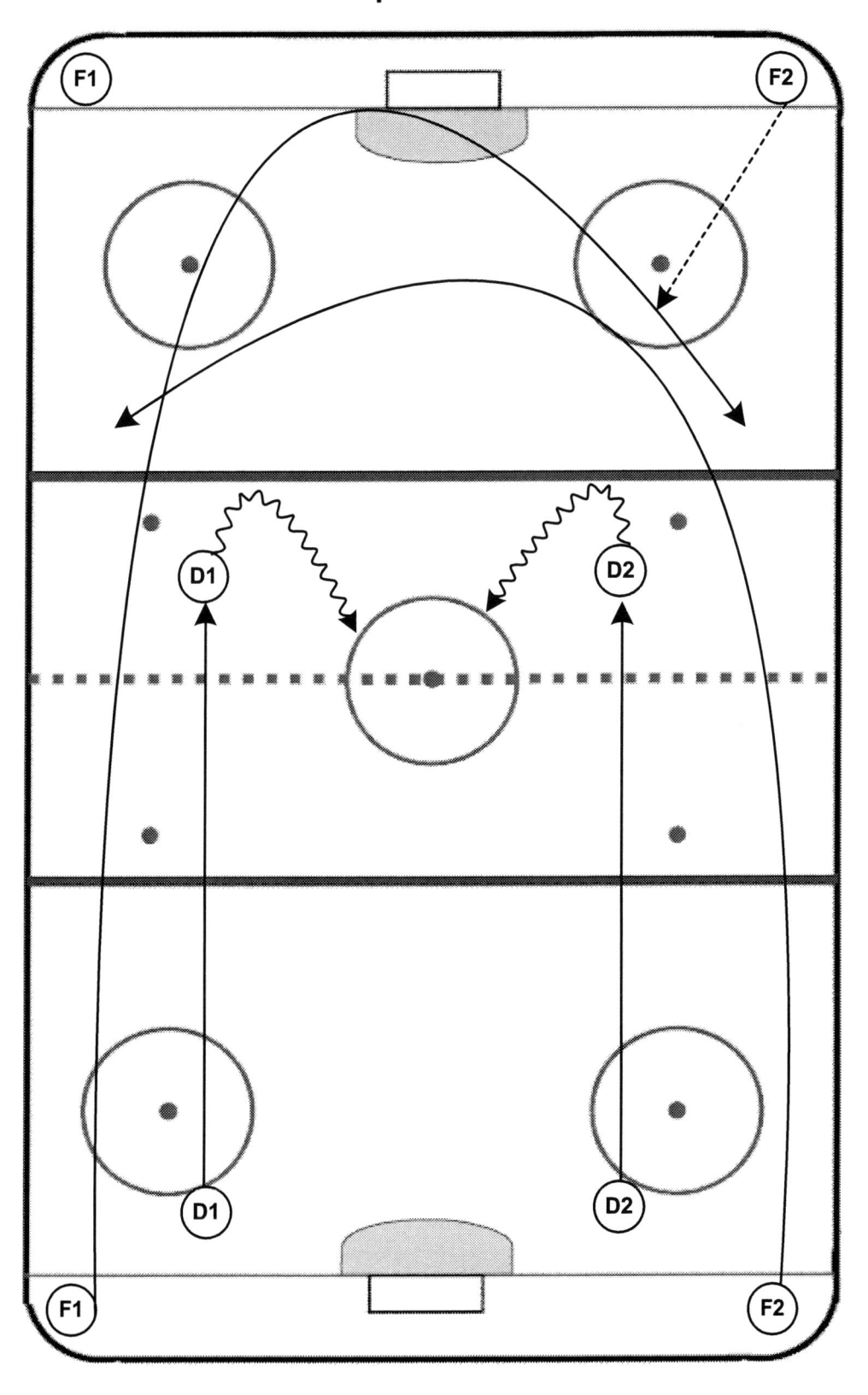

# 61     The Eagle, Shoot and Attack 2 v 2

### Emphasis and Objective
    Full ice 2 v 2 attack drill.

### Drill Set-Up
- F1, F2 on the wall in the neutral zone, D1 and D2 on opposite blue-lines, D3 and D4 positioned at the opposite side of the red-line in the neutral zone.
- F1, F2 and D1 skate down the wall and shoot on goal.
- F2 cuts across the zone to receive a pass from C, F1 makes a high curl in the neutral zone and prepares to regroup with D3 and D4.
- After receiving the pass from C, F2 hits D4 with a pass, D4 passes to D3 who looks for a regrouping F1 or F2.
- F1 and F2 attack D1 and D2, who have skated to the neutral zone, 2 v 2.

### Key Teaching Points
- Full speed.
- Maintain Gap control.
- F's attack at angles and with speed.
- Play until the whistle.

### Recommended Progressions
- 3 v 2.

# The Eagle, Shoot and Attack 2 v 2

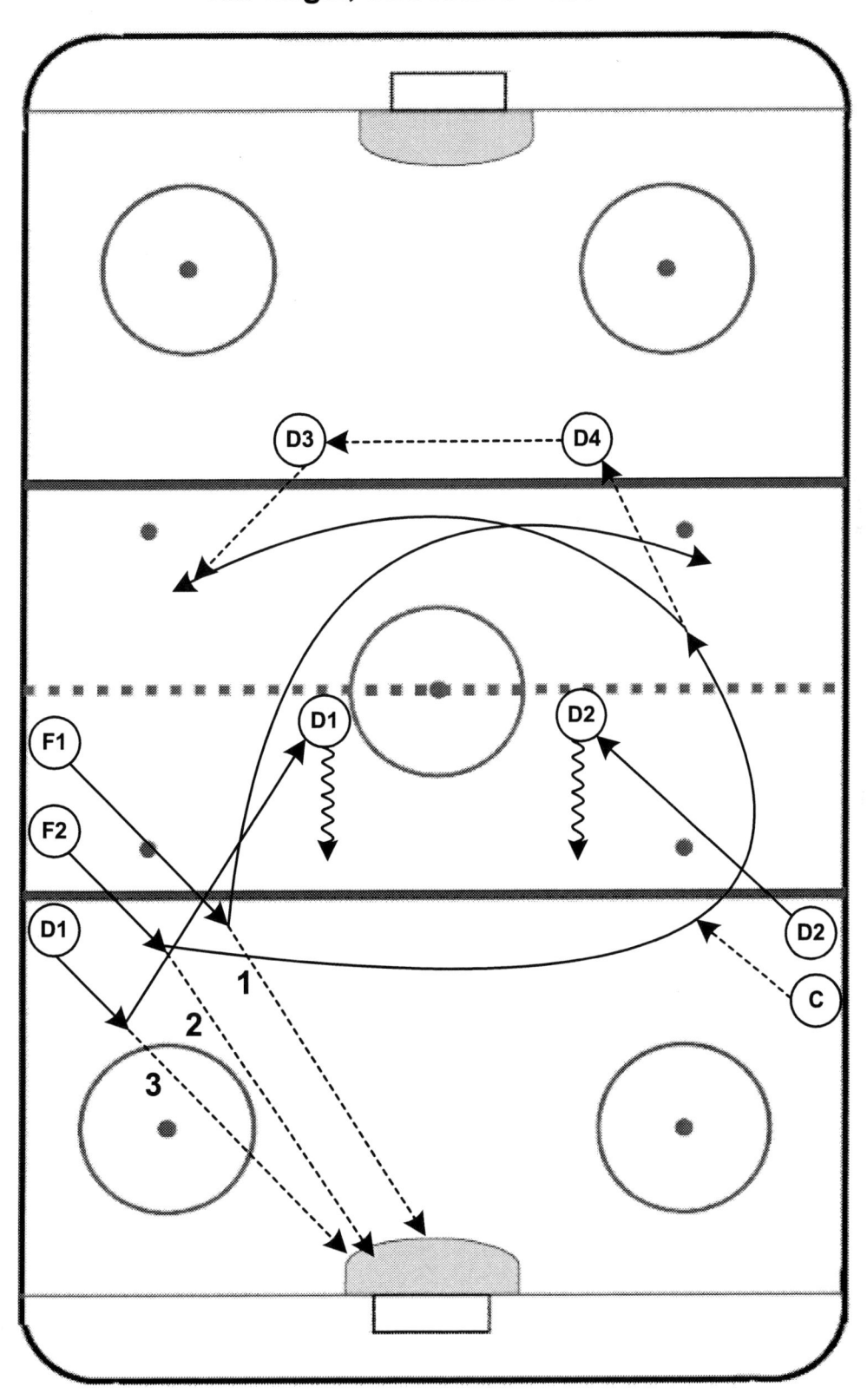

# 62 — Half Ice Curl and Attack

## Emphasis and Objective

Drill designed to improve neutral zone 2 v 2 attacks.

## Drill Set-Up

- F's at opposite blue-lines in two groups.
- D's in the neutral zone.
- X1 and X2 take off down the wall, curl in the neutral zone and receive a pass from C. X1 and X2 attack D1 and D2 2 v 2.
- D1 and D2, sprint to the blue-line, pivot and meet the 2 v 2 attack.
- Alternate sides.

## Key Teaching Points

- Good Gap control.
- Full speed.
- Make plays in the offensive zone.

## Recommended Progressions

- None.

# Half Ice Curl and Attack 2 v 2

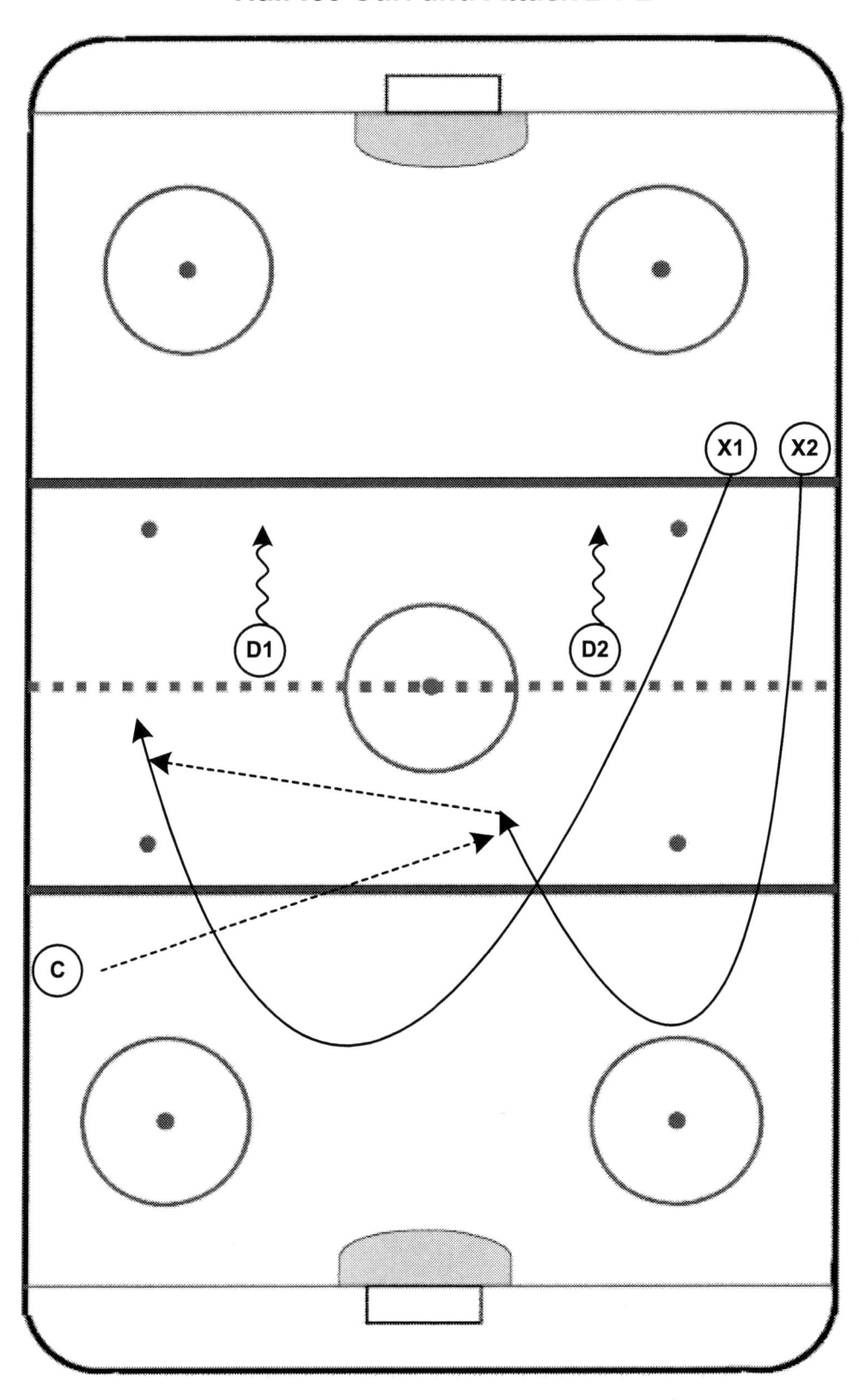

# 63 — Split Second 2 v 2

## Emphasis and Objective
Work on 2 v 2 attack and defend skills in a half ice situation.

## Drill Set-Up
* F's in each corner with pucks, D even with the face-off spot on the goal-line. C on the center red-line.
* F1 and F2 skate to the neutral zone, pass to C, regroup and attack D1 and D2 2 v 2.
* D1 and D2 skate to the blue-line, pivot and defend the 2 v 2.
* Both ends.

## Key Teaching Points
* Good regroups.
* Stay onside.
* Make split second offensive and defensive decisions.
* Play to the whistle.

## Recommended Progressions
* None.

**Split Second 2 v 2**

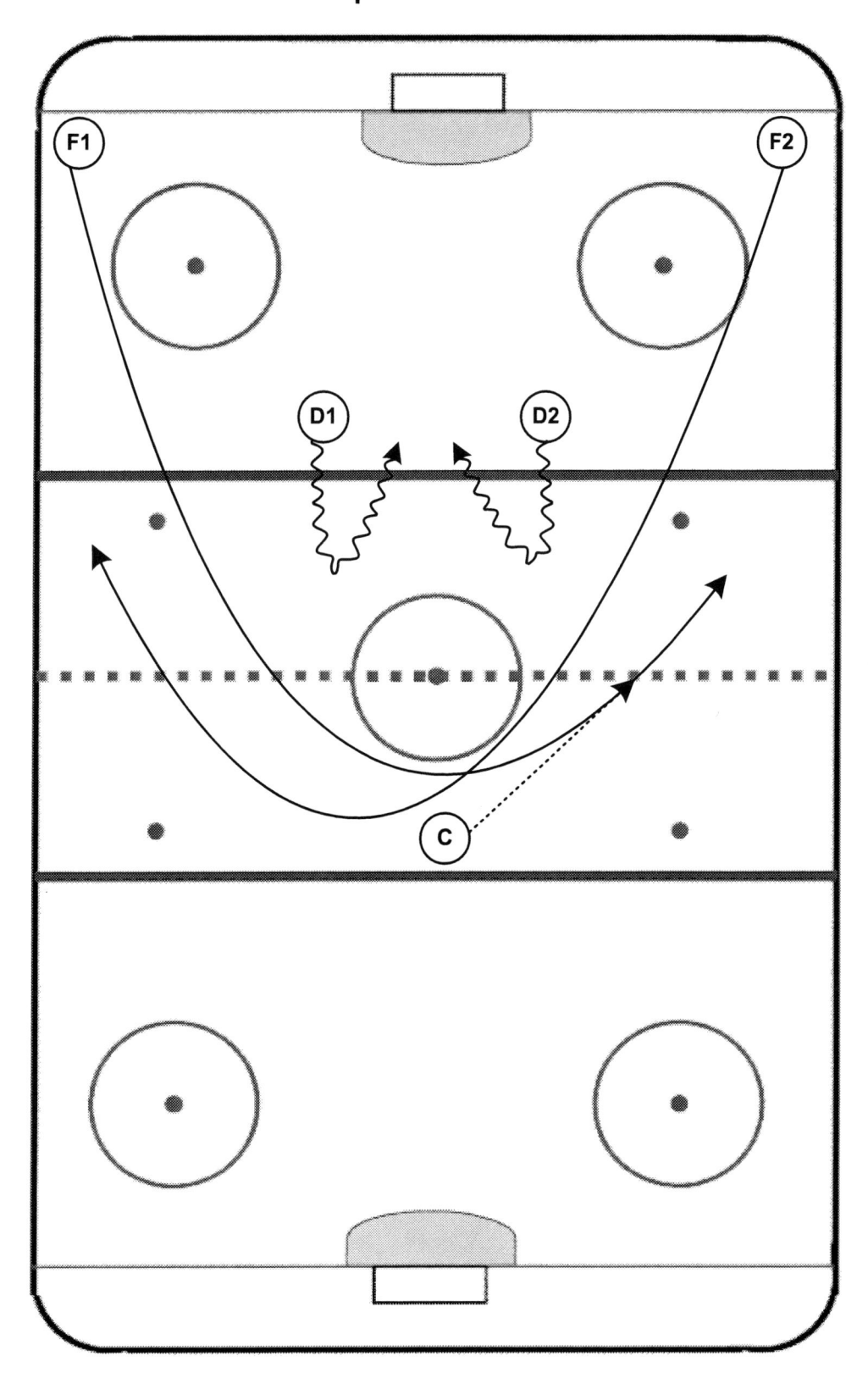

# 64. Russian Battle: 1 v 1, 2 v 2 to a 3 v 3

## Emphasis and Objective

Work on a series of competition drills to improve offensive and defensive skills.

## Drill Set-Up

* One offensive F in each corner, remaining linemate at the blue-line, all with pucks. One D opposite each F in the corner. One defensive F at the blue-line.
* On the 1st whistle, both corners will battle 1 v 1, players at the blue-line pass the puck.
* On the 2nd whistle, 2 corner forwards attack the 2 D 2 v 2.
* On the 3rd whistle, the F on the blue-line shoots on net while the 2 corner F's crash the goal for rebounds and tips. After shooting, both players from the blue-line join the play for a 3 v 3.
* Play 30-45 second shifts and add pucks when cleared.

## Key Teaching Points

* Puck protection.
* Competition.
* Picks, screens and cycling.

## Recommended Progressions

* Add defense for a 3 v 1 or 3 v 2.

**Russian Battle: 1 v 1, 2 v 2 to a 3 v 3**

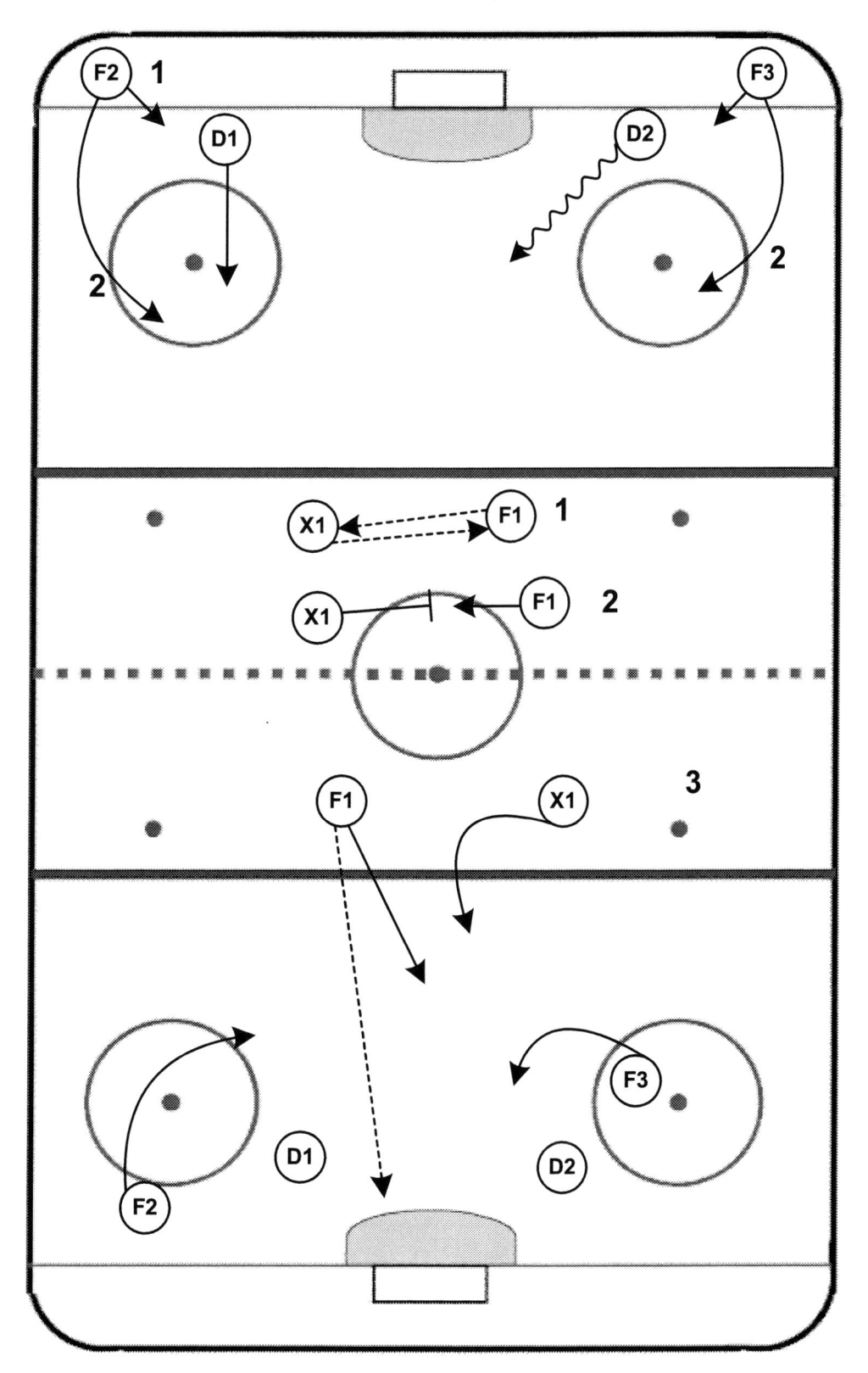

## 65 — 3 v 3 Chaser

### Emphasis and Objective
3 v 3 backchecking drill, ideal for reading the rush and the backcheck.

### Drill Set-Up
* F1, F2 and F3 on the red-line, D1 and D2 in the neutral zone, X1, with pucks, on the blue-line.
* On the whistle, X1 passes to one of the F's who attack D1 and D2, 3 v 2.
* After passing, X1 backchecks the play making it a 3 v 3 in the zone.
* Play until the whistle.

### Key Teaching Points
* Puck protection.
* Backcheck with a purpose.
* Communicate.

### Recommended Progressions
* None.

# 3 v 3 Chaser

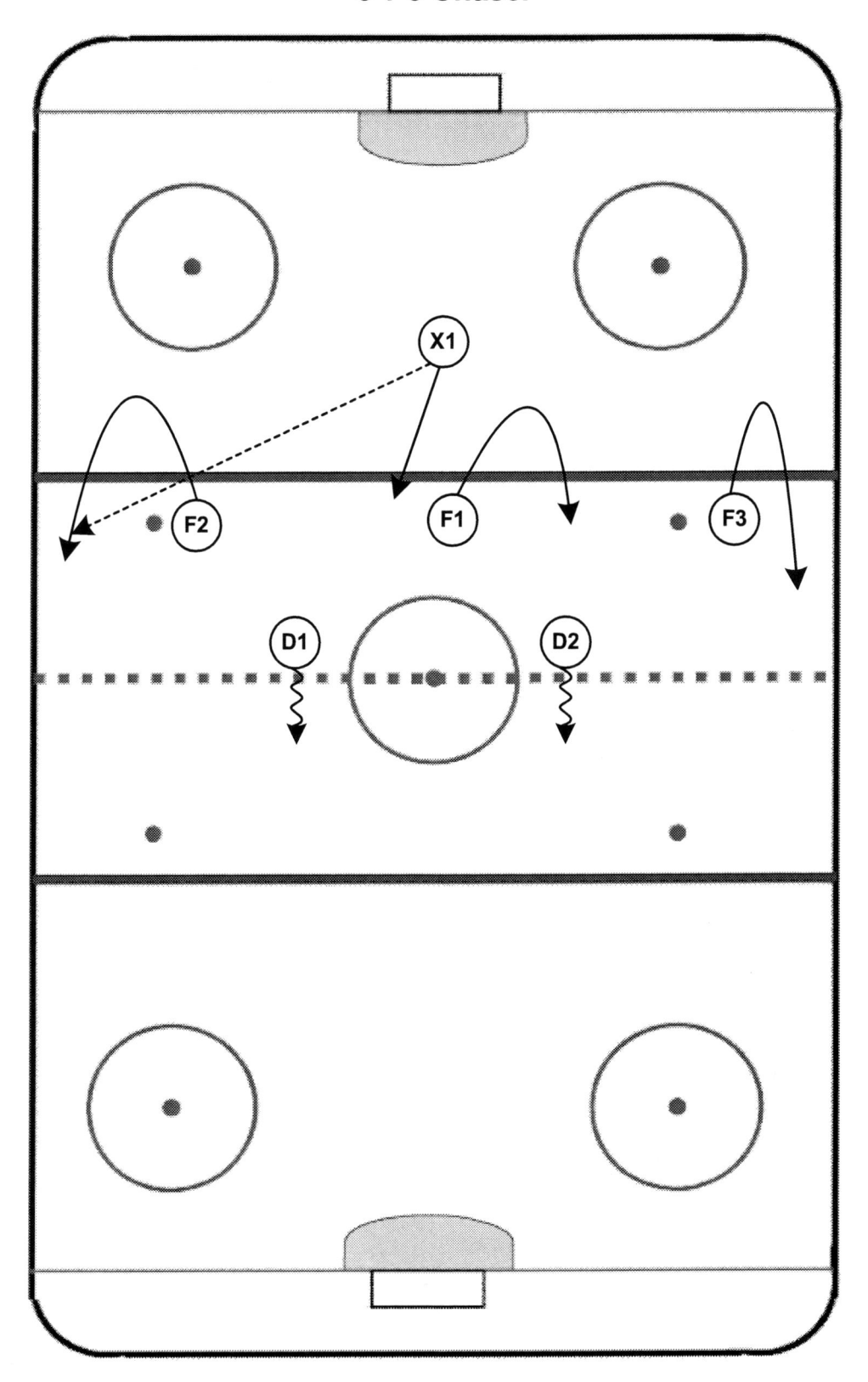

# 66 — 3 v 3 Down Low Coverage

## Emphasis and Objective

3 v 3 man to man coverage in a confined area.

## Drill Set-Up

* F1, F 2 and F3 positioned in offensive position, D1, D2 and X1 in defensive position. Remaining players form an area to play 3 v 3.
* C dump into corner, F's attack against D1, D2 and X1.
* When puck is cleared, dump a new puck.
* 30-45 second shifts.

## Key Teaching Points

* Puck protection.
* Cycling, picks and screens.
* Defensive positioning.
* Angling.

## Recommended Progressions

* None.

# 3 v 3 Down Low Coverage

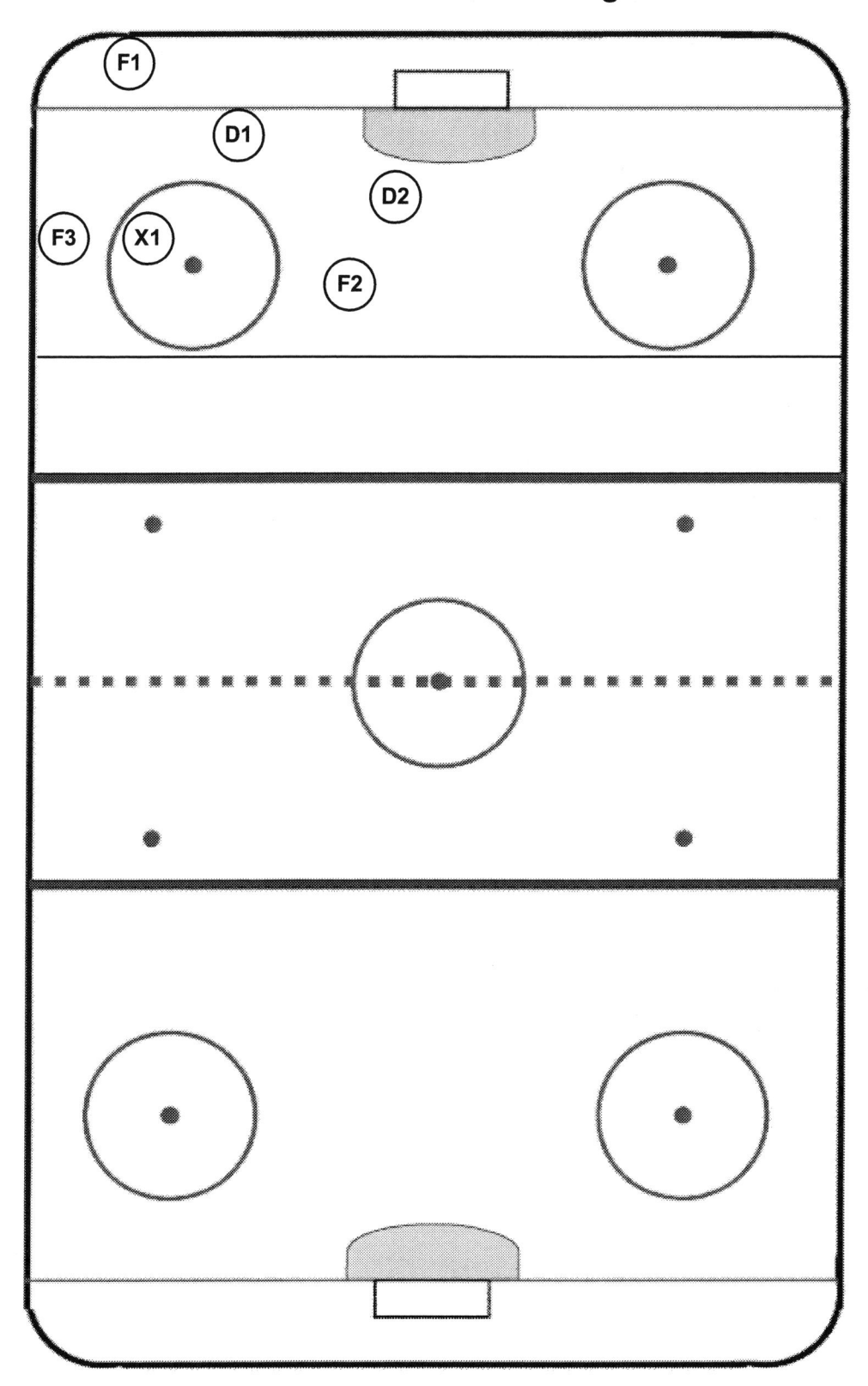

# 67 Neutral Zone Counter to a 3 v 3

## Emphasis and Objective

Neutral zone regrouping concepts and 3 v 3 attacks and defense.

## Drill Set-Up

- F1, F2 and F3 on red-line. D1, D2, D3 and D4 in pairs, one pair at each blue-line. X1 on the center face-off dot.
- C places puck behind one set of D's, X1 forechecks hard and the D counter attack with the 3 F's, 3 v 2.
- X2 backchecks into the zone making it a 3 v 3.
- Play until the whistle.

## Key Teaching Points

- Read forecheck.
- Good passing angles.
- Support the puck throughout the neutral zone.
- Puck protection.

## Recommended Progressions

- None.

# Neutral Zone Counter to a 3 v 3

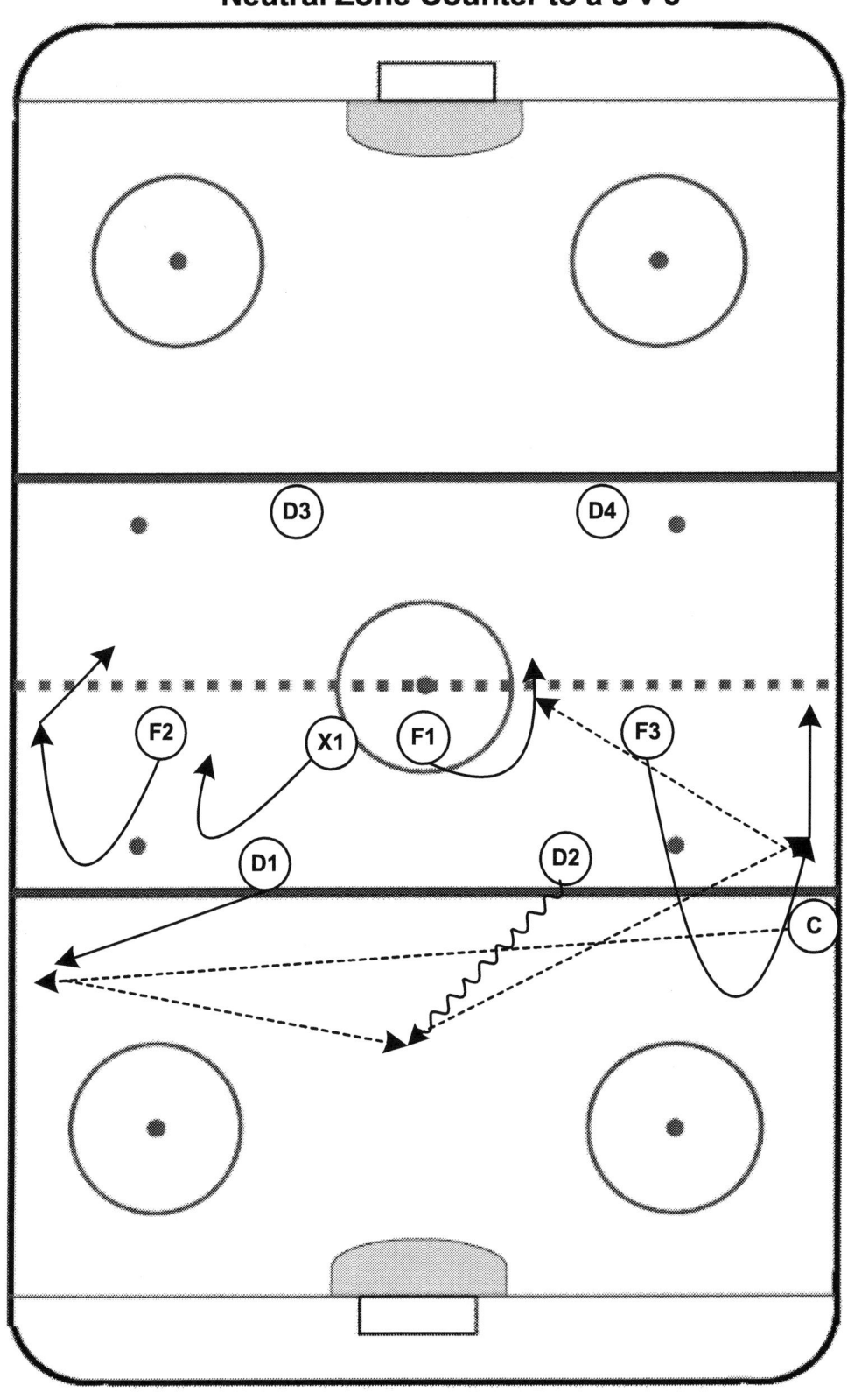

# 68   Full Wheel, 3 v 3

## Emphasis and Objective
Full ice 3 v 3 attack drill.

## Drill Set-Up
- F's in each corner with pucks, D on the face-off dots.
- F1, F2, F3 skate full speed, they cross in the opposite zone and receive a pass from X1, X2 or X3.
- D1 and D2 and X1 skate forward to the far blue-line, pivot and meet the 3 v 3 attack.
- Alternate ends.

## Key Teaching Points
- Full speed.
- Maintain Gap control.
- F's attack at angles and with speed.
- Play until the whistle.

## Recommended Progressions
- None.

# Full Wheel 3 v 3

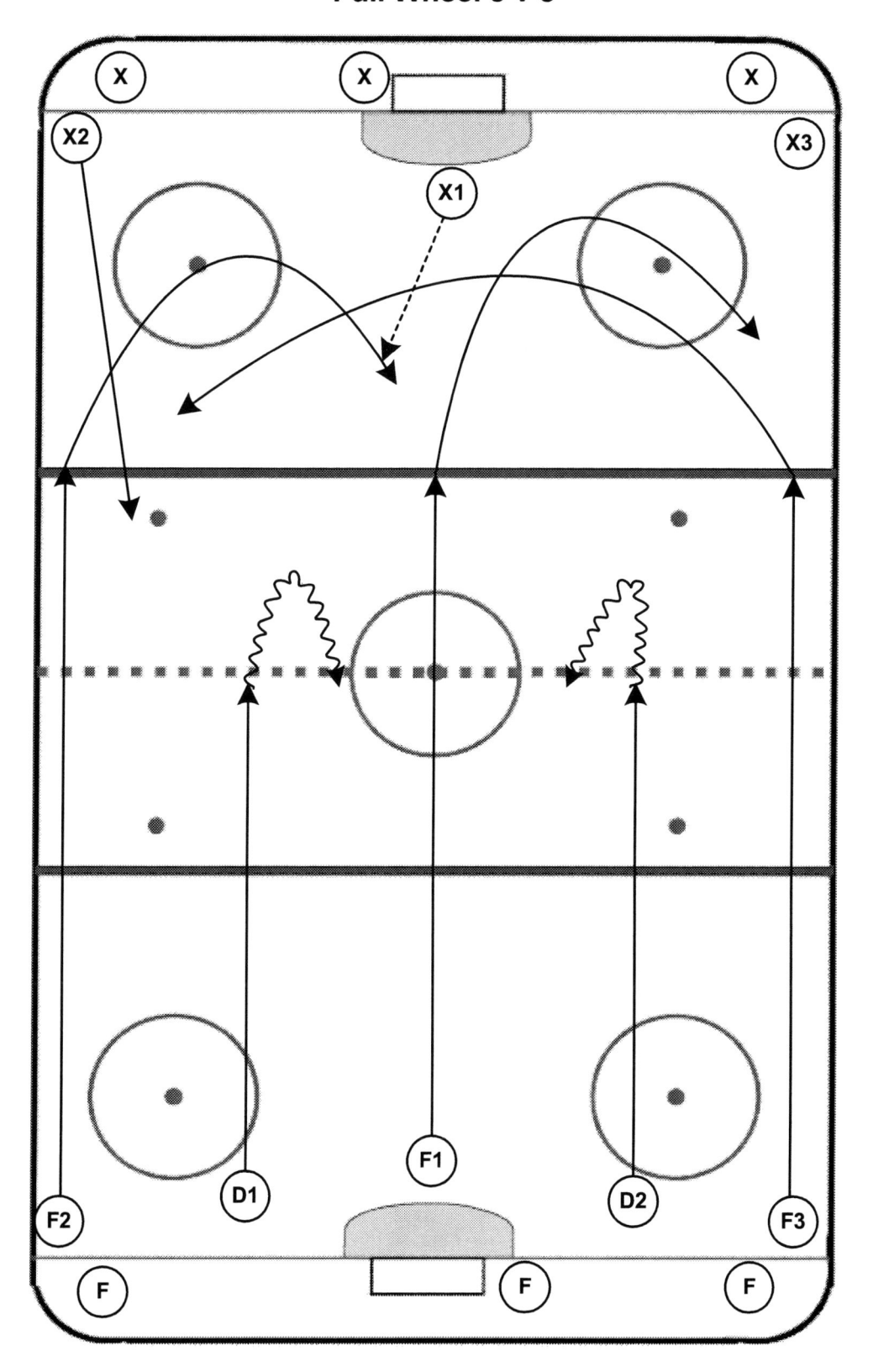

# 69. The Skipper, 3 v 3 Late Attack

## Emphasis and Objective

Excellent drill to recognize the late attacker.

## Drill Set-Up

* F1 and F2 perform a neutral zone regroup with D1 and D2.
* F1 and F2 skate through the neutral zone, pass to F3 who is stationed at the opposite blue-line and counter attack against D1 and D2.
* Once F3 makes the regrouping pass, F4 comes off the wall to backcheck and F3 jumps into the play making it a 3 v 3.
* Play until the whistle.

## Key Teaching Points

* Speed through the neutral zone.
* Support the puck.
* Maintain proper Gap control.
* Keep shooters to the outside.
* Protect the puck.

## Recommended Progressions

* None.

# The Skipper, 3 v 3 Late Attack

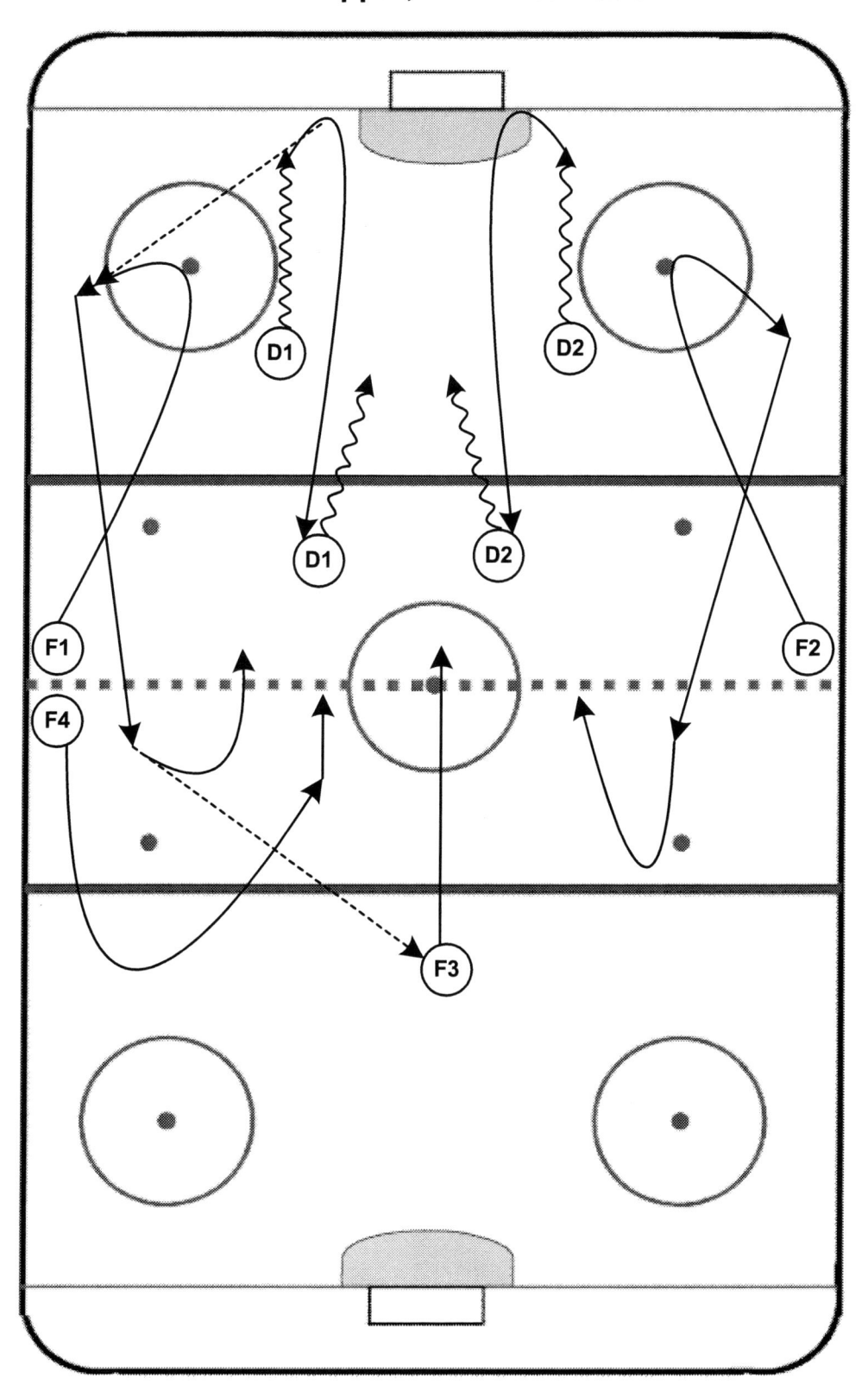

Photo courtesy of Dave Eggen & Dick Carlson of Inertia Pro Event Imaging and The Sioux Falls Stampede

# 4

## Odd Numbered Attacks

Who can make plays? Who are difference makers on a team? Answers, the players that can create convert odd numbered attacks! Players that can create and convert 2 v 1's are in high demand. A player with this ability will have much success and a team with play makers will succeed!

This section focuses on the odd numbered attack both from an offensive and defensive approach. While the glory often goes to the player and team that can convert these situations, it is also critical to learn to defend and diffuse these odd numbered attacks quickly.

Hockey is a game of mistakes and often times an out numbered attack or rush can decide the game. Work on these situations in all 3 zones of the ice. Be it a 2 v 1, 3 v 1, 3 v 2 or 4 v 3, the ability to recognize and create these situations from both an offensive and defensive standpoint are critical to development.

Be sure to incorporate odd numbered attacks in your everyday practice routine. Proficiency in this area will provide great dividends!

## D Up, 2 v 1

### Emphasis and Objective
A quick 2 v 1 forcing D to move feet and gain position and forwards to make quick offensive decisions.

### Drill Set-Up
- Goalies in net.
- F1 and F2 just inside the defensive blue-line, D1 positioned 10 feet in front of middle F.
- On 1st whistle, F1 and F2 skate against D1, 2 v 1.
- D1 must hurry and gain position between the attacking F's.

### Key Teaching Points
- D's dictate flow of play and puck.
- Force puck wide using lateral skating skills.
- Do not permit shot in high percentage area (slot).
- Stay inside face-off dots.
- Goaltender has the shooter.
- Force bad angle shot.

### Recommended Progressions
- Vary position of F's and D's.

# D Up 2 v 1

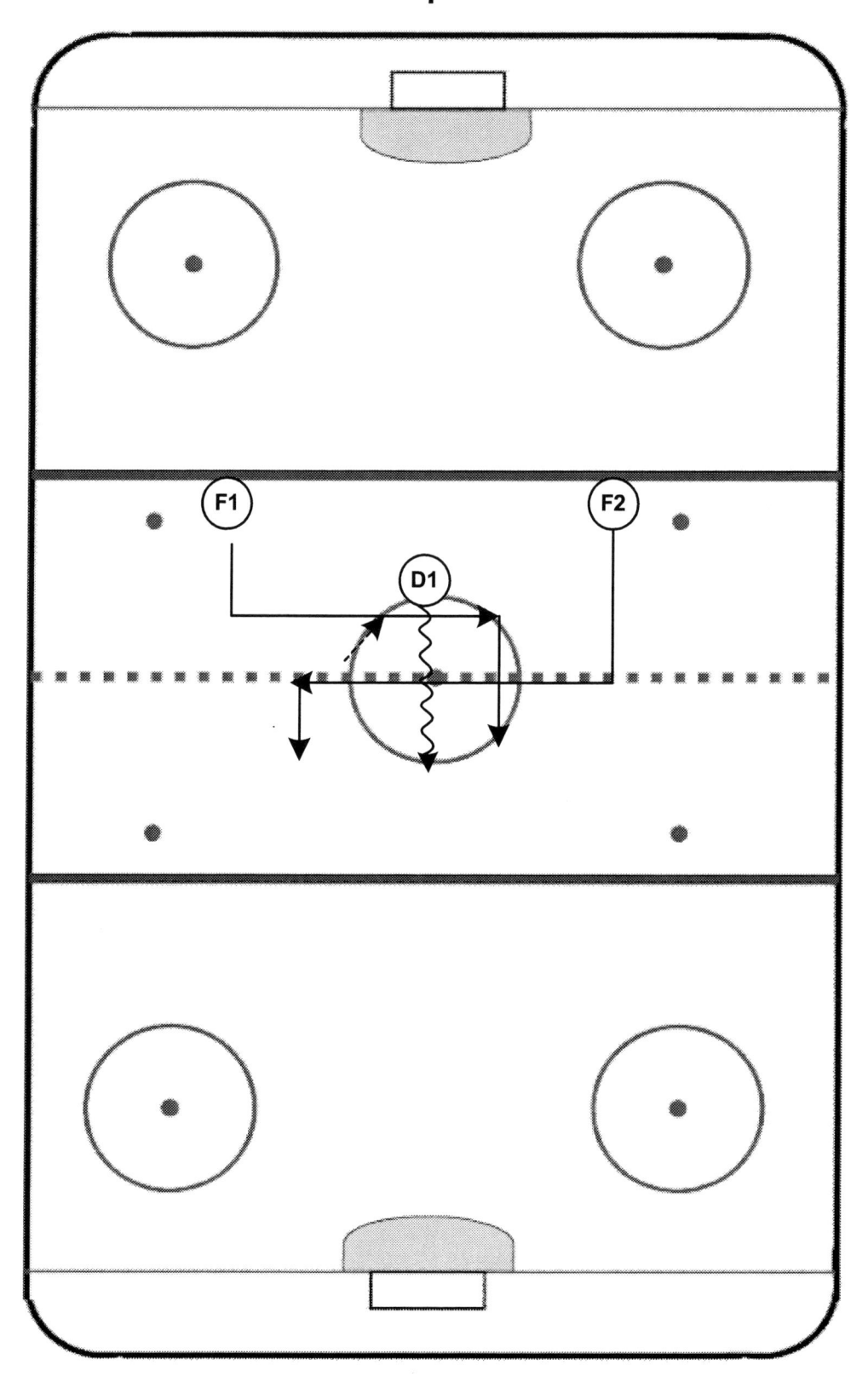

# 71 Hornet 2 v 1

## Emphasis and Objective

Puck support to a 2 v 1 rush.

## Drill Set-Up

* Position F's in each corner in both ends, D's on in zone face-off spot with pucks.
* On the 1st whistle, D1 exchanges passes with F1, F1 passes to F2 breaking down the wall. D1 follows play up in the middle of ice.
* F1 and F2 circle in opposite zone and regroup with D2 for a 2 v 1 attack against D1.
* After regroup, F's must skate and support puck through the neutral zone.
* D2 follows play for a point shot and support.

## Key Teaching Points

* Close puck support.
* D force puck to the outside.
* Maintain 2 stick length gap.
* Create scoring opportunities.

## Recommended Progressions

* 3 v 1.
* 3 v 2.

# Hornet 2 v 1

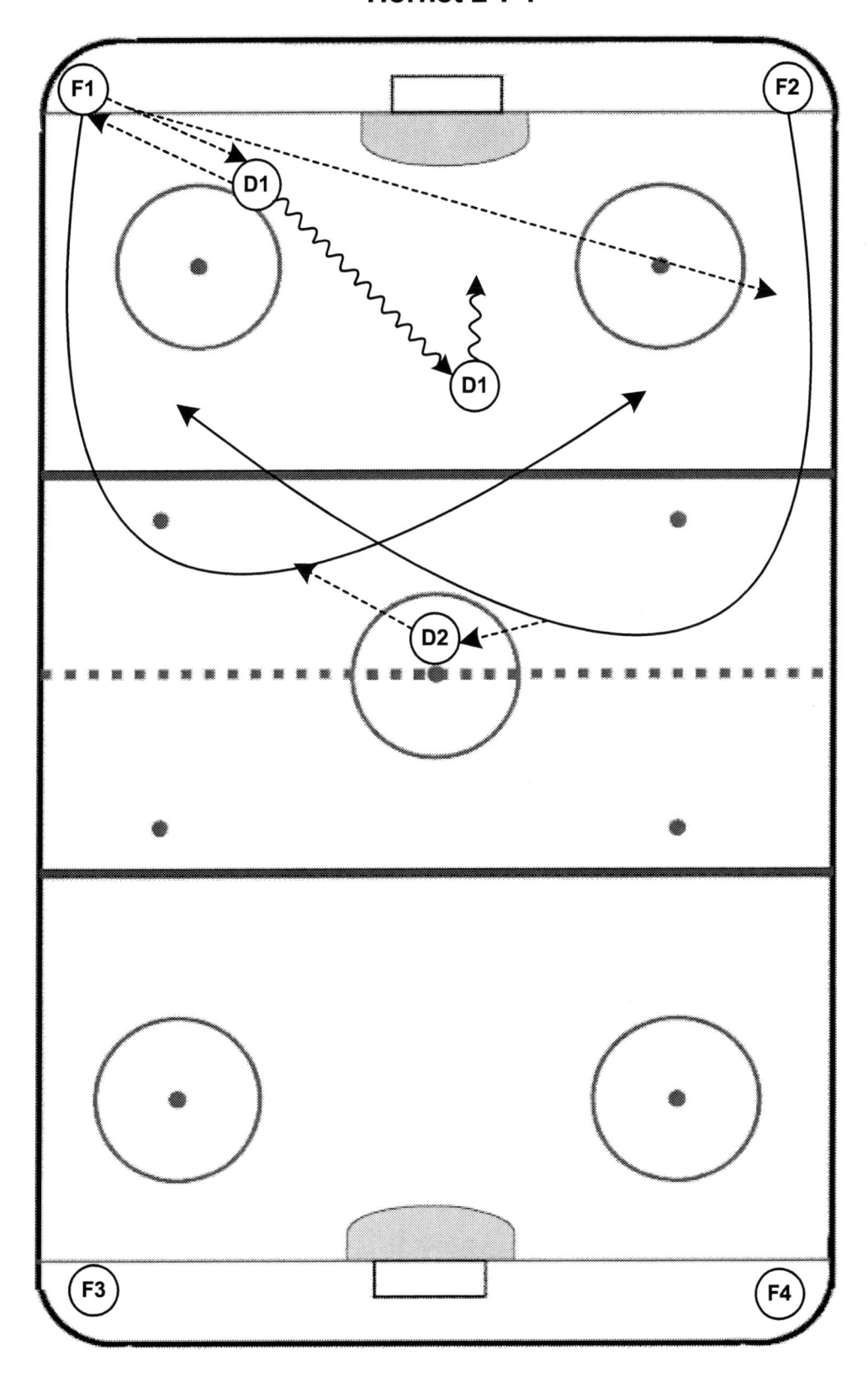

# 72     2 v 1, Down Low

## Emphasis and Objective

Goal-line attacks and out numbered attack and power play skills.

## Drill Set-Up

* Drill done at both ends.
* C inside blue-line with pucks, F1 below the goal-line, F2 on half board hash mark, D in the middle.
* C passes to F1 or F2 and they read off one another and attack the goal.
* D always careful to stay between F's and discourage high percentage shot.

## Key Teaching Points

* Give and go.
* Use picks and screens.
* Puck protection.
* High percentage shots.

## Recommended Progressions

* 2 v 2.
* 3 v 2.
* 3 v 3.

# 2 v 1 Down Low

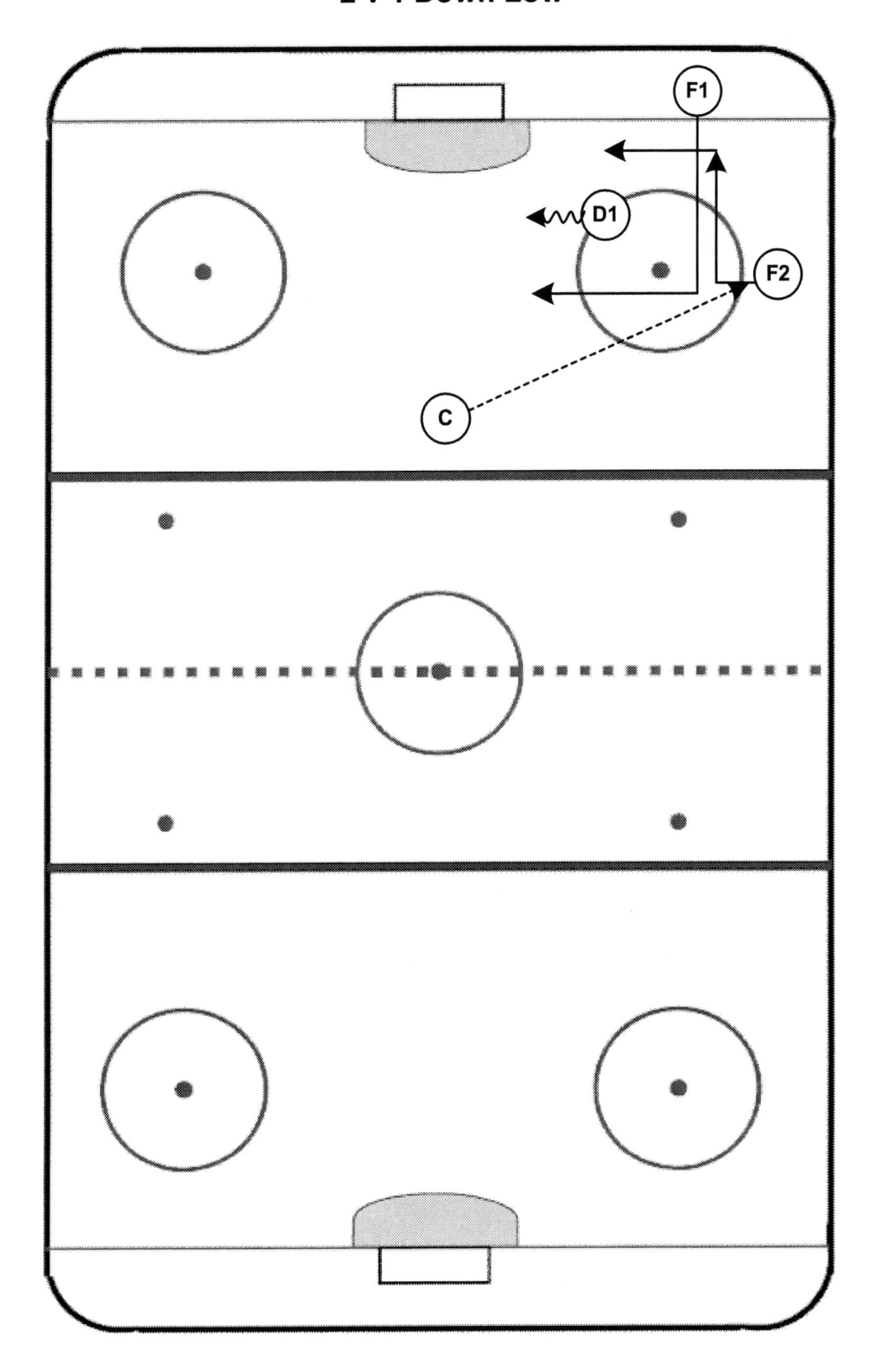

# 73 — 2 v 1, Breakout Counter Attack

## Emphasis and Objective

Work on breakouts and neutral zone counter attacks.

## Drill Set-Up

* Pucks behind each net.
* On whistle, D1 skates backwards to the hash marks, pivots and picks up puck behind net starting a breakout with F1 and F2 who have moved into breakout position.
* F1 and F2 pass and carry the puck through the neutral zone, at the red-line, they pass to D2 who immediately transitions the puck back to F1 and F2.
* F1 and F2 attack 2 v 1 against D1.
* D2, after transitioning the puck, skates backwards and starts the drill in the other direction.

## Key Teaching Points

* Support the puck.
* Pass in stride.
* Good depth in transition.
* Drive the net.

## Recommended Progressions

* 2 v 0, 3 v 0, 3 v 1, 3 v 2.

# 2 v 1 Breakout Counter Attack

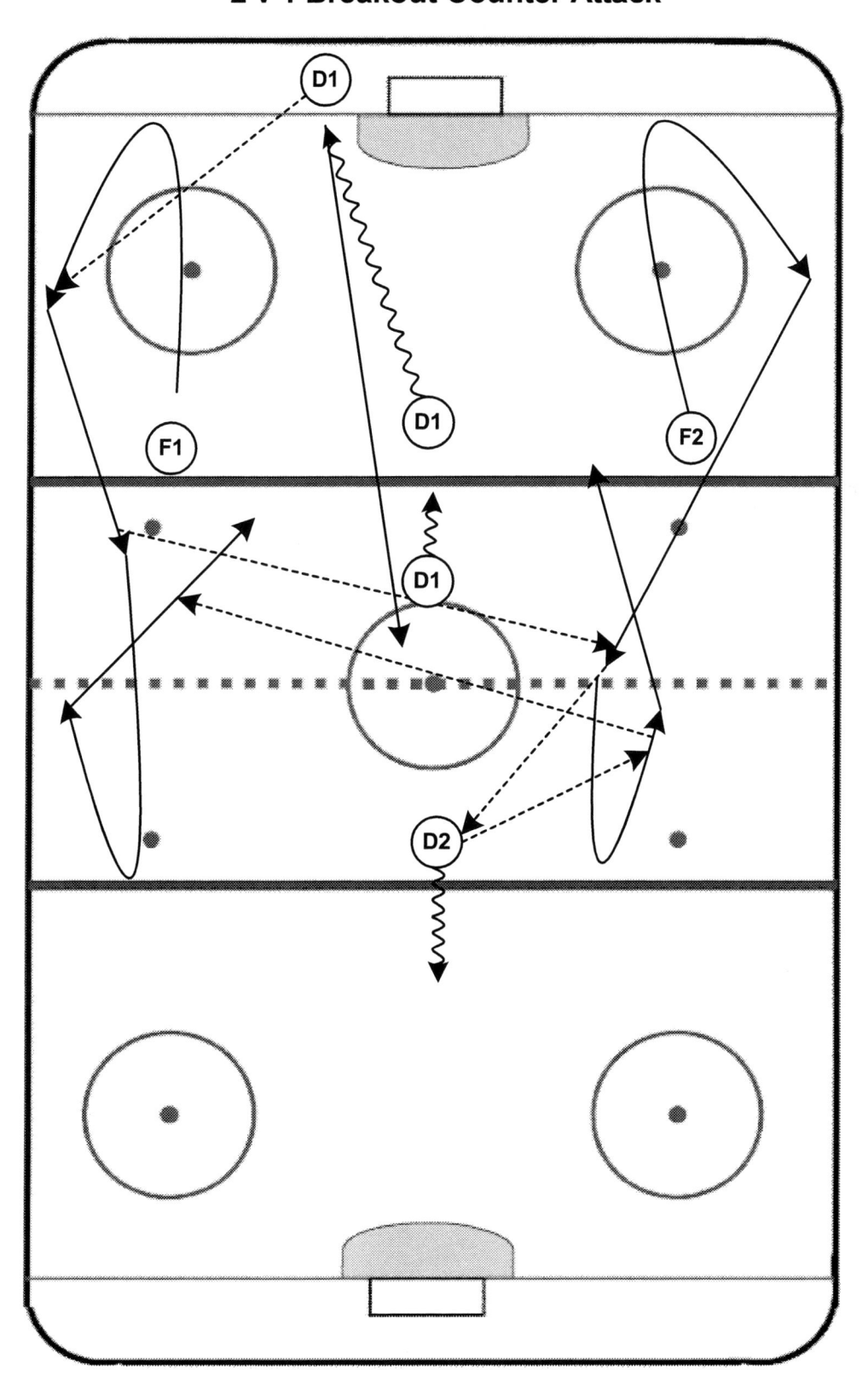

# 74     Terrier 2 v 1

## Emphasis and Objective

Continuous 2 v 1 utilizing long and short passes.

## Drill Set-Up

* F's in opposite corners, D's in opposite corners with pucks.
* D1 skates to F1 and they skate down the wall passing 2 v 0. D2 and heads to middle ice, F2 skates behind the net at full speed.
* F1 continues skating, stretching the D, D2 steps out and passes to either F1 or F2 for a 2 v 1 against D1.
* D2 continues the drill by activating a 2 v 1 with opposite line of F's.

## Key Teaching Points

* Good passes.
* Puck support.
* Stretching the offense.
* Offensive and defensive positioning.

## Recommended Progressions

* None.

# Terrier 2 v 1

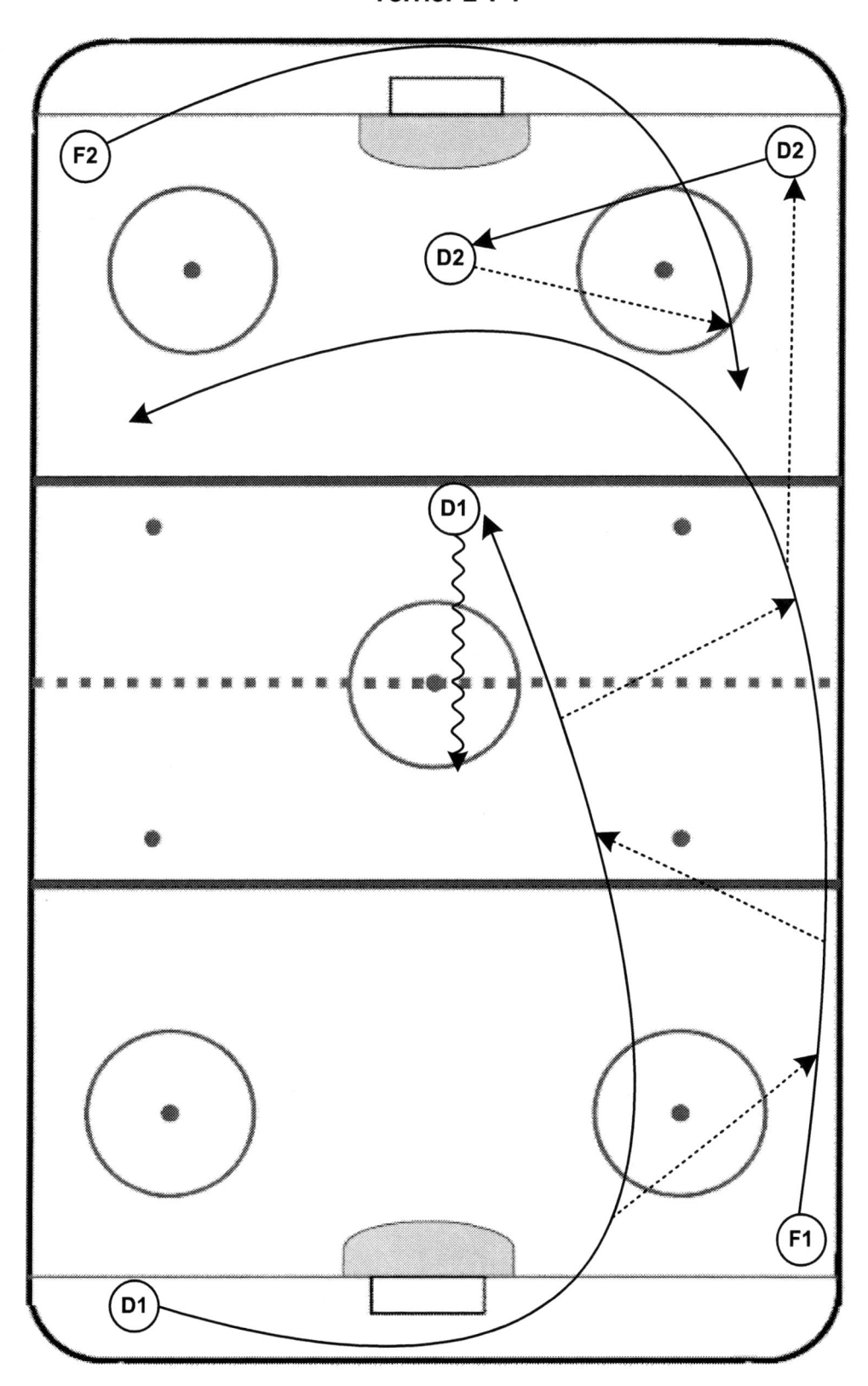

# 2 v 1 Quick

## Emphasis and Objective
To have players make quick decisions in a variety of situations.

## Drill Set-Up
* F's in both ends, positioned at the tops of the circles. D's in the neutral zone.
* On 1st whistle, F's in one end begin skating in a figure 8. D skate in the neutral zone forward to the blue, backward to the red.
* On the 2nd whistle, F's attack the neutral zone looking for a pass form C. D react quickly, close the Gap and play the 2 v 1.
* Play continues to the offensive zone until 3rd whistle.
* That 3rd whistle activates the next two F's who begin skating figure 8's while the next D in the neutral prepares for the attack.
* On the next whistle, F's take off to the neutral zone and the drill repeats.
* Drill is continuous.

## Key Teaching Points
* Keep feet moving.
* Stagger the offensive attack.
* Maintain good Gap control.
* Attack with speed.
* Protect the puck.
* Stay onside.
* C vary the timing of the initial pass.
* Score and attack under pressure.

## Recommended Progressions
* 2 v 2, 3 v 2.

# 2 v 1 Quick

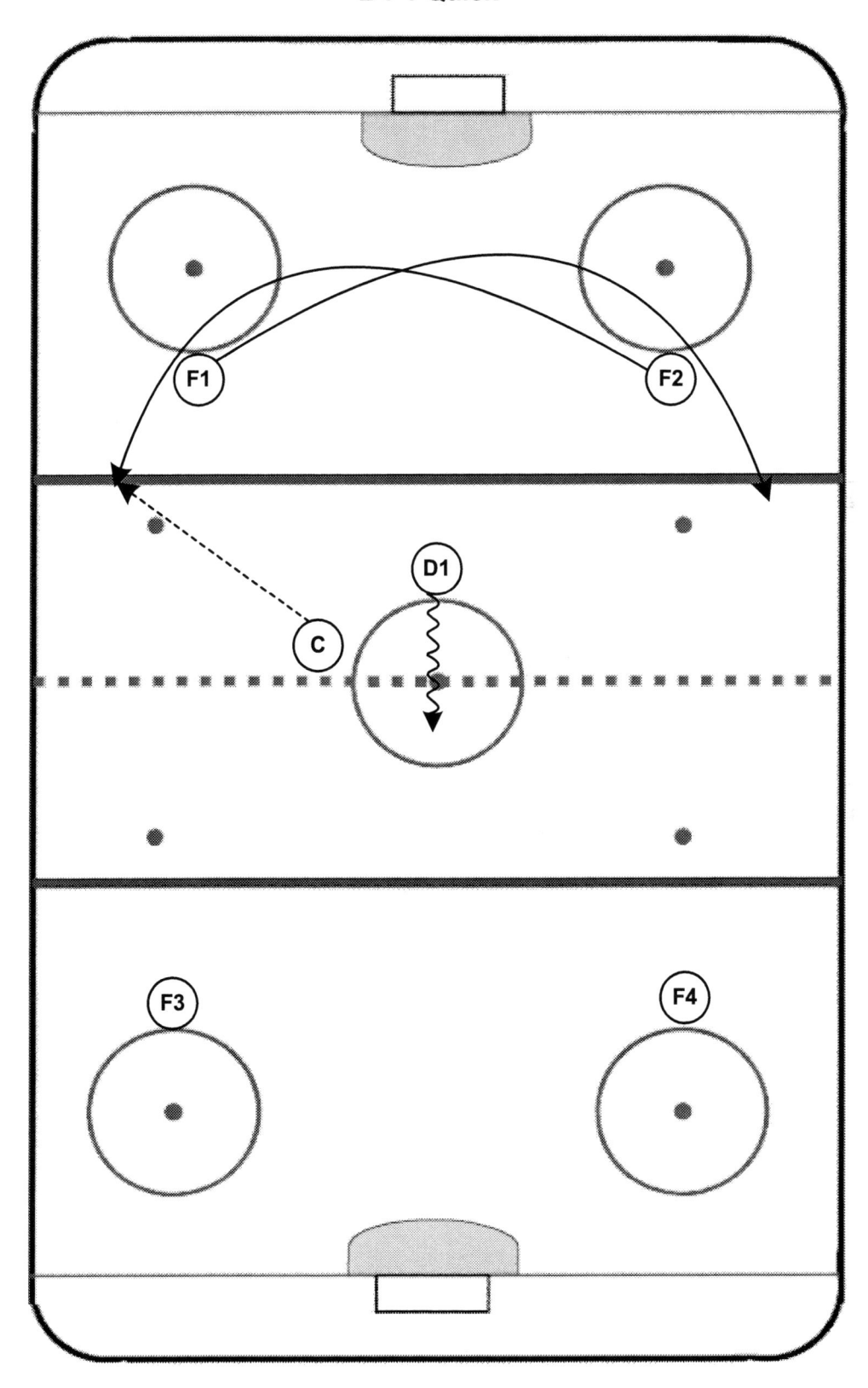

# 76 — 2 v 1, 4 Blues

## Emphasis and Objective
Give forwards and defense different 2 v 1 situations.

## Drill Set-Up
* F's in 4 groups, one at each blue-line, with pucks.
* D divide into 4 groups, 1 D facing each group of F's.
* 2 F's in each group attack D's, 2 v 1 to a shot.

## Key Teaching Points
* Alternate sides.
* Quick decisions in confined areas.
* Gap control, 2 stick length.
* Use screens to take away space.
* Stop in front of the net.

## Recommended Progressions
* None.

# 2 v 1, 4 Blues

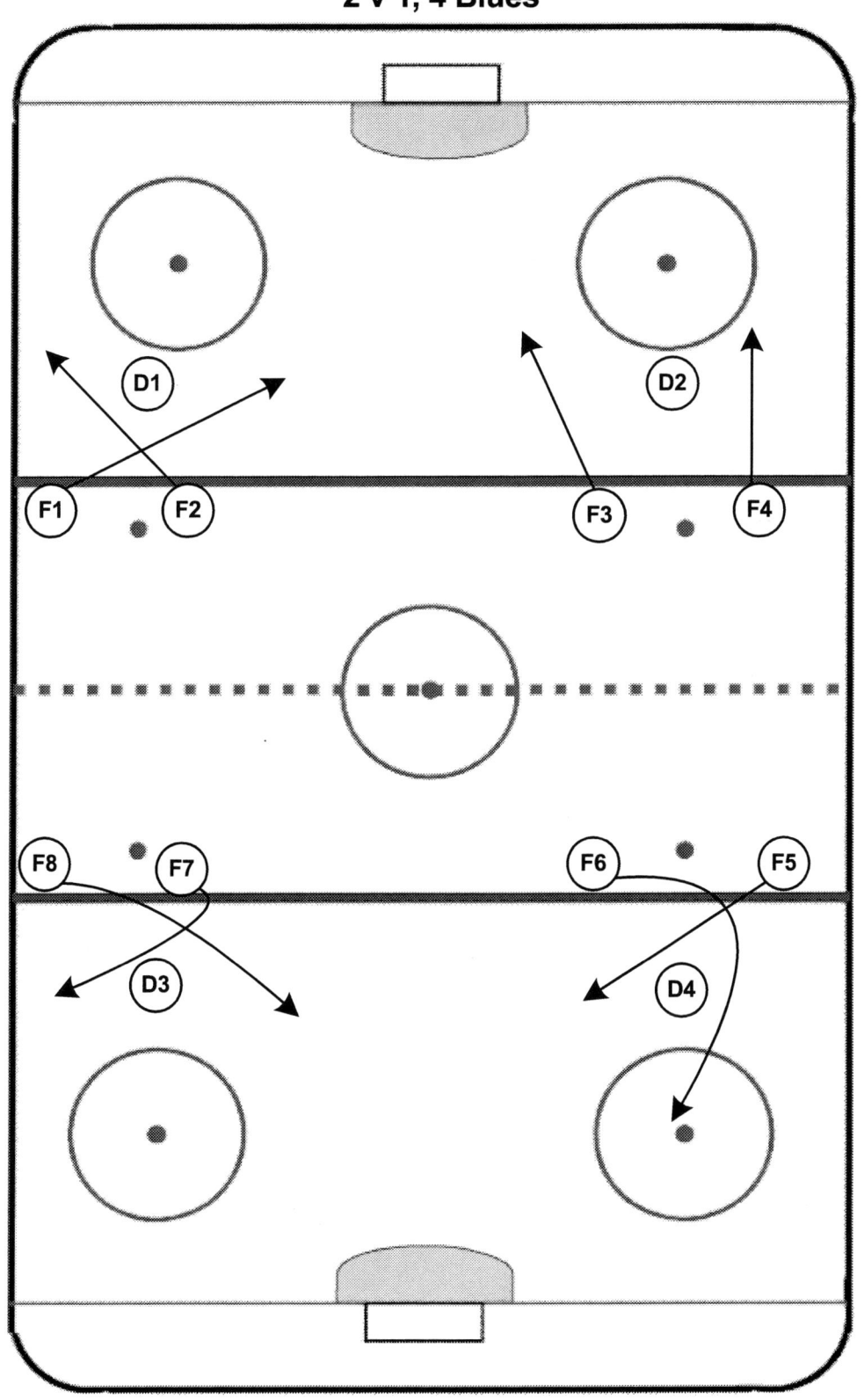

# 77            The Yukon: 2 v 1

## Emphasis and Objective
Defending and attacking a 2 v 1 at full speed with recovery.

## Drill Set-Up
* F's in opposite corners with pucks, D on both sides of the center circle, cones on neutral zone face-off dots.
* D's on their knees at the red-line.
* On the whistle, D get up and skate forward to the cone, pivot and defend against the 1st 2 F's in each line 2 v 1. F's be sure to take off immediately on the whistle.
* F's must stay on their half until they enter the offensive zone.

## Key Teaching Points
* Good, quick feet, don't cheat.
* Balance.
* Gap control, 2 stick lengths.
* Keep shooter to the outside lane.
* Full speed offensive attack.
* Both ends in unison.

## Recommended Progressions
* Can also be done as a 1 v 1.

# The Yukon 2 v 1

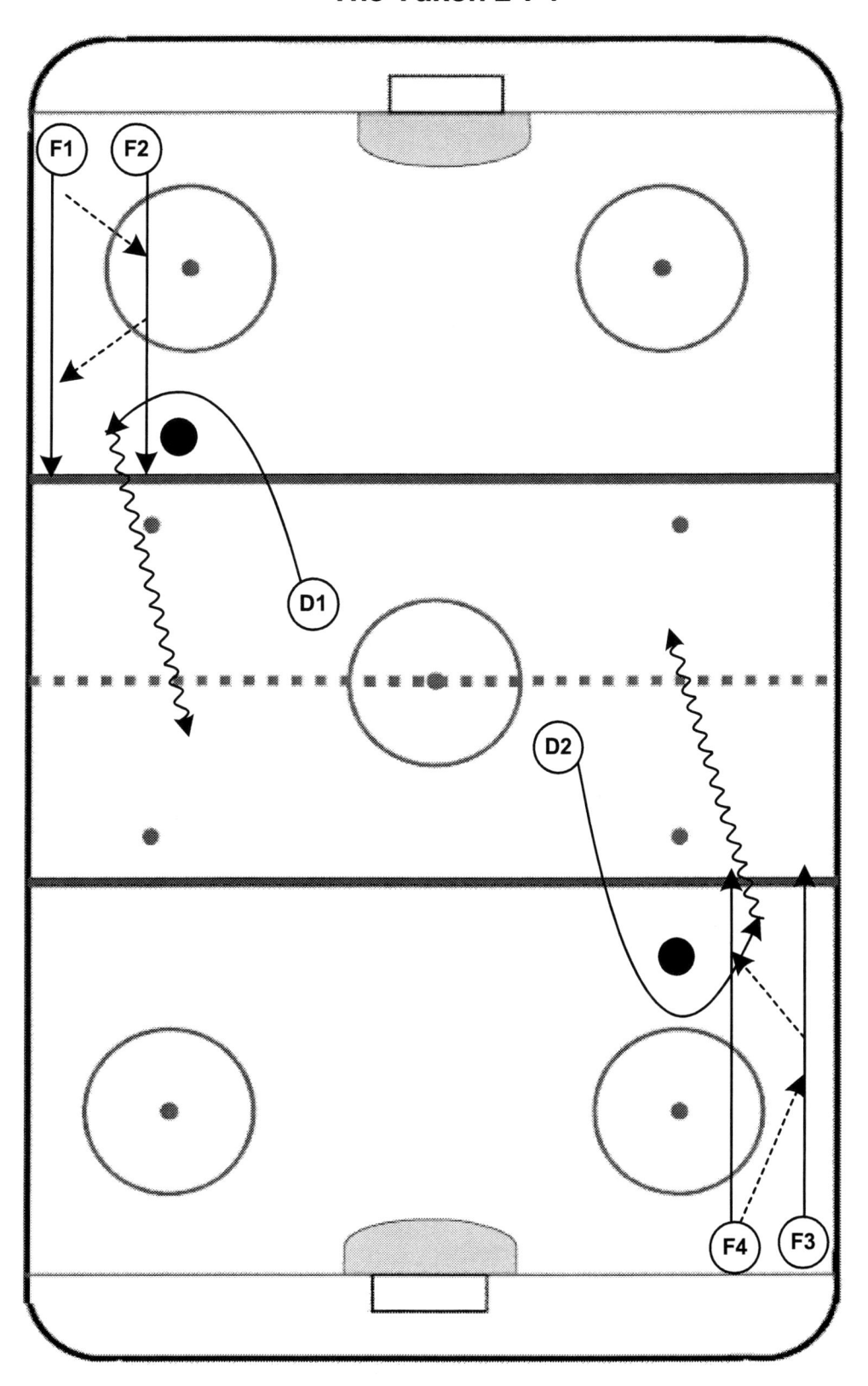

# 78     The Buck: 2 v 1 Fast Offense

## Emphasis and Objective

Puck support, timing and 2 v 1 play.

## Drill Set-Up

* Players in 5 groups positioned as diagrammed. X1 on blue-line, X2 on red-line, X3 and X4 in neutral zone on red-line, D1 inside the blue-line.
* On the whistle, X1 shoots on net and proceeds to pick up a puck in the corner, D1 backwards skates to the goal-line looking for a pass from X1.
* X1 passes to D1. D1 passes to X3 who has curled deep in the center zone supporting the puck.
* X3 one touches the puck to X2 who has come back in the zone in good break out position. X2 attacks the zone down the wall.
* X3 regroups in the center with X4, receives a pass from the C and attacks D1, 2 v 1.
* X2 performs an escape in the offensive zone and hits a breaking X1 who has joined the rush for a shot.

## Key Teaching Points

* Timing.
* Puck support.
* Full speed.

## Recommended Progressions

* None.

# The Buck, 2 v 1 Fast Offense

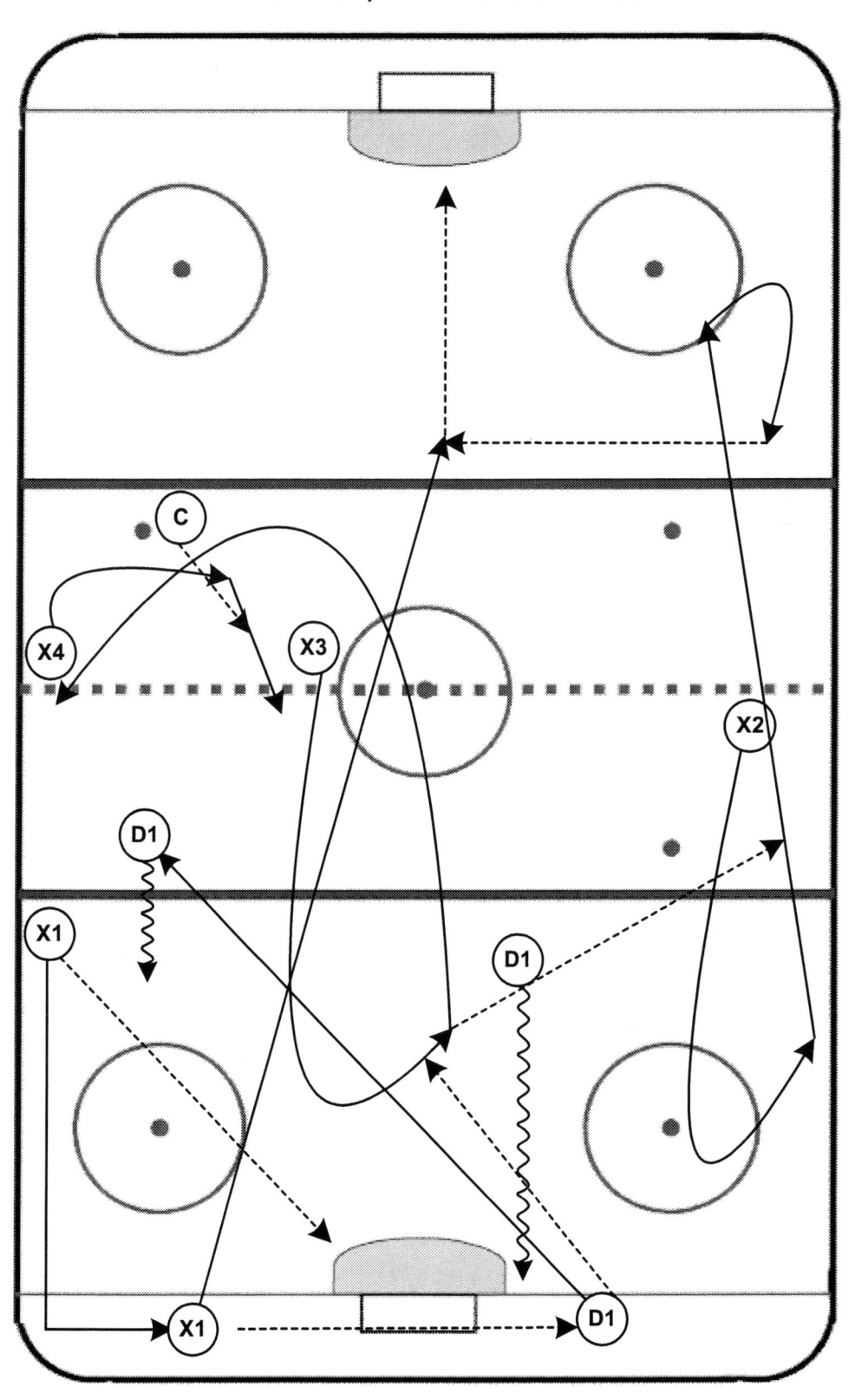

# 79 — 2 v 1 Mirror, Full Ice

### Emphasis and Objective
Work on Gap control, foot work and attack skills.

### Drill Set-Up
* F's in two line in both corners. D at the blue-line.
* F1 and F2 on the goal-line with one puck. F1 skates with the puck around the top of the near circle proceeding to the bottom of the far circle, F2 performs the same action as they attack the D1.
* D1 mirrors the puck carrier maintaining a proper Gap and defends the full ice 2 v 1.

### Key Teaching Points
* Keep feet moving at all times.
* Maintain 2 stick length Gap.
* Support the puck through the neutral zone.
* Keep shooter to the outside.
* Speed and staggered attack through the neutral zone.

### Recommended Progressions
* 3 v 1.

**2 v 1 Mirror Full Ice**

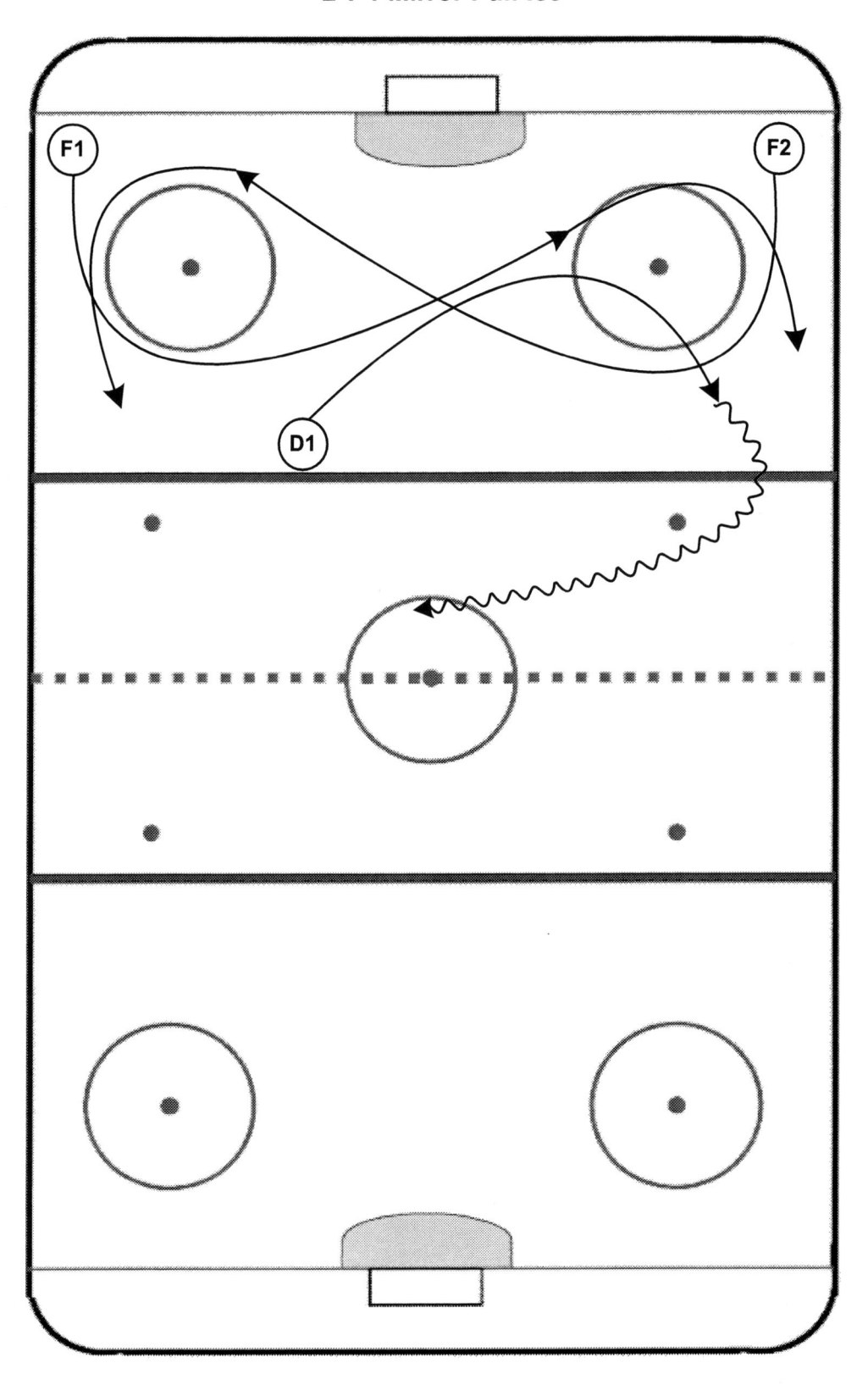

# 80 — Half Ice Attack, 2 v 1

## Emphasis and Objective

Work on attacking and defending 2 v 1 in a confined area.

## Drill Set-Up

* F's in 4 lines, 1 on each side of the red-line. D in 4 groups, one on each blue-line.
* Both sides at the same time, F1 passes to D1, D1 backwards skates around the circle, F1 and F2 curl in the zone and receive a pass from D1 and attack 2 v 1 on their half of the ice against D2.
* Be sure that F3 and F4 are regrouping with D3 and attacking D4 at the same time.

## Key Teaching Points

* Good foot work.
* Puck control and puck support.
* Maintain good two stick length gap.
* Keep shooter to the outside.
* Drive the net.

## Recommended Progressions

* None.

# Half Ice 2 v 1 Attack

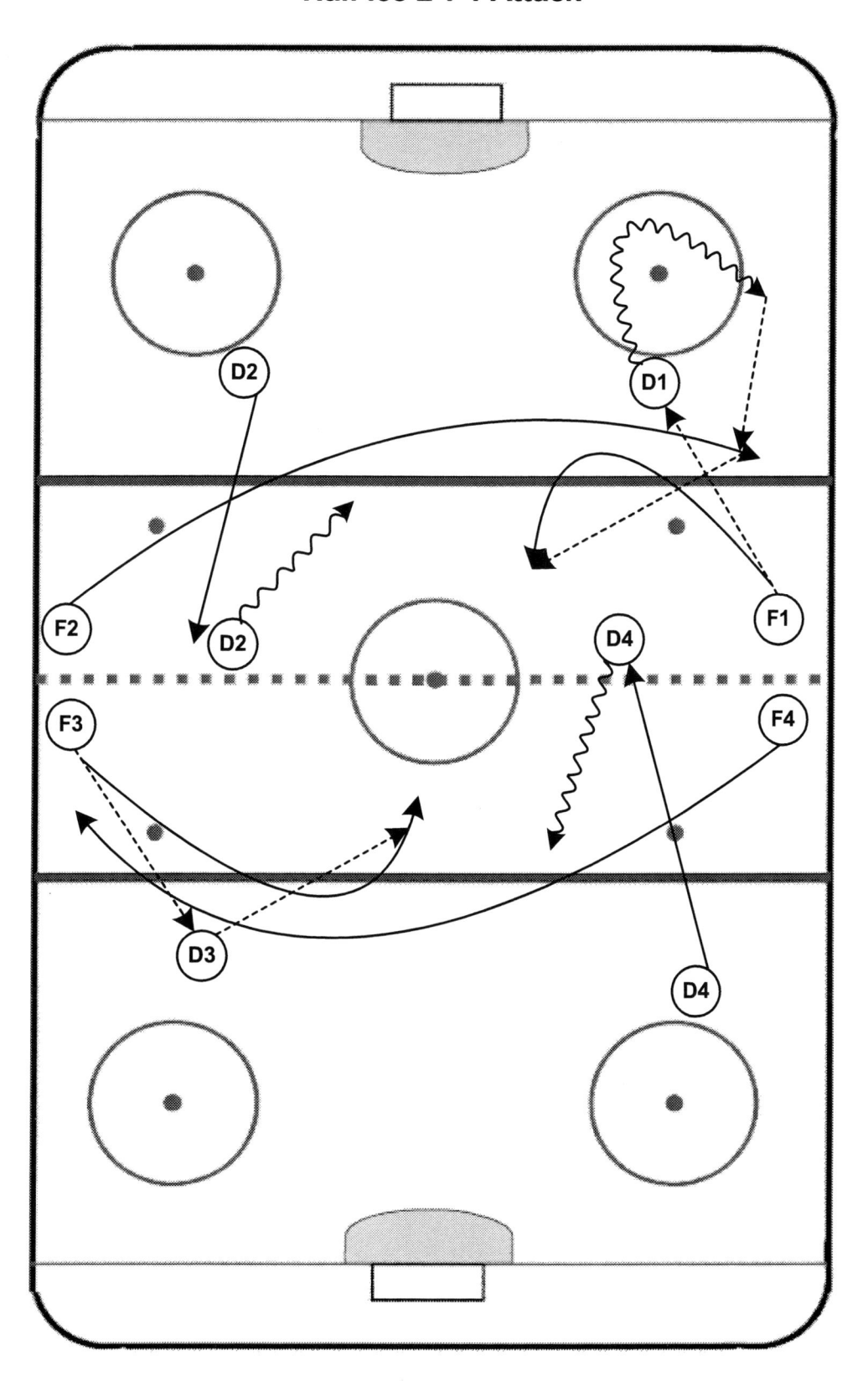

# 2 v 1, Defense Join the Rush

## Emphasis and Objective

Work on defensemen transitioning from defense to offense.

## Drill Set-Up

* Forwards in each end at opposite corners with pucks, D in the neutral zone.
* Drill starts with F1 attacking D1, 1 v 1.
* On the whistle, D1 immediately drops off and joins F2 who has taken off and attacking D2, thus creating the 2 v 1. F1 finishes the offensive play.
* On the whistle, D2 drops off and joins F3 for a 2 v 1 and the drill repeats.

## Key Teaching Points

* Read the rush.
* Forwards must be patient to create the 2 v 1.
* React immediately on the whistle.
* Communication.
* Shoot to score.
* One attack shown.

## Recommended Progressions

* 2 v 1 to a 3 v 1.
* 2 V 2 to a 3 v 2.

# 2 v 1 D Join the Rush

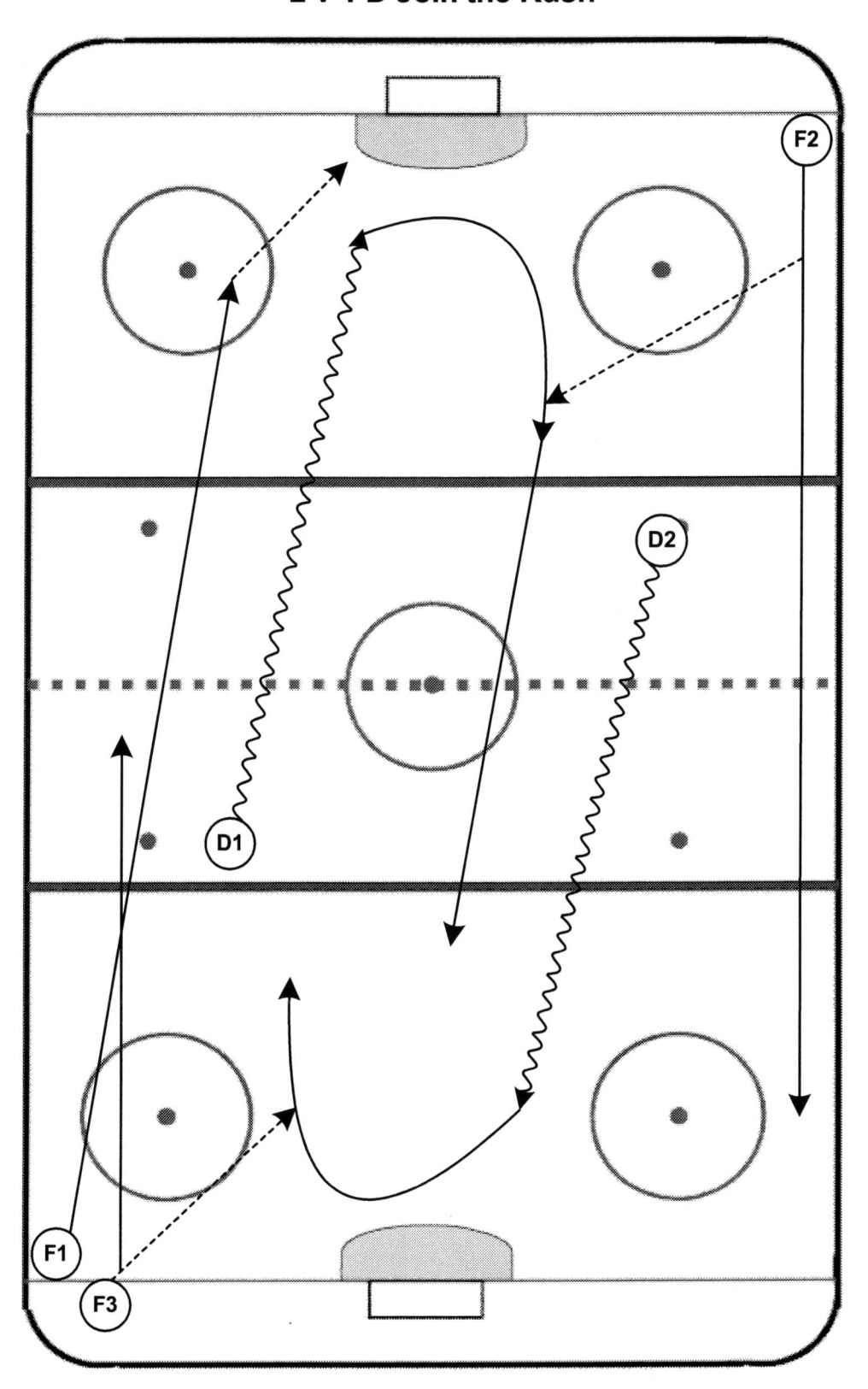

# 82 — Both Ways From Center, 2 v 1

## Emphasis and Objective

Work on foot work and 2 v 1 attacks.

## Drill Set-Up

* F's in 4 lines at each blue-line, D's at the center face-off dot.
* F pass to D in the center, D catches the puck, pivots backwards and leaves the puck.
* One F from each line cross in the center, picks up the puck and attacks the D, 2 v 1.

## Key Teaching Points

* Good footwork, work on pivots.
* Stay on sides.
* Keep shooter to the outside.
* Goalie has the shot.
* Good 2 stick length gap, force play before hash marks.
* One end diagrammed.

## Recommended Progressions

* None.

# Both Ways From Center 2 v 1

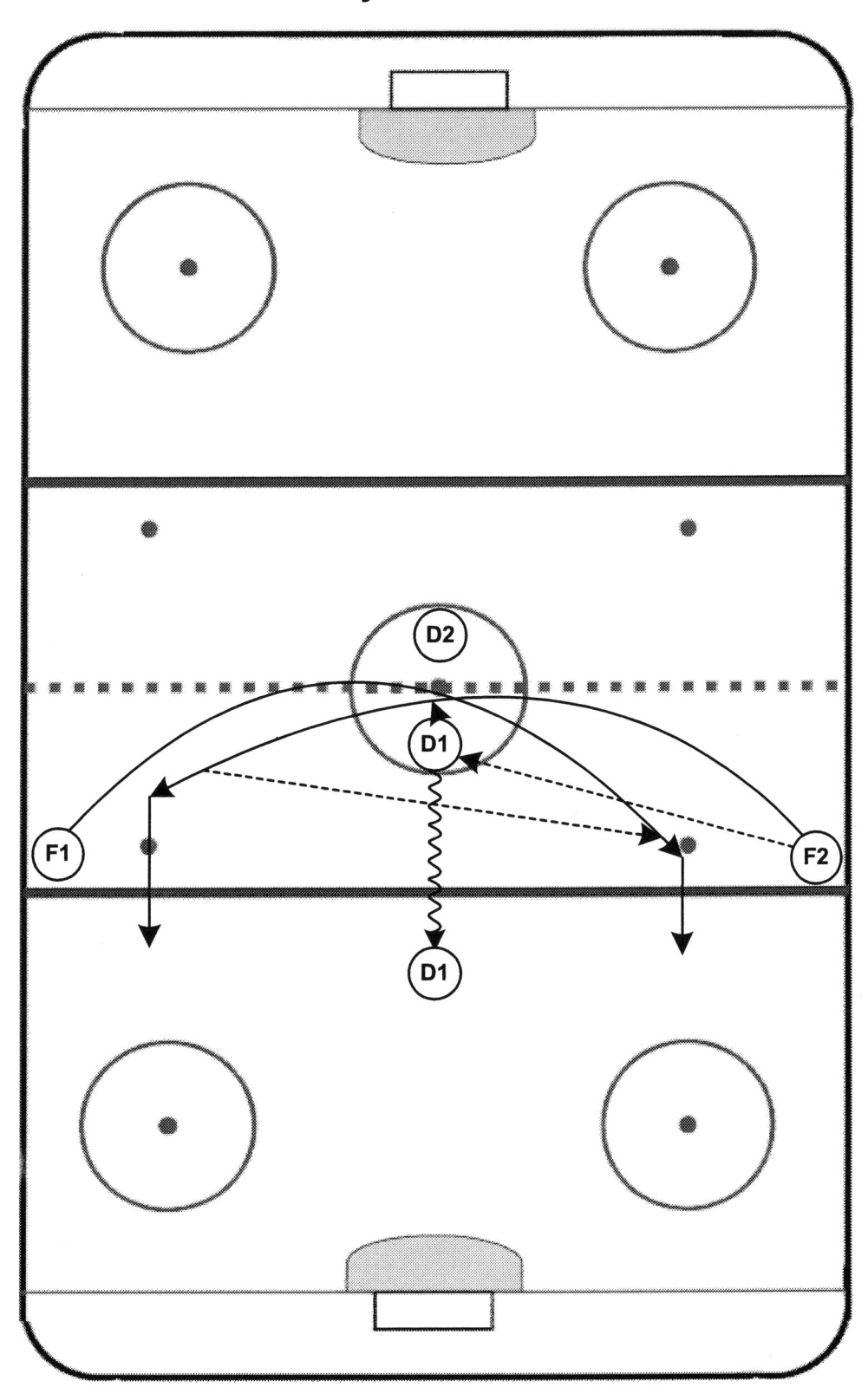

# 83 The Snap 3 v 1

## Emphasis and Objective

3 v 1 drill requiring defensemen to react and prepare to defend the rush in a snap.

## Drill Set-Up

* F1, F2 and F3 positioned on the red-line, D1 and D2 on the blue-line, C in the opposite corner.
* F3 passes to D1, D1 passes to D2, while counter attacking with D2, D1 races to the red-line and prepares to meet the rush 3 v 1.
* D2, after regrouping with F1, F2 and F3, follows the play up to the attacking blue-line and on the whistle, receives a pass from C, F1, F2 and F3 position themselves for a tip and rebound.
* Alternate ends.

## Key Teaching Points

* Quick transition.
* Good offensive attack angles.
* Tips, screens and rebounds

## Recommended Progressions

* None.

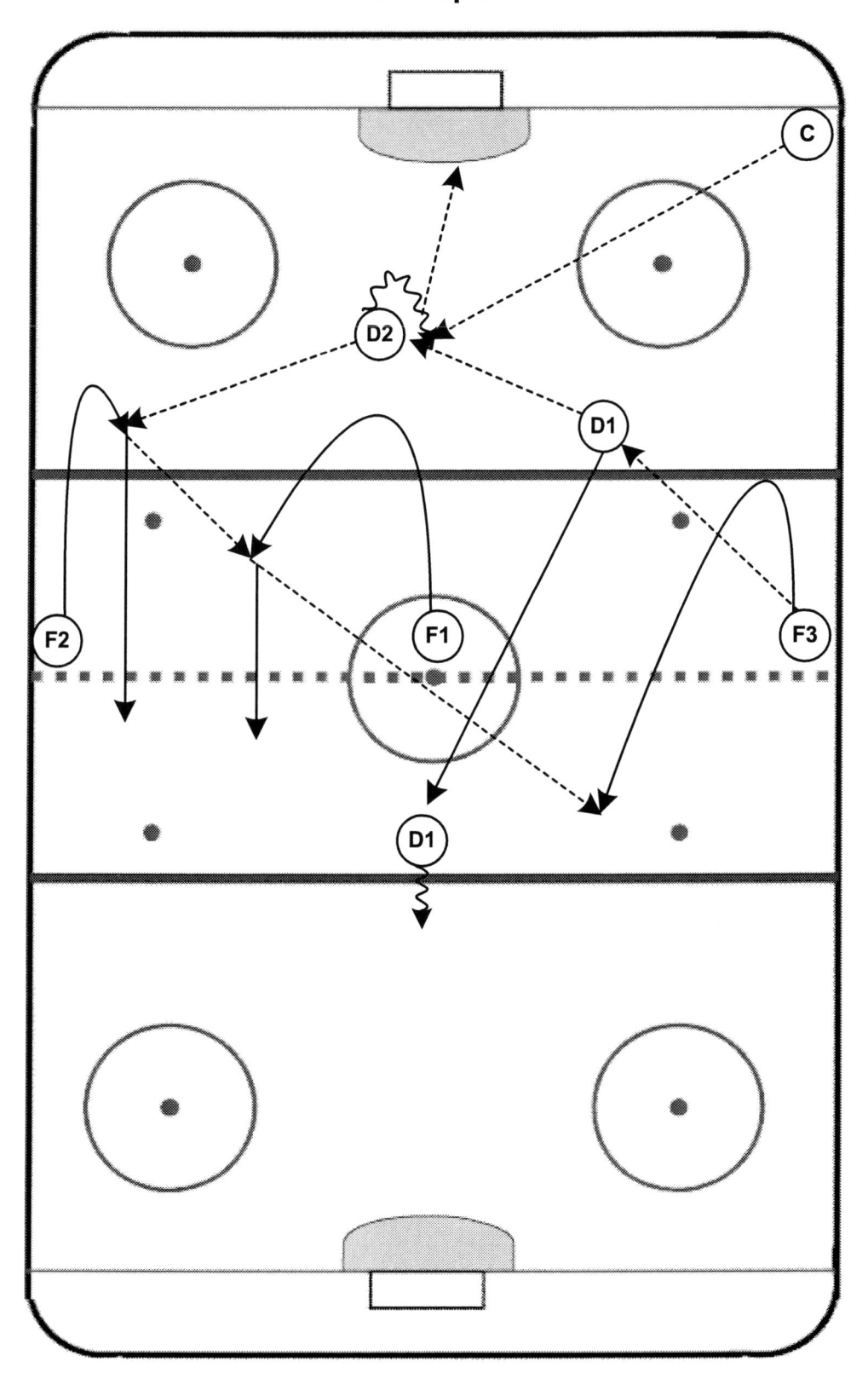

# The Snap 3 v 1

# 3 v 2 Breakouts

## Emphasis and Objective
Continuous drill for breakout and 3 v 2 attack and defend skills.

## Drill Set-Up
* F1, F2 and F3 breakout with D1 and D2 attacking D3 and D4, 3 v 2.
* Once F1, F2 and F3 move through the neutral zone, X1, X2 and X3 move into breakout position.
* On the whistle, D3 and D4 breakout X1, X2 and X3 against original D1 and D2.

## Key Teaching Points
* Make good, crisp breakout passes.
* Movement through the neutral zone.
* Quick recognition and counter attacks.

## Recommended Progressions
* None.

# 3 v 2 Breakouts

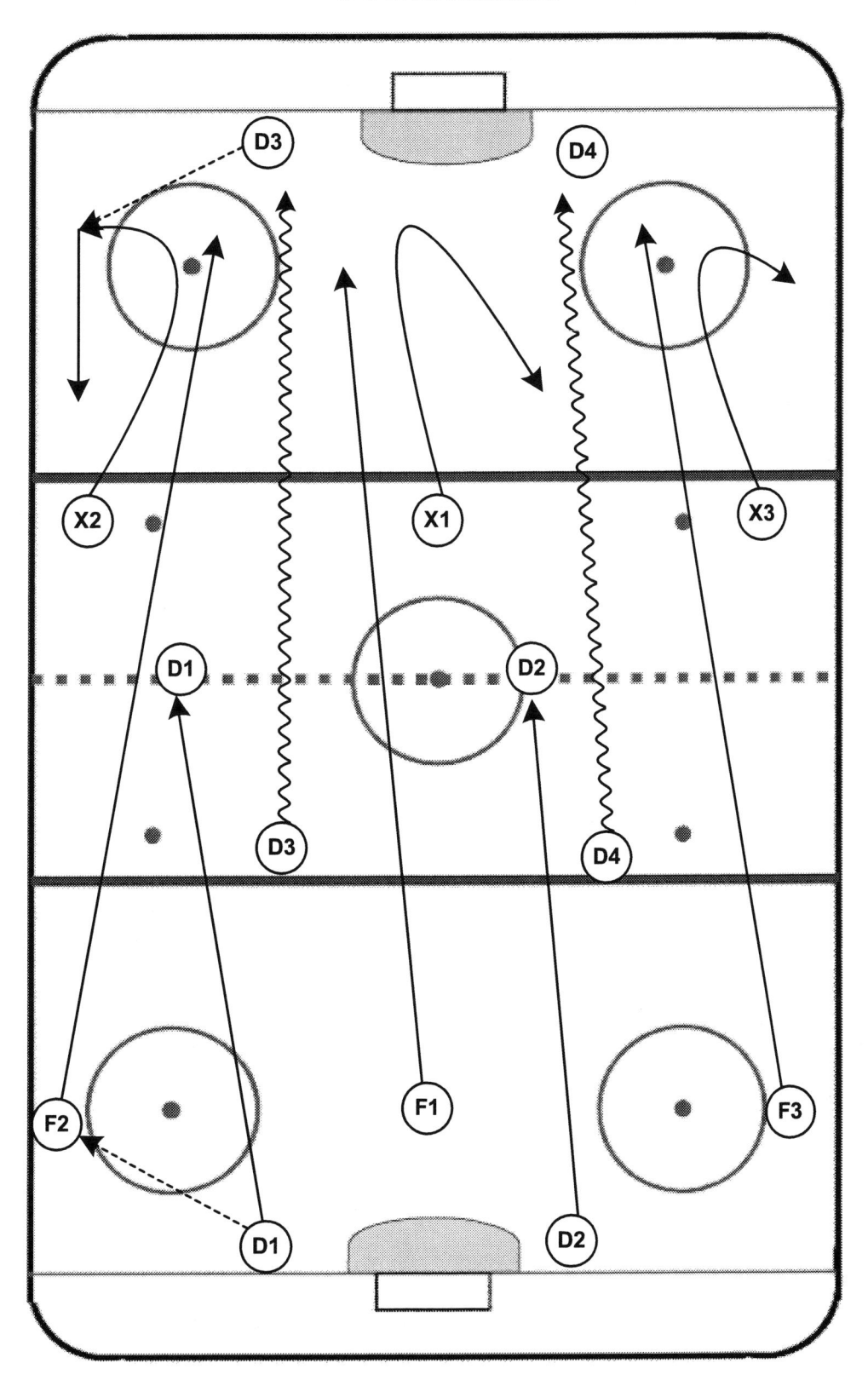

# 85 — Free Flow, 3 v 0 to a 3 v 2

## Emphasis and Objective
To improve speed and passing through the neutral zone.

## Drill Set-Up
* F1, F2 and F3 on blue-line, D1 and D2 on opposite blue-line.
* F's curl off the wall and receive a pass from C. F1, F2 and F3 proceed through the neutral zone attacking 3 v 0.
* On the whistle, D1 and D2 jump into the neutral zone, F's receive a long pass from C and attack the opposite end, 3 v 2.
* Both ends, switch sides.

## Key Teaching Points
* Speed and decision making in the neutral zone.
* Maintain proper Gap.
* Create scoring opportunities.

## Recommended Progressions
* None.

# Free Flow 3 v 0 to a 3 v 2

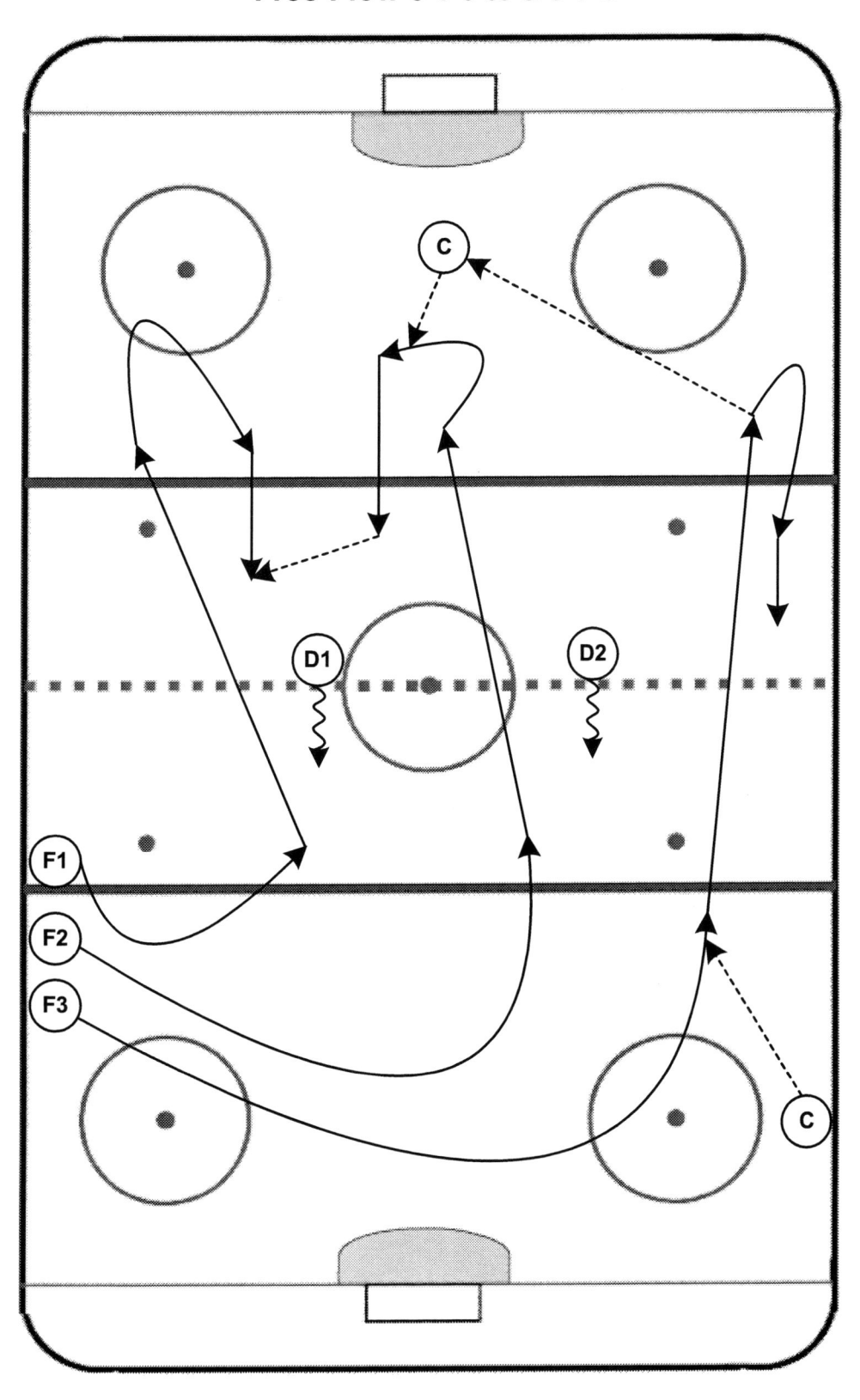

## 3 v 2 with a Backchecker

### Emphasis and Objective
Full ice 3 v 2 with a backchecker emphasizing reading the rush.

### Drill Set-Up
* C in the corner, F1, F2 and F3 on the blue-line, X1 in center.
* F's curl into the defensive zone, receives a pass from C and attack 3 v 2 against D1 and D2.
* After the pass, X1 backchecks the play into the zone for a 3 v 3.

### Key Teaching Points
* Read the backcheck.
* Speed through the neutral zone.
* Puck protection.

### Recommended Progressions
* None.

# 3 v 2 with a Backchecker

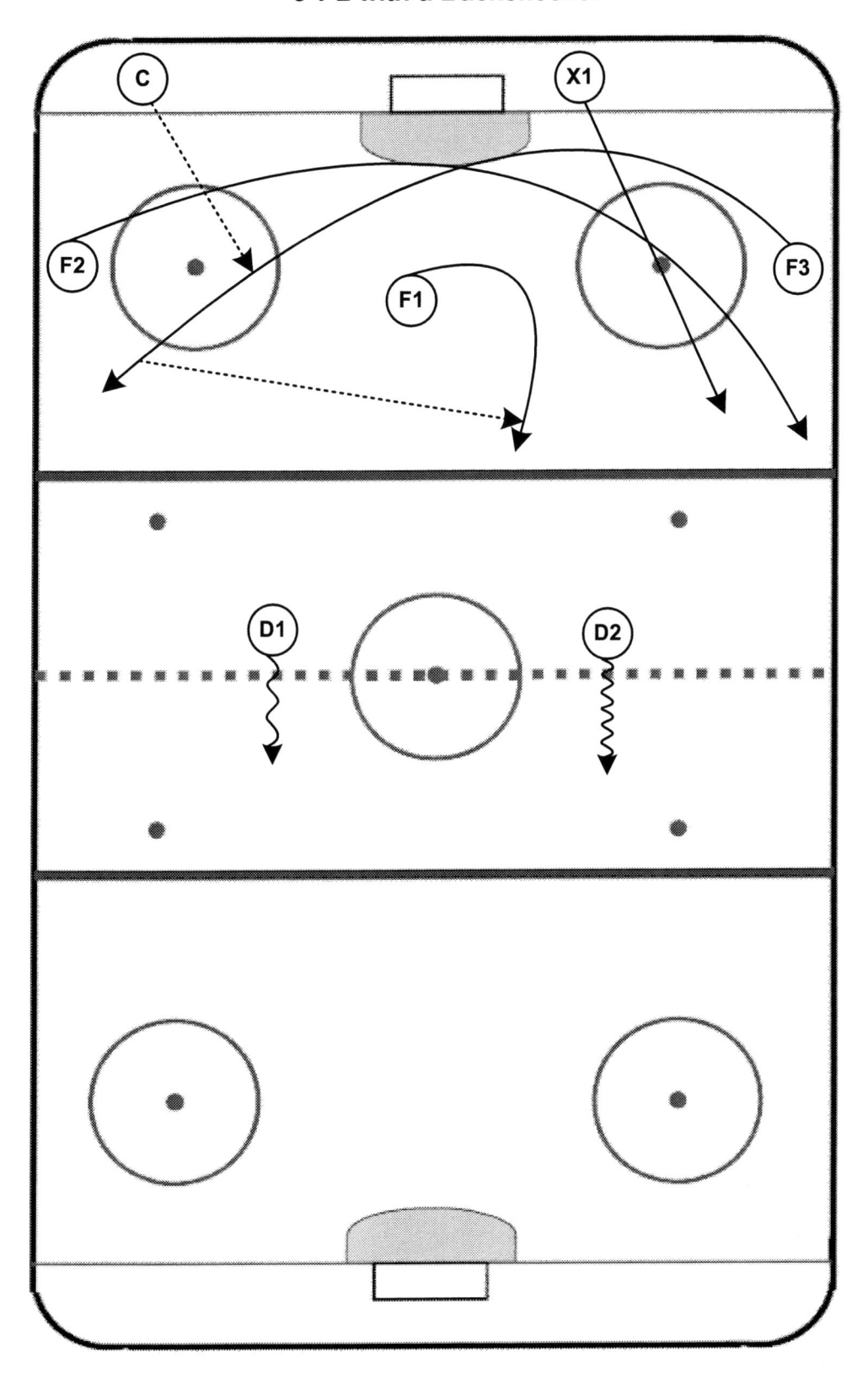

# 87     Quick Shot and Backcheck

## Emphasis and Objective

Excellent shooting drill designed to incorporate skating, passing, receiving and shooting.

## Drill Set-Up

* C in corner, F1, F2 and F3 in breakout position. X1 in the slot, D1 and D2 on blue-line.
* On the whistle, C passes to X1 who shoots on goal, F1, F2 and F3 take off and attack D2 and D2, 3 v 2.
* After scoring a goal, F1 takes off and backchecks the play making it a 3 v 3.
* Play continues in the offensive zone until the whistle, use multiple pucks.

## Key Teaching Points

* Score goals under pressure.
* Read the rush.
* Communicate.
* Backcheck with a purpose.
* Defensive in-zone play.

## Recommended Progressions

* None.

# Quick Shot and Backcheck

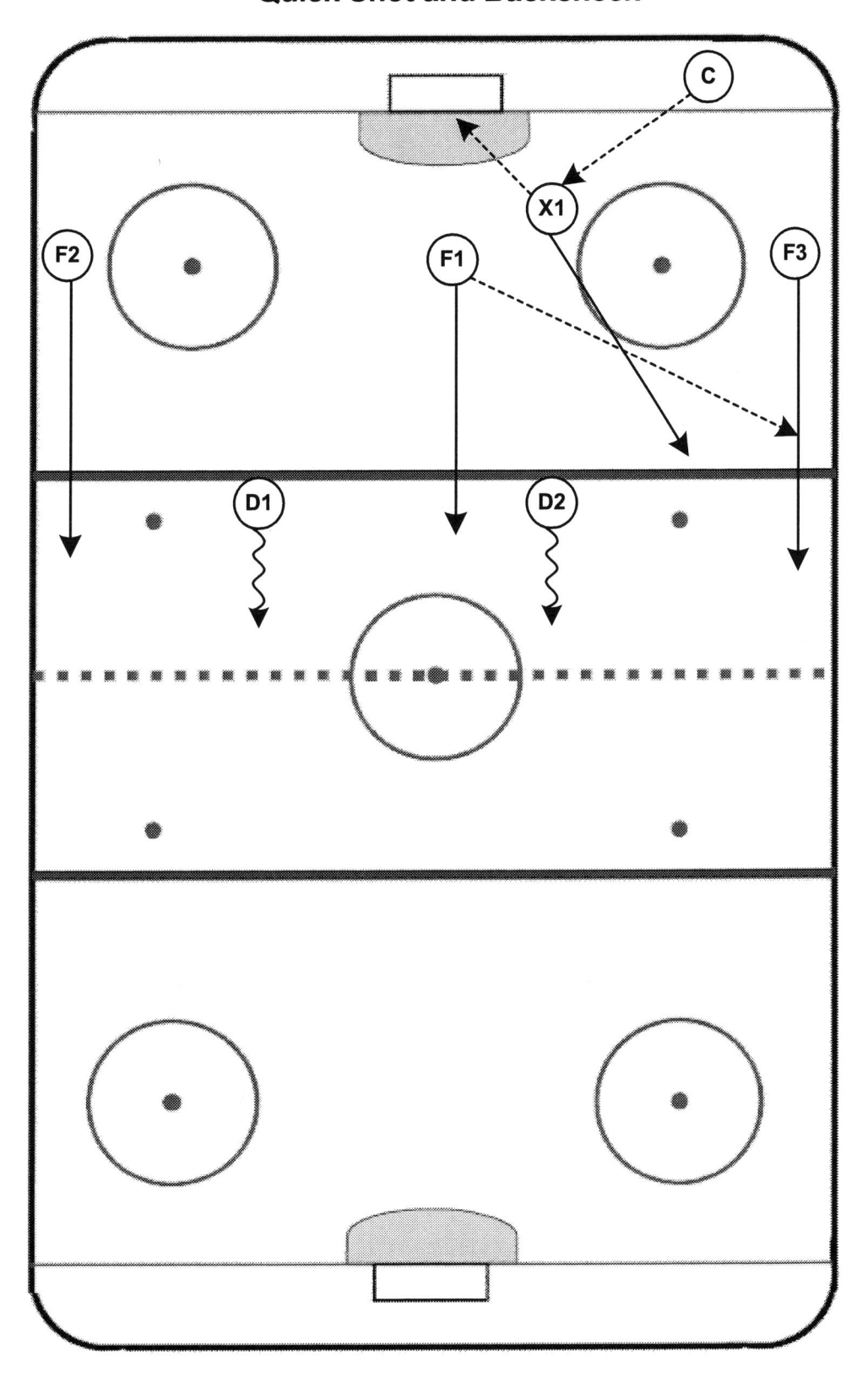

# 88 — 3 v 2, Attack

## Emphasis and Objective
Teach attacking and defending skills of a 3 v 2 rush.

## Drill Set-Up
* F's in 3 lines just inside defensive blue-lines with pucks, D1 and D2 in neutral zone.
* On 1st whistle, 1st 3 F's attack D1 and D2, 3 v 2.
* Play continues to a frozen puck or turnover.

## Key Teaching Points
* Force puck wide using lateral skating skills and position.
* Maintain Gap (2 stick lengths) between attackers and partner.
* Force the play before the blue-line.
* Communicate.
* Do not concede middle of ice.

## Recommended Progressions
* Position F's inside red-line for quicker pace and a more confined area.

# 3 v 2 Attack

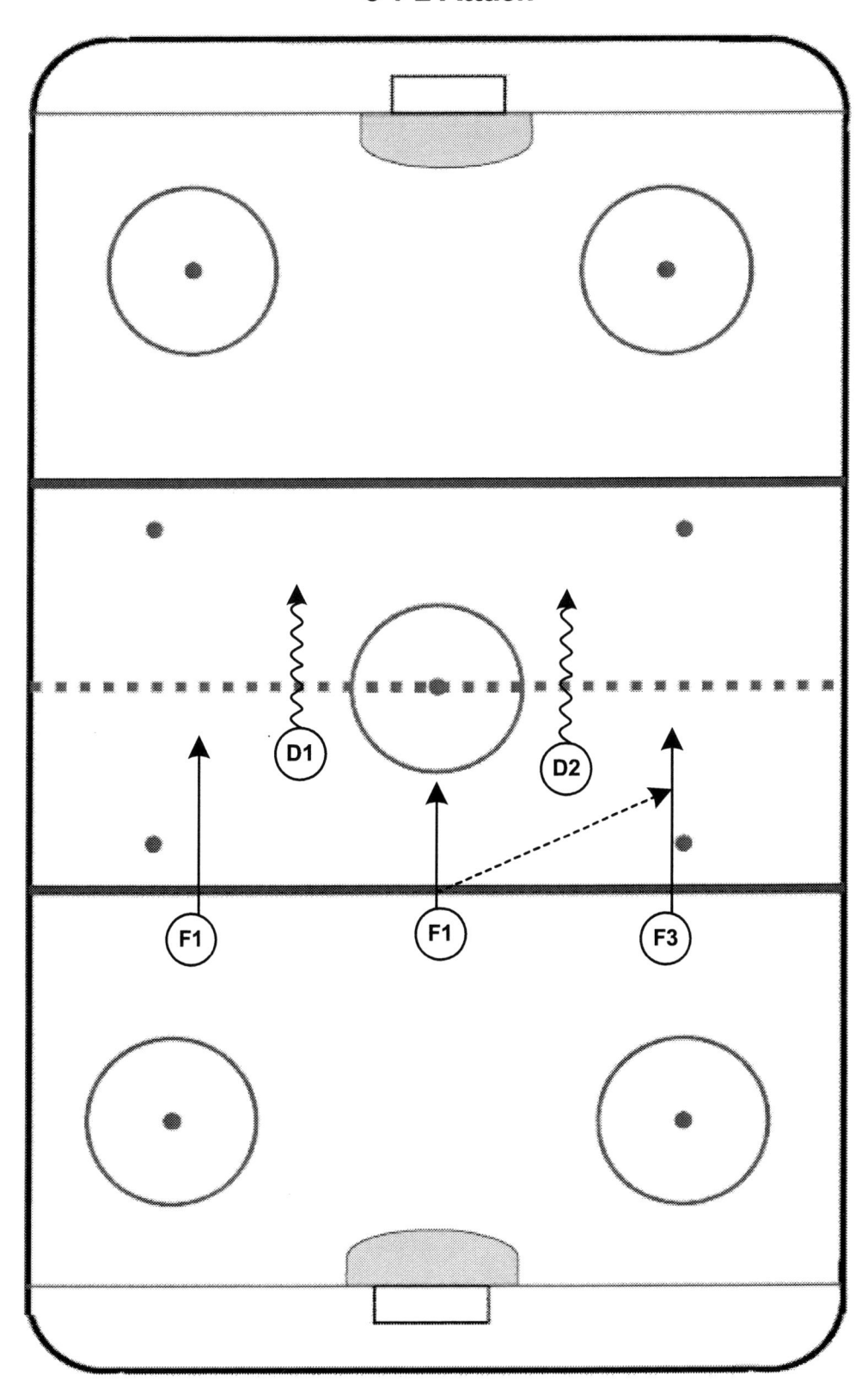

# 89. Tri-Angle Attack

## Emphasis and Objective
Improve goal scoring in a variety of situations.

## Drill Set-Up
* C in the corner with pucks, players in 3 lines at the red line facing each direction.
* On the whistle, 1st group of 3 attack the zone. C passes to 1 of the players at the blue-line who immediately shoots on net. All 3 players drive the net for a rebound or puck recovery and play until a goal is scored.

## Key Teaching Points
* Offensive triangulation.
* Stop in front of the net.
* Communication.
* Good shooting position.
* Rebound control.
* One end shown in diagram.

## Recommended Progressions
* 3 v 1, 3 v 2.

# Tri Angle Attack

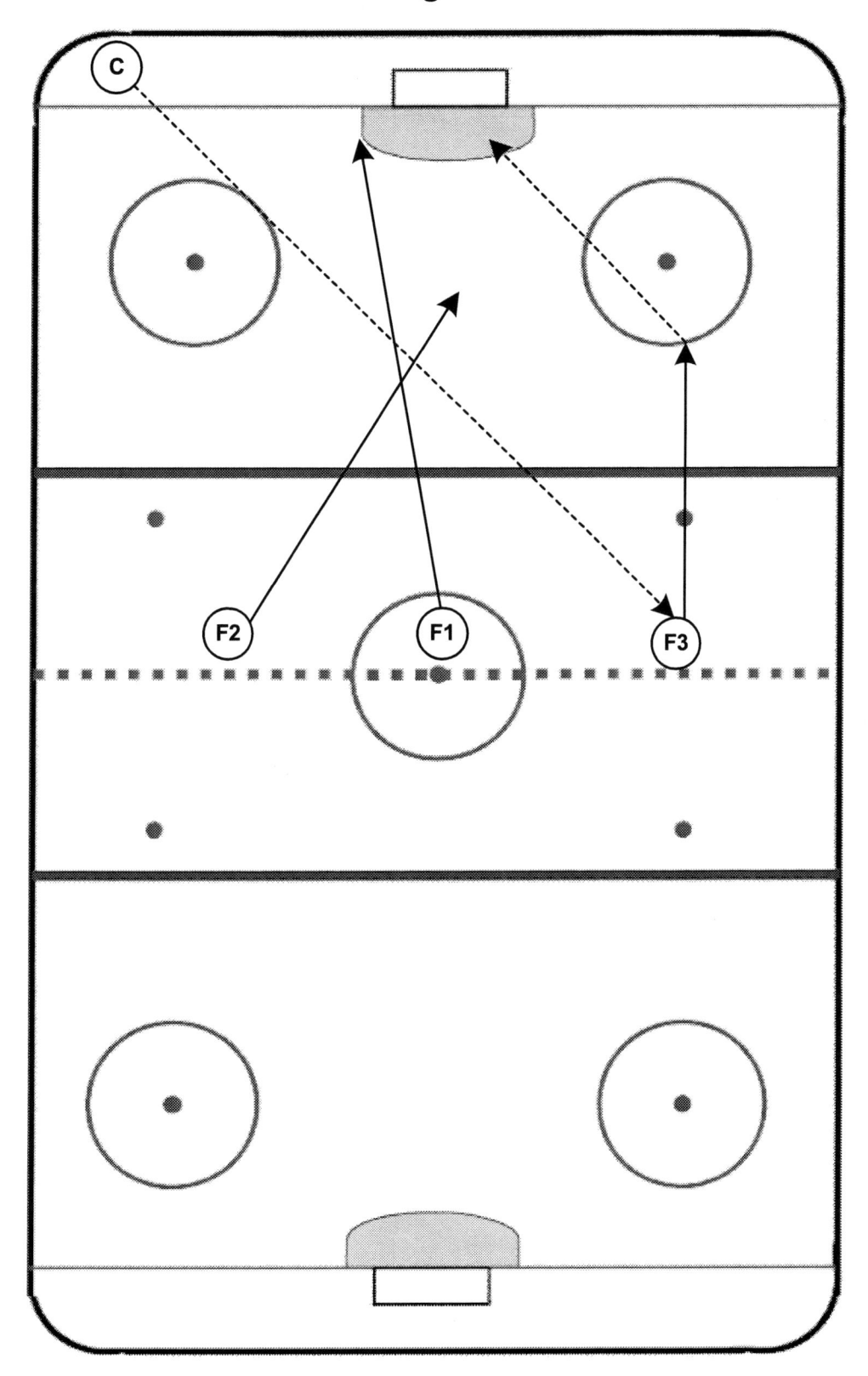

## 3 v 2, Delayed Cycle

### Emphasis and Objective
To work on the concept of cycling against opposition.

### Drill Set-Up
- Work both ends at the same time.
- 2 lines of 3 F's in the neutral zone, each facing opposite ends, 1 set of 2D on each blue-line.
- On the whistle, F's dump a puck into their offensive zone and gain possession. D, skate backwards and allow the F's to gain the puck.
- Once the F's gain control, D's pressure and F's begin to control the puck by cycling in the offensive zone.
- Maintain control of the puck and play until the whistle.

### Key Teaching Points
- Puck protection and control.
- Use picks, screens and quiet areas.
- Communication.
- D maintain good Gap and positioning.

### Recommended Progressions
- 3 v 3.

# 3 v 2 Delayed Cycle

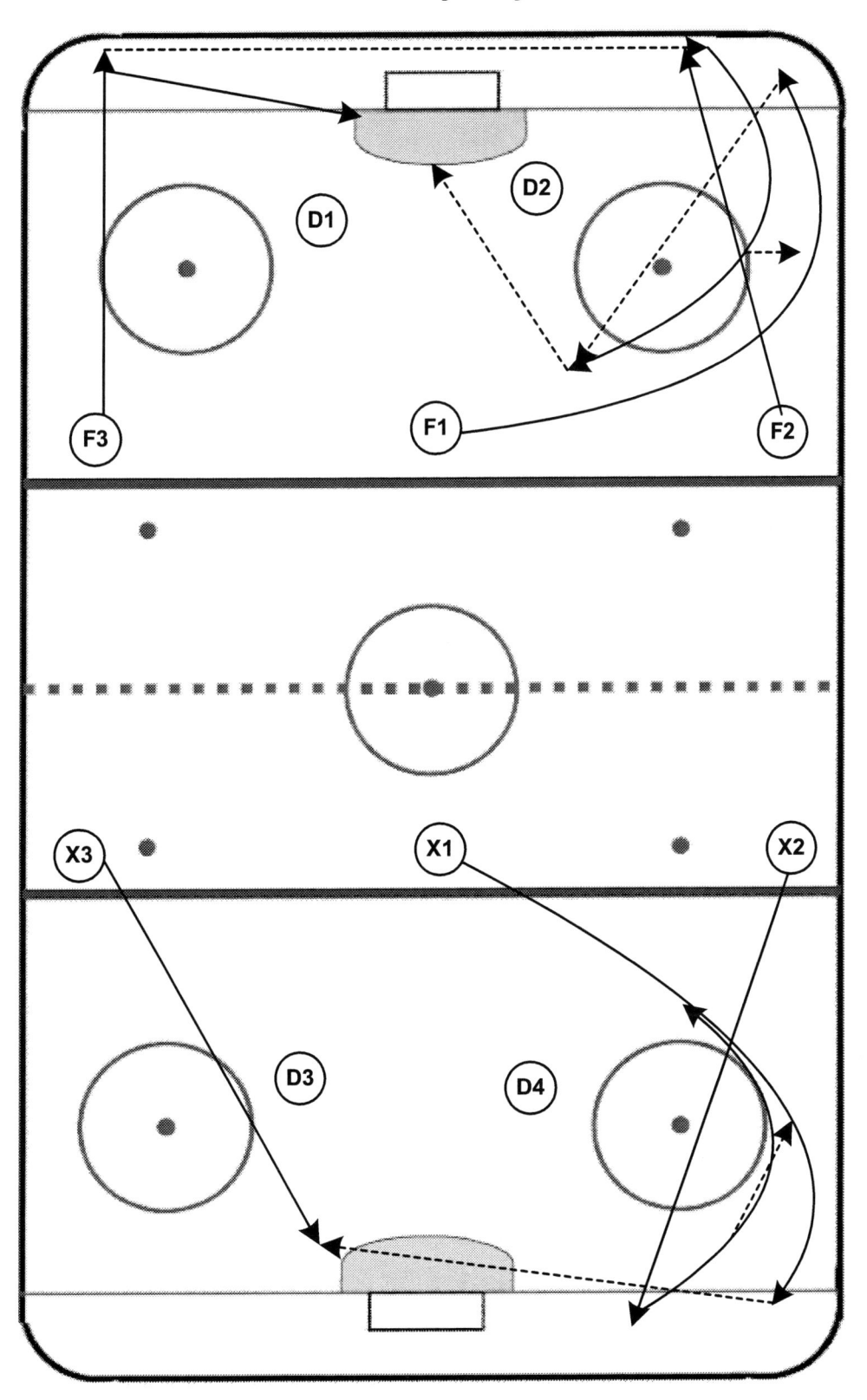

Photo courtesy of Mike Thill

# 5

## Special Teams

This section deals with the aspects of special team play. That is, power play skill development, penalty killing skills and unique situations including pulling the goaltender.

Rather than focus on a type or system of power play, this section places an emphasis on the skills necessary to be improve power play concepts and provide exposure to a number of different situations.

In theory, your power play players must be outstanding 2 v 1 players. They must have the ability to create and recognize the 2 v 1, have the ability to shoot off the pass, 1 time the puck as well as possess the competitive nature to win the battles for loose pucks.

Penalty killing is hard work and discipline. The ability to stop and start, stay in shooting lanes, ice the puck and of course, win face-offs and get a big save are critical to successful penalty killing. Use the drills in this section to improve skills for effective penalty killing.

Special teams can win games. Give all your players a chance to be special teams players as it will foster camaraderie and improve team chemistry. Place an emphasis on your practice session to improve this area, it will pay off in the won loss column!

# 91     3 v 2 High

## Emphasis and Objective
Develop out numbered situations and power play skills.

## Drill Set-Up
* C in neutral zone, 3 F's or combination of F's and D's in high zone in triangle form.
* 2 defenders positioned to between attackers.
* C passes to one of the 3 attackers.
* The 3 attackers look for seams to pass or for shooting opportunity.

## Key Teaching Points
* Ice vision.
* Anticipation skills.
* Head up at all times.
* Shoot off the pass.
* Look to create seams in defense.

## Recommended Progressions
* Move attackers and defenders to the side for side board 3 v 2.

# 3 v 2 High

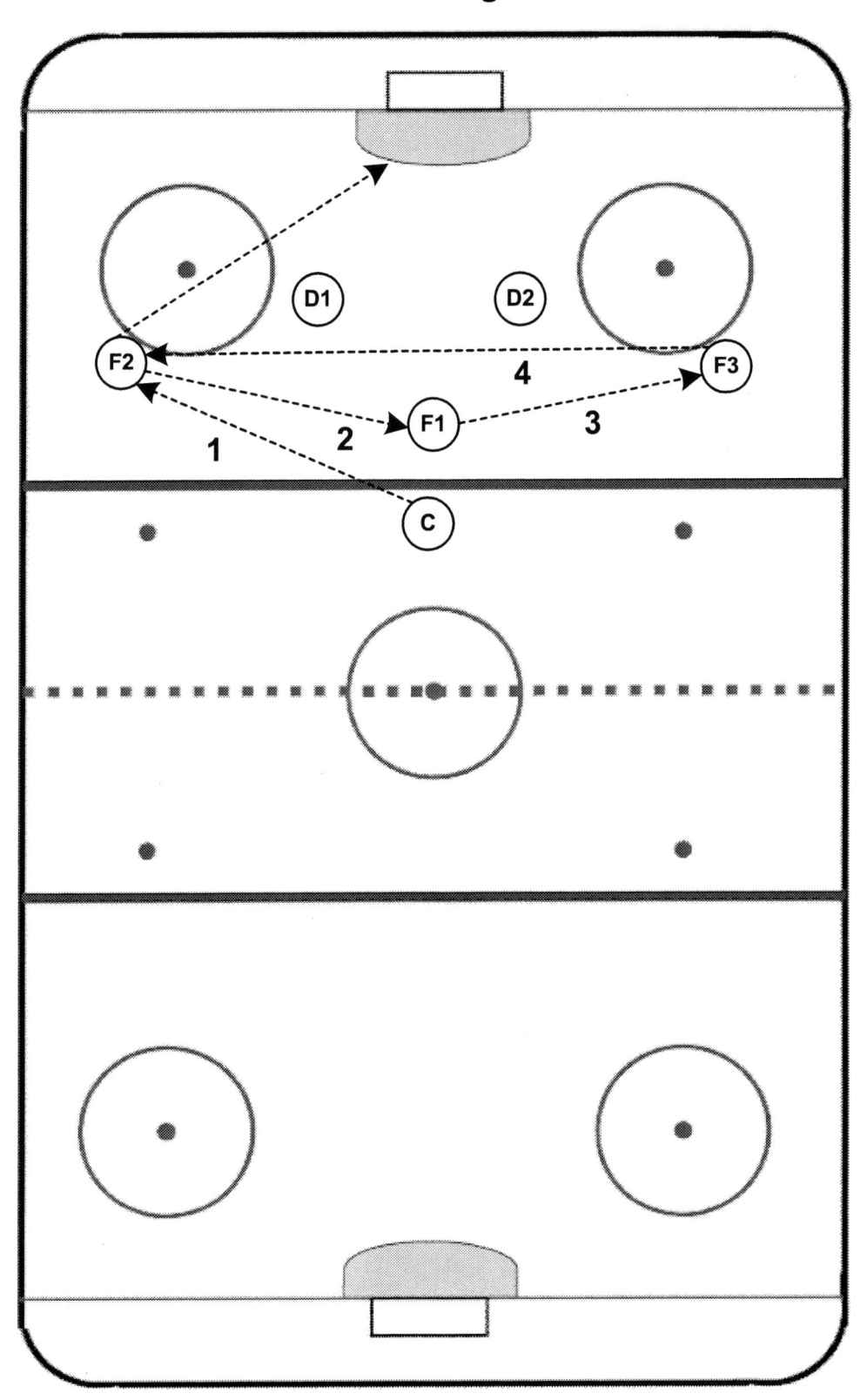

# 92 — 3 v 2, Win the Battle!

## Emphasis and Objective

Develop puck pursuit and power play skills.

## Drill Set-Up

* C outside blue-line with pucks, 3 F's outside blue-line, 2 D just inside blue-line.
* C dumps puck into corner and the 3 attacking F's attempt to gain control of the puck. Once control is established, the 3 F's attack for a scoring opportunity.

## Key Teaching Points

* Win the race and battle for the loose puck.
* Head up at all times, see your teammates.
* Handle puck under control.
* Communicate with your partners.
* Use picks and screens to get best shot.
* Use your body to protect the puck.
* D use good body position.
* Use area behind the net.

## Recommended Progressions

* 3 v 3 for defensive coverage.

# 3 v 2 Win the Battle

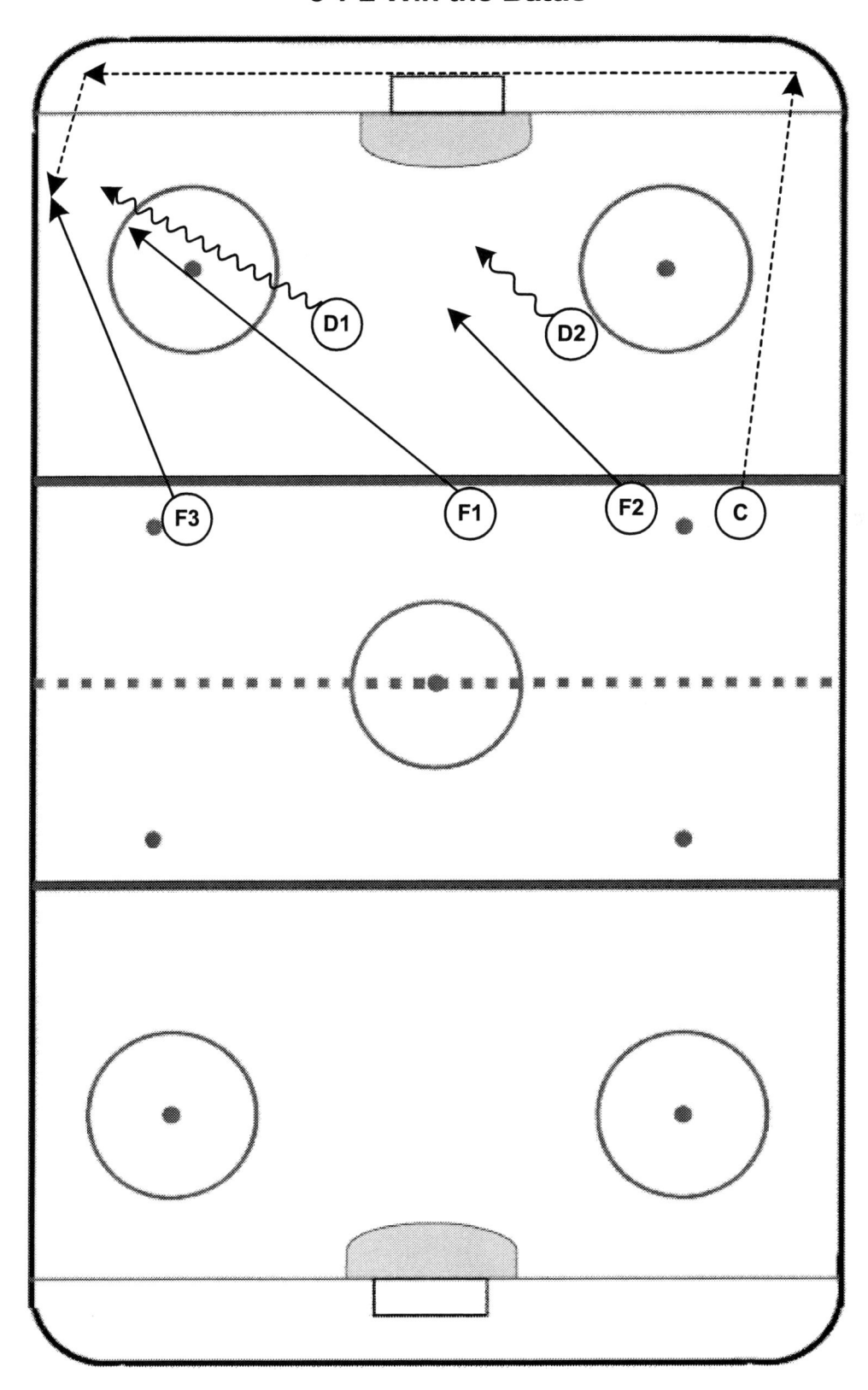

# Continuous Power Play

## Emphasis and Objective
Give all players experience in power play situations.

## Drill Set-Up
* Power play unit #1 in one zone, power play unit #2 in neutral ice, 4 penalty killers in each zone.
* On 1st whistle, power play #1 begins 5-4, play continues until puck is cleared to neutral ice by the killers.
* Power Play #2 gathers the puck and attacks the opposite end for a 5-4, again, play continues until the puck is cleared to neutral ice activating Power play #1 in the opposite end.
* Be sure to have all players play in all situations.
* Play is continuous.

## Key Teaching Points
* Great for power play practice and evaluation.
* PP players read and react, create 2 v 1's.
* Create good scoring chances under pressure.
* Excellent for PK practice.
* Use glass, see open lanes for clears.
* One time the puck.
* Battle for position and puck possession.

## Recommended Progressions
* 5 v 3, 4 v 3 and 6 v 5 goalie out.
* Add conditions, keep score.

# Continuous Power Play

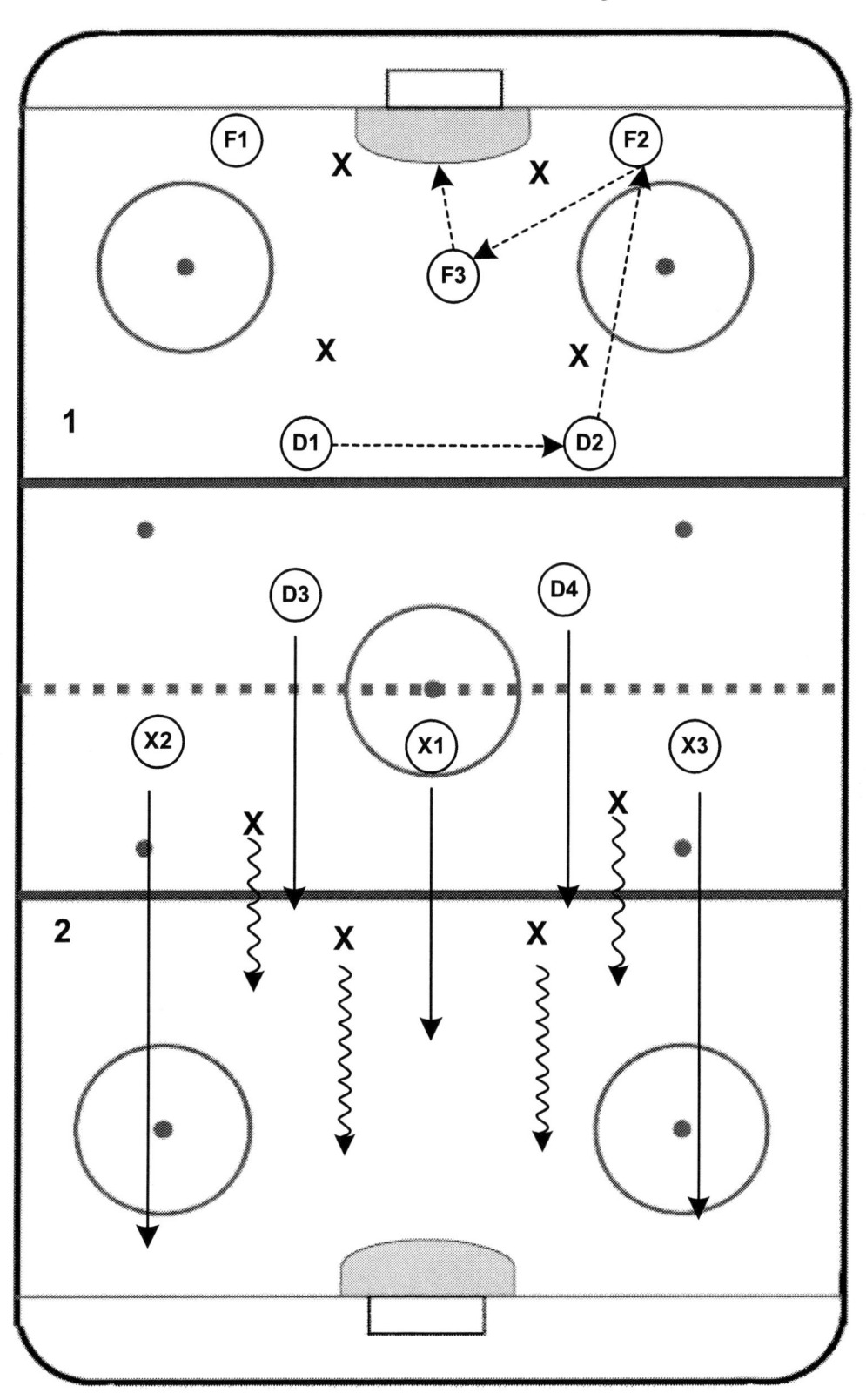

# 2 Man Point Shot

## Emphasis and Objective
Power Play shooting and attacking skills.

## Drill Set-Up
* F's in each corner on their off side.
* Alternating sides, F's pass to D on the wall who immediately move across the blue-line to the prime shooting area.
* Passing F, supports the puck up the half board and gains position on the top of the circle in a good shooting position.
* D can either shoot or pass to the F for a 1 time shot.

## Key Teaching Points
* Make good passes.
* Present at good angles.
* Hard shots, low and accurate.
* Practice 1 timers.

## Recommended Progressions
* Can be done utilizing both sides, 2 F's and 2 D's.
* Add conditions, bad pass control etc.

# 2 Man Point Shot

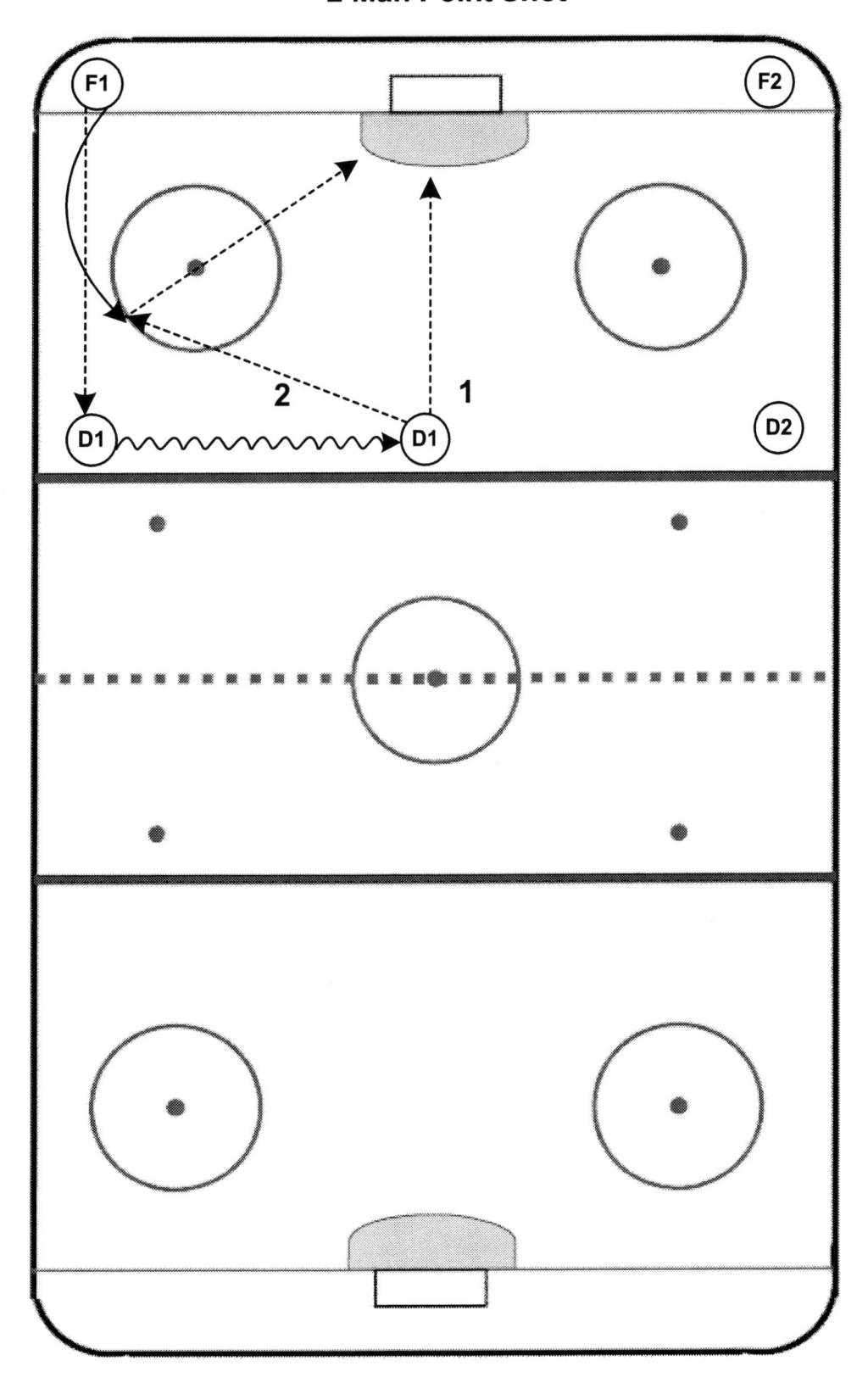

# 95 — 3 Puck Power Play

## Emphasis and Objective

Work on components and skills necessary for the power play.

## Drill Set-Up

* Can be done at both ends.
* F1 on the half board hash mark on off side with pucks, F2 below the goal-line, D1 on the blue-line, even with the face-off dot.
* 1st puck, F1 to F2 for a quick walk out on the goalie.
* 2nd puck, F1 to D1, D1 walks to shooting area and shoots, F2 can screen, deflect and rebound.
* 3rd puck, F1 to D1 return pass back to F1 who drives the lane and shoots.

## Key Teaching Points

* Hard accurate passes.
* Take high percentage shots.
* Point shot must be low for deflections and rebounds.

## Recommended Progressions

* Switch sides.

# 3 Puck Power Play

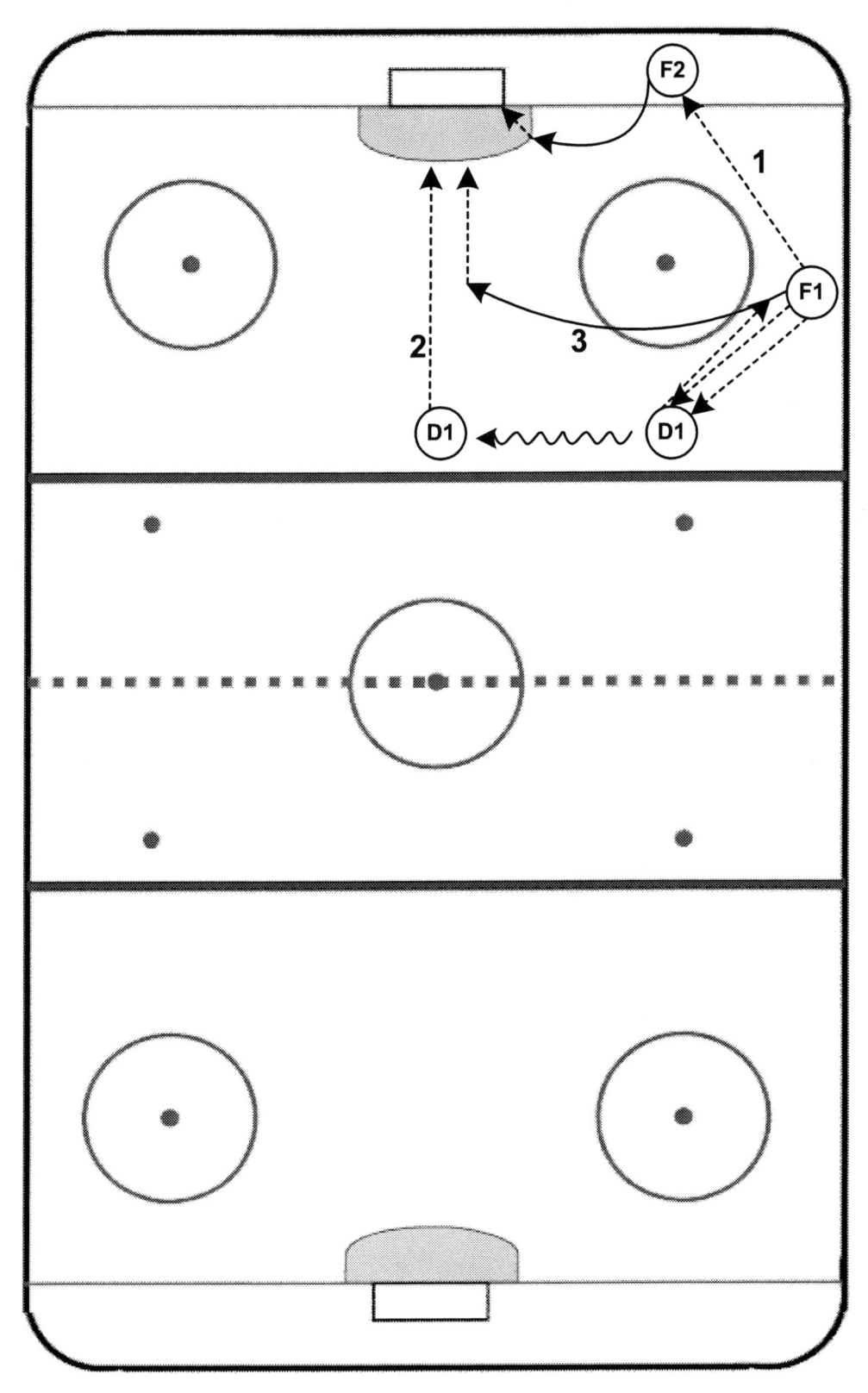

# 96 | 3 Puck, 45 Second Power Play

## Emphasis and Objective

Power play practice under varied conditions.

## Drill Set-Up

* Start drill with 5 v 4 in zone.
* On 1st whistle, play 5 v 4 until clear or goalie freeze.
* On 2nd whistle, C dumps a puck to the far end for a Power Play breakout against a full ice Penalty Kill forecheck. Attack and play 5 v 4 until clear or goalie freeze.
* On the 3rd whistle, C dumps or rims puck around boards for a final 5 v 4 against high pressure.
* After 45 seconds, next 2 units take ice for a similar action.

## Key Teaching Points

* Recognize 2 v 1's.
* PK in shooting lanes, clearing puck 200 feet.
* Full speed and competition.
* Vary forechecking and break-out schemes.
* 1 touch passing and 1 time shooting.

## Recommended Progressions

* 5 v 3, 4 v 3, 6 v 5.
* Keep score, make it competitive.
* Evaluate all players in these situations.

**3 Puck, 45 Second Power Play**

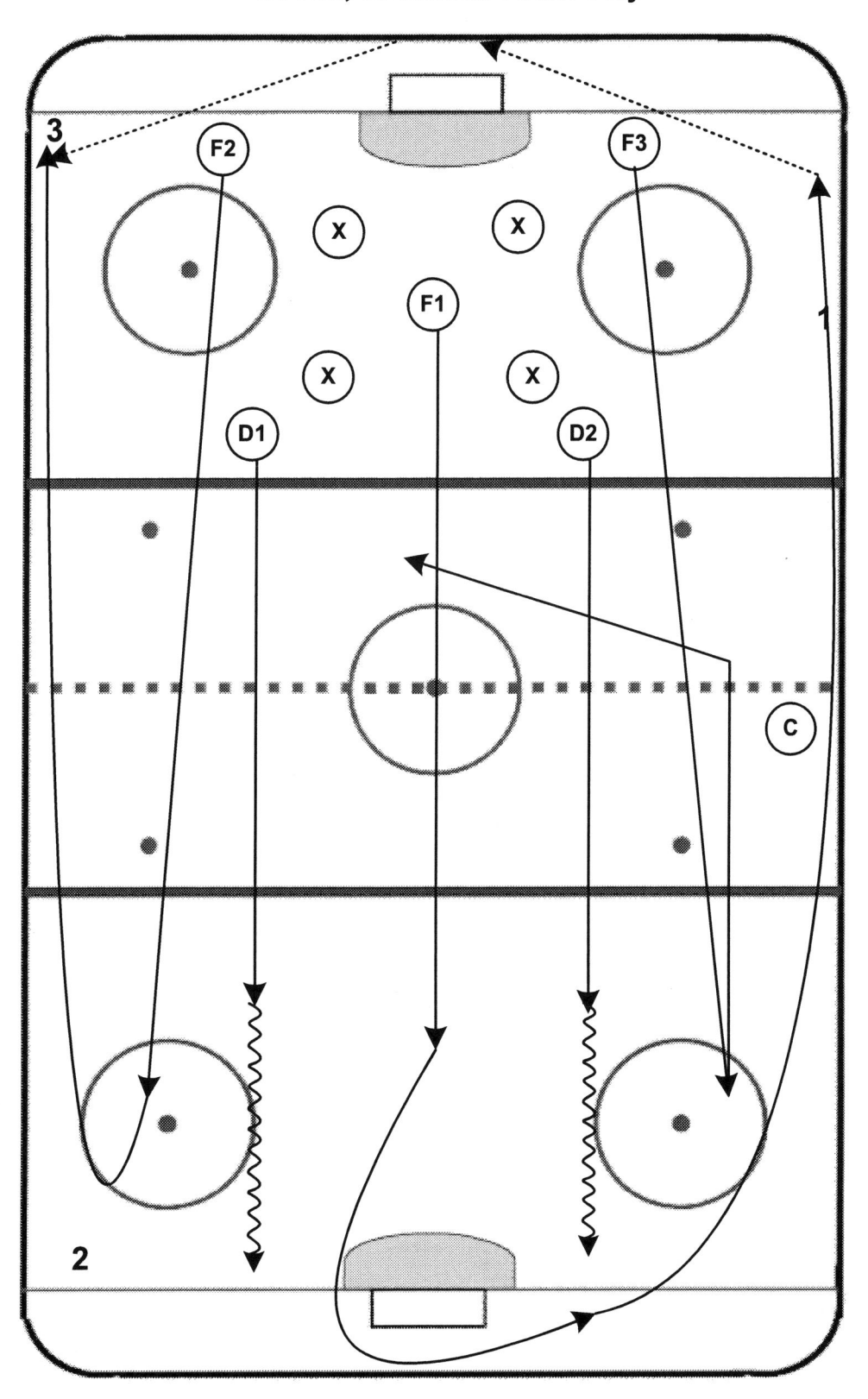

## 97 Canada Power Play: 5 v 0, 5 v 4

### Emphasis and Objective
Power play development in a variety of situations.

### Drill Set-Up
- Players in units of 5. C with pucks.
- At one end, one unit of 5 execute a power play 5 v 0. At the opposite end, another unit of 5 execute a 5 v 4 power play.
- On the 1st whistle after 30 seconds, the 5 v 0 unit executes a power play breakout started by a C dump in. The offensive unit at the other end waits as defenders (4 players) and plays a 5 v 4. The initial defending unit goes to the box and another unit of 5 plays 5 v 0 at the far end.

### Key Teaching Points
- Create 2 v 1's.
- 1 touch passes and shots.
- Penalty killers fill shooting lanes.
- Outnumber opposition.
- Attack the zone with speed.
- Puck protection and control.

### Recommended Progressions
- 5 v 3, 4 v 3, 4 v 4, 6 v 5.

# Canada Power Play, 5 v 0, 5 v 4

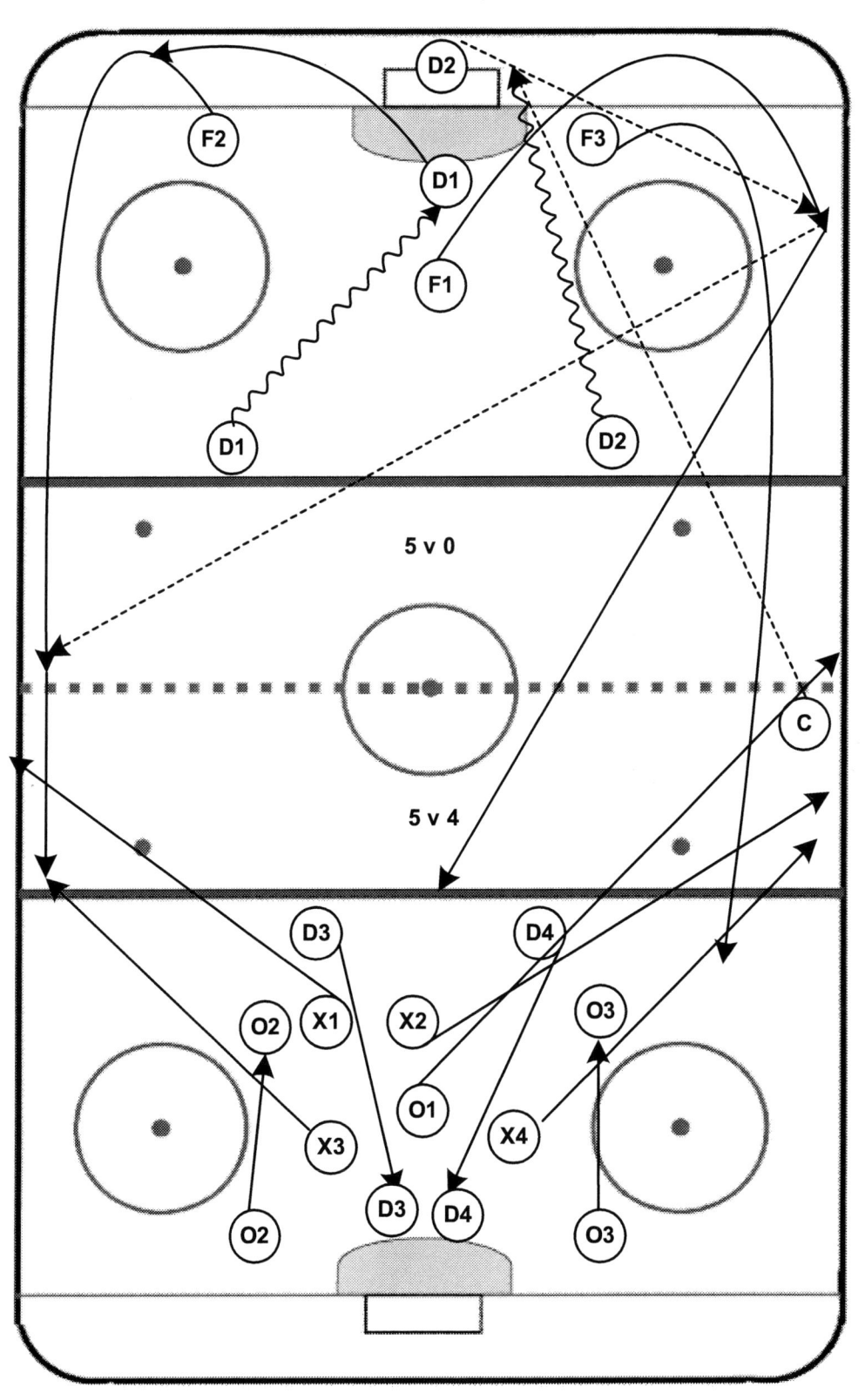

## 98 — 2 v 1, Gain Control

### Emphasis and Objective
Improve puck pursuit and possession skills. Develop out numbered situational awareness.

### Drill Set-Up
* C outside blue-line with pucks, 2 F's outside blue-line, D just inside blue-line.
* C dumps puck into corner and the 2 attacking F's attempt to gain control of the puck. Once control is established, the 2 F's attack for a scoring opportunity.

### Key Teaching Points
* Win races and battles for the puck.
* Head on a swivel, know where our partner is at all times.
* Quick attack to the net.
* Use picks and screens.

### Recommended Progressions
* 2 v 2.

# 2 v 1 Gain Control

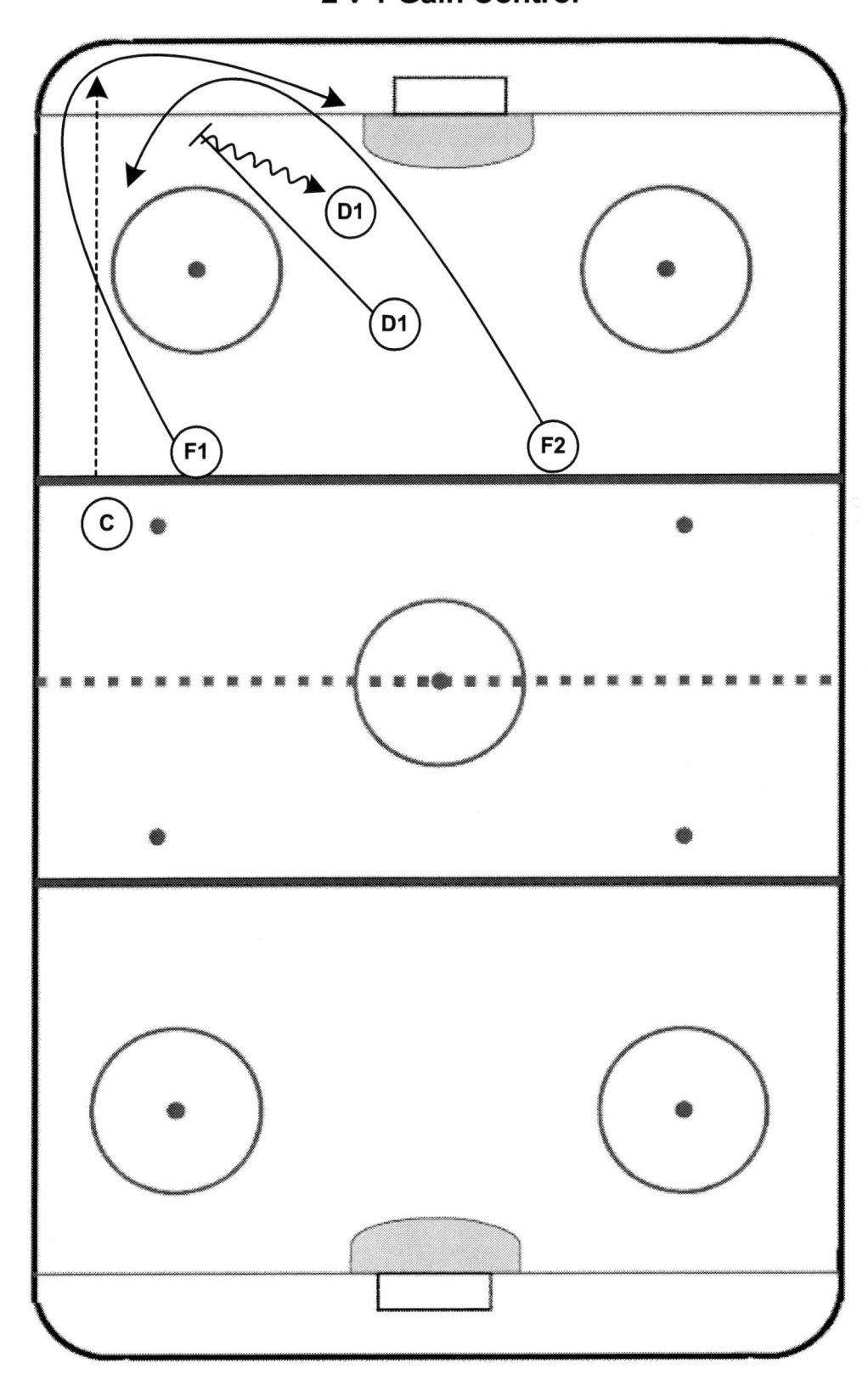

# 99 PK Skill Work

## Emphasis and Objective

To work on the skills necessary for effective penalty killing.

## Drill Set-Up

* Drill is done on 1 end of ice, in two situations.
* Situation 1 with D, cones below the goal-line and on the half board.
* D starts in front of net, pressures the cone below the goal-line progressing the the half board and back to the front of the net.
* Situation 2 with F's, cones at the point and on the half board.
* F skates up and back fronting point shot and taking away passing and shooting lanes from point and half board.

## Key Teaching Points

* Keep play in front of player, NEVER turn your back on the play.
* Sticks must remain active, denying passing and shooting lanes.
* Simulate shot and pass blocking.

## Recommended Progressions

* Alternate sides.
* Replace cones with players for live situations.

# PK Skill Work

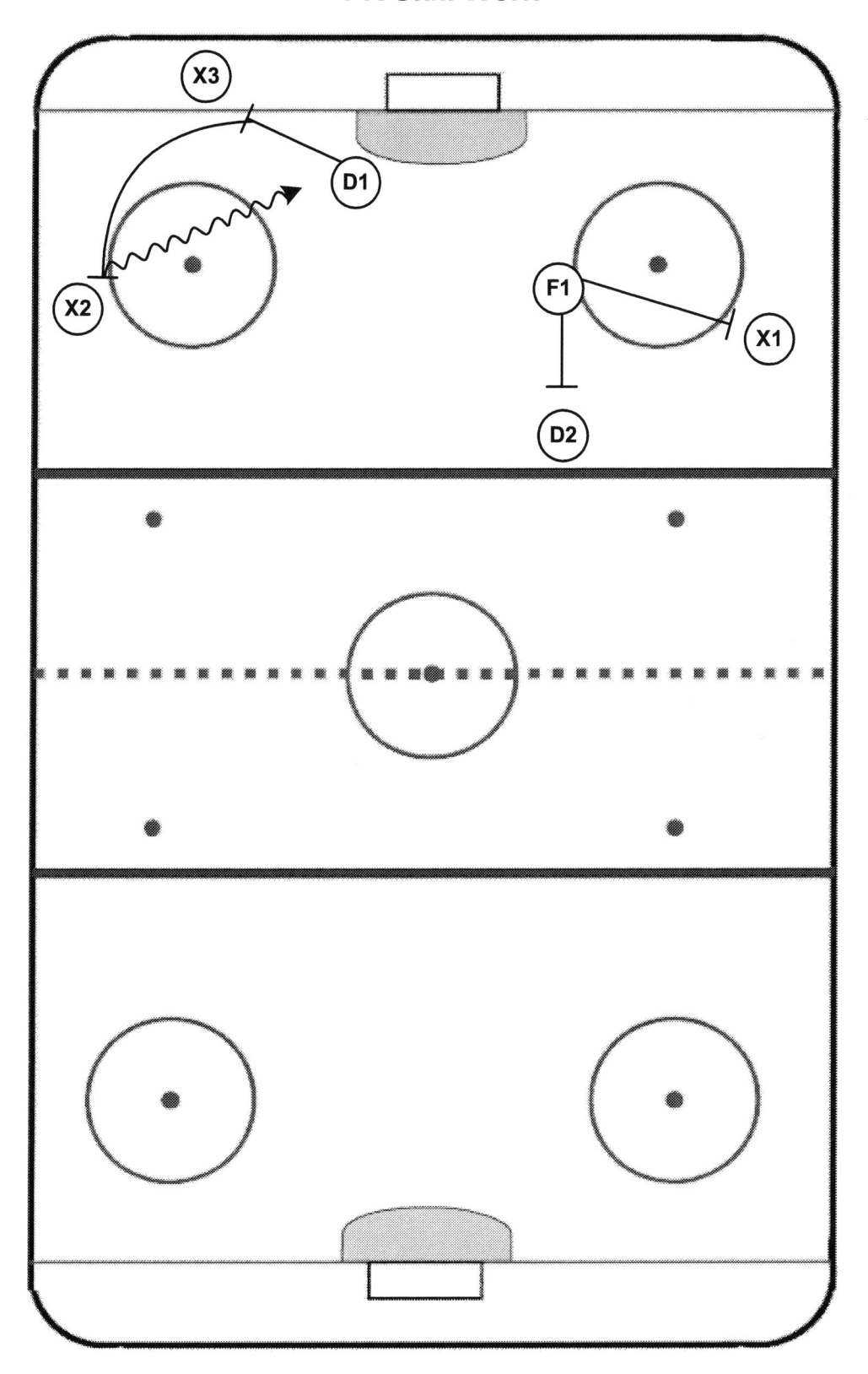

Photo courtesy of Dave Eggen & Dick Carlson of Inertia Pro Event Imaging and The Omaha Lancers

# 6

## Drills for Forwards and Scoring

This section is specifically designed to improve the skills of forwards and to challenge scoring skills. Included in this section are game like shooting drills that will test the ability of your forwards to score and perform in pressure situations. That is, when being challenged by an opponent.

In addition, this section also introduces and develops the concept of cycling, puck possession and using the width and depth of the offensive zone.

These drills can be done in a specialized time during practice or these concepts can be introduced and taught to all team members.

# 100     Behind the Net Bump Pass

## Emphasis and Objective

To practice using the area behind the net and work on shooting position.

## Drill Set-Up

* C with pucks on blue-line. 1 line of F's at the each blue-line.
* C passes to either F, both F's break down the boards, F with puck passes off the back boards behind the net, F receives pass, either bumps it back to the original F or passes to the slot for a quick shot. After making the pass, F gains position in front of the net.
* After the 1st shot, both F's to the net, C shoots on goal for screens and deflections.

## Key Teaching Points

* Know the boards.
* Touch with the puck.
* Shooting position.
* Movement without the puck.

## Recommended Progressions

* Add a 3rd F.

# Behind the Net Bump Pass

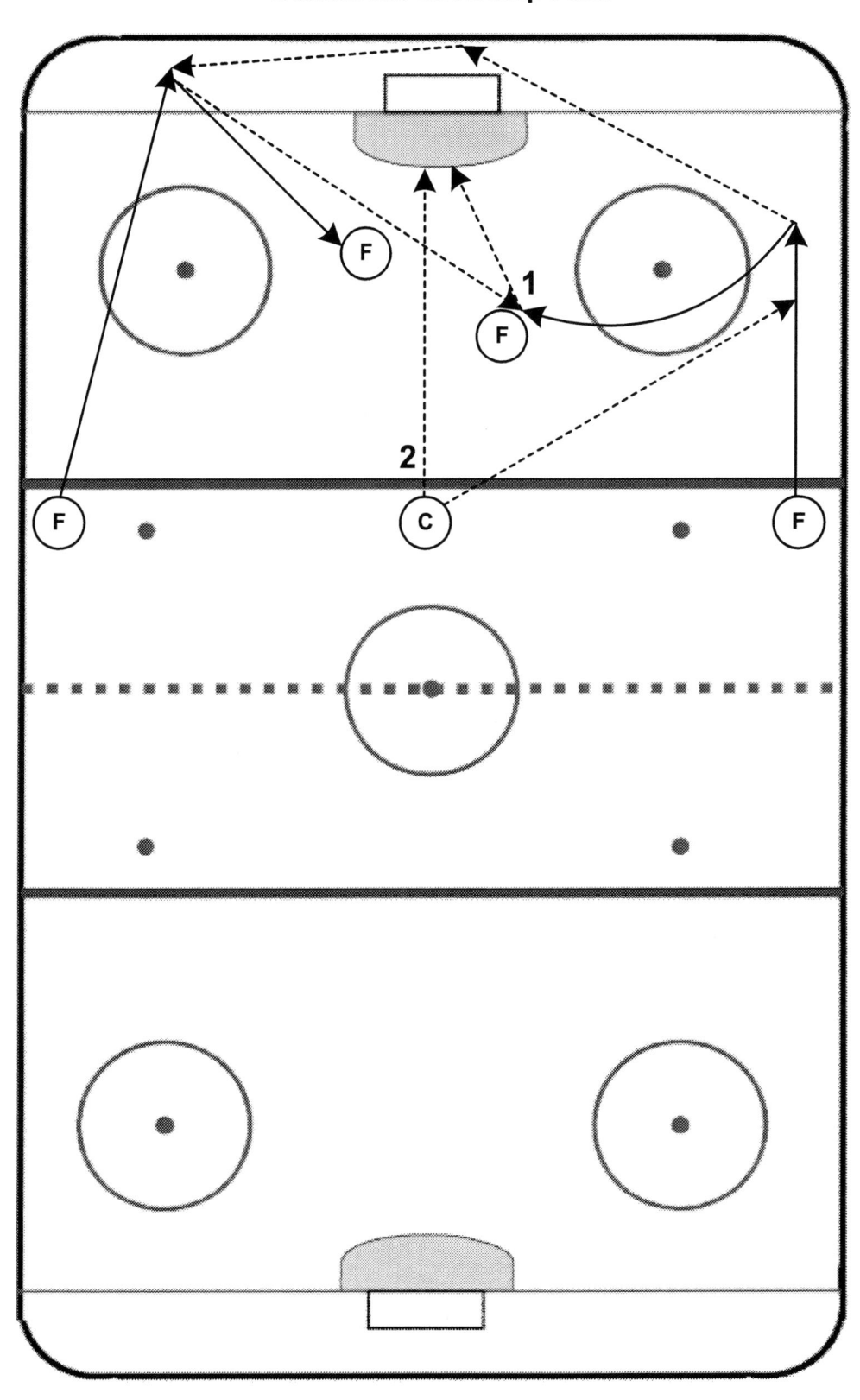

# 101                Deke and Shoot

## Emphasis and Objective

Work on receiving passes, dekes and shooting at full speed.

## Drill Set-Up

- Need 8 cones or tires, positioned on face-off dots.
- Players in 4 groups, each side of the red-line.
- On 1st whistle, F1 and F2 skate forwards and receive a pass from opposite F3 or F4.
- After receiving the pass, players deke around each cone or tire on their side of ice and take a quick shot on net.
- On 2nd whistle, 1st shooters go to opposite line and F3 and F4 begin again.

## Key Teaching Points

- Keep feet moving.
- Head up at all times.
- Shoot in stride.
- Use forehand and backhand shots.

## Recommended Progressions

- None.

# Deke and Shoot

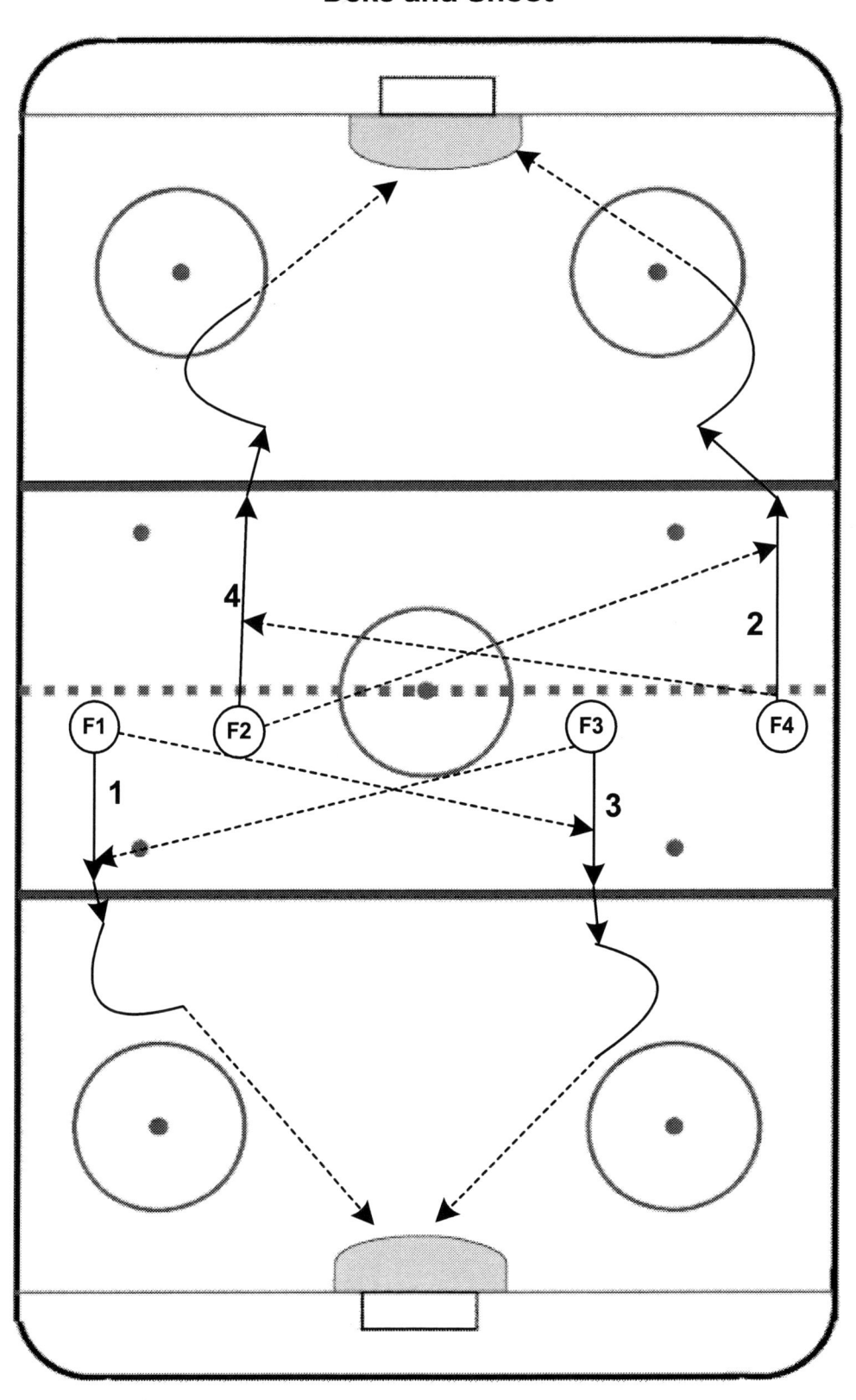

## Hamilton Quick 4

### Emphasis and Objective

4 quick shots at different angles.

### Drill Set-Up

* Players at center ice facing both directions, pucks at center, behind net and in corners.
* Shot 1: X1 skates down the middle and shoots from the hash mark.
* Shot 2: X1 curls to the corner, picks up a puck, skates around the circle and shoots.
* Shot 3: X1 proceeds to the opposite circle for a shot.
* Shot 4: X1 picks up a puck behind the net and tries a wrap around.
* After 4th shot, X1 picks up a puck behind the net and feeds the next person in line.

### Key Teaching Points

* Keep feet moving.
* Shoot in stride.
* Head up.
* Use all shots.

### Recommended Progressions

* None.

**Hamilton Quick 4**

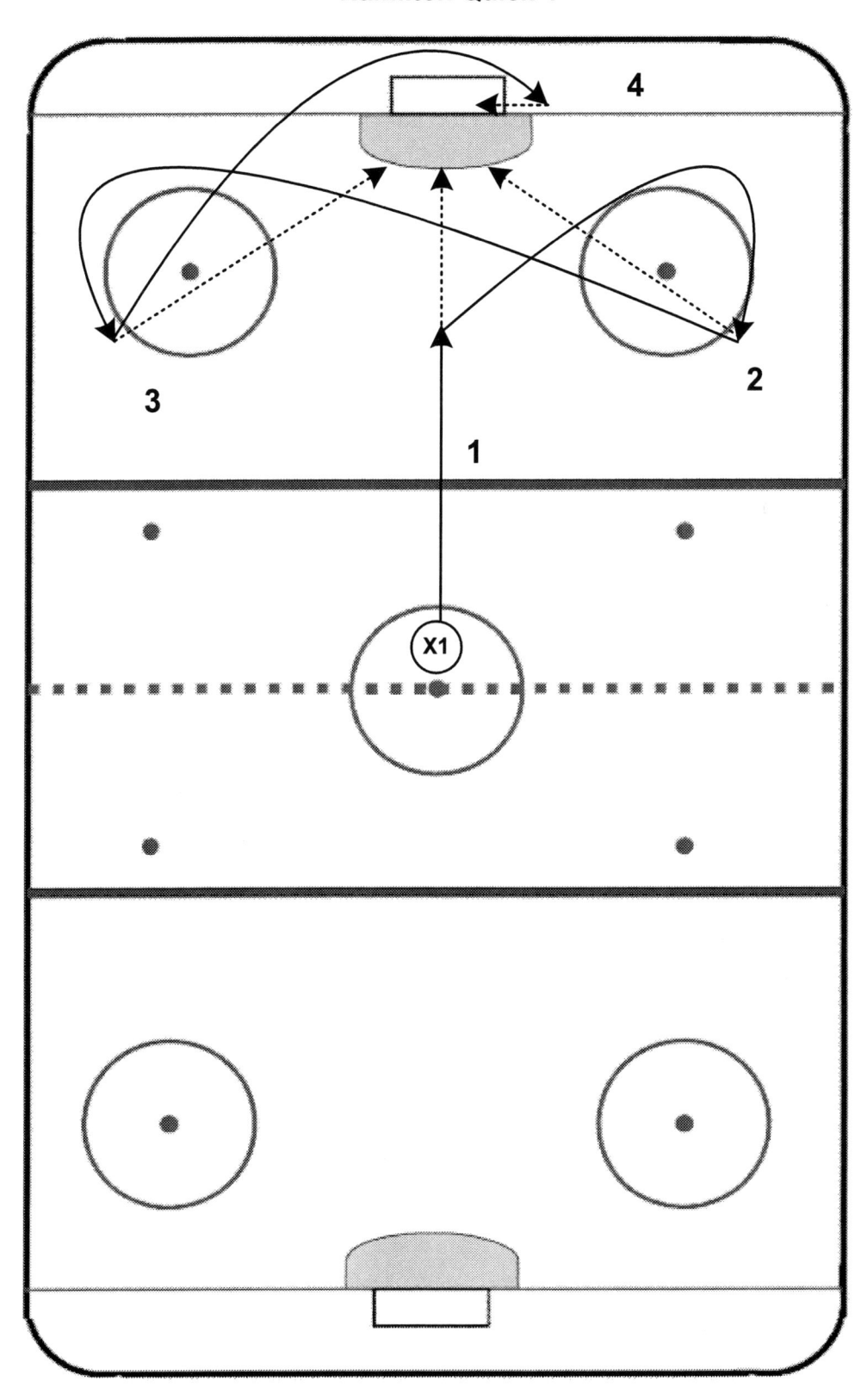

# 103 Scoring Under Pressure, 1 v 1

## Emphasis and Objective

Fun drill to develop scoring techniques and acceleration.

## Drill Set-Up

* 2 lines of players facing each direction at the red-line. C with pucks in the middle.
* On the C's signal, C places puck in zone.
* 2 players race for the puck, player that gets to the puck first is on offense trying to score, other player on defense trying to prevent the goal.
* Use both ends.

## Key Teaching Points

* Protect the puck.
* Quick starts and acceleration.
* Scoring skills.
* Competition.

## Recommended Progressions

* None.

# Scoring Under Pressure 1 v 1

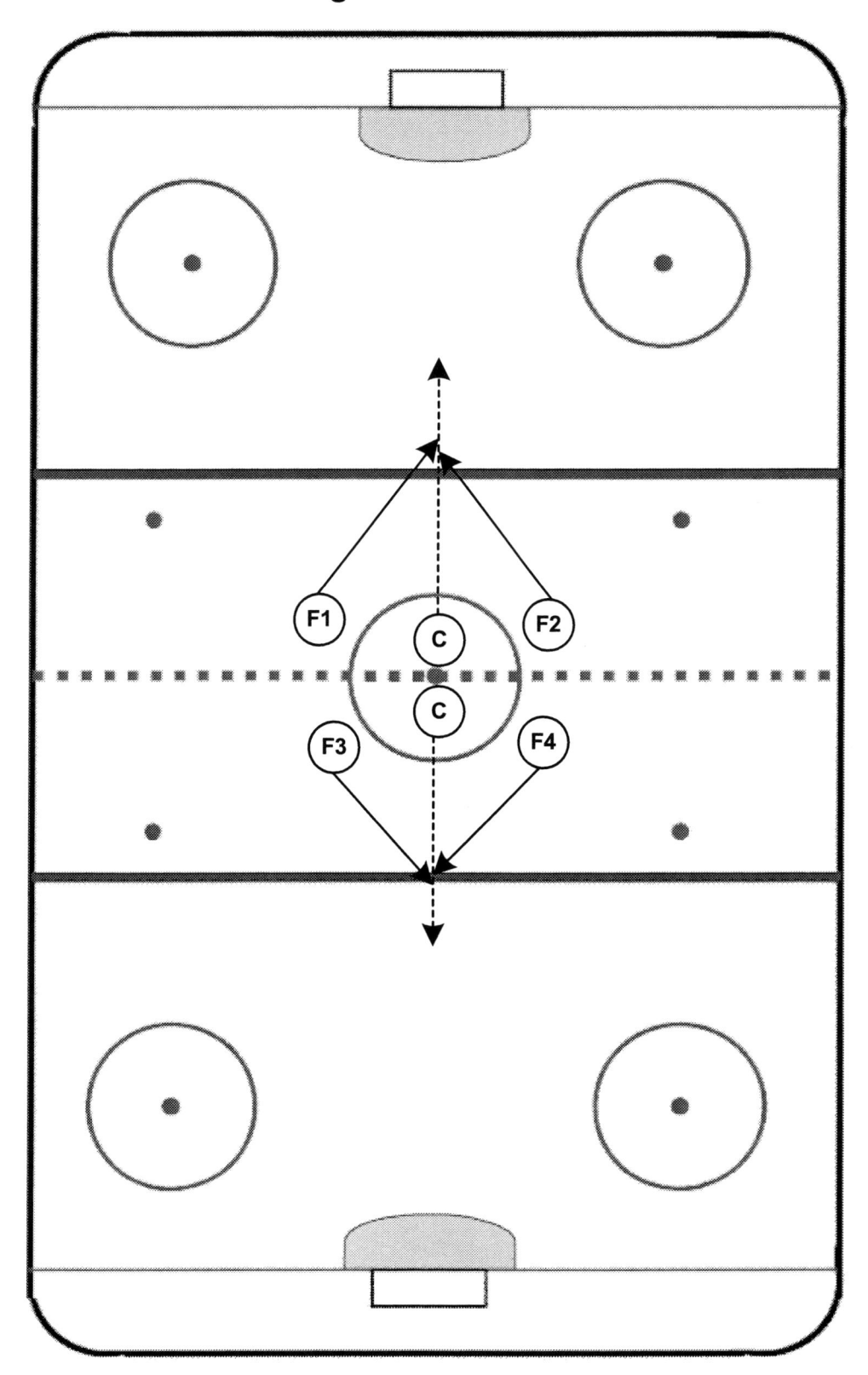

# 104          Hard Around

## Emphasis and Objective

Improve handling passes and missed shots hard around the boards.

## Drill Set-Up

* C on one hash mark with pucks, F's on the opposite inside hash mark in a defensive position.
* C fires puck hard around the boards, F must race to the boards, control the puck and skate to the slot for a shot.
* Be sure to alternate sides.

## Key Teaching Points

* Control the puck first before moving to slot.
* Anticipation.
* C vary speed of rims.

## Recommended Progressions

* None.

# Hard Around

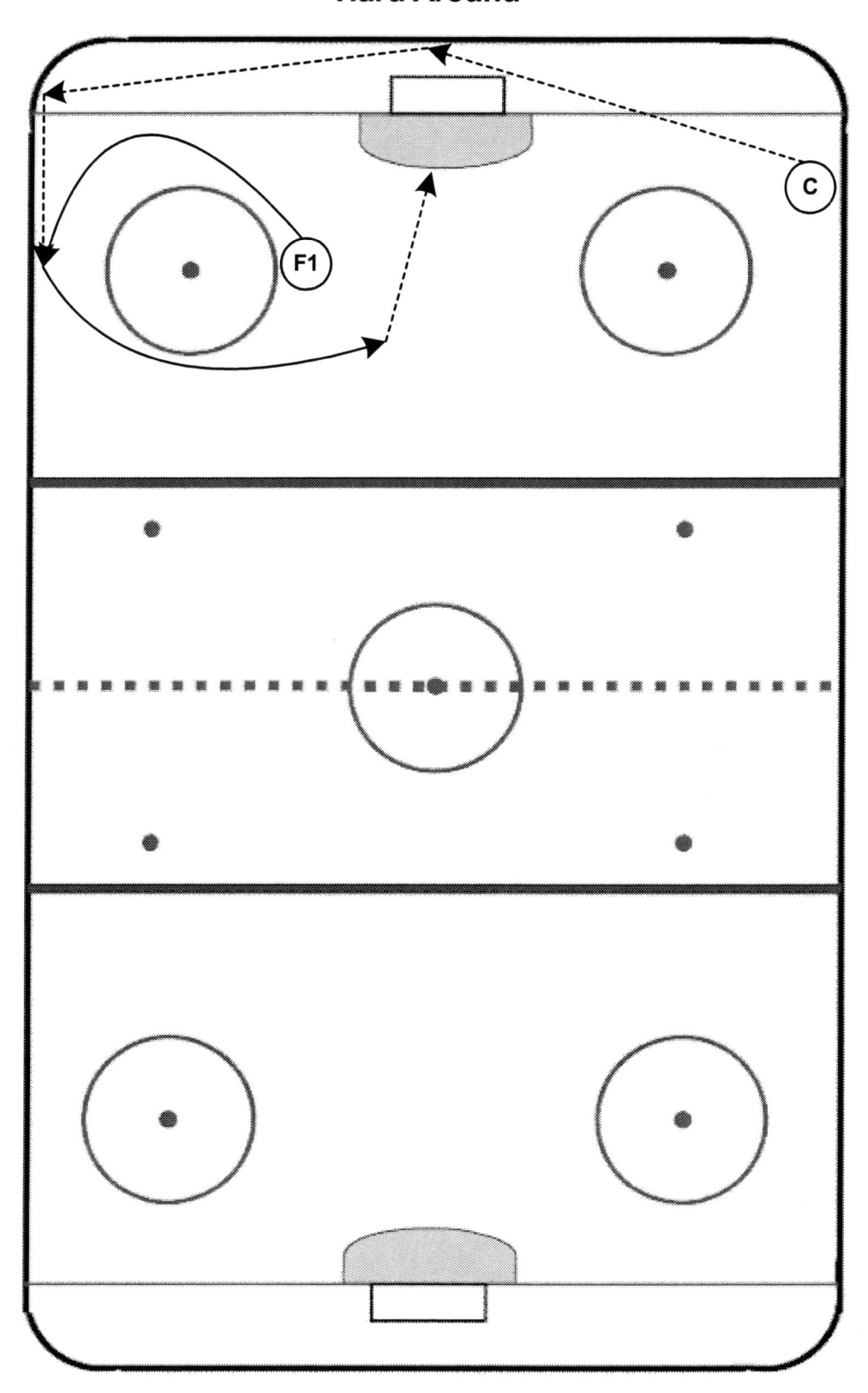

## 105 "Own the Wall"

### Emphasis and Objective
Work on and improve puck protection along the wall.

### Drill Set-Up
- F's in pairs, divided in the zone.
- On the whistle, F along the wall has the puck, F tries to gain control.
- F uses equipment and body position to protect the puck, F attempts gain possession within the rules.
- Switch roles.

### Key Teaching Points
- Keep body between the puck and attacker.
- Use strength to shield player.

### Recommended Progressions
- None.

## "Own the Wall"

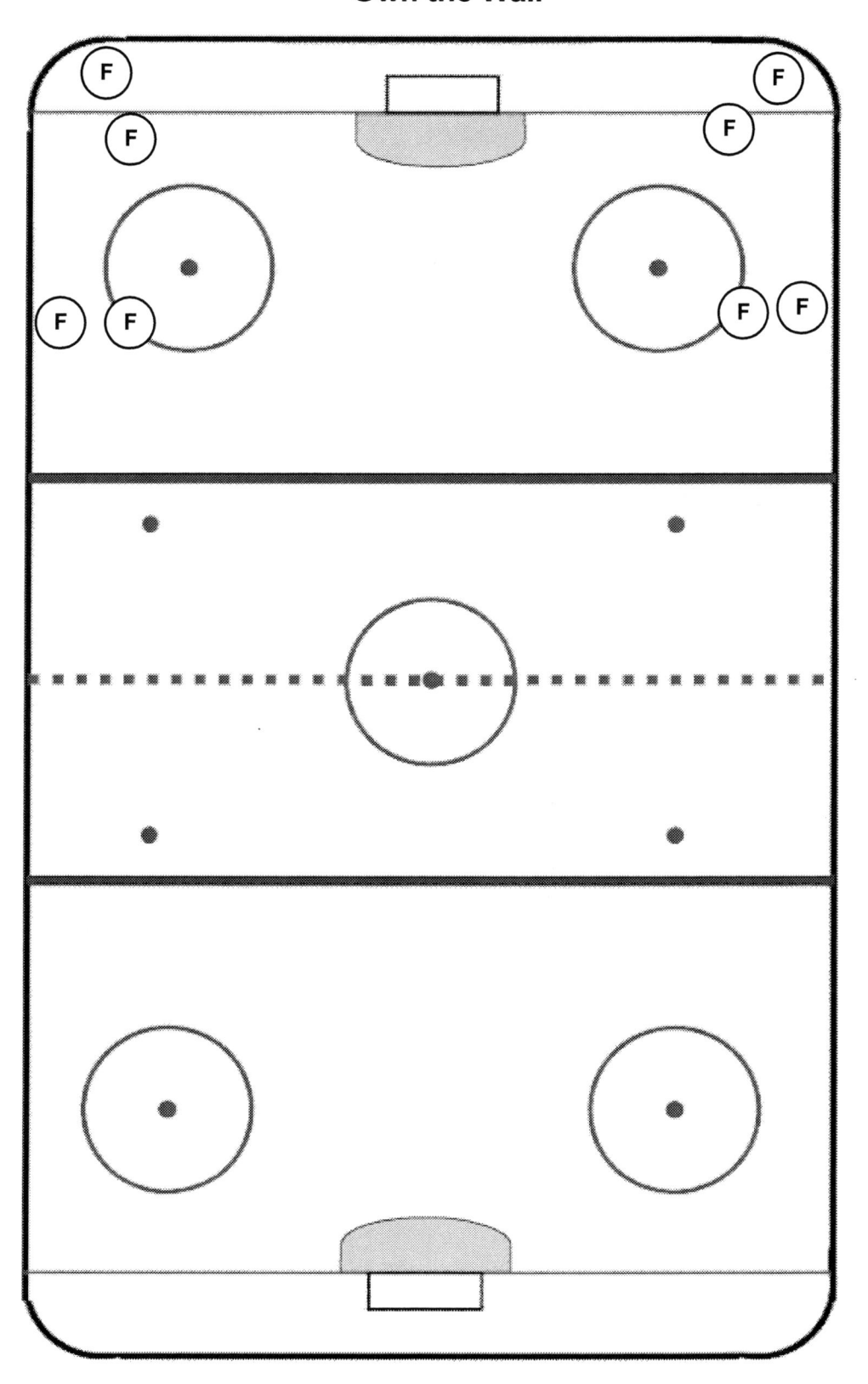

# 1 Time Quick Shot

## Emphasis and Objective
Work on redirecting the puck on goal while attacking full speed.

## Drill Set-Up
* C with pucks on the inside hash mark, F's at the blue-line.
* On the whistle, F's break hard to the far post and attempt to 1 time the pass from C on goal.

## Key Teaching Points
* Stick on the ice.
* Use forehand and backhand shots.
* Strong on sticks.

## Recommended Progressions
* None.

# 1 Time Quick Shot

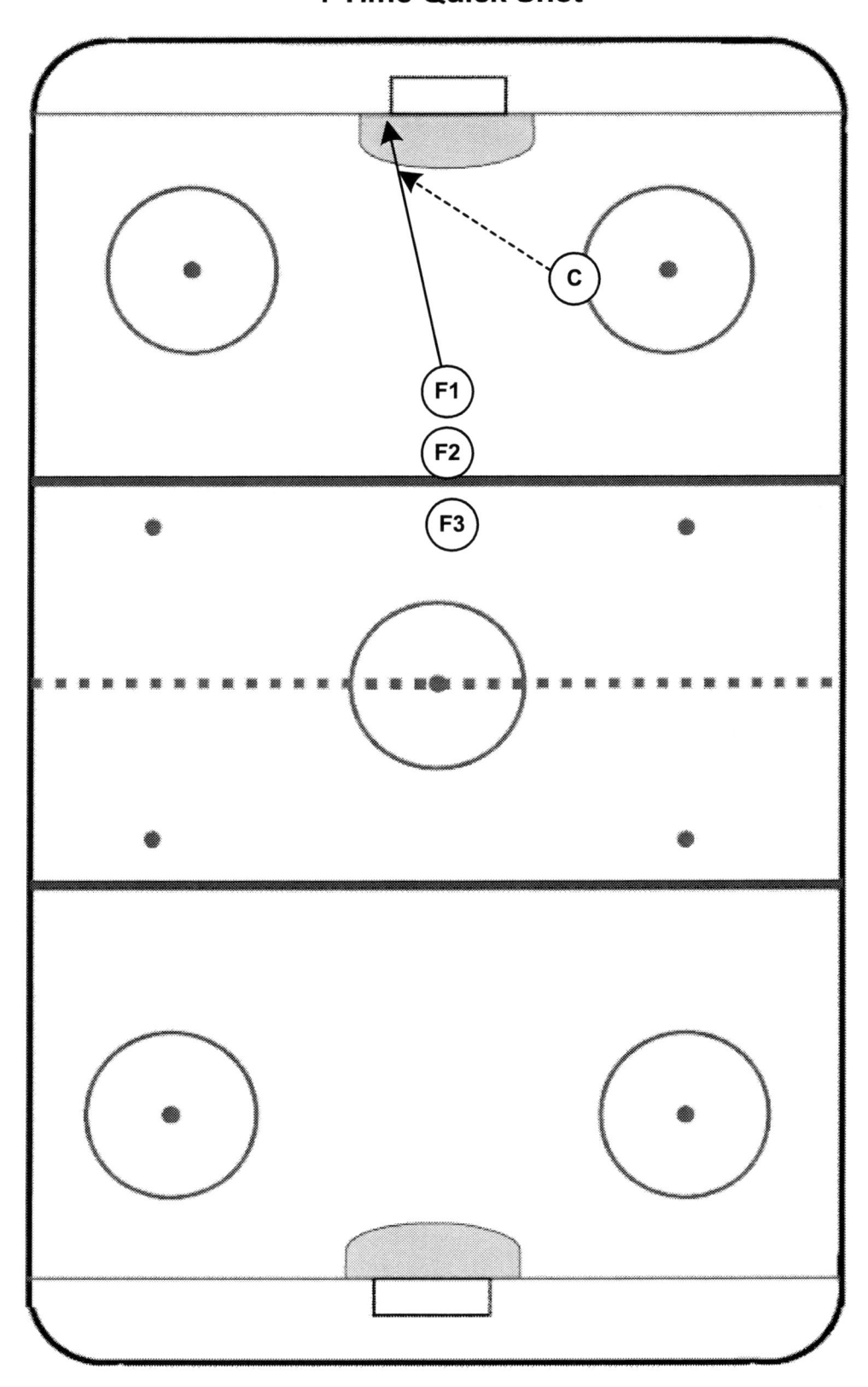

# 107 Finish in Tight

## Emphasis and Objective
Improve hands and rebound skills.

## Drill Set-Up
* C in the slot with pucks, G in the net on side, pads together, F's facing C at the top of the crease.
* On the whistle, C fires puck into G pads, F turns, finds the loose puck and tries to score.
* Stay in until a goal is scored.

## Key Teaching Points
* Quick hands.
* Good scoring positioning.
* Goal scoring skills.

## Recommended Progressions
* None.

# Finish In Tight

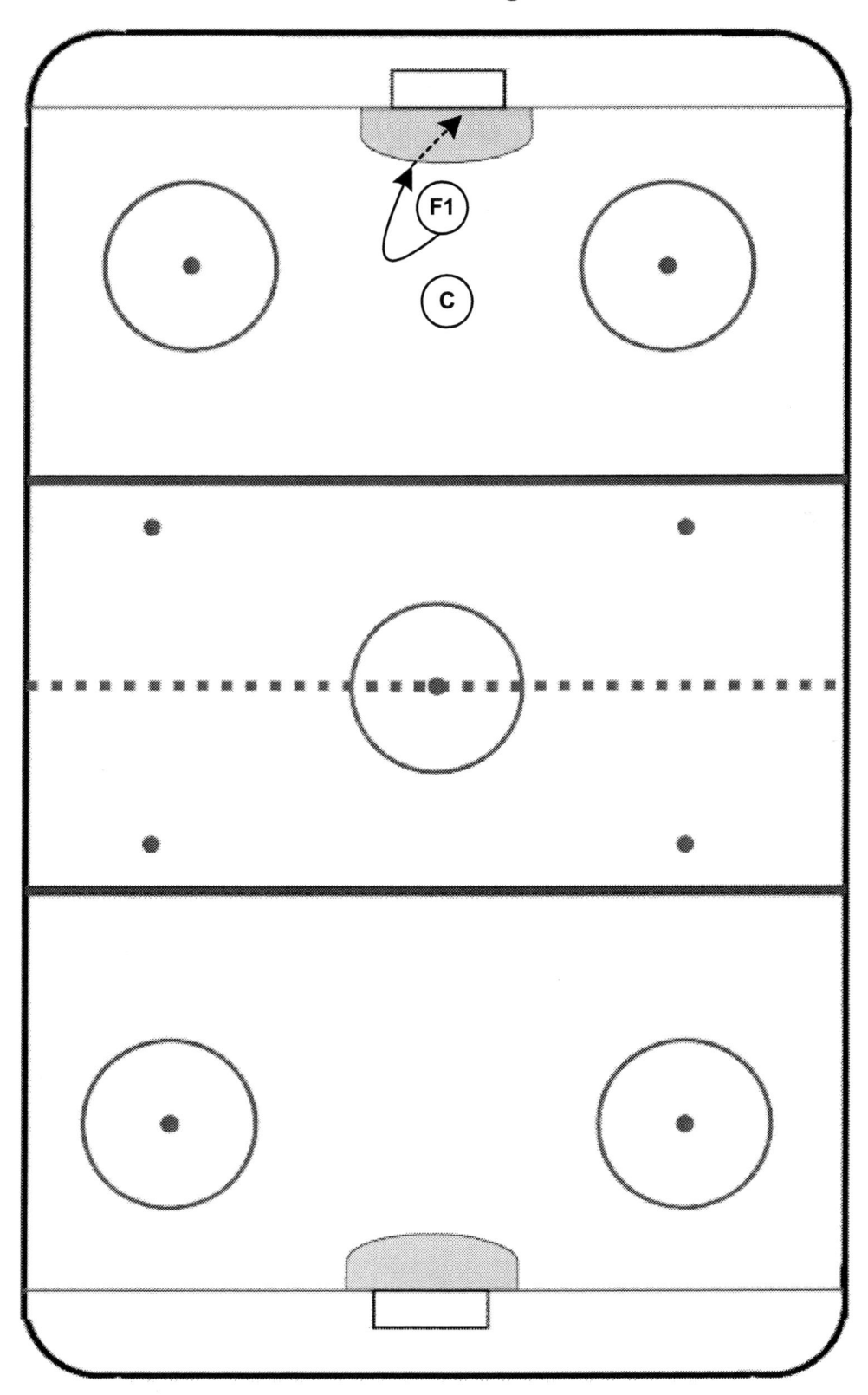

## 3 v 0 Cycle Behind the Net

### Emphasis and Objective

Introduce cycling and and improve puck possession skills.

### Drill Set-Up

* C in center circle with pucks, F1, F2 and F3 in attack position on the blue-line.
* C dumps puck into the offensive zone, F2 races to the puck and carries behind the net, F3 circles behind the net, receives a board pass from F2 and proceeds to the hash mark.
* At the hash mark, F3 escapes toward the boards, attacks the goal-line and hits F2 in the slot. F1 has moved into a defensive position.

### Key Teaching Points

* Movement.
* Puck protection.
* Puck support.
* Score goals.

### Recommended Progressions

* None.

# 3 v 0 Cycle

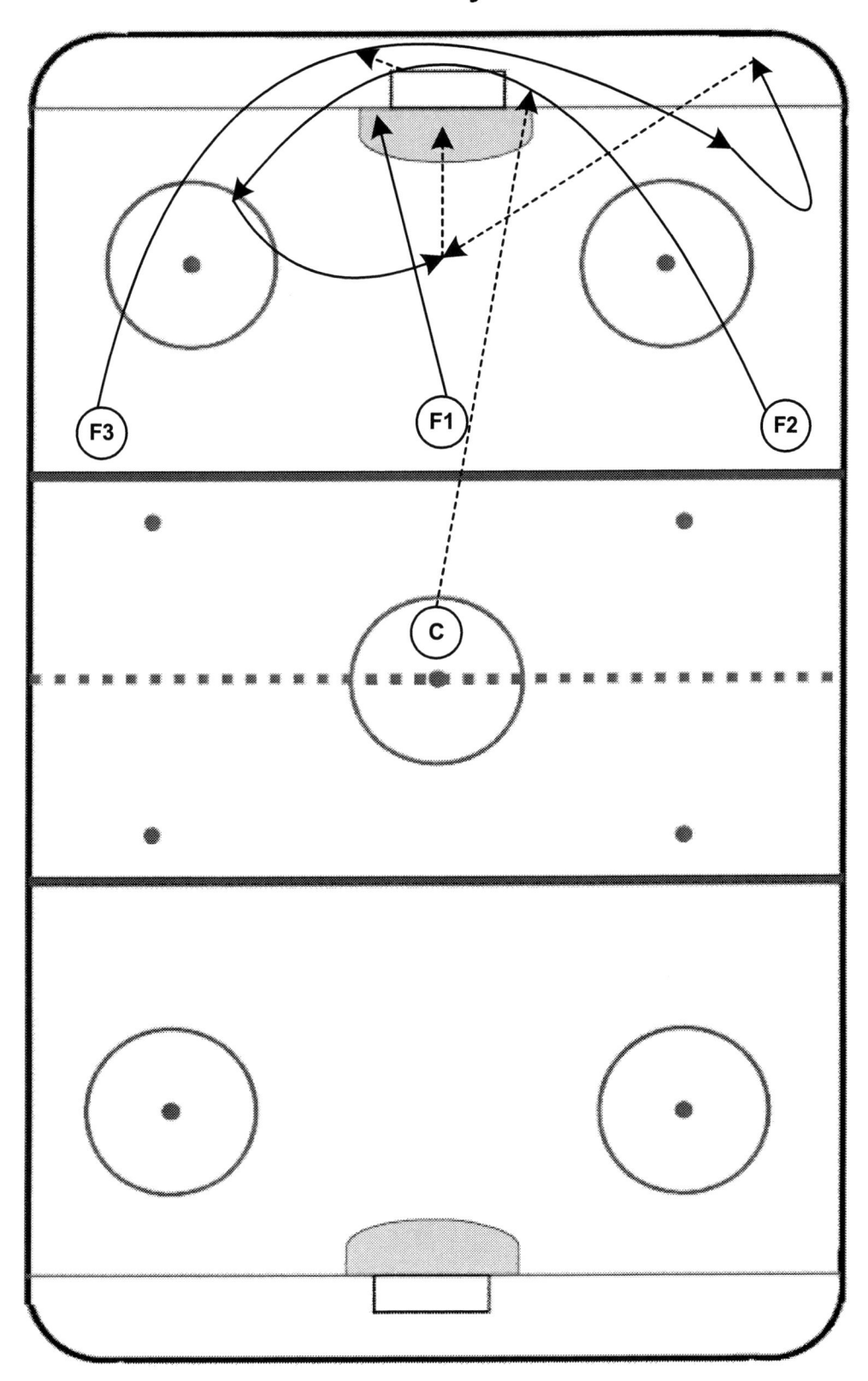

## 3 v 0, Double Cycle

### Emphasis and Objective
Cycling skills and puck protection.

### Drill Set-Up
- C in center circle with pucks, F1, F2 and F3 in attack position on the blue-line.
- C dumps puck into the offensive zone, F2 races to the puck and curls up the near half board, F1 follows down the wall, receives a board pass from F2 and drives the net. F3 proceeds to the slot and receives a pass from F1.
- F3 takes the puck to the far corner and curls up the half board, F2 follows down the wall, receives a board pass from F3 and drives the net. F2 hits F1 or F3 for a shot on goal.

### Key Teaching Points
- Puck movement.
- Puck protection.
- Puck support.
- Communication.
- Be sure 1 F is always in defensive position.

### Recommended Progressions
- None.

# 3 v 0 Double Circle

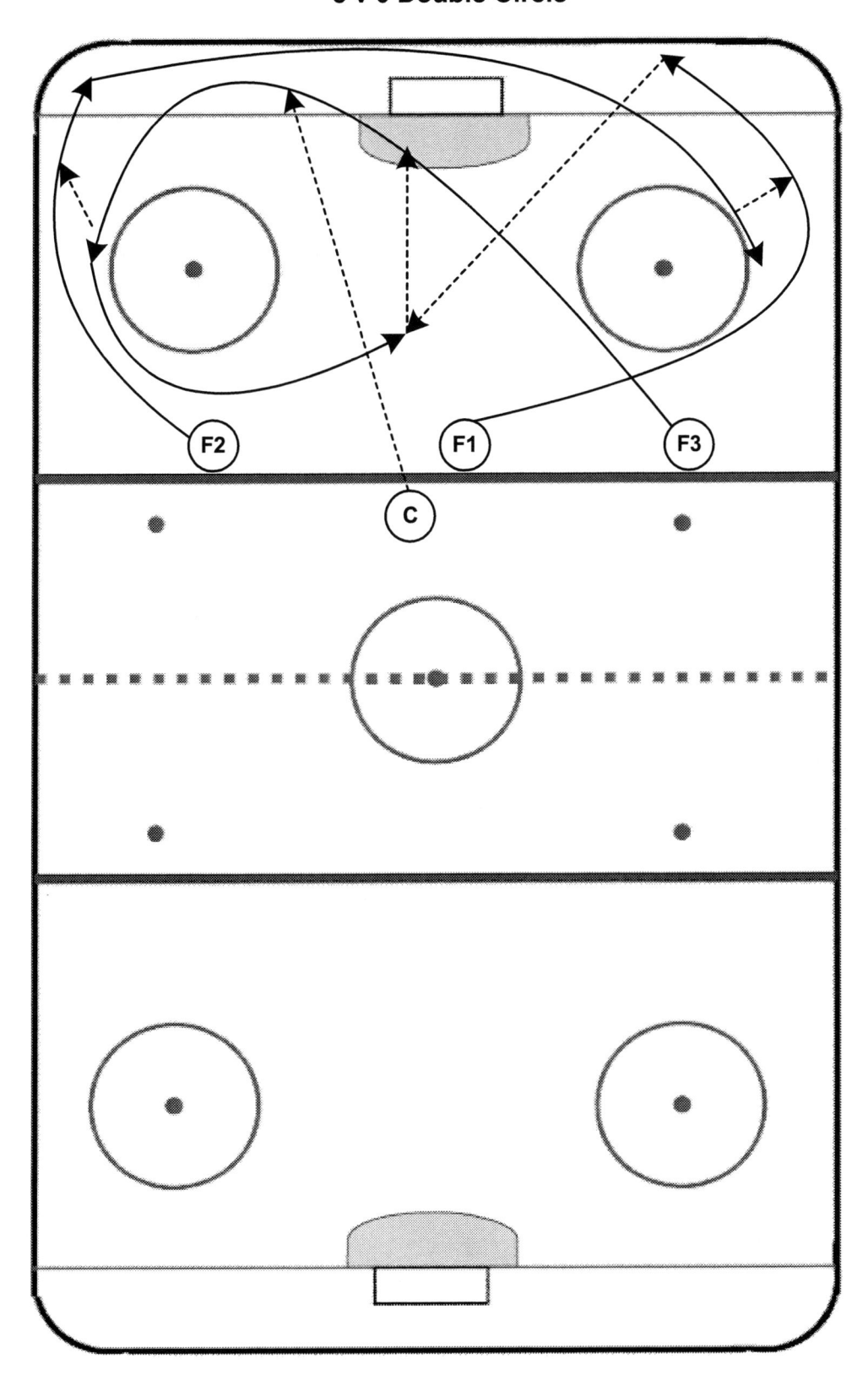

## In the Slot, Quick Shot

### Emphasis and Objective
Work on scoring skills and shot release.

### Drill Set-Up
* C behind net with pucks, F's in two lines in slot.
* C passes to F1 or F2 who quick releases a shot on net.
* F be sure to follow shot to a rebound.

### Key Teaching Points
* Score goals under pressure.
* Quick release.
* Soft hands.

### Recommended Progressions
* None.

# In the Slot, Quick Shot

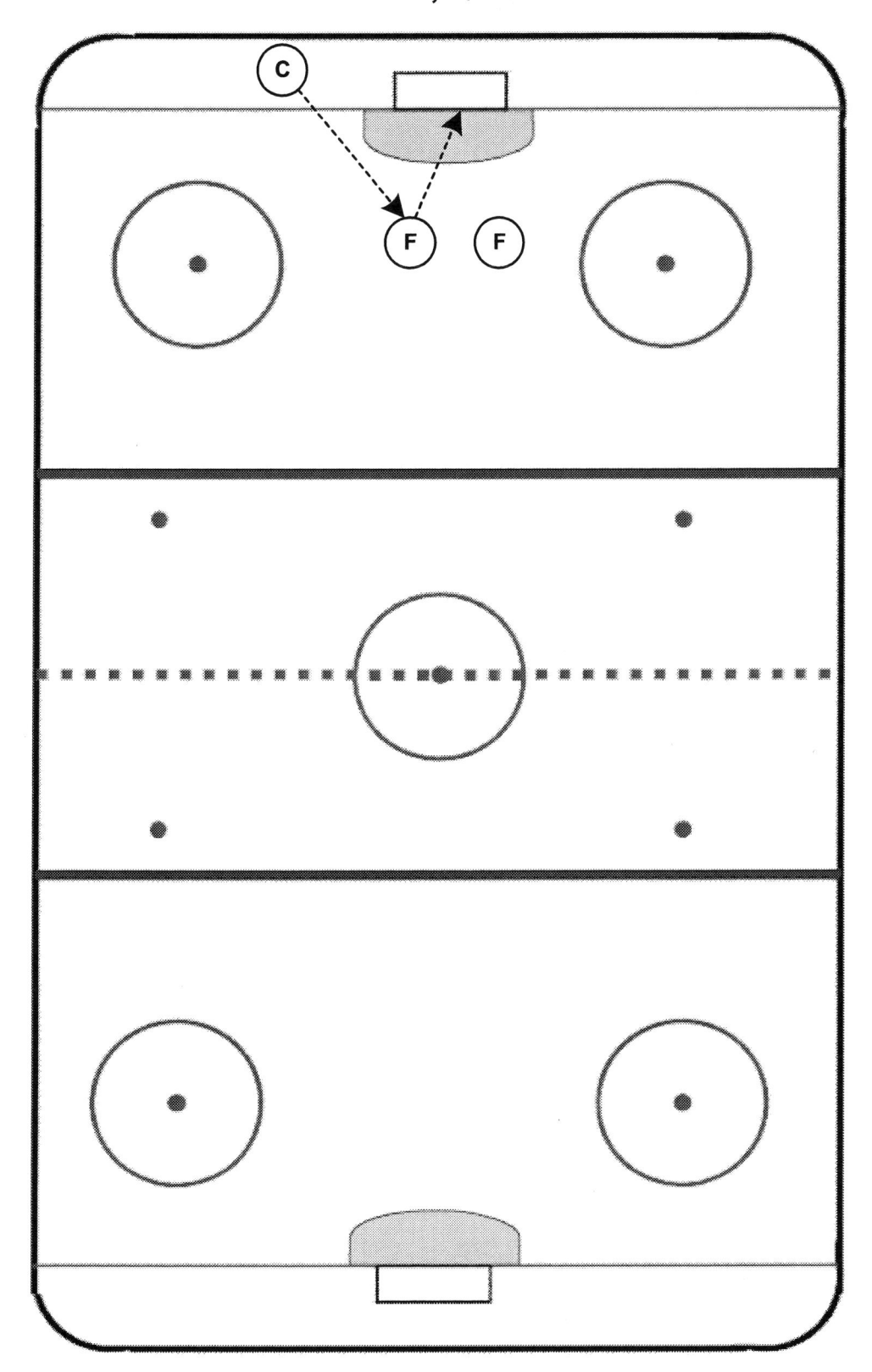

# 111 Face-Off Challenge

### Emphasis and Objective
Improve face-off skills and techniques.

### Drill Set-Up
- F's in groups of 3 divided in the zone.
- F1 and F2 face-off with F3 dropping the puck.
- Change roles.

### Key Teaching Points
- Quick hands.
- Timing, anticipation.
- Body position.
- Take opponents stick away.
- Win it clean or go for the tie.

### Recommended Progressions
- Crown a champion.

# Face-Off Challenge

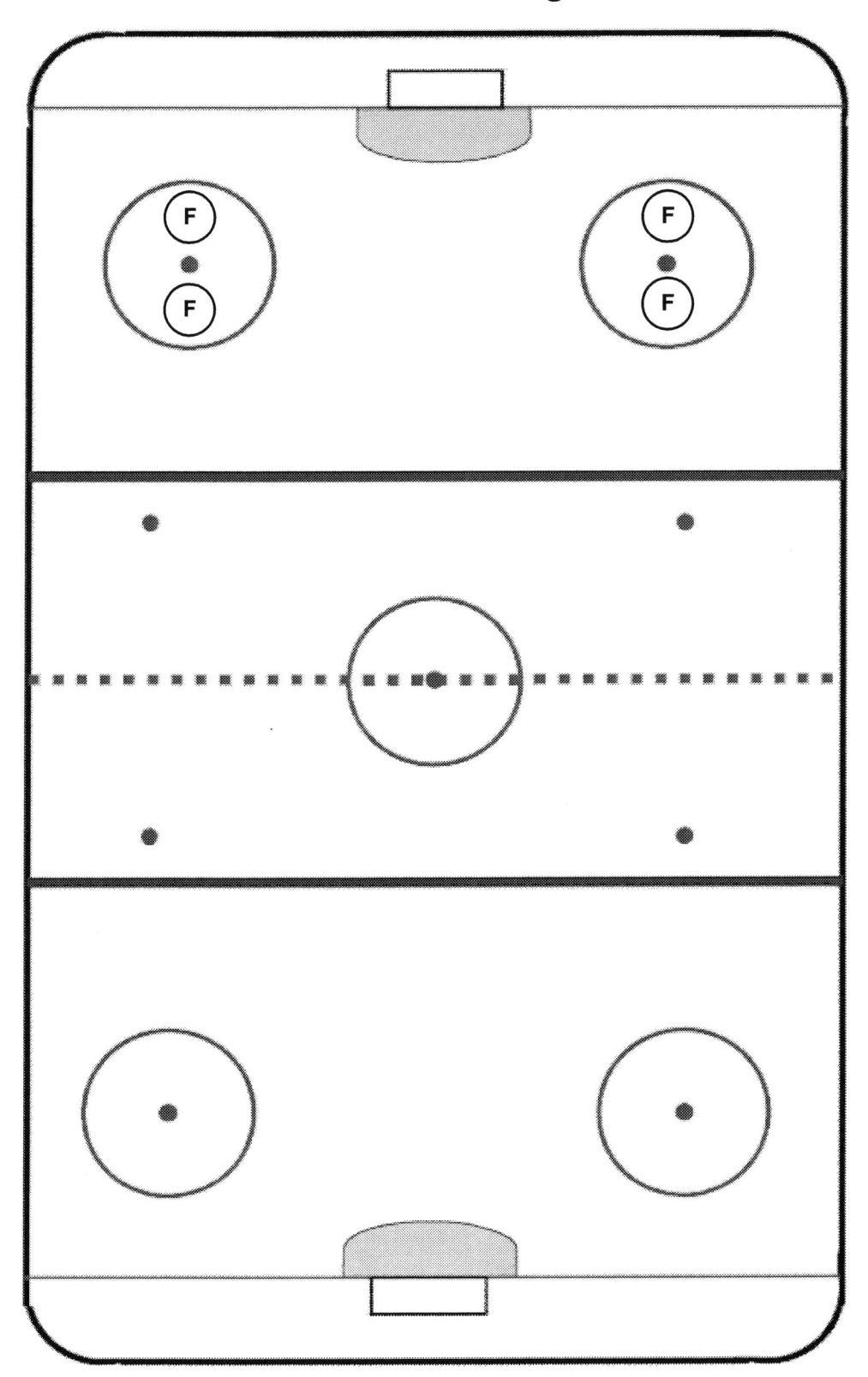

## 112     2 v 0 Out of the Corners

### Emphasis and Objective
Work on attacking and goal scoring skills.

### Drill Set-Up
- Two lines of F's in the corner, one below the goal-line, one even with the bottom of the circle.
- F1 and F2 attack the goal 2 v 0.
- After the initial shot, F1 and F2 proceed to the opposite corner

### Key Teaching Points
- Move the puck.
- Attack at a good shooting angle.
- Quick shots.
- Vary attack options.

### Recommended Progressions
- None.

**2 v 0 Out of the Corners**

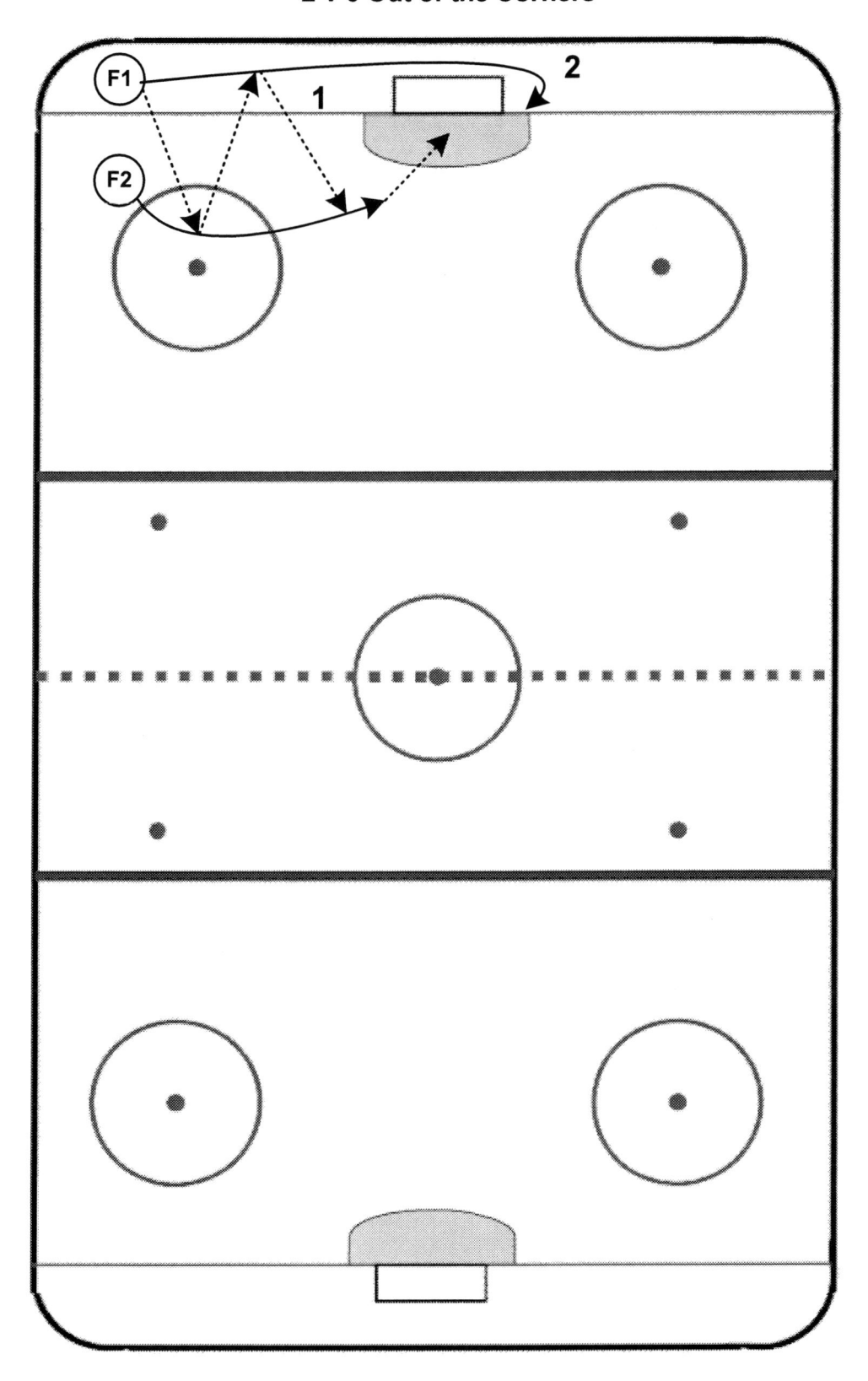

# 113 Two Shot, Double Circle

## Emphasis and Objective

Work on shooting in stride and goal scoring skills.

## Drill Set-Up

- F's divided in two groups, one in each corner.
- F1 skates to the top of the near circle, receives a pass from F3 and shoots in stride on goal.
- After the shot, F1 skates to the opposite circle, exchanges passes with F2 and moves to the high slot.
- F2 hits F1 in the slot and begins a similar action.

## Key Teaching Points

- Score goals.
- Shot in stride.
- Ice vision.
- Develop soft hands.

## Recommended Progressions

- None.

# Two Shot Double Circle

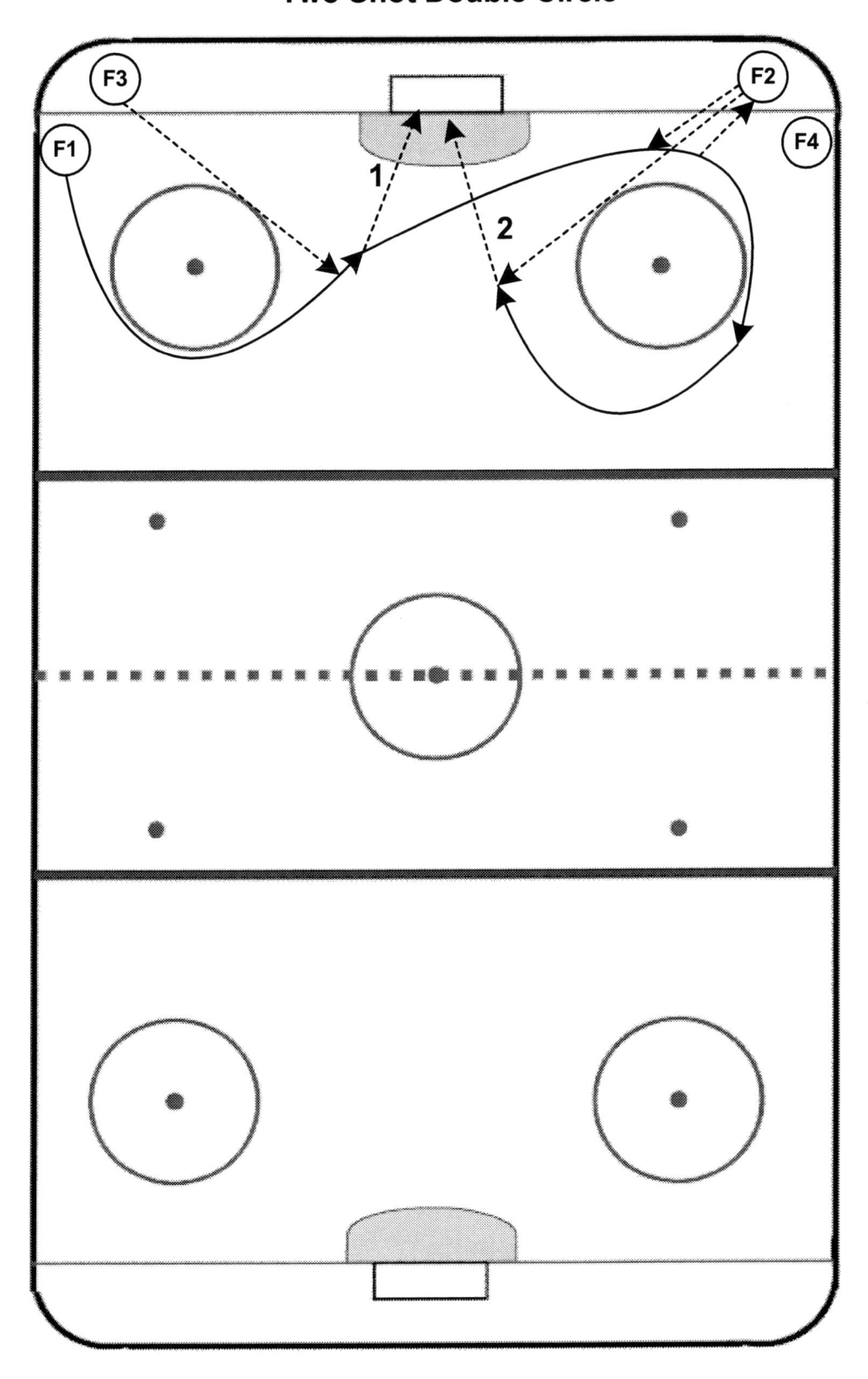

Photo courtesy of Dave Eggen & Dick Carlson of Inertia Pro Event Imaging and The Sioux Falls Stampede

# 7

## Defensemen Specific Drills

The development of the defensemen and the skills necessary for the position are stressed in this section.

Defense is a highly specialized position and constant attention to the skills and fundamentals of defensive play should be stressed.

Skating, shooting, passing and footwork are the concepts that should constantly be developed and improved. Naturally, these concepts are stressed in each phase of a regular practice, this section is an ideal supplement to the regular practice phase.

Use these drills in a half ice situation or challenge the entire team. The fundamentals of the defense position will enhanced the development of the total player.

# 114    Quick Tip and Cover

## Emphasis and Objective

Work on point shot deflections and slot coverage.

## Drill Set-Up

- Position F's in each corner, D on blue-line and one corner.
- On the C's 1st whistle, F1 passes to D1 at point.
- D1 receives pass and moves to shooting lane for a shot on net. After the initial pass, F1 attacks goal for a screen and deflection.
- D2 joins the play picking up F1 for coverage in the slot.
- On the C's 2nd whistle, F1 and D2 battle for position while F2 looks to pass to F1 for a second shot.
- Both ends, alternate sides.

## Key Teaching Points

- Hard, low accurate shots from points.
- Proper screens and deflection techniques.
- Rebound control.
- 1 v 1 defensive coverage and positioning skills.
- Competition for loose pucks.

## Recommended Progressions

- None.

# Quick Tip and Cover

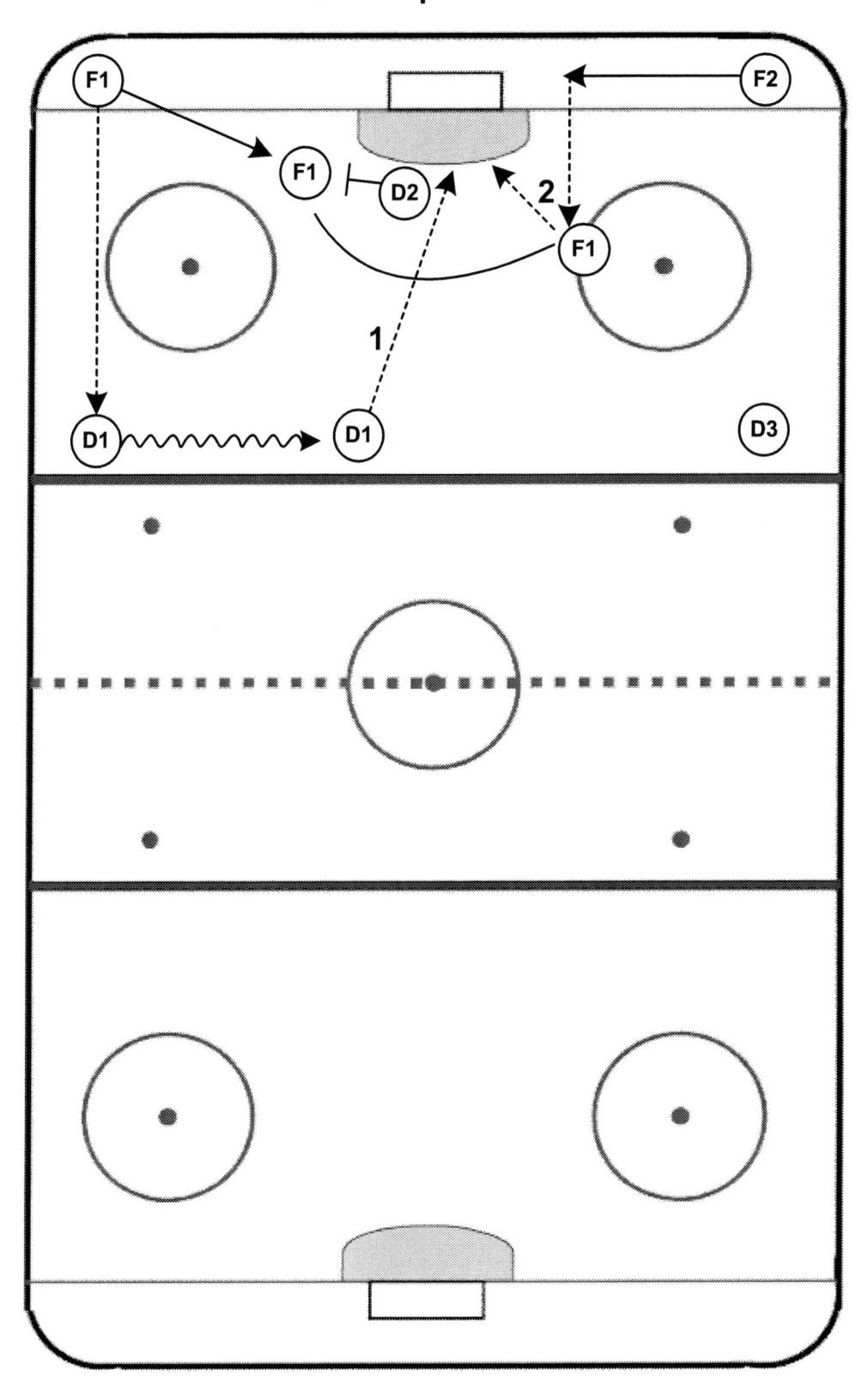

# 115     Shin-Hi Shooting

## Emphasis and Objective

Get defensemen to shoot point shots shin-hi over defenders sticks.

## Drill Set-Up

- Need 6-8 extra sticks placed end to end extending across the tops of each face-off circle.
- D1's and D2's on each blue-line and D3's and D4's in a passing position at the hash marks.
- D3 passes to D1 who catches the puck and moves 3-4 strides to the shooting area.
- D1 then shoots the puck Shin-Hi making sure to avoid the sticks on the ice.

## Key Teaching Points

- Head up at all times.
- Get the puck to the net.
- Use quick wrist shots.
- Move to avoid shot blocker.
- Shoot from scoring area.

## Recommended Progressions

- One-time shots from D-D pass.

# Shin-Hi Shooting

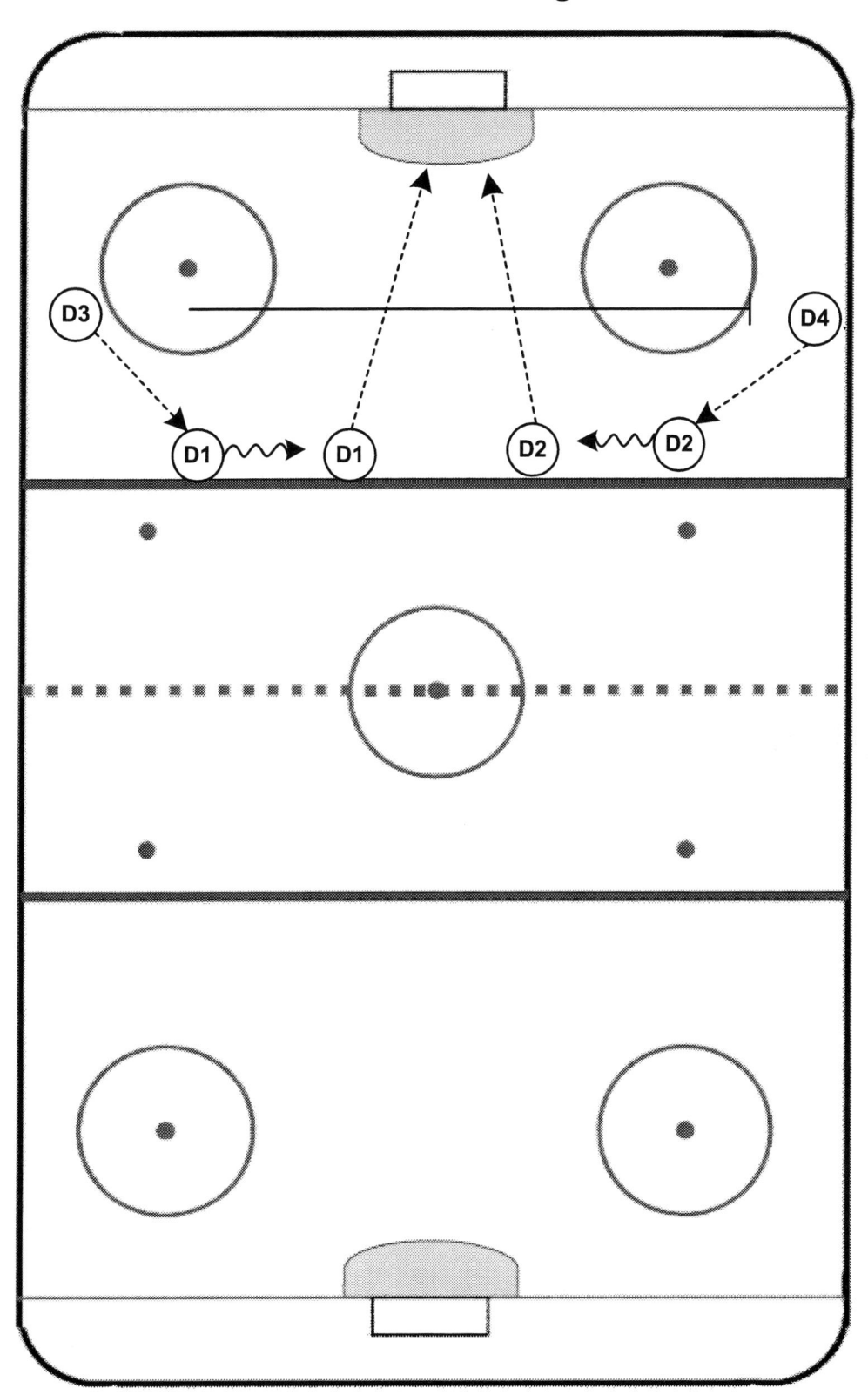

# 116 Lateral Movement

## Emphasis and Objective
Work on defensemen lateral skating skills.

## Drill Set-Up
- D in one end of ice.
- Cones positioned on the center face-off circle, neutral zone face-off spots and in the high slot area.
- On the signal, skate in and out of the cones.
- Finish in the corner, stop and sprint to back of the line.

## Key Teaching Points
- Always keep feet moving.
- Head up at all times.
- Stick down in front of body.
- Balance and wide skating base.

## Recommended Progressions
- Have D carry a puck while skating.

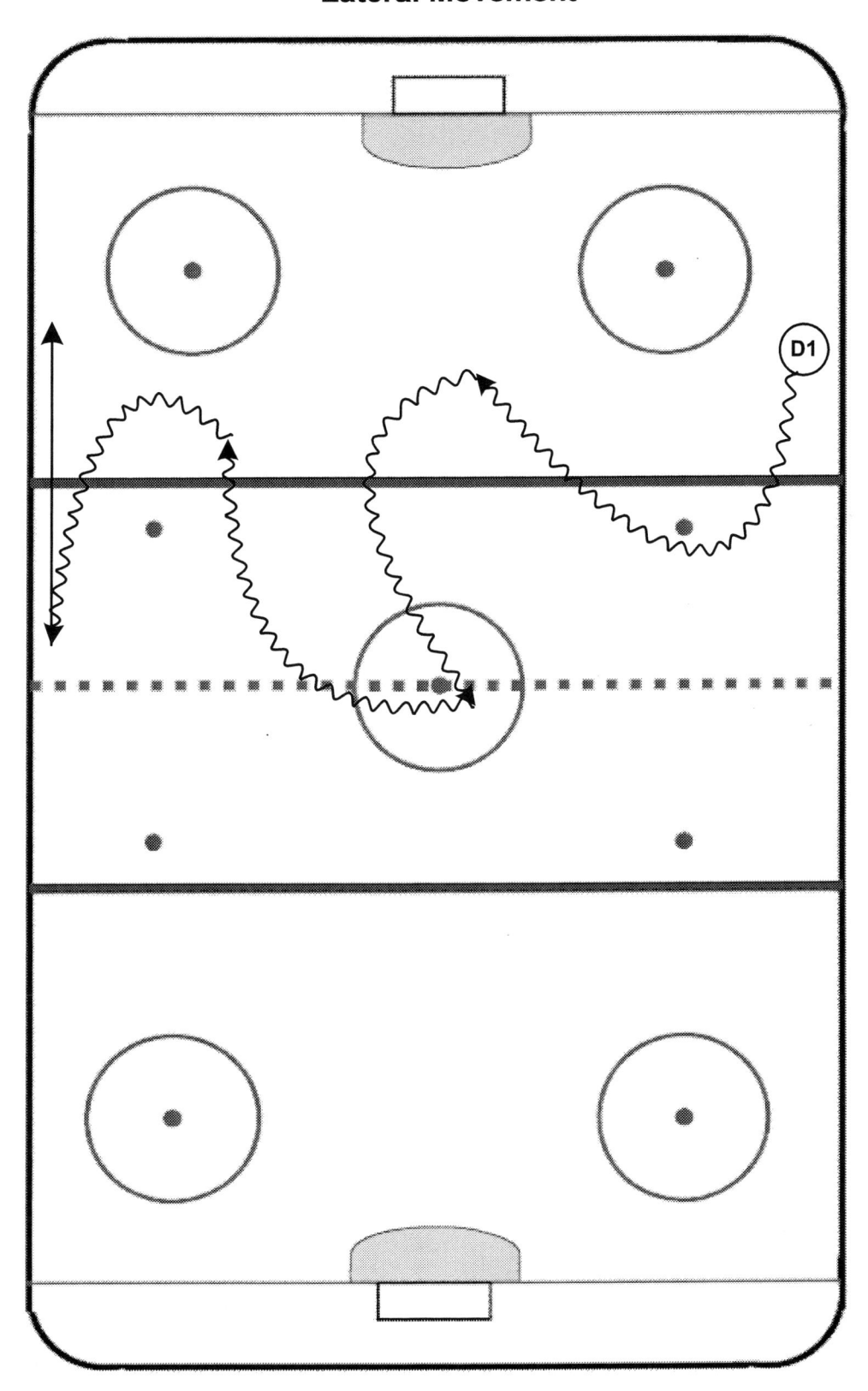

# Lateral Movement

# 117     Defensive Angling

## Emphasis and Objective

Introduce and teach the concept of angling.

## Drill Set-Up

* 3 stations.
* F1's in end corner, F2's in opposite end corner and F3's on blue-line, each with pucks.
* D1's positioned just inside blue-line in front of F1's. D2's in corner with F2's and D3's on the neutral zone face-off spot facing F3's.
* On the C's 1st whistle, F1 takes off down the wall full speed, D1 must skate backwards and angle F1 to the boards before blue-line. F2 attacks the net while D2 gains position between F2 and goal, F3 takes off down the wall full speed outside of cone driving the net. D3 must skate backwards angling F3 to near post or corner.
* F's and D's rotate positions, be sure to switch sides of ice.

## Key Teaching Points

* Full speed.
* Insist on backwards skating.
* Use stick position to deny the middle of the ice.
* Drill can be done with staggered whistles to activate goaltenders.

## Recommended Progressions

* None

# Defensive Angling

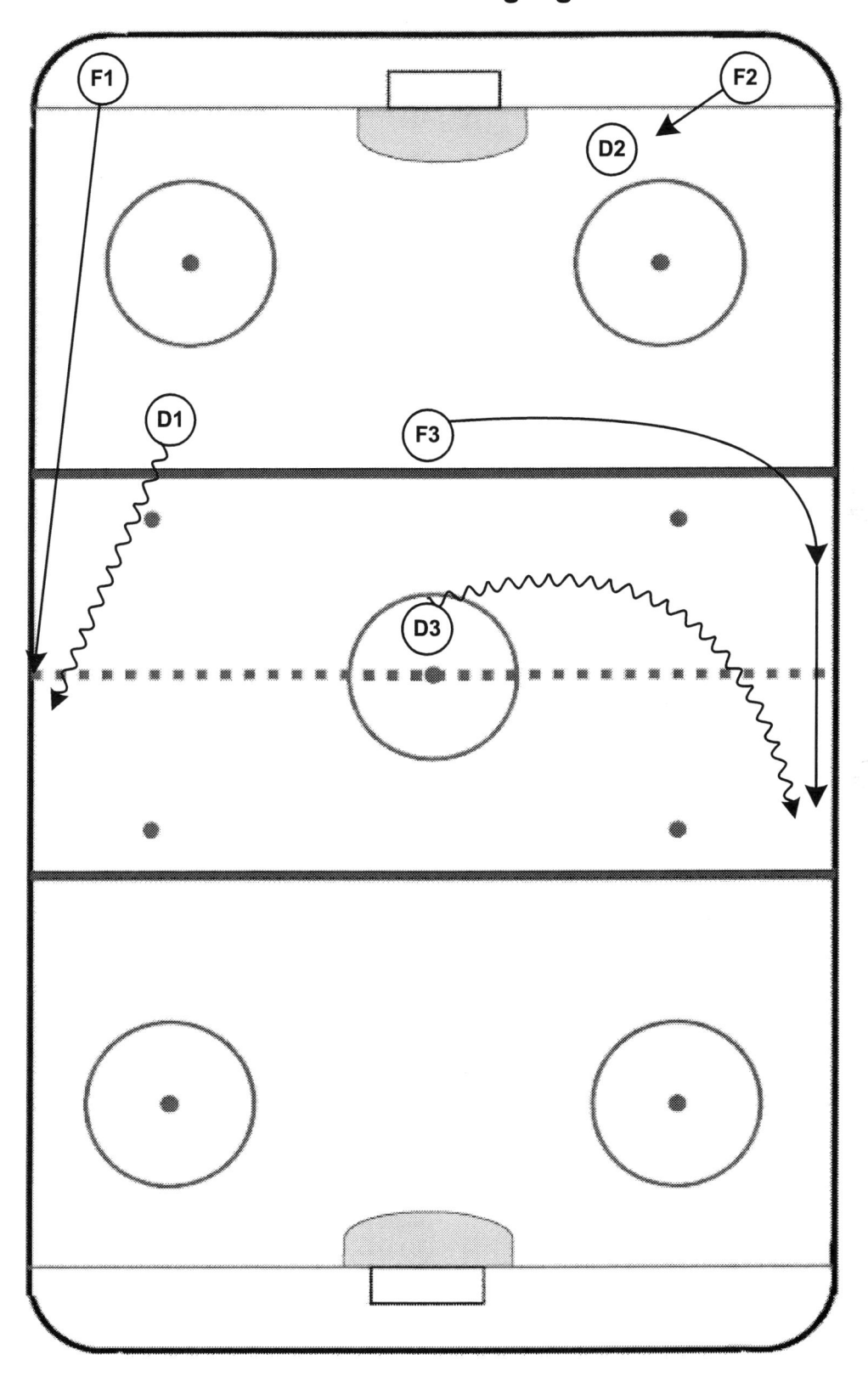

# 118     D to D Puck Support

## Emphasis and Objective

D positioning supporting puck and partner.

## Drill Set-Up

* F's in opposite corners, D's with partners on each side of center red-line.
* F1 makes a long pass to D1 who catches pass and gives a pass to supporting D2 behind and at mid-ice, F1 proceeds up the wall.
* D2 hinges and skates up ice, D1 supports behind and at mid-ice.
* D2 passes back to D1 who immediately looks and passes to F1 who proceeds back down the wall for a shot.
* Action is done at both ends at the same time.

## Key Teaching Points

* Keep feet moving.
* Good, hard passes.
* Pass at good angles.
* F's come back deep.

## Recommended Progressions

* None.

# D to D Puck Support

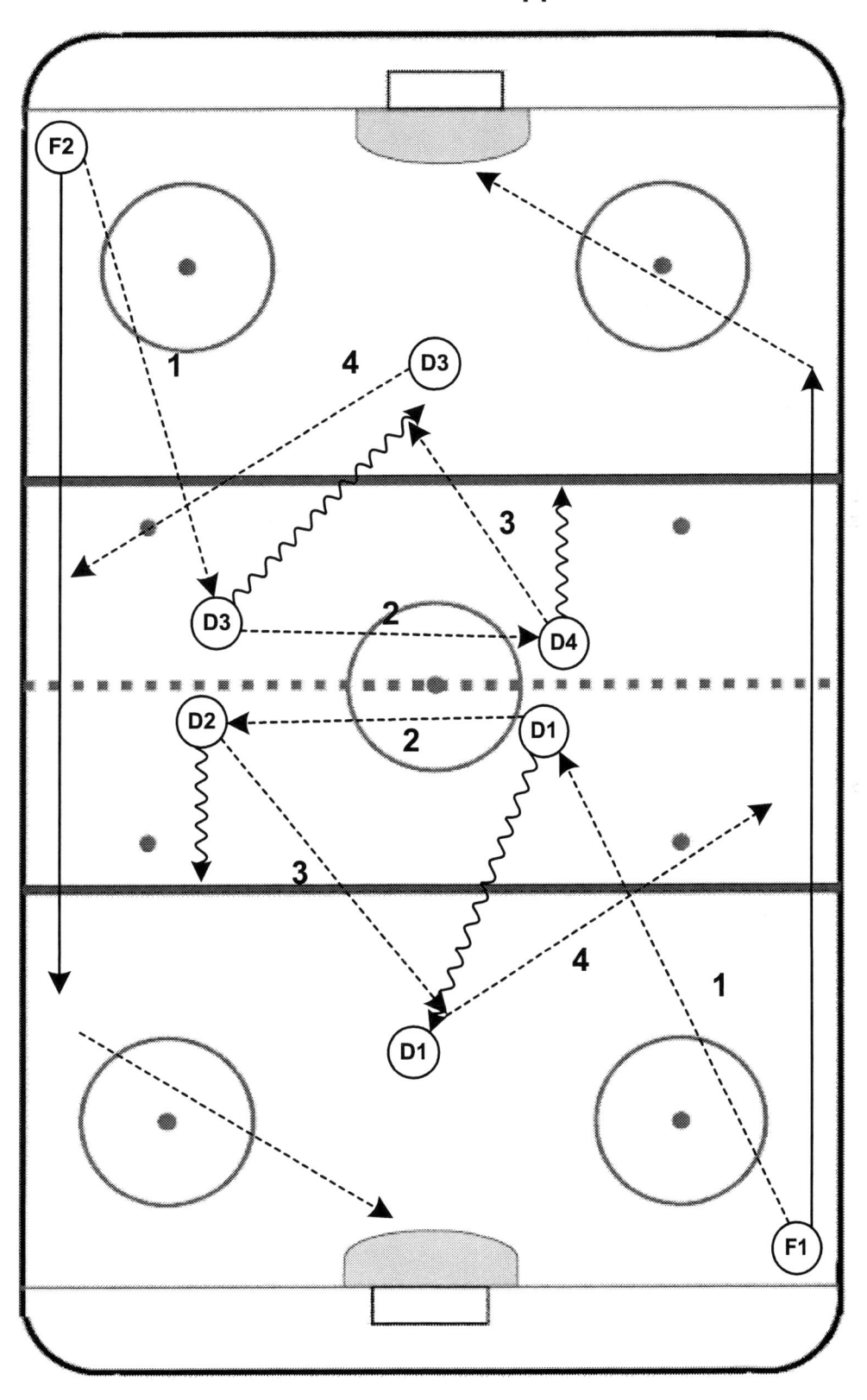

## 119     Oslo Multi-Purpose Containment

### Emphasis and Objective
Work on defensive situations, angling and competition.

### Drill Set-Up
* F1 and F2 in opposite corners, F3 in neutral zone. D1 facing F1, D2 facing F2.
* On 1st whistle, F1 attacks D1 1 v 1.
* On 2nd whistle, 1st 1 v 1 ends and F2 attacks D2 1 v 1.
* On the 3rd whistle, F3 attacks zone 1 v 2 against D1 and D2.
* On the 4th whistle, F1, F2 and F3 attack D1 and D2, 3 v 2.
* After each 1 v 1, F"s go to neutral zone preparing for 3 v 2.

### Key Teaching Points
* Angling.
* Containment.
* Defensive skills.
* Competition.
* Puck protection.

### Recommended Progressions
* Mix in a 2 v 2.

# Oslo Multipurpose Containment

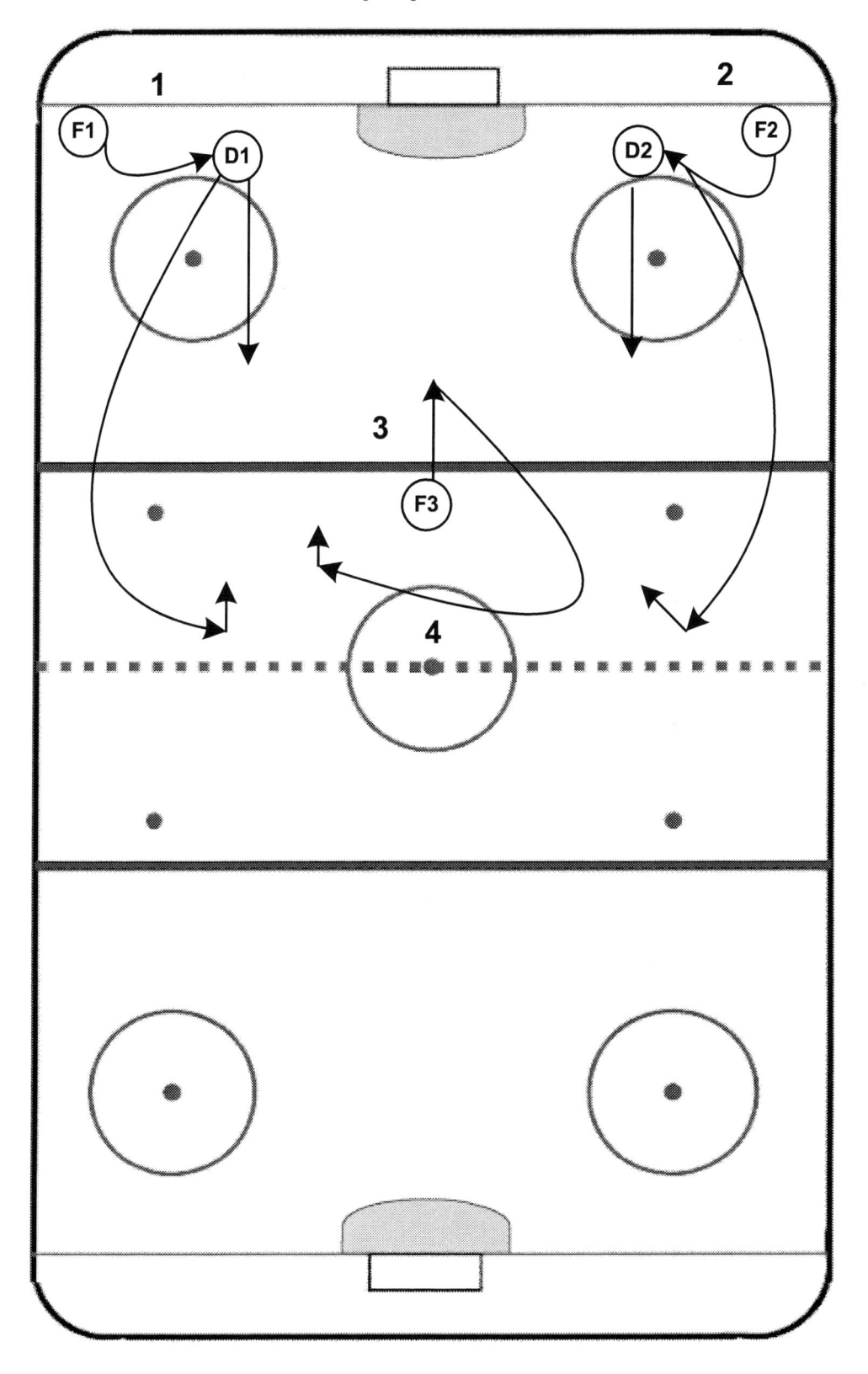

## 120 Half Ice Winger Breakouts

### Emphasis and Objective
Breakout passing and positioning.

### Drill Set-Up
* Goalies with centers in one end for shooting, wingers and defense at opposite end.
* Two lines each of F's and D's on the blue-line even with the neutral zone face-off spot.
* Working independently and in pairs, F's dump the puck into their corner, D skate backwards, pivot properly picking up the puck and breaks out with F.
* F supports the D in good backchecking position, pivots to the corner and gets in good break out position. After receiving the pass from the D, F skates up the wall and passes to the next F in line who repeats the breakout sequence.

### Key Teaching Points
* Support the D.
* Head on a swivel.
* Open up and give D a passing target.
* Good passes.

### Recommended Progressions
* Go through all breakout options.
* Partner with opposite line to work on 4 v 4 breakout.
* Increase the number of passes required.
* Centers can be shooting on the goaltenders in opposite end.

# Half Ice Winger Breakouts

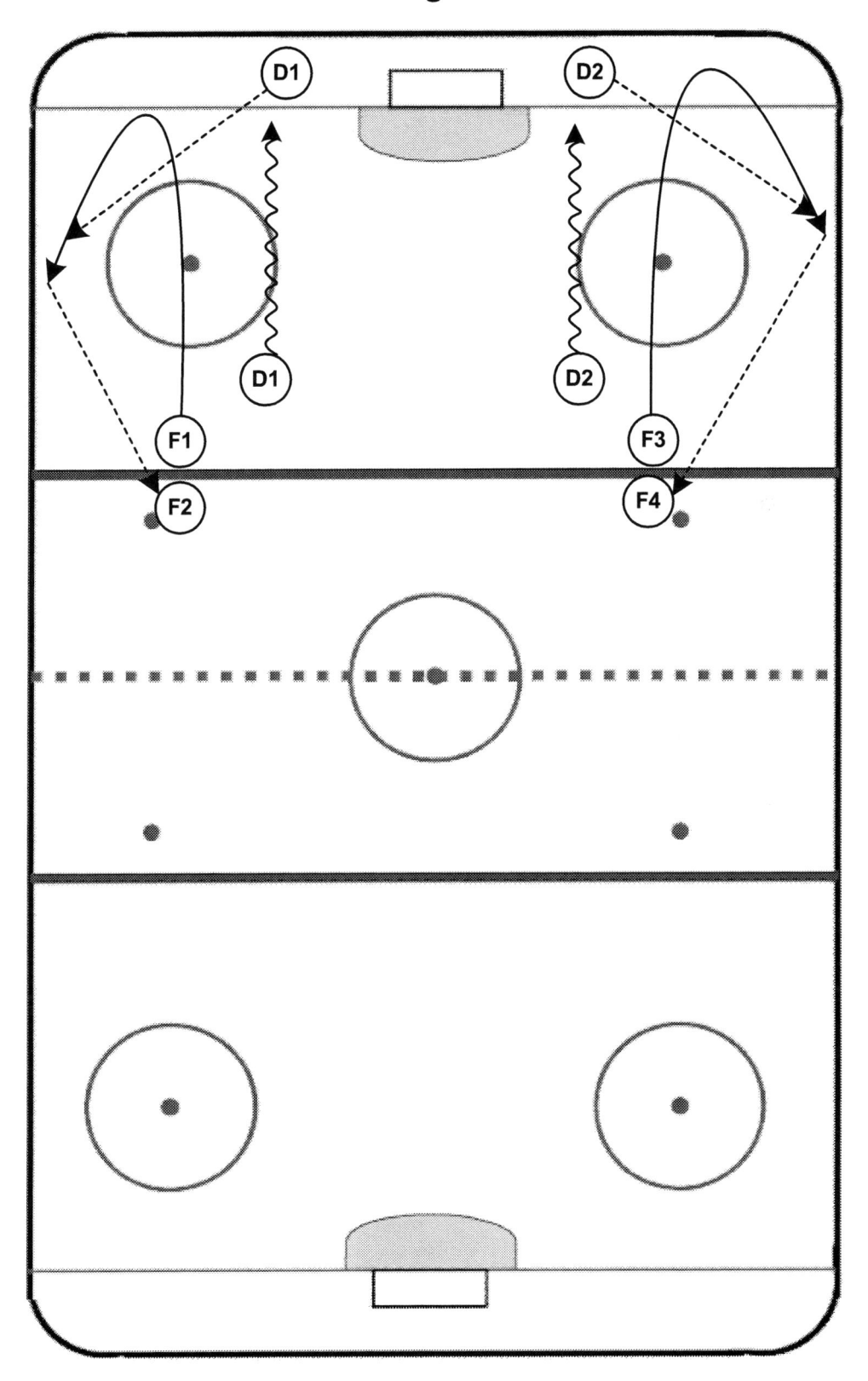

# 121 — 3 One Timers

## Emphasis and Objective
Work on one-time shooting at a variety of angles.

## Drill Set-Up
* C with pucks at hash marks. shooters (D's) at each blue-line.
* C passes to D, D return and gets into shooting position, C returns pass for a one-time shot.
* After the shot, coach gives the D another puck, they exchange for another one-time shot.
* Repeat for 3rd shot.

## Key Teaching Points
* Good passes.
* Proper weight transfer.
* Keep shots low.
* Work on foot work.
* Vary the positioning.
* Realistic passes, not too slow.

## Recommended Progressions
* None.

# 3 One-Timers

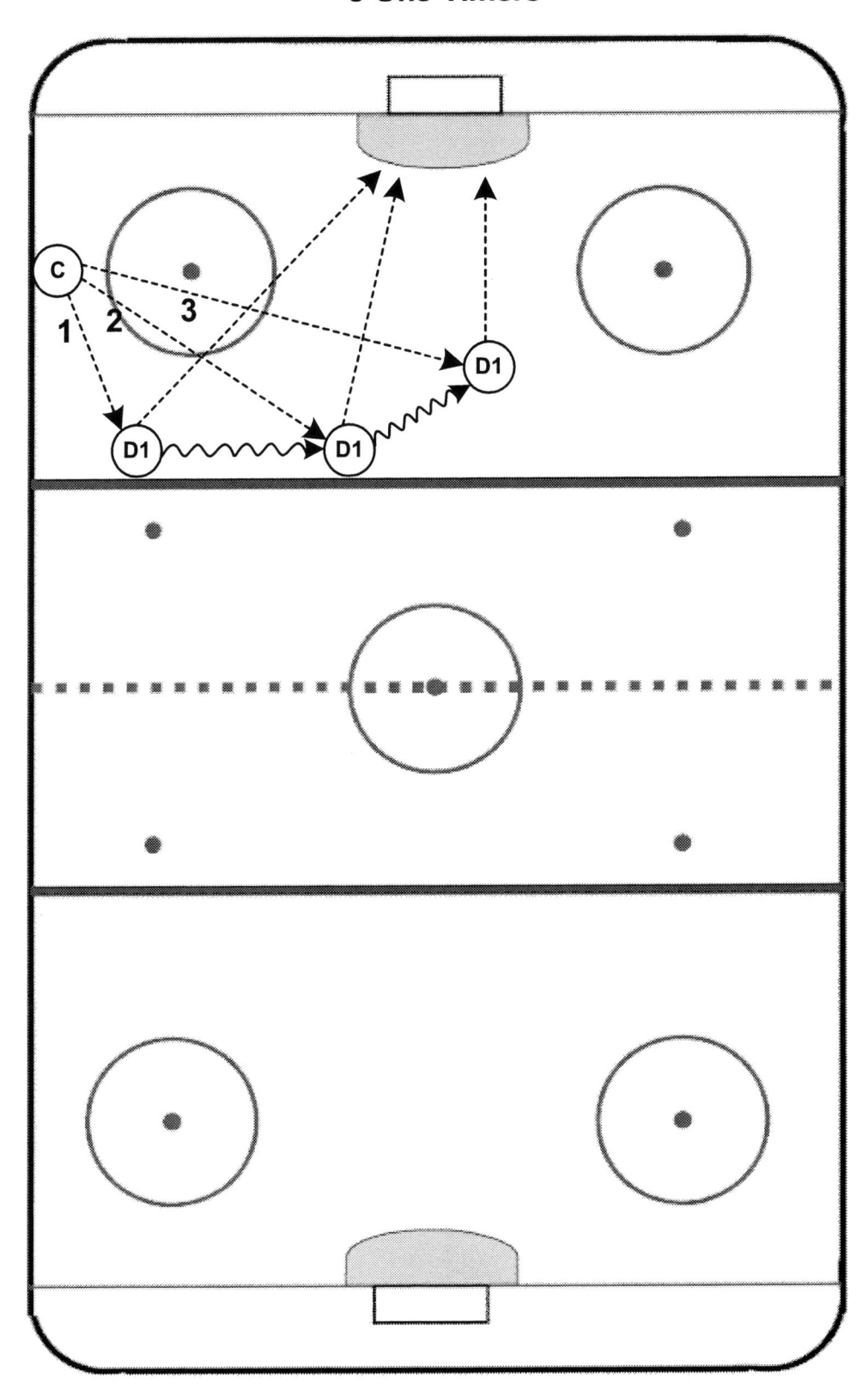

## Defensive Pins, 3 v 3

### Emphasis and Objective
Work on defensive positioning and attacks from a pin.

### Drill Set-Up
- 2 D and 1X on defense, 3 F's on offense.
- D1 in front of net with F3, D2 and X in corner with F1 and F2.
- Drill starts with D1 pinning F1 in the corner and X in defensive position on F2
- On the whistle, play begins with F's attempting to score. D1, D2 and X on defense attempt to break the puck out of the zone.
- 30-45 second shifts.

### Key Teaching Points
- Puck protection and control.
- Defensive side positioning.
- Don't get beat back to the front of the net.
- Competition.

### Recommended Progressions
- None.

# Defensive Pins 3 v 3

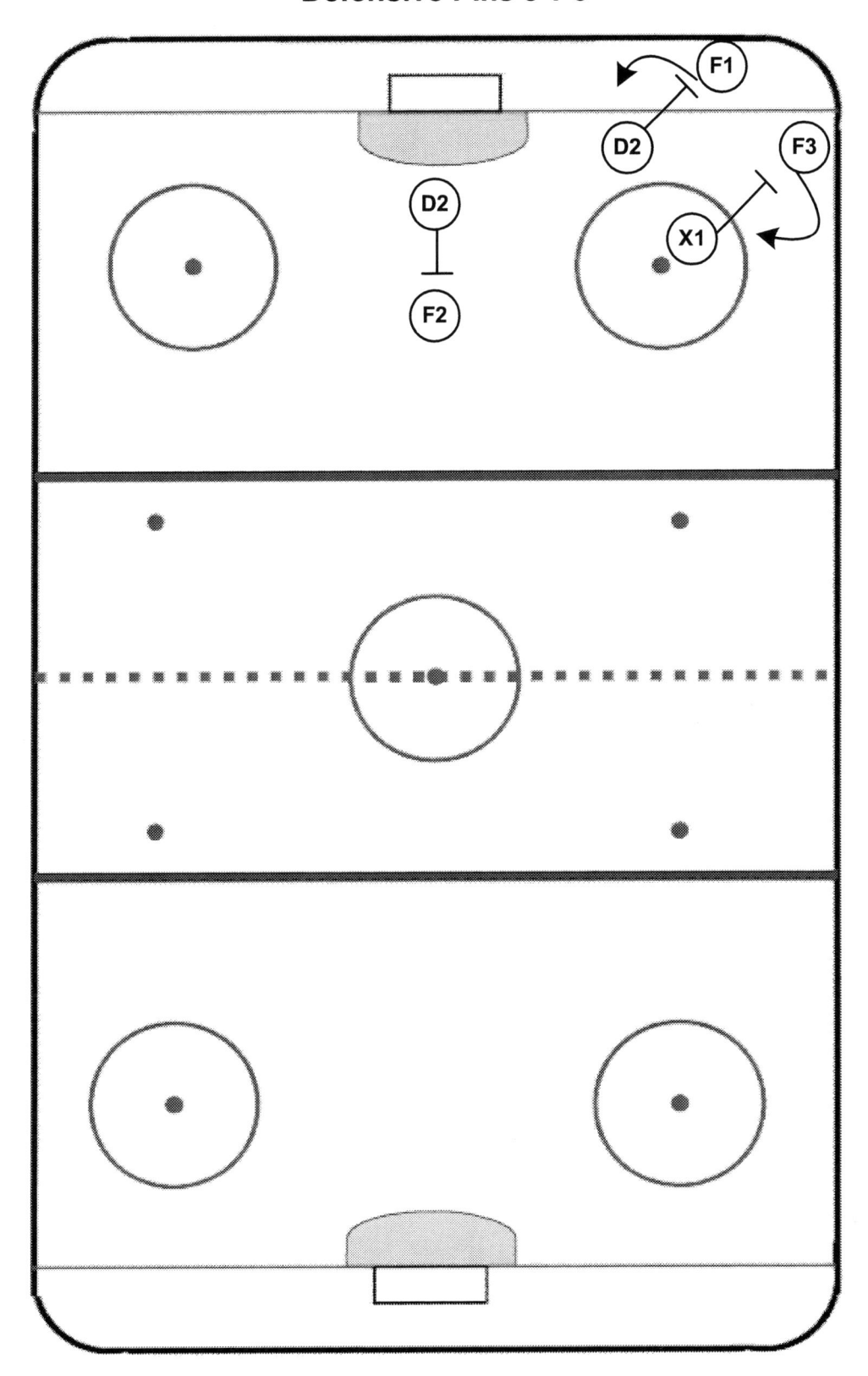

# 123 — "Read the Pinch"

## Emphasis and Objective
Read and react to aggressive defensemen and create a breakouts.

## Drill Set-Up
* F's in zone in defensive positions, 2 D's at blue-line.
* On the whistle, F3 passes the puck up the wall to F2, D1 pinches aggressively, F1 communicates where the puck should be placed ("boards" or "center'), D1 finishes check and gets back up ice, F1 and F3 attack D1.

## Key Teaching Points
* Read the situation.
* D time the pinch.
* Communication.
* Puck movement.

## Recommended Progressions
* Add an additional back checking forward creating a 3 v 3.

# "Read the Pinch"

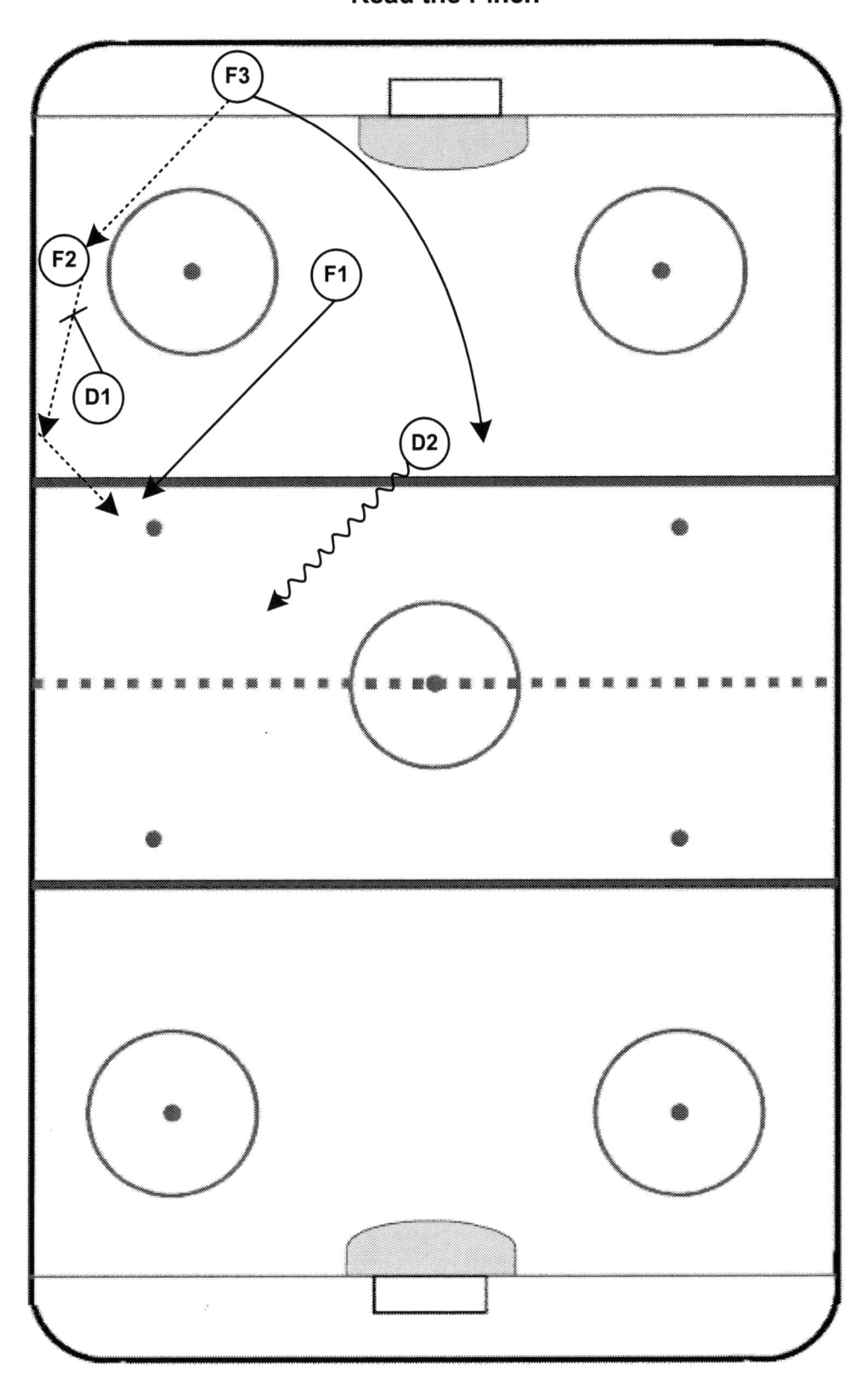

# 124     Pivot and Shoot

## Emphasis and Objective

Improve skating and shooting skills of defensemen.

## Drill Set-Up

- D positioned on both sides at the blue-lines, cones on the hash marks and top of circles.
- D skates forwards to the hash mark cone, simulates a poke check, pivots around the cone, moves laterally to the inside cone, skates to the blue-line, picks up a puck and moves laterally across the blue-line for a point shot.
- Alternate sides.

## Key Teaching Points

- Head up.
- Quick feet.
- Balance.
- Lateral movement to the shooting area.

## Recommended Progressions

- None.

**Pivot and Shoot**

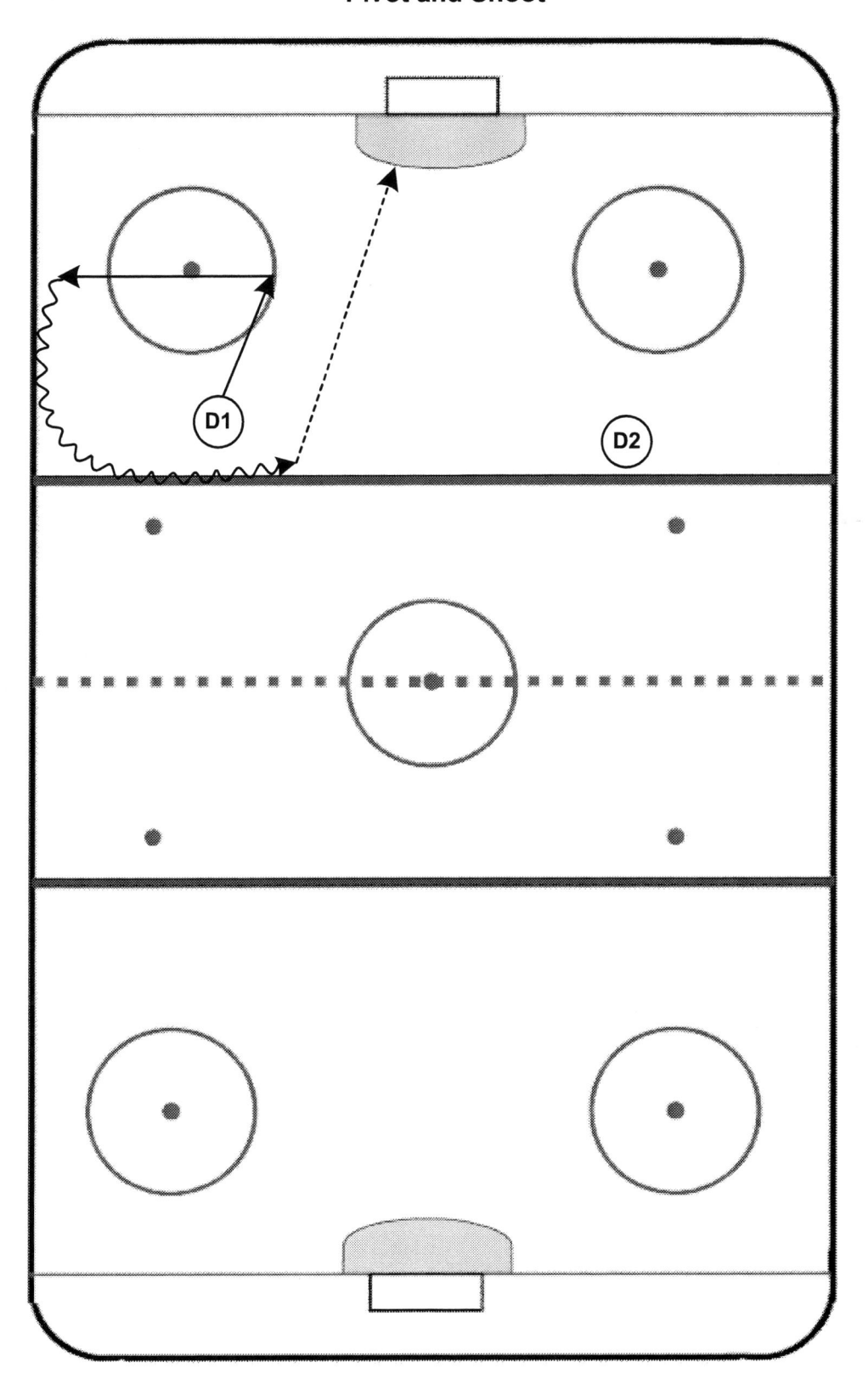

# 125     Quick Feet and Pass

## Emphasis and Objective
Work on foot speed and passing skills of defensemen.

## Drill Set-Up
* D's divide into groups at each face-off circle.
* D1 on the face-off spot with pucks, D2 facing D1 on the edge of the circle.
* D1 starts drill by skating to the top of the circle, giving a pass to D2 and skating backwards to the dot.
* D1 continues by skating laterally and backwards in the circle exchanging passes with D2.

## Key Teaching Points
* Quick feet.
* Head up.
* Forehand and backhand passes.
* Drill diagram enlarged to show detail.

## Recommended Progressions
* None.

# Quick Feet and Pass

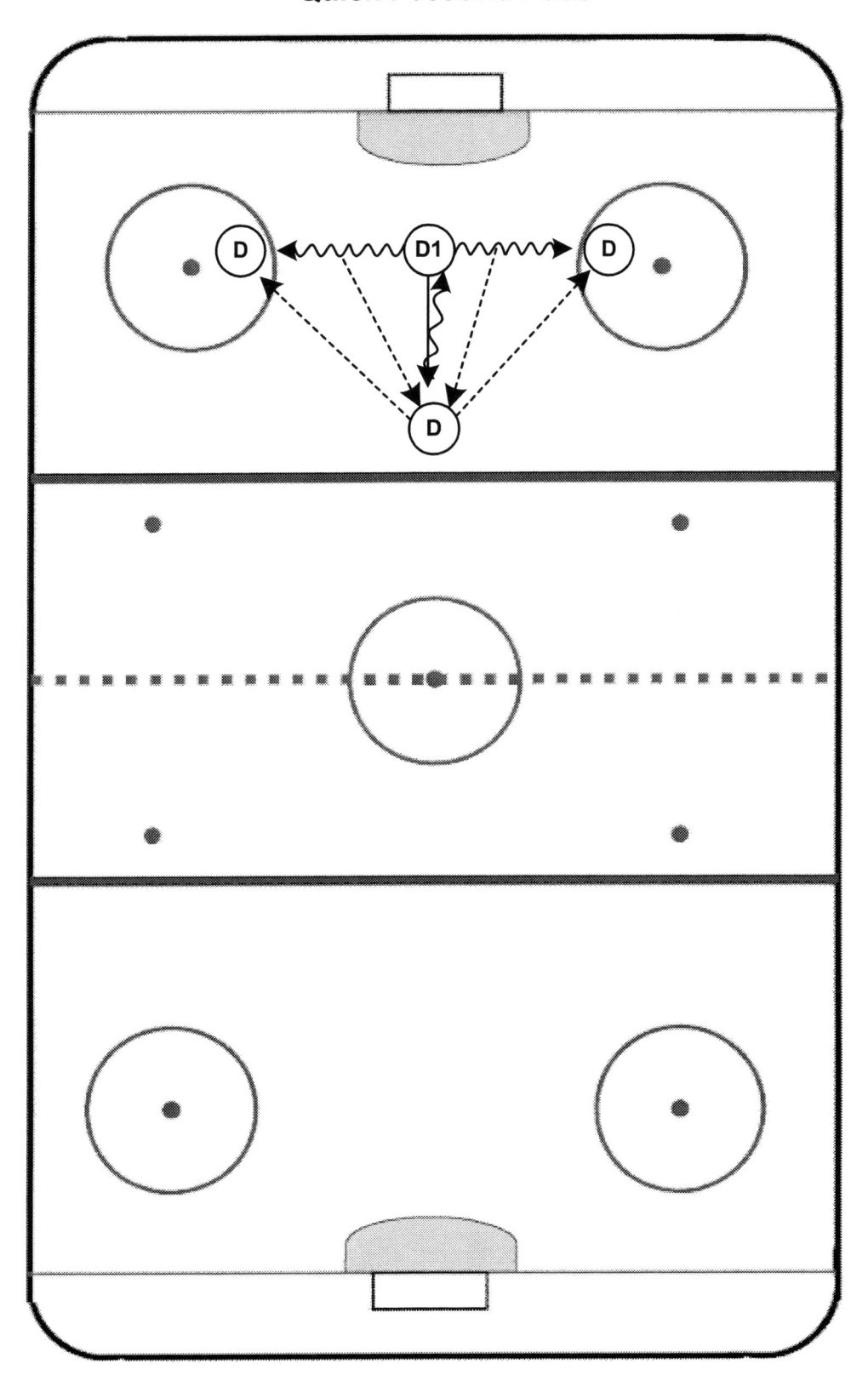

# 126 D Agility Skate and Shoot

## Emphasis and Objective
Drill to work on defensemen's agility skating and handling the puck.

## Drill Set-Up
- C behind the goal-line with pucks, D in the corner on the goal-line.
- D begins drill by skating backwards to the top of the near circle, proceeding to the bottom of the far circle and on to the blue-line.
- Once the D gets to the hash mark on the far wall, C rims a pass to the D. D must control the hard around, move to the shooting area and shoot on net.
- Be sure to switch sides.

## Key Teaching Points
- Head up.
- Quick feet.
- Move to shooting areas.
- Shots on target.

## Recommended Progressions
- None.

# D Agility Skate & Shoot

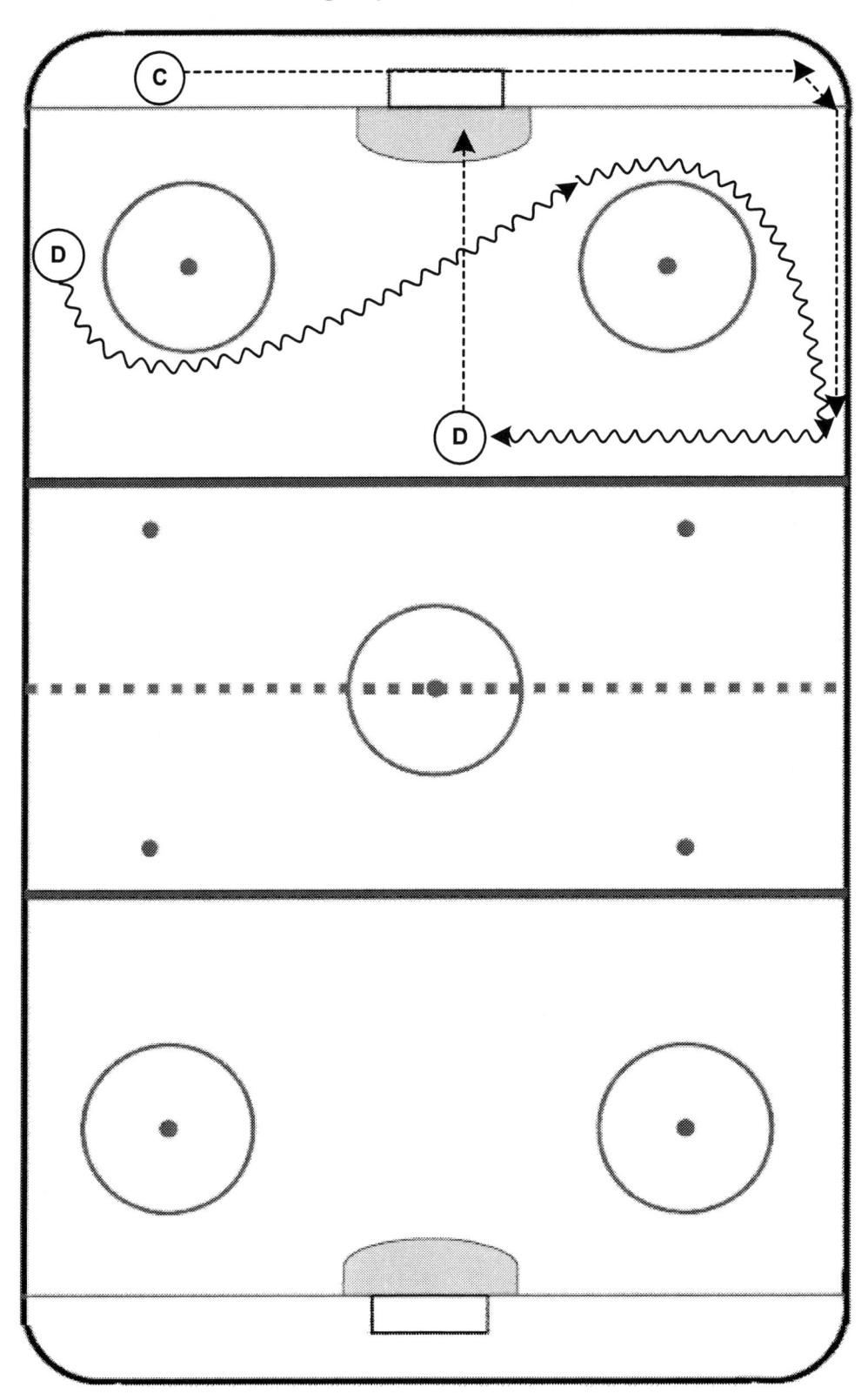

## Double Fake Point Shot

### Emphasis and Objective
Drill for quick feet and shooting.

### Drill Set-Up
* Pucks on the wall, 15-20 feet inside zone, D even with the face-off dot.
* D skates to loose puck, skates backwards to blue-line, moves laterally to the shooting area, fakes a shot, changes the shooting lane for a shot on goal.
* After D skates to the opposite boards and performs a similar action.

### Key Teaching Points
* Quick feet.
* Head up.
* Handle puck while moving.
* Hard shots on target.

### Recommended Progressions
* None.

# Double Fake Point Shot

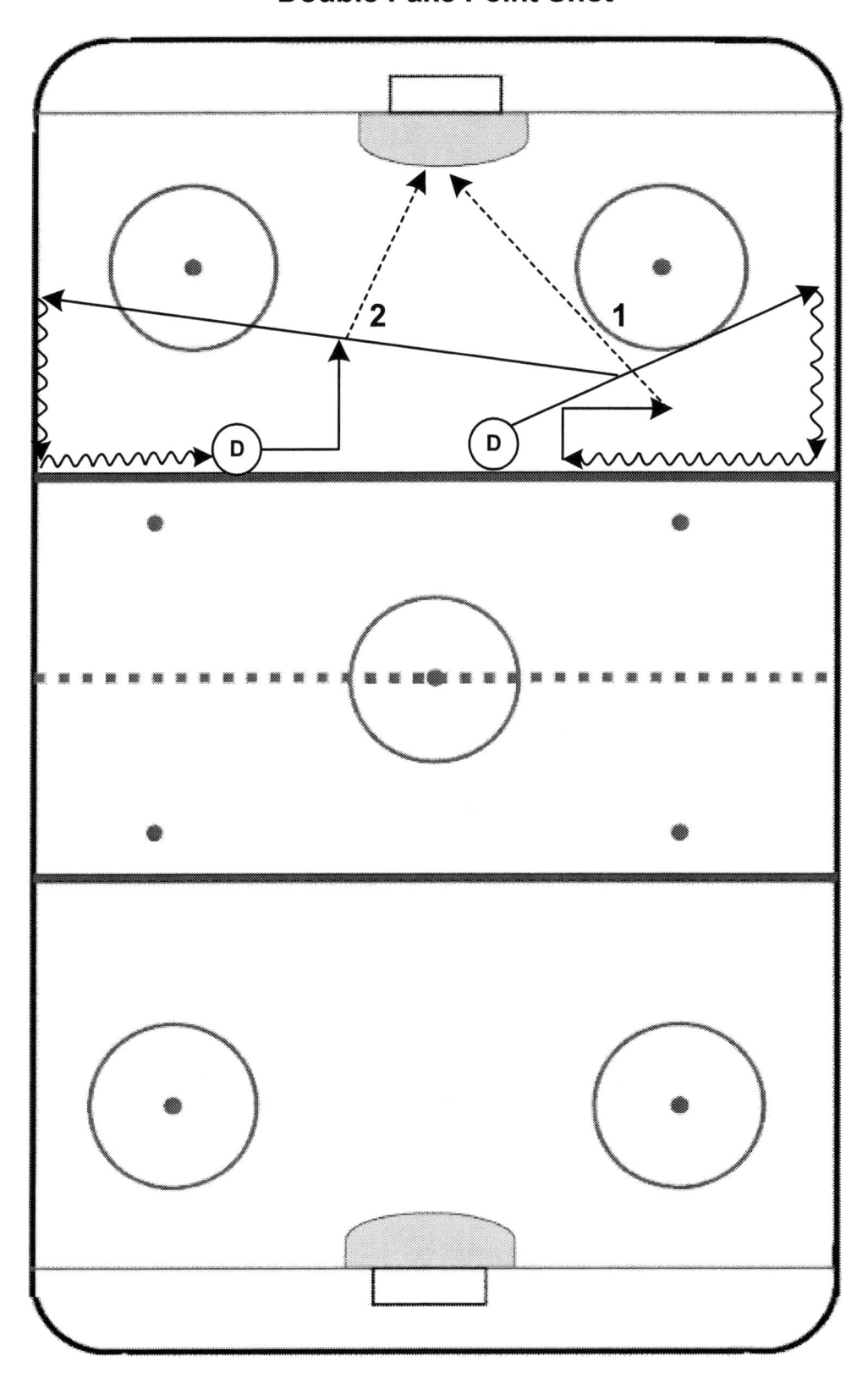

# 128        Spartan 3, 1 v 1

## Emphasis and Objective

Work on 1 v 1 skills from different spots in the offensive zone.

## Drill Set-Up

* C on the blue-line with pucks. F1 positioned in the corner, F2 at the opposite half board and F3 inside the blue-line. D1 in front of net, even with the hash marks.
* C will start the drill by passing to either F1, F2 or F3 who then attack the goal with D1 defending 1 v 1.
* On 1st whistle, D1 gets back to his original position and the C C passes to 1 of the remaining F's for a 1 v 1 attack.
* On the 2nd whistle, C passes to the remaining F for the 3rd 1 v 1.

## Key Teaching Points

* D keep feet moving while defending.
* D angle F to the corner.
* F's protect the puck and attack.

## Recommended Progressions

* 2 v 1, 2 v 2.

# Spartan 3 1 v 1

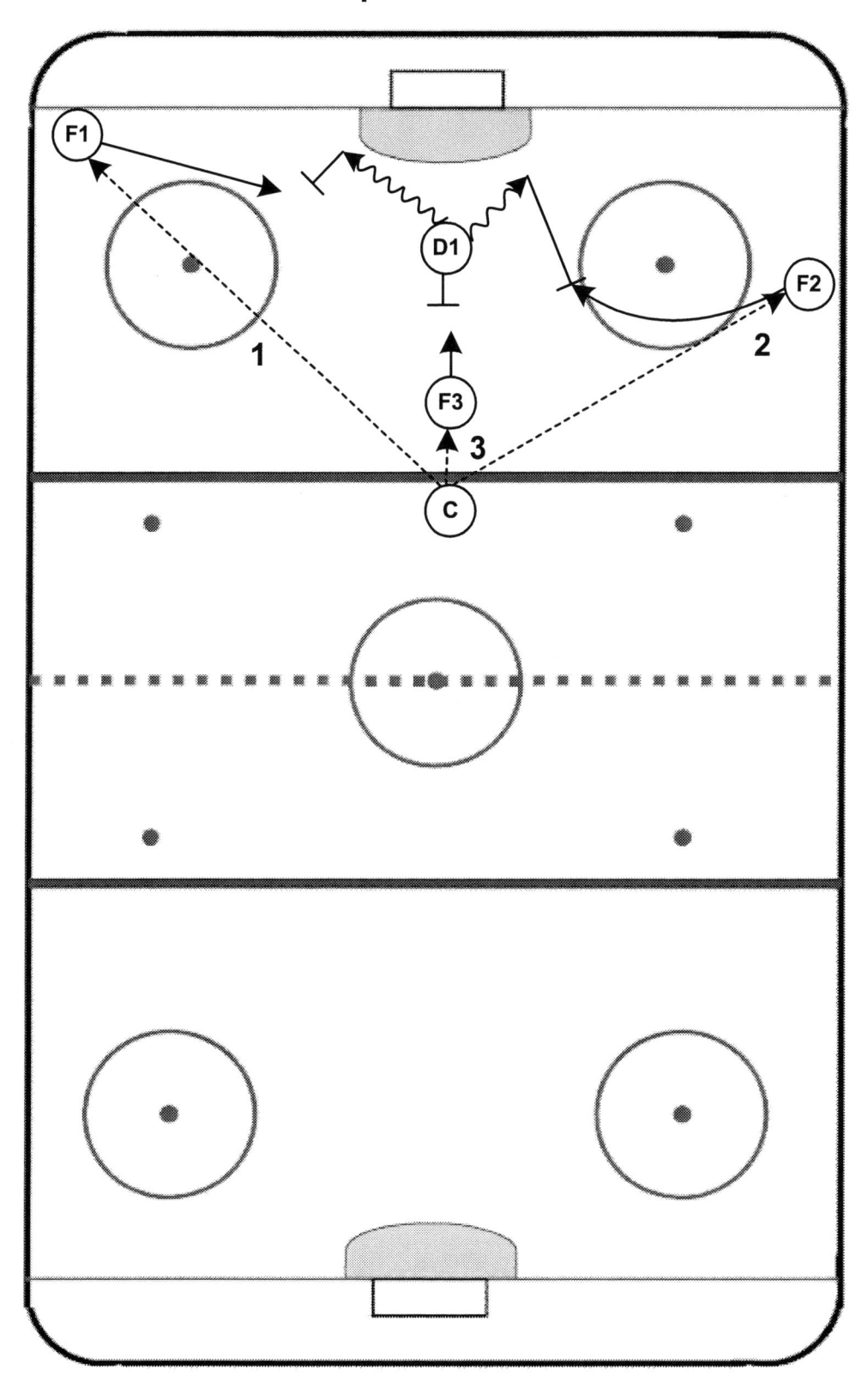

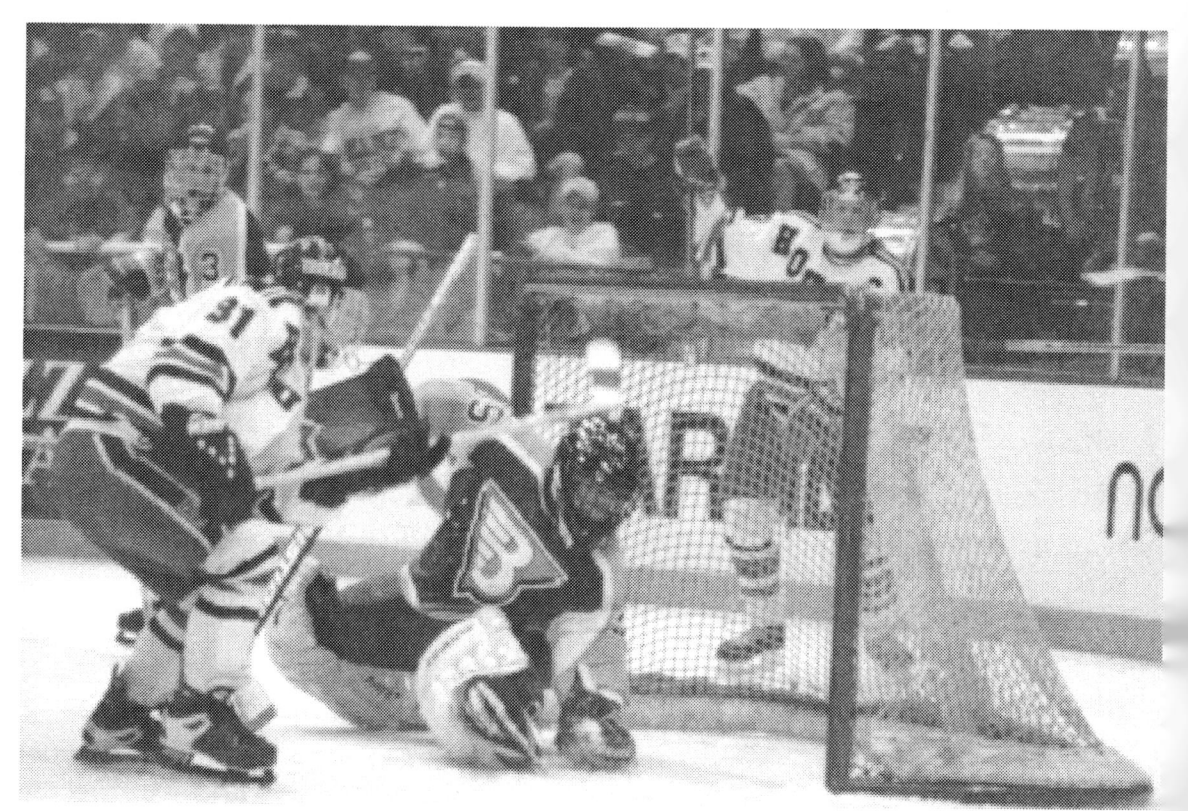

Photo courtesy of Mike Thill

# 8

# Specialized Goaltender Drills

It is true that goaltenders do get work in practice in each and every full ice team drill. However, goaltenders, like forwards and defensemen, need specialized attention.

This section provides for that specific attention. While team drills test the mettle and concentration skills of your goaltenders, these drills reinforce and stress the necessary fundamentals for the position.

Goaltending is a highly critical and specialized position and the skills and fundamentals can always be improved. At all levels, the basics of the position and base fundamentals should be reinforced. Once the fundamentals of the position are learned, continued development can occur.

Be sure to have your goaltenders participate in your team skating and stickhandling drills. Skating and puck handling are key components for today's goaltender.

Challenge and require your goaltenders to be good in practice. Keep track of saves and make them compete in all drills. Good practice habits for goaltenders determine their performance in games and spur development.

## 129 Behind the Net, Pass and React

### Emphasis and Objective

Present goalies with passes from behind the goal line in preparation for a variety of shots.

### Drill Set-Up

* Two nets, back to back.
* 6 shooters, 3 in front of each net.
* Players pass the puck to players stationed in front of opposite net.
* Player can shoot or return a pass to opposite side.

### Key Teaching Points

* Goalies must react to pass.
* Challenge the shooter.
* Angles.
* Goaltender foot work.
* Quick shots.

### Recommended Progressions

* None.

# Behind the net, Pass & React

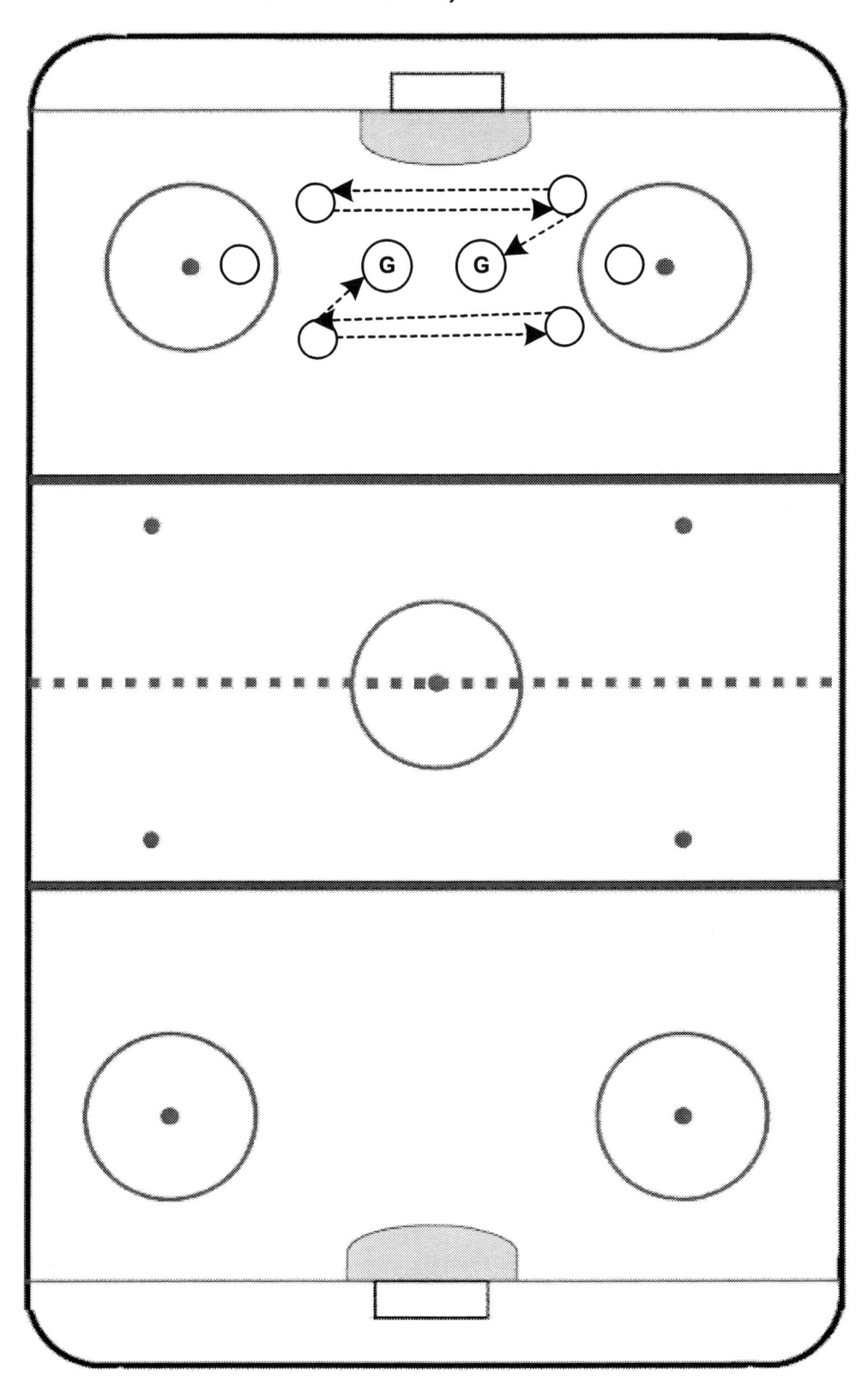

# 130     Goal-line Drive

## Emphasis and Objective

Work on offensive plays from a goal-line drive. Improve ice vision.

## Drill Set-Up

* F1's positioned in corner, F2's on hash mark of opposite in zone face-off circle.
* Pucks in F1's corner.
* On the whistle, F1 drives the goal-line while F2 positions to receive a pass and shoots.
* F1 has 4 options:
    1. Drive the goal-line and pass to F2 immediately.
    2. Skate behind the net and pass to F2.
    3. Skate around the net and walk out for shot.
    4. Use a wrap-around attack.

## Key Teaching Points

* Keep feet moving.
* Head up at all times.
* F2 must be available as an option at all time in good shooting position.
* Goaltender must move laterally and use angles.

## Recommended Progressions

* Add a defenseman for a 2 v 1.

# Goal-line Drive

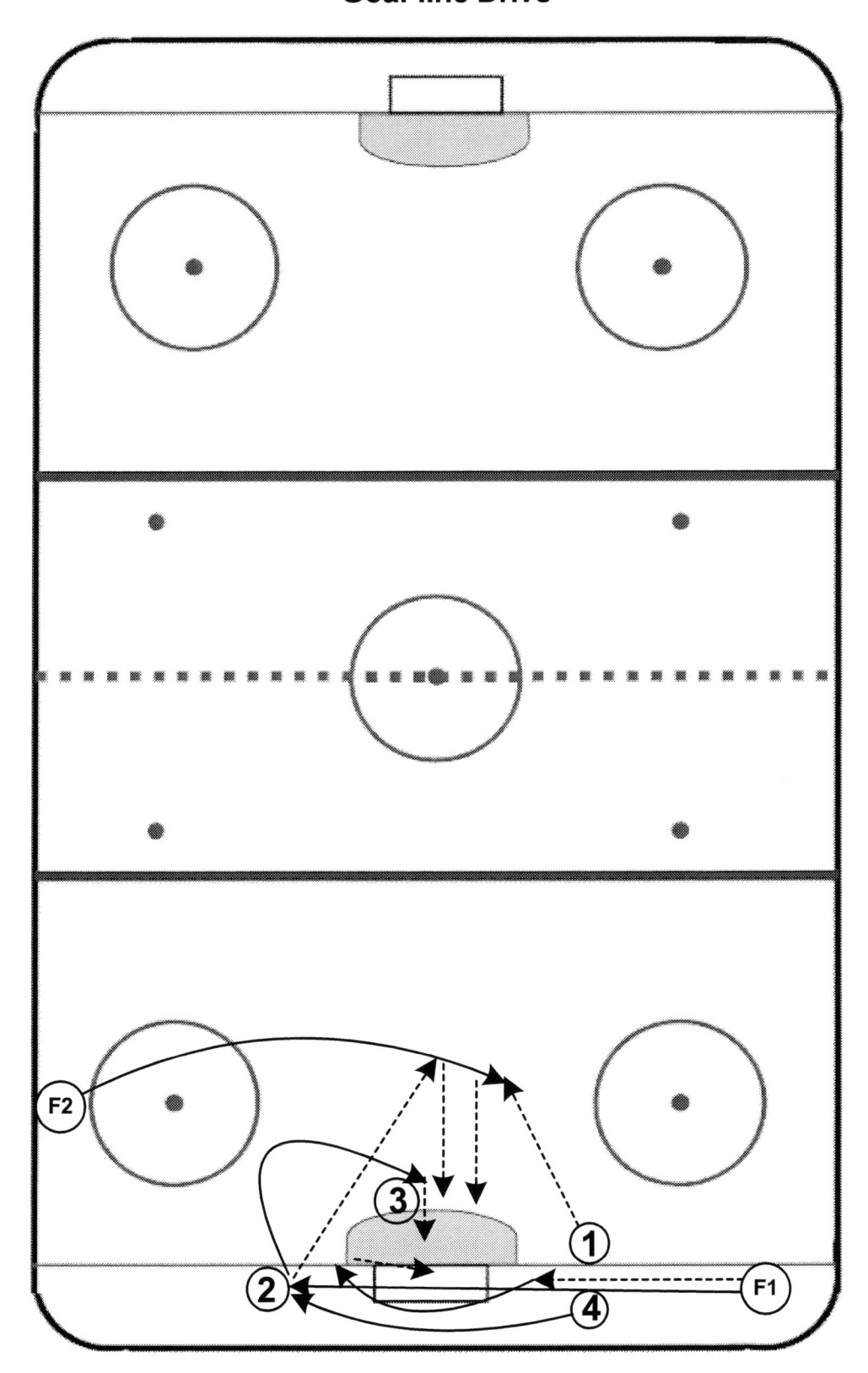

# 131 — 1 Touch Rapid Fire

## Emphasis and Objective
1 time shooting, 1 time passing.

## Drill Set-Up
- Goalies in net, use both ends.
- C on the blue-line with pucks, X's on the top of circles on off sides.
- C passes to either side, player receives pass and one touch passes across ice to partner for a 1 time shot.

## Key Teaching Points
- Good hard passes.
- Keep shots low and on net.
- Work on weight transfer.

## Recommended Progressions
- Add additional passes.

# 1 Touch Rapid Fire

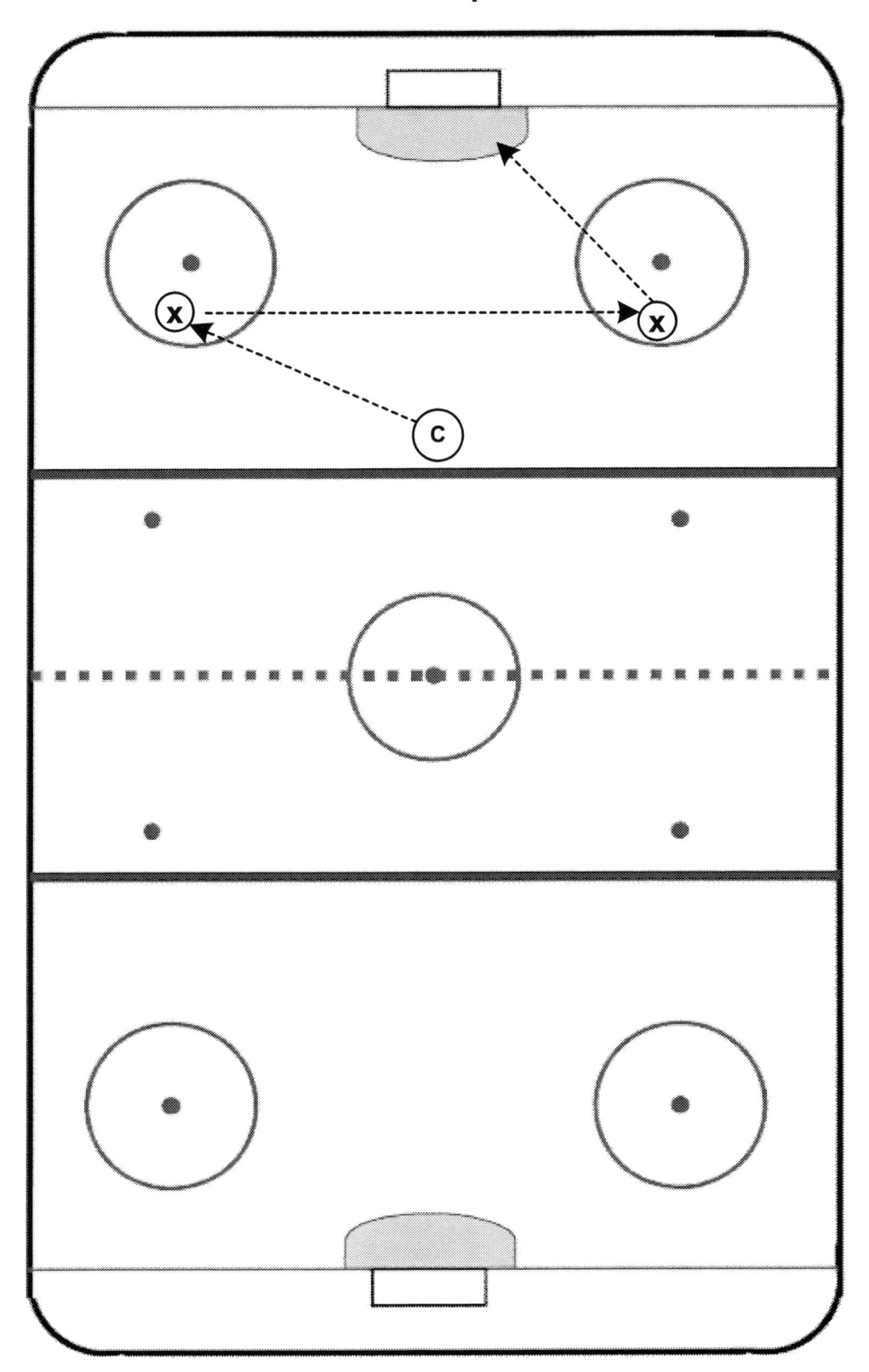

# 132     Triangle 3 Man 1 Touch

## Emphasis and Objective

    1 time passing, 1 time shooting.

## Drill Set-Up

- Goalies in net.
- 3 players positioned in triangle formation on blue-line and tops of circles.
- Players 1 touch the puck around the triangle alternating shooters.
- Be sure all players operate on all 3 sides of the triangle.

## Key Teaching Points

- 1 touch passes a must.
- Passes must be tape to tape.
- Shots low and on net.
- Learn comfort zone for passing and shooting.

## Recommended Progressions

- None

# Tri-Angle 3 Man 1-Touch

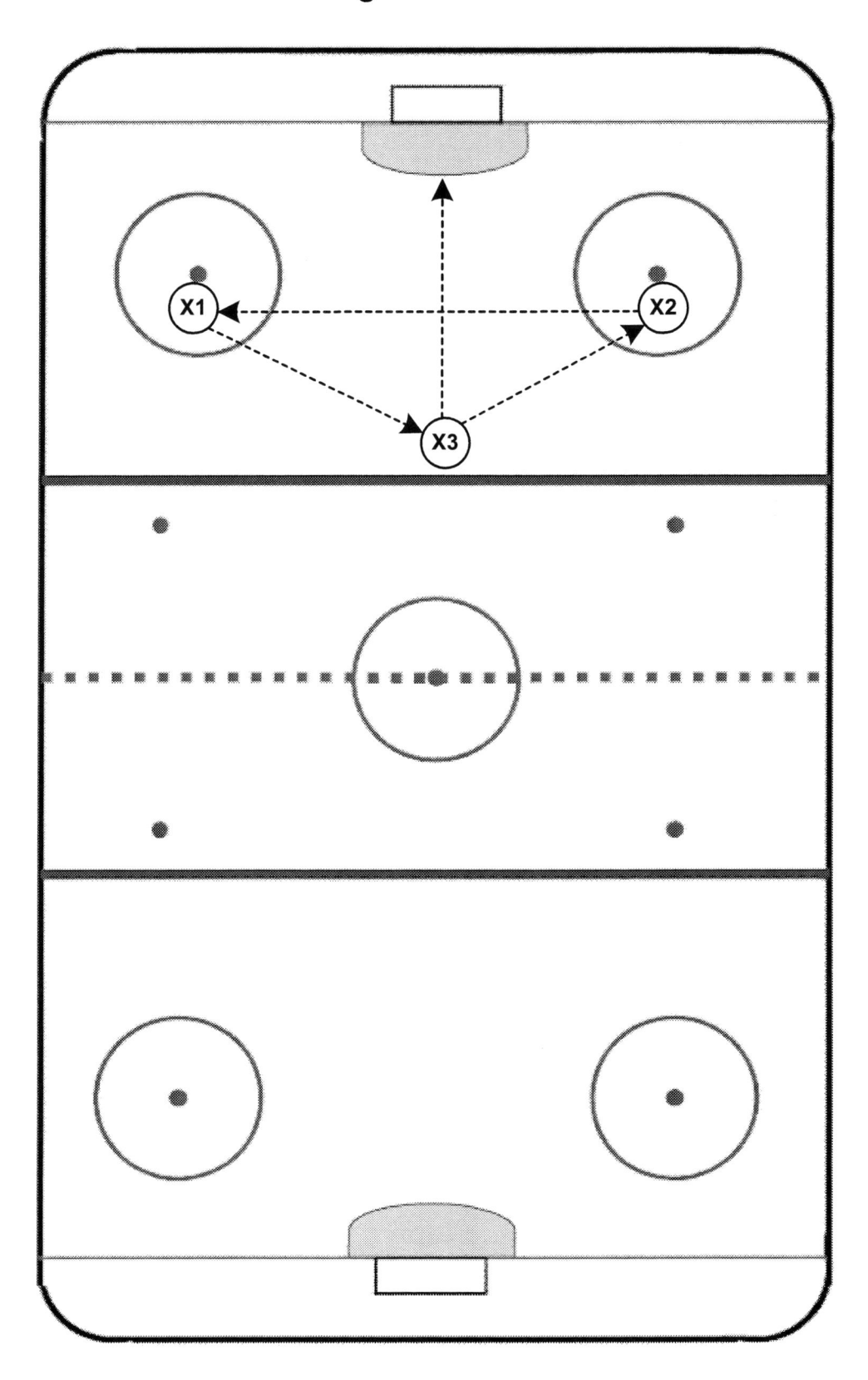

# 133 — 3 Dekes

## Emphasis and Objective

Work on dekes from various angles.

## Drill Set-Up

- Players in 3 lines, (on the boards, in the middle and at the opposite boards) on each blue-line with pucks.
- Alternating lines, players attack the goaltender in their lane and attempt to deke and score.

## Key Teaching Points

- Head up, puck in front of the shooter at all times.
- Allow goaltender to recover from previous shooter.
- Be shooters alternate lines.

## Recommended Progressions

- Add a chaser.

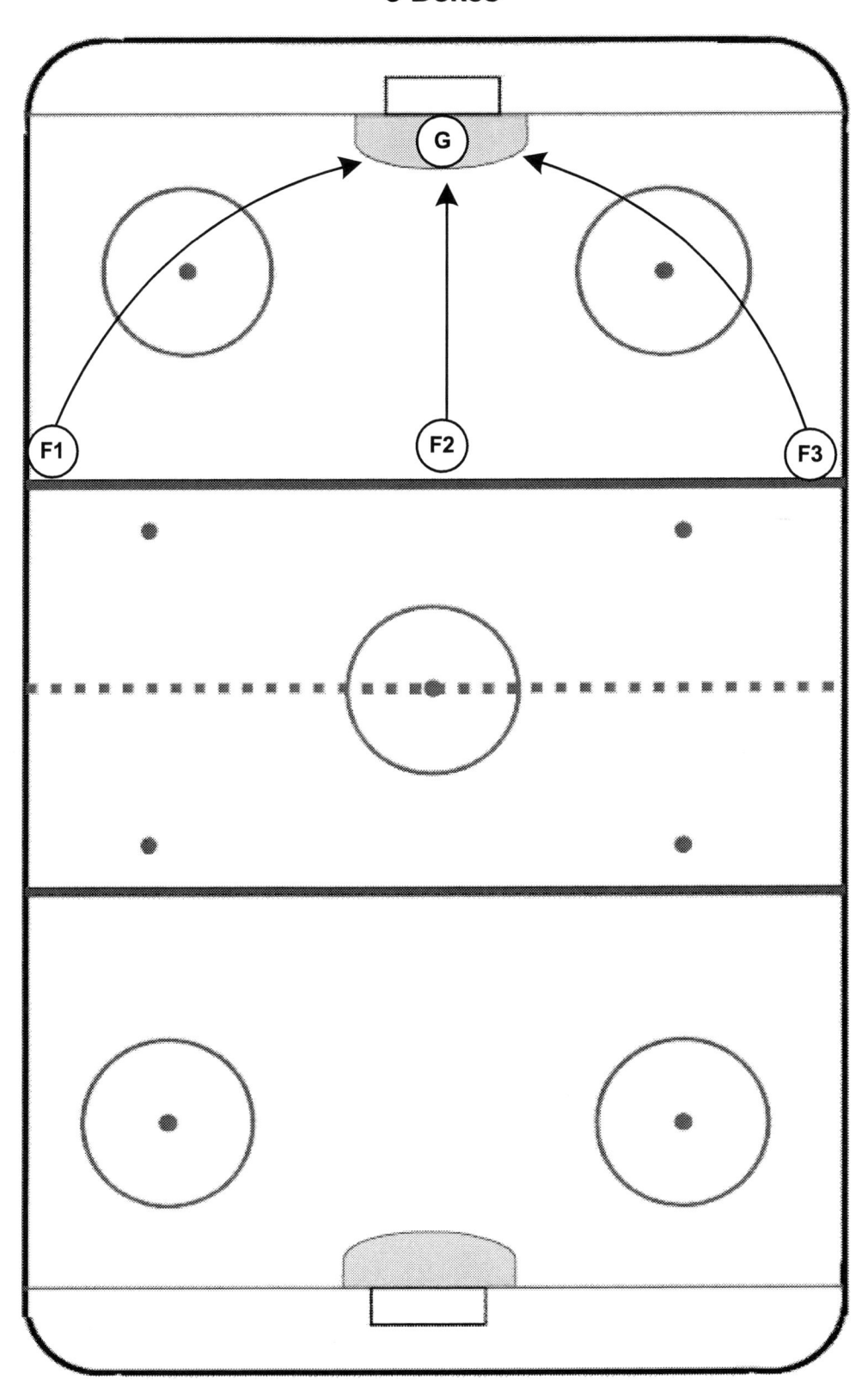

# 3 Dekes

# Corner 3 v 1

## Emphasis and Objective

Work on goaltender and forward movement in a small area.

## Drill Set-Up

- Nets moved the to bottom of the in zone face-off circles, each facing the corners, puck in the crease with C.
- One F always behind the net, 2 F's and 1 D in front.
- C passes to the F behind the net who has all options available: wrap around, pass, give and go etc.
- One F must always be behind the net, players must rotate and make plays quickly.

## Key Teaching Points

- Head on a swivel.
- Positioning.
- Goaltender movement.
- Forwards must move to get open.

## Recommended Progressions

- Add another D for a 3 v 2.

**Corner 3 v 1**

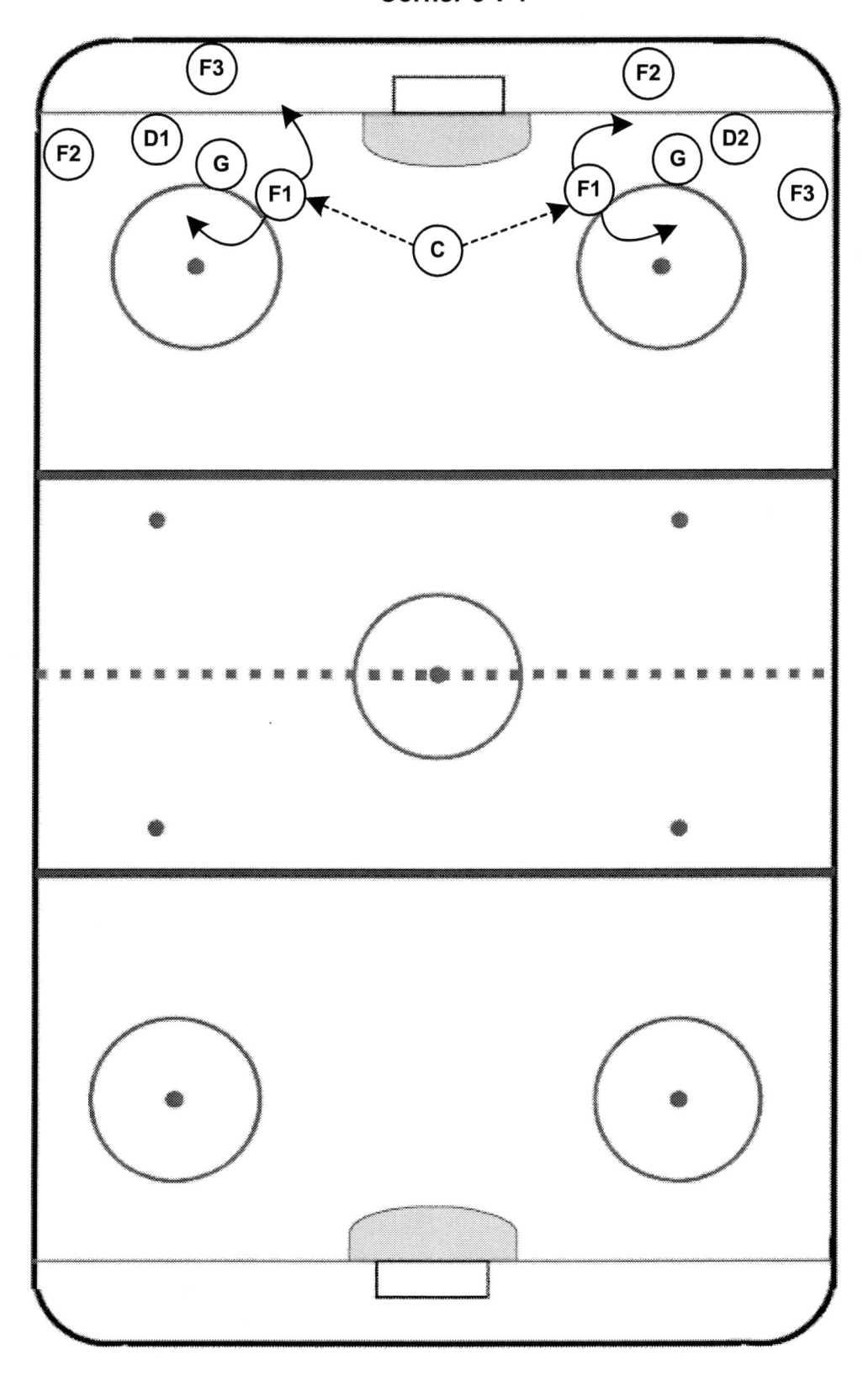

## 135 — Attack the Goal Line, 2 Shots

### Emphasis and Objective
Give shooters and goaltenders work on shots from different angles.

### Drill Set-Up
* 2 lines of shooters (F1 and F2), 1 on each face-off dot.
* F1 skates to the outside of the face-off circle, receives a pass from the next person in line and drives the goal-line for a shot.
* After taking the first shot, F1 back peddles and gets into shooting position and receives a pass from F2 in the high slot.
* F2 then skates to the outside of the face-off circle, receives a pass from the next person in line and drives the goal-line for a shot and continues.

### Key Teaching Points
* Handle and move the puck quickly.
* Challenge the goaltender.
* Shoot to score, realistic shots and opportunities.

### Recommended Progressions
* None.

# Attack the Goal Line, 2 Shots

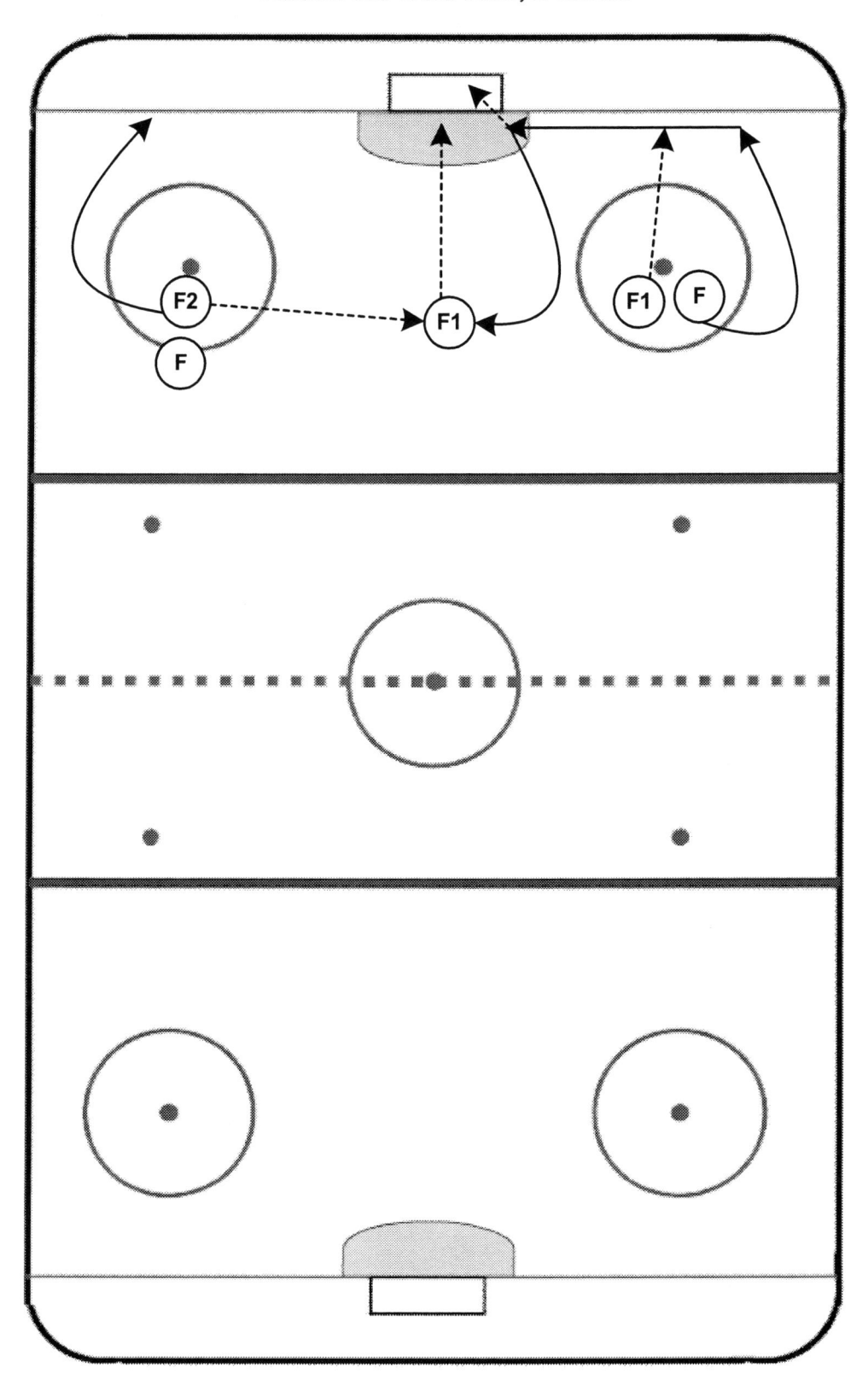

# 136     Drive the Net

## Emphasis and Objective

Work on footwork, passing, driving the net while protecting the puck and scoring.

## Drill Set-Up

* F's in opposite corners, D in 2 lines at opposite sides of the red-line.
* On the whistle, D1 touch passes to a backwards skating D2 and D3 touch passes to a backwards skating D4.
* D2 and D4 pivot or escape controlling the puck and looking to pass to F1 and F2.
* Timing the play so they receive the pass prior to the blue-line and at full speed, F1 and F2 take off down the wall, receive a pass, accelerate through the neutral zone and drive the net.
* F's attempt to score on the rush.
* On the whistle with goaltenders in position, next group proceeds.

## Key Teaching Points

* Foot work.
* Timing to receive a pass full speed.
* Puck protection.
* Goaltender challenge the shooter.

## Recommended Progressions

* 1 v 1 with passing D defending opposite attacking F.

# Drive the Net

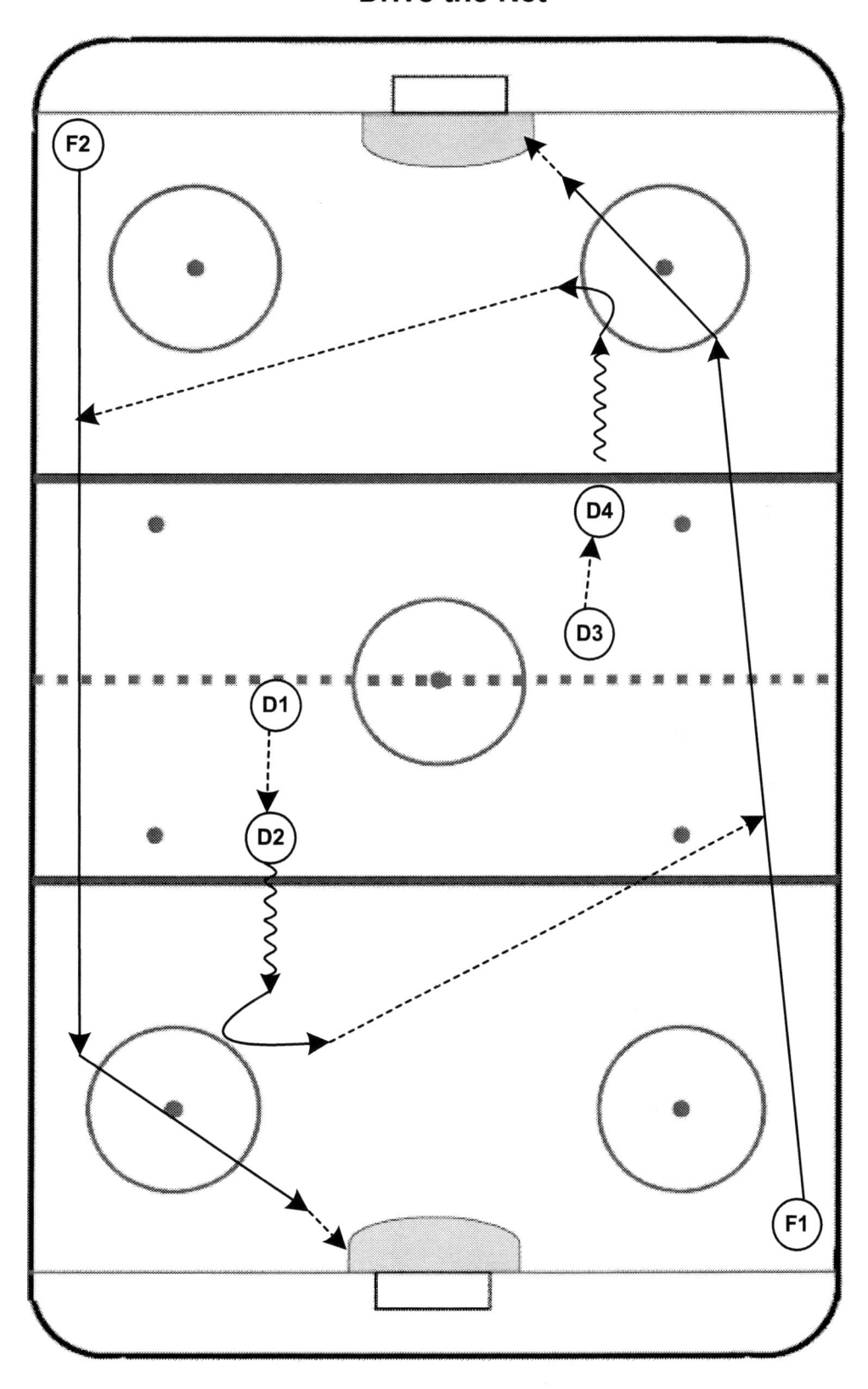

# 137 — High Slot, Drive Across

## Emphasis and Objective
Goaltender drill for shots and recovery.

## Drill Set-Up
- F1, with speed drives the shooting lane, cuts at the hash marks and shoots on goal from the slot.
- After a quick G recovery, F2 drives the shooting lane and cuts across the crease for a shot.

## Key Teaching Points
- G must track and challenge the shooter.
- Quick recovery under control.
- Controlled movement side to side.
- Rebound control.

## Recommended Progressions
- None.

# High Slot, Drive Across

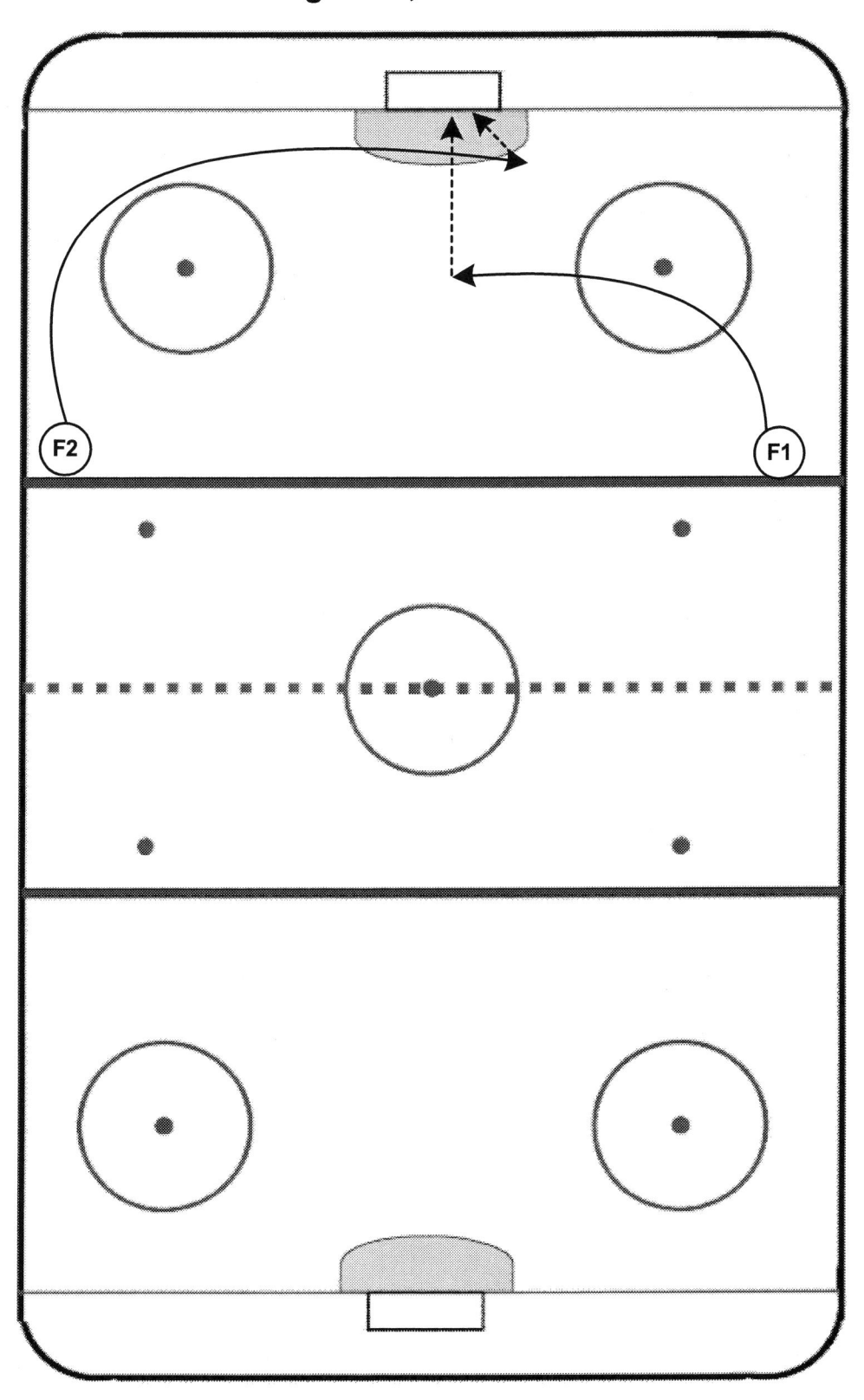

# 138 — Drive the Lane and Tip

## Emphasis and Objective
Goaltender drill for movement and recovery.

## Drill Set-Up
* C in center with pucks, X's in two groups, one at each blue-line.
* On the whistle, X1 drives the shooting lane, shoots in stride and follows the shot to the slot.
* While in front of the net and screening the goaltender, C fires a shot on goal for a tip/screen.
* Play until the whistle.

## Key Teaching Points
* Goaltender movement.
* Challenge the shooter.
* Square to the shooter.
* Rebound control.

## Recommended Progressions
* None.

# Drive the Lane and Tip

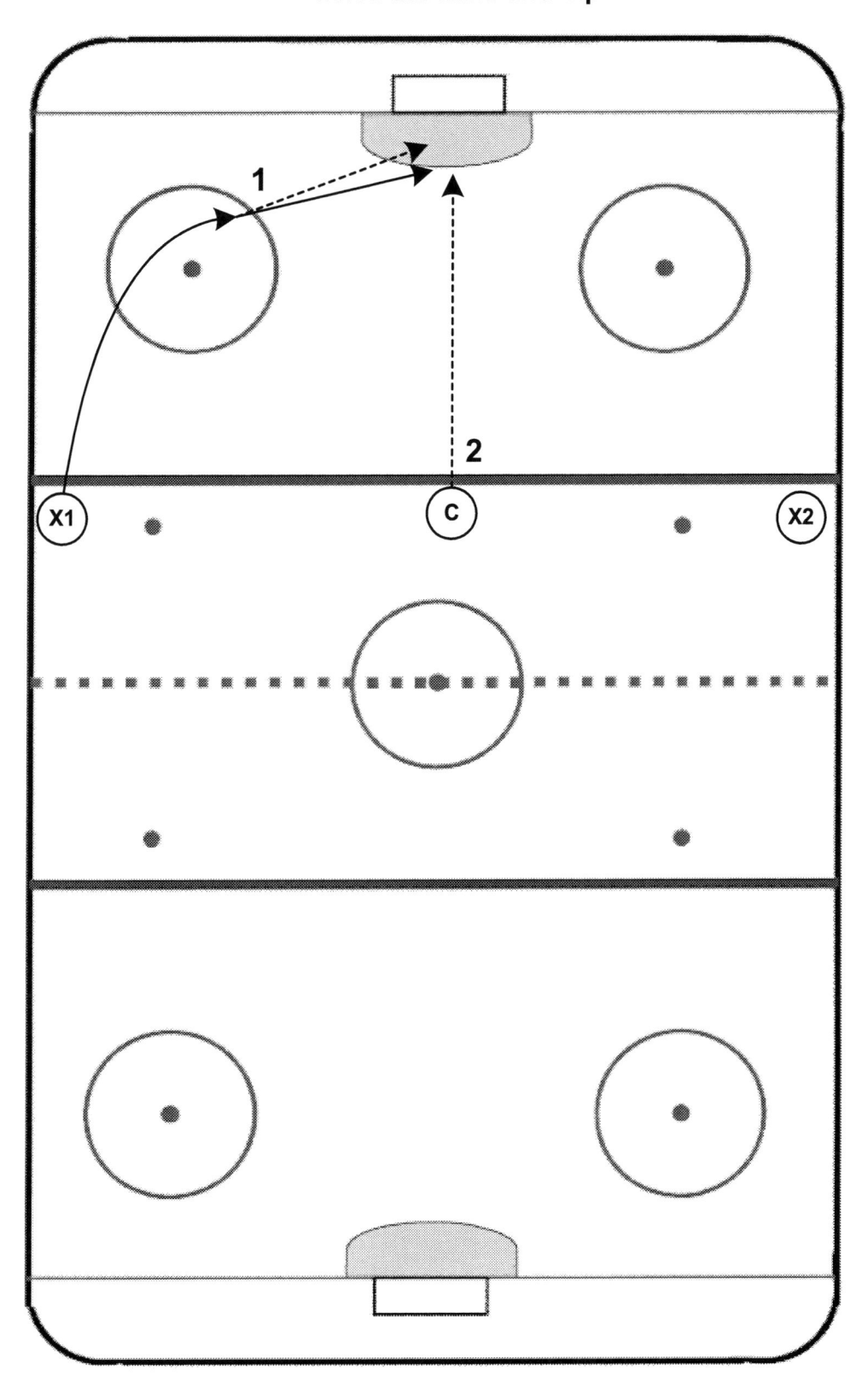

# 139     Side to Side

## Emphasis and Objective

Goaltender drill for side to side movement.

## Drill Set-Up

* X1 on blue-line, even with face-off dot, X2 on the opposite hash mark, pucks with X1 and behind goal.
* X1 drives the shooting lane and shoots on the angle.
* After shooting, X1 picks up a puck behind the goal and looks for a breaking X2.
* X2 shoots on goal.
* Alternate sides.

## Key Teaching Points

* Square to the shooter, move side to side.
* Recovery and rebound control.

## Recommended Progressions

* None.

# Side to Side

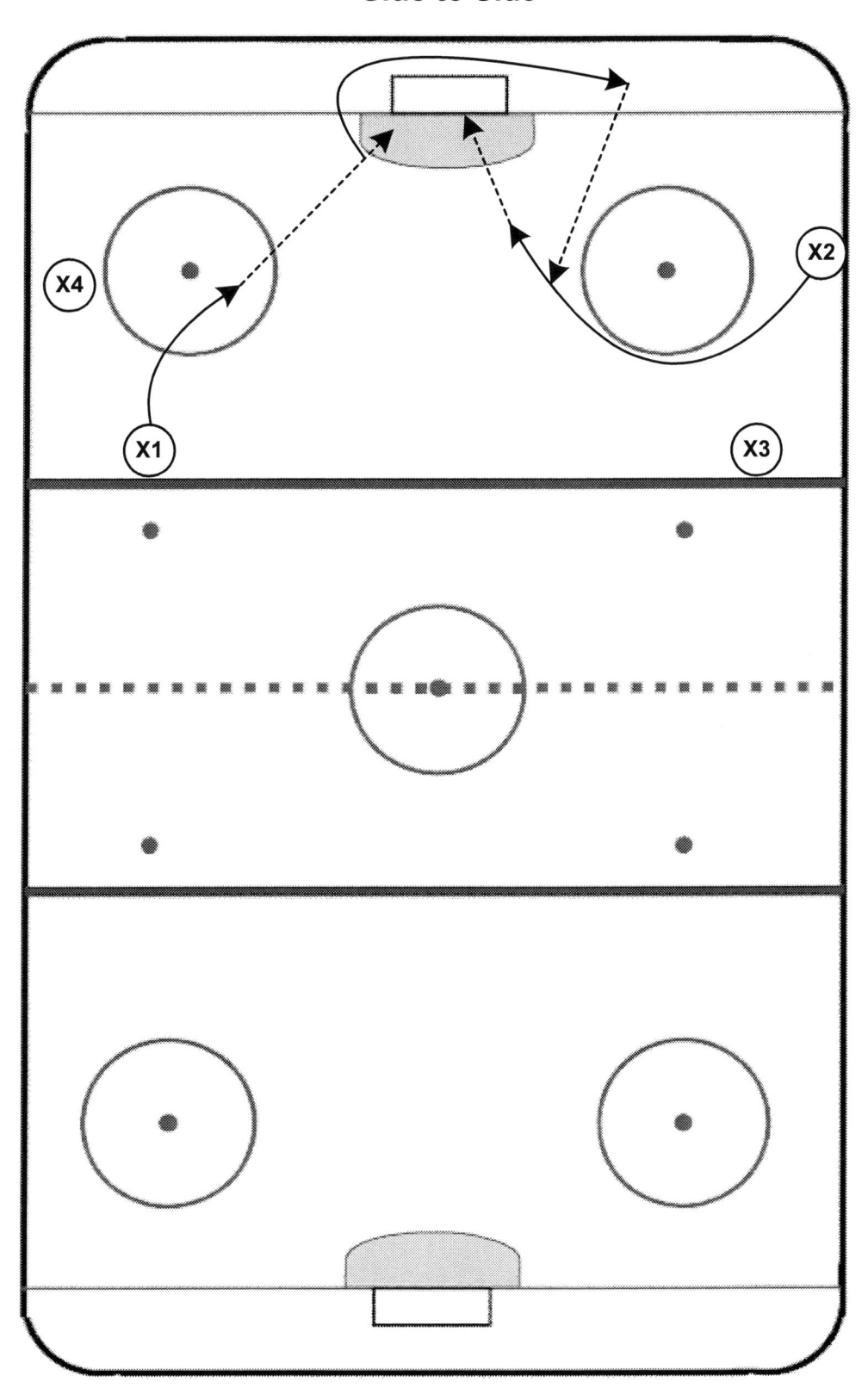

# 140     Long Shot, Rebound

### Emphasis and Objective
    Goaltender drill for rebound control.

### Drill Set-Up
- C behind goal-line with pucks, X's in two groups, one at each blue-line.
- X1 passes across ice to X2, X2 drives the lane and shoots on an angle.
- After initial shot, X2 goes to the front of the goal and receives a rebound pass from C.
- Play until the whistle on the rebound shot.
- Be sure to switch side of attack.

### Key Teaching Points
- Goaltender movement.
- Rebound control.
- Square to the shooter.
- Challenge and control rebound shot.

### Recommended Progressions
- None.

# Long Shot, Rebound

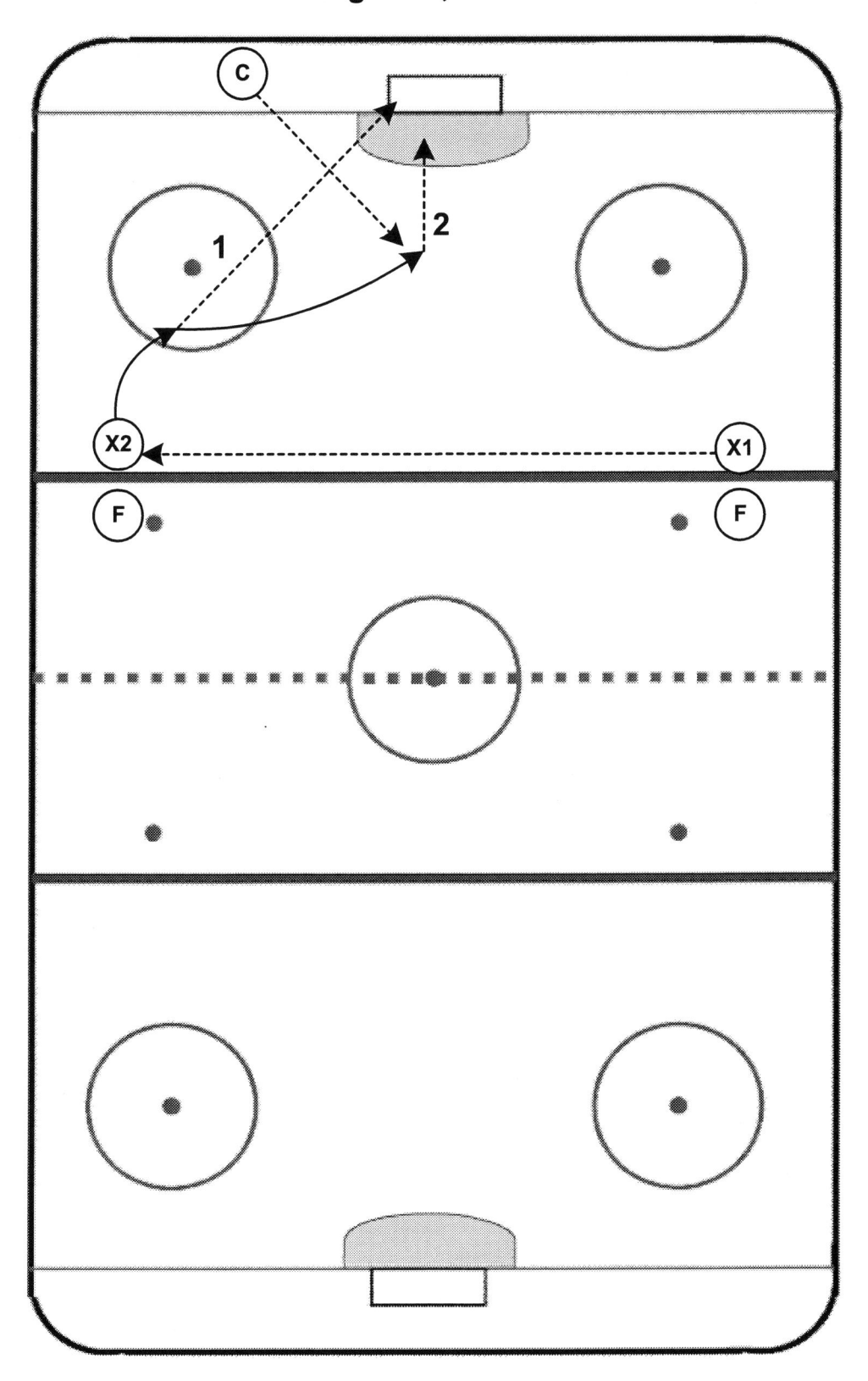

# 141 — Breakout, Breakaway 1 v 1

## Emphasis and Objective

Goaltender drill for rebound control, puck handling and breakaway skills.

## Drill Set-Up

* X's in two groups, one at each neutral zone face-off dot.
* X1 shoots and long shot on goal, X2 moves into breakout position.
* G makes the save, controls the rebound and makes a breakout pass to X2 on the wall.
* X2 catches the pass, skates into the neutral zone and challenges G on a breakaway 1 v 1.

## Key Teaching Points

* Rebound control.
* Handle the puck.
* Challenge the shooter.
* Footwork.

## Recommended Progressions

* None.

# Breakout, Breakaway 1 v1

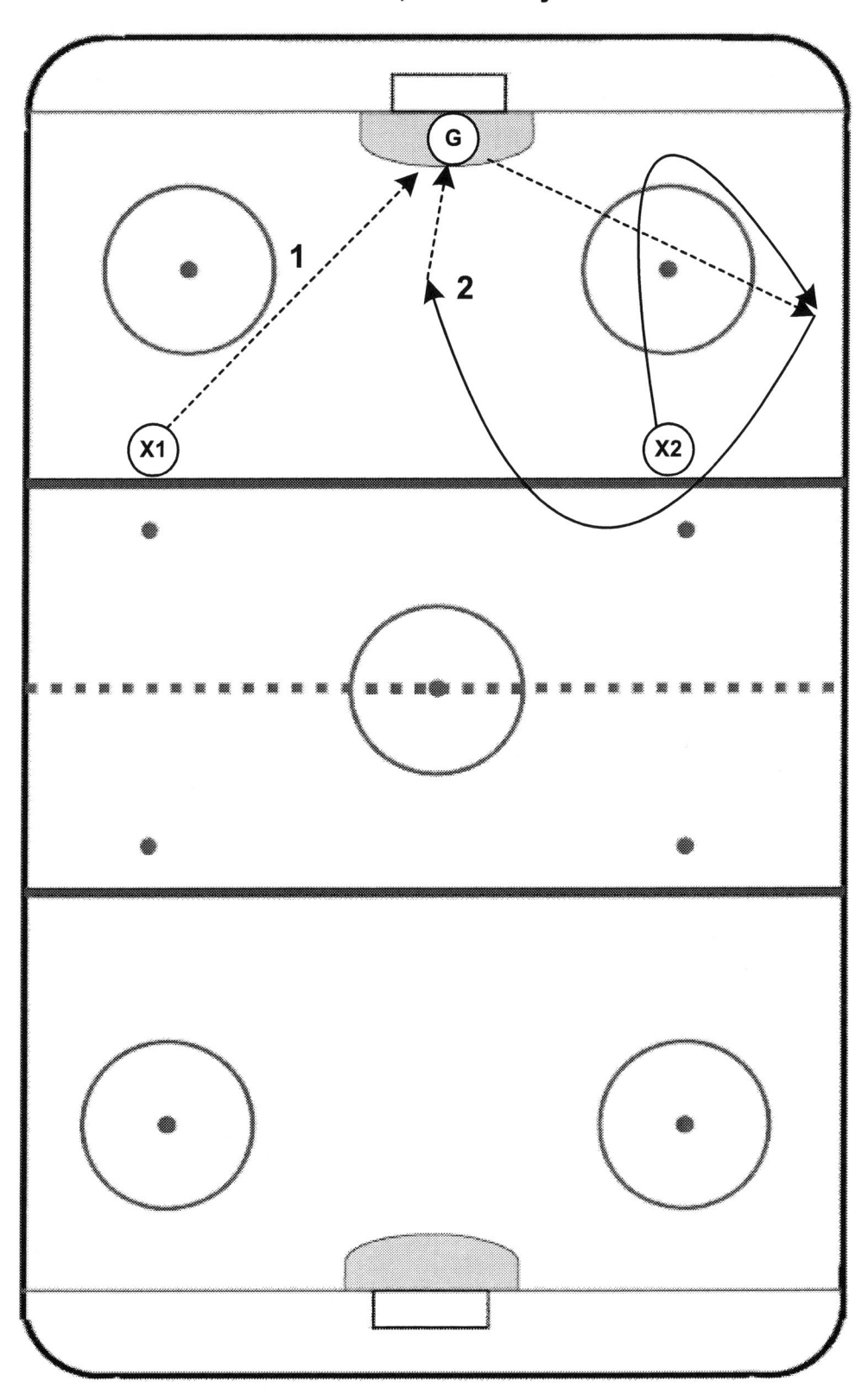

# 142 — Save and Quick Rim

## Emphasis and Objective

Goaltender drill for rebound control and stopping pucks behind goal and passing.

## Drill Set-Up

* X's in two groups, one at each blue-line.
* X1 shoots a long shot on goal, G stops it and immediately passes to X2 outside the blue-line.
* After the first pass, X1 rims the puck hard around the boards, G goes behind the net, controls the puck and immediately sends it up the boards and off the glass to X1.
* Alternate sides.

## Key Teaching Points

* Goaltender puck control.
* Control the puck behind the goal.
* Footwork.

## Recommended Progressions

* None.

# Save and Quick Rim

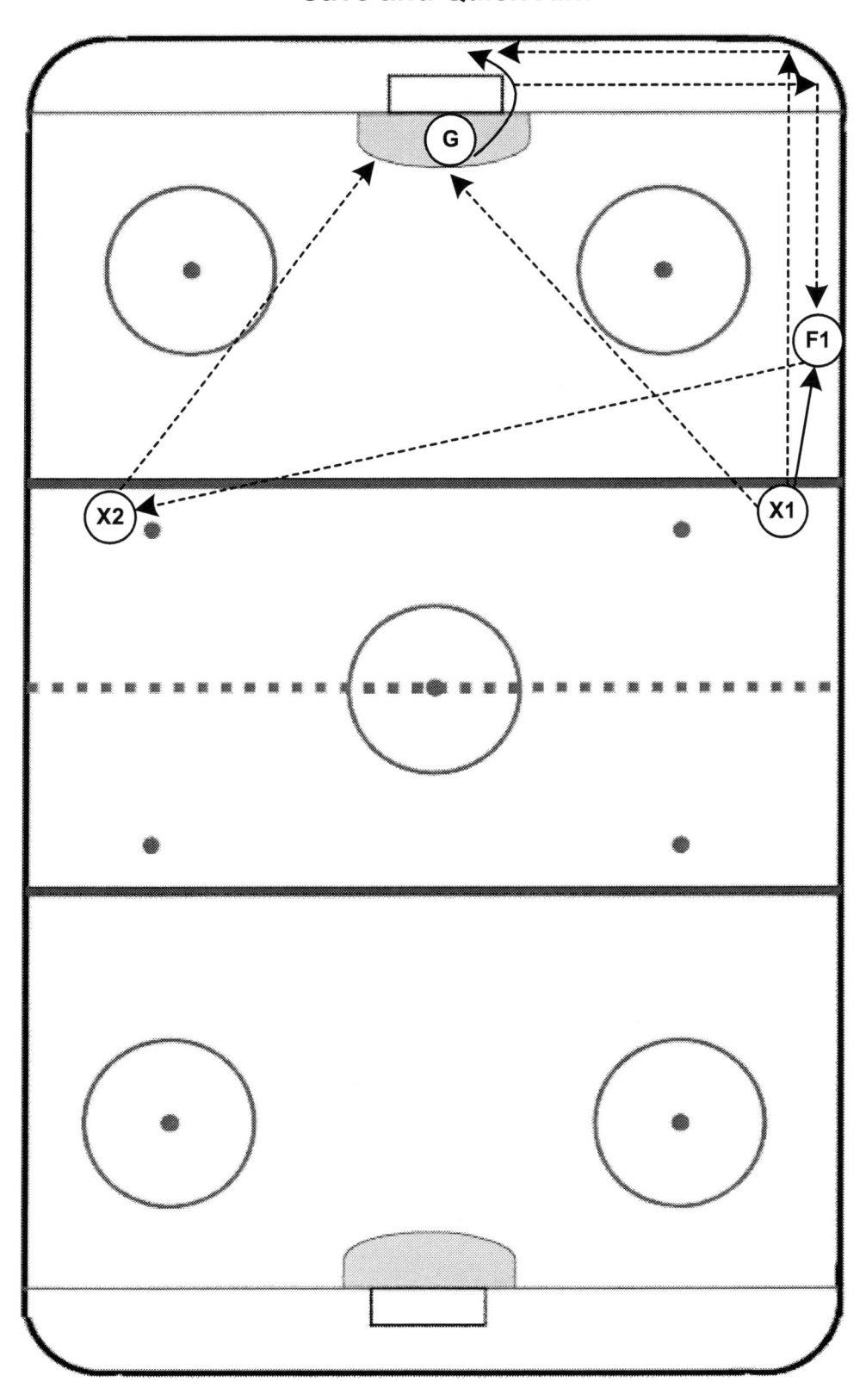

# 143 Rim and Recovery

## Emphasis and Objective
Goaltender drill for puck control and recovery.

## Drill Set-Up
- F's in two groups, one at each blue-line.
- F rims the puck around the boards, G goes behind the net, controls the puck and passes back to F.
- Once F receives the pass, G returns to the net and faces a quick recovery shot.
- Alternate sides.

## Key Teaching Points
- Goaltender movement.
- Puck control.
- Recovery.

## Recommended Progressions
- None.

# Rim and Recovery

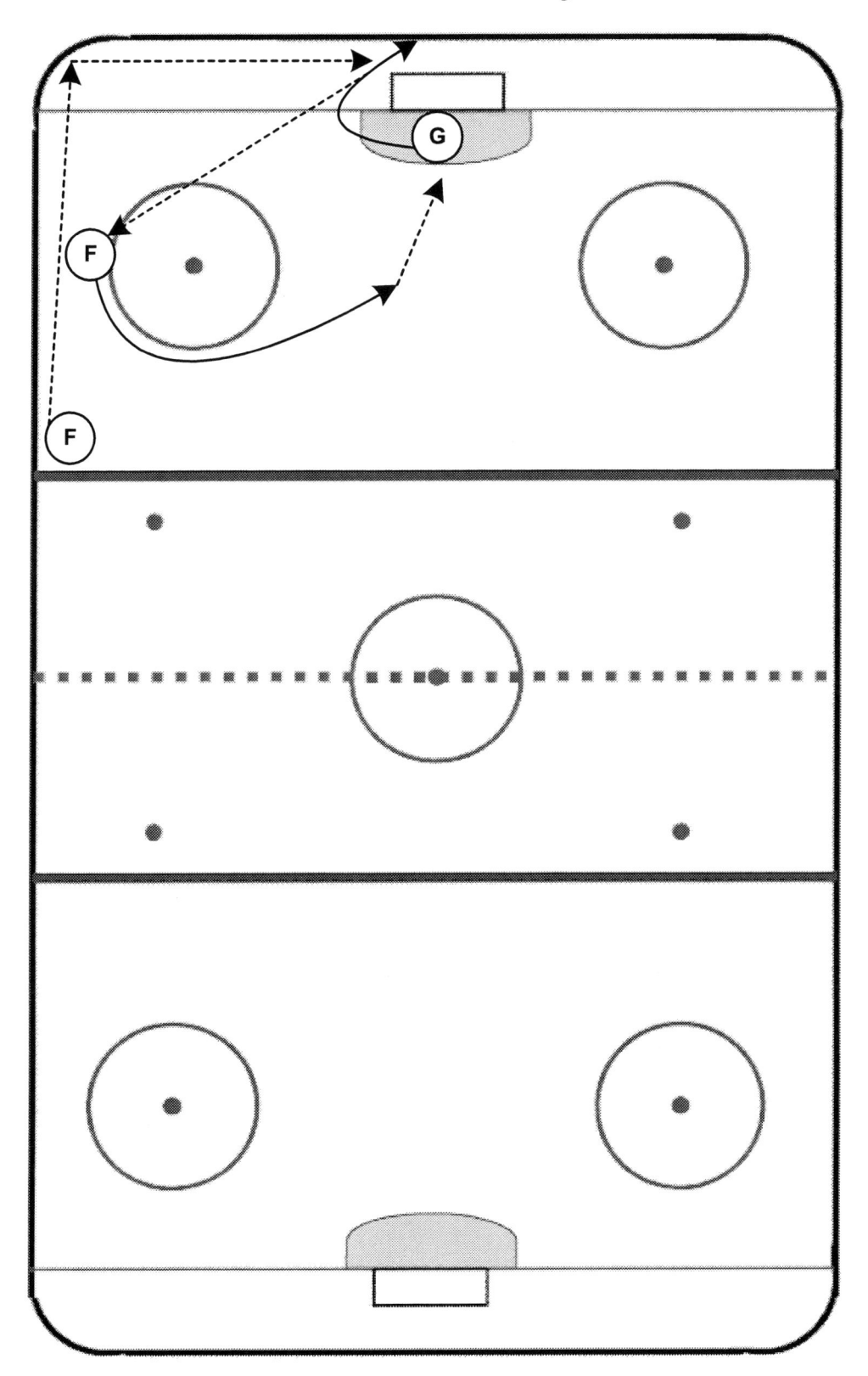

# 144                 Rapid Fire

## Emphasis and Objective

Challenge goalies with quick shots from different angles, work on rebound control.

## Drill Set-Up

* Goalies in net, can be done at both ends.
* Position shooters in zone at 5 spots, assign each spot a number 1 through 5.
* C calls out a number and the corresponding shooter places a quick shot on net.

## Key Teaching Points

* Goalies stay up, control rebounds.
* Have goalies return to crease after each save.
* Shooters hit the net.
* Shooters vary type of shot used.

## Recommended Progressions

* Play out any rebounds.

# Rapid Fire

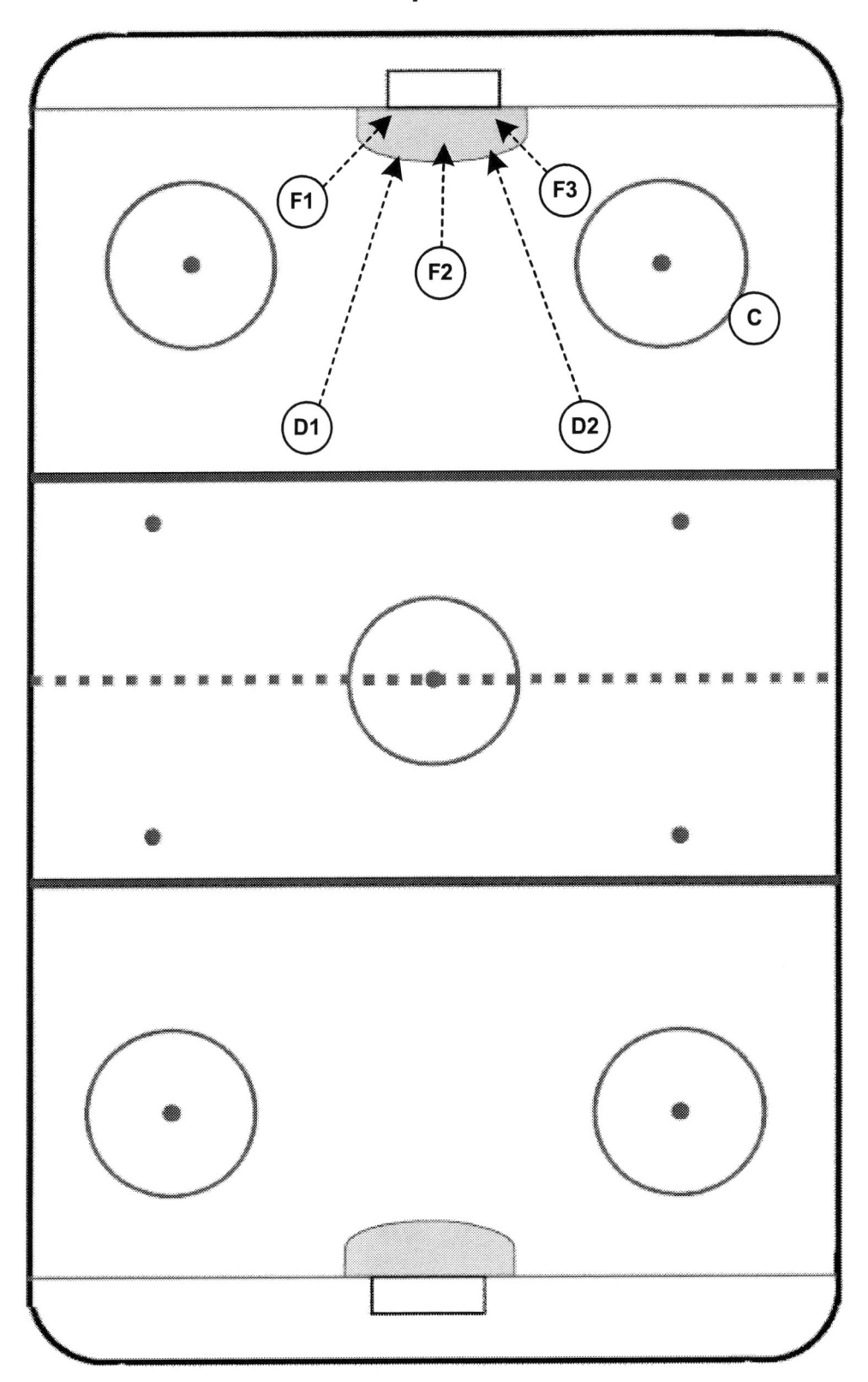

Photo courtesy of Dave Eggen & Dick Carlson of Inertia Pro Event Imaging and The Tri-City Storm

# 9

## **Fun and Games**

Competition and the drive for that competition fuels and separates athletes. Design your practices in a fashion that competition is routine and positively reinforced.

This section, while titled fun and games, should be taken seriously. Competition is the name of the game and these drills test and challenge the competitive nature of your participants.

Use these drills at anytime during practice but insist on full out play. Coaches can learn a great deal about the make-up of the individuals and their team by how they respond to these drills. Competitive, yet fun, these drills are the game within the game. Use them as a conditioning method or for a whole practice. Players love them and will respond and coaches will see results!

## 145 — 3 v 3, 2 Pass Minimum

### Emphasis and Objective
Puck support in a competitive game situation.

### Drill Set-Up
* Played in each zone, goalies in net.
* Game starts with a 3 v 3 in each end.
* Each team must complete a minimum of 2 clean, non deflected passes prior to shooting.
* The instant the puck is touched by the opposition or the goaltender saves a shot, the team gaining possession must complete a minimum of 2 passes prior to shooting.
* No scoring off rebounds.

### Key Teaching Points
* Support the puck.
* Set picks and screens for teammates.
* Defensive positioning.
* Compete.
* Score goals under pressure.
* See the ice, use all areas.
* Cycling.
* Rebound control for goaltenders.

### Recommended Progressions
* Keep score, crown a champion
* Great for conditioning.

# 3 v 3, 2 Pass Minimum

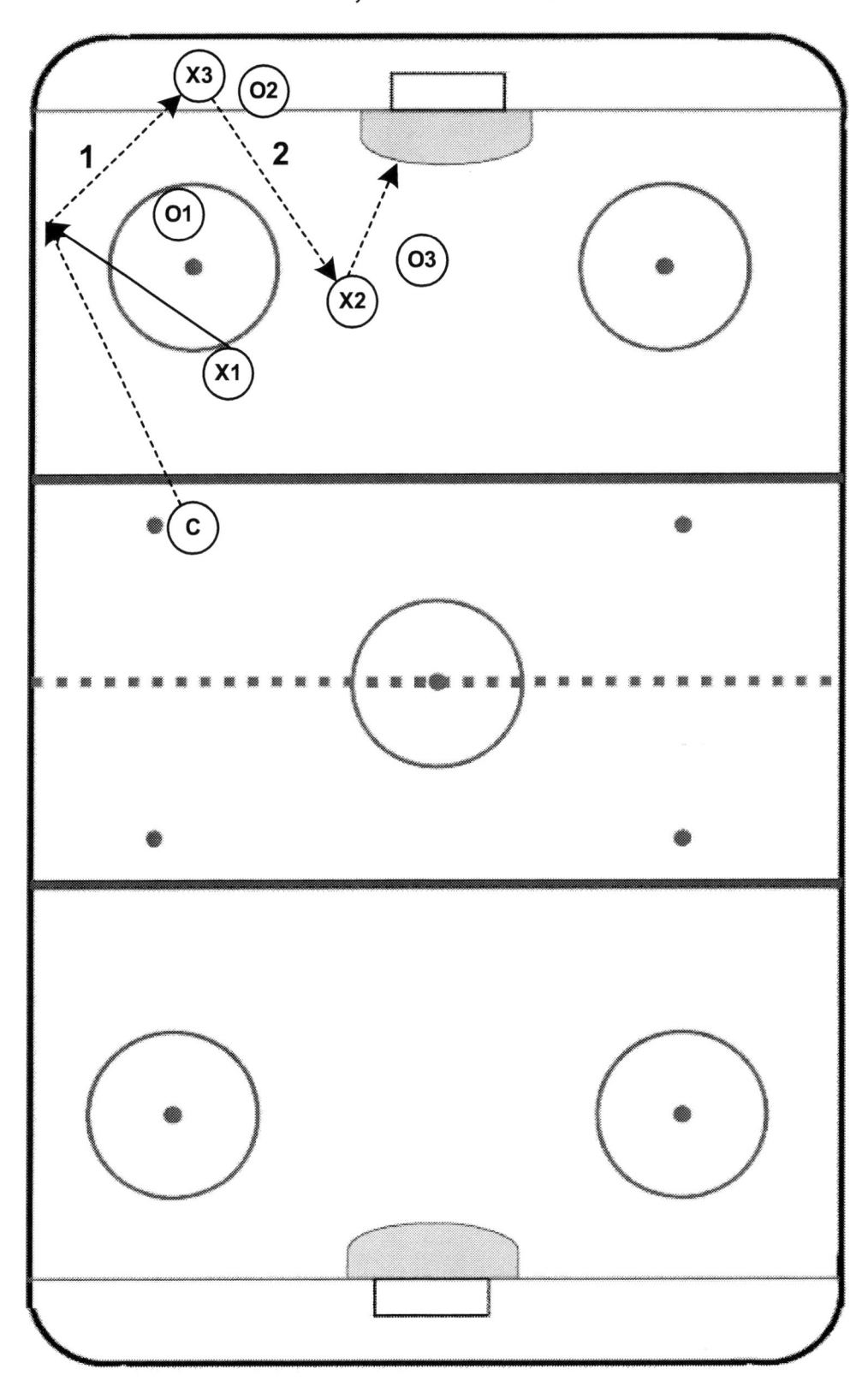

## 146     3 v 3 Across Ice

### Emphasis and Objective
Improve offensive, defensive and competition skills.

### Drill Set-Up
* 2 nets in each end, 2 teams of 3 prepared to compete cross ice.
* Game starts when C dumps the puck into the zone and possession is gained.
* Play 3 v 3 for 60 second shifts or until a goal is scored.

### Key Teaching Points
* Support the puck and teammates.
* Recognize defensive responsibilities.
* Set picks and screens for teammates.
* Handle puck and make plays under pressure.
* Use the whole zone.
* Rebound control for goaltenders.

### Recommended Progressions
* Keep score, crown a champion.

# 3 v 3 Across Ice

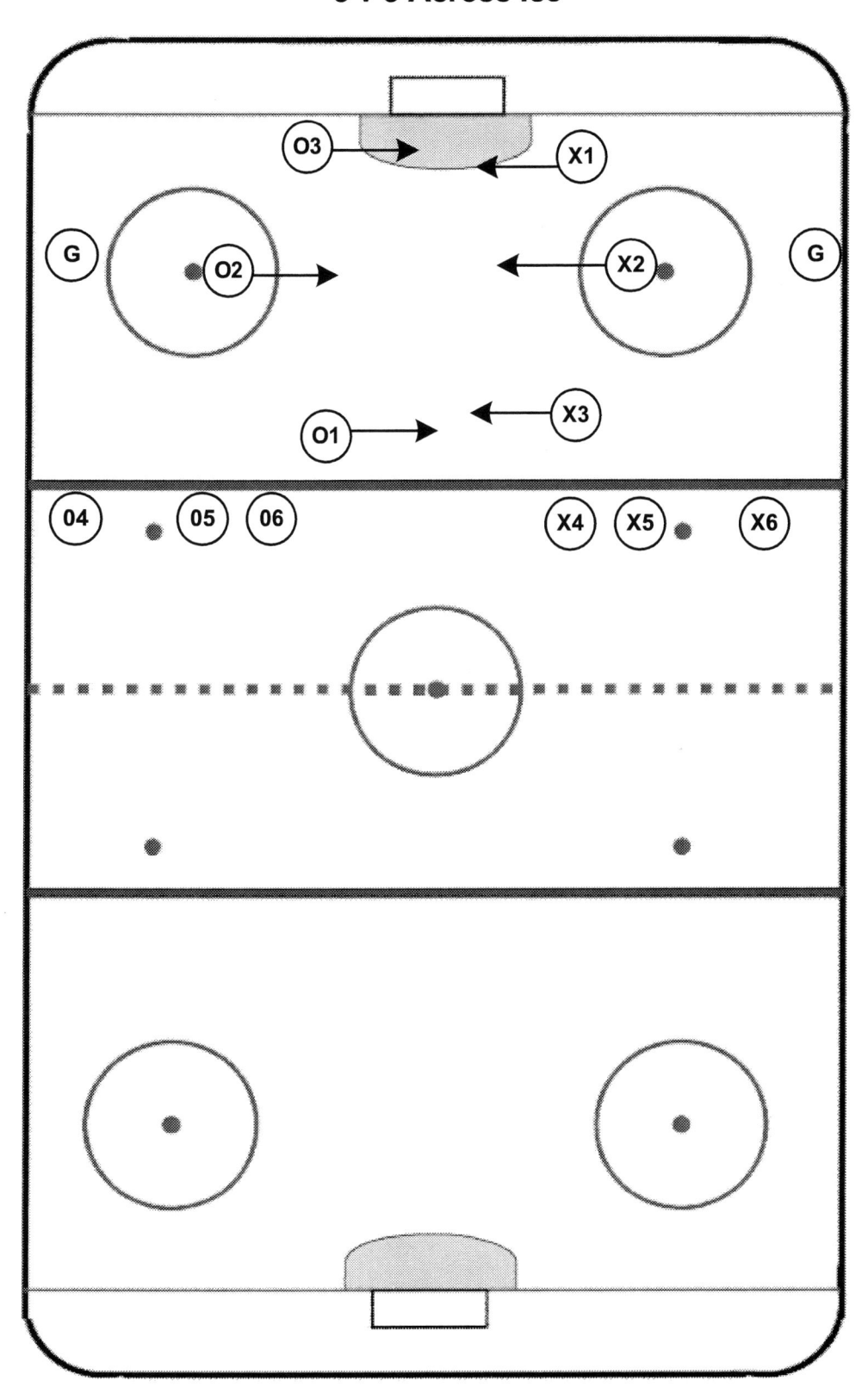

# 147 — 3 v 2 Back to Back Nets

## Emphasis and Objective

Competition game to develop 3 v 2 offensive and defensive awareness.

## Drill Set-Up

* 2 nets in each zone positioned back to back, 15-20 feet apart.
* 2 groups of 3 in each zone, Team A and Team B.
* One player each from Team A and Team B must remain on their half of the ice thus creating a 3 v 2 situation.
* Passes can be made from all areas of the ice.
* Play 3 v 2 for 60 second shifts or until a goal is scored.

## Key Teaching Points

* Read the situation.
* Make high percentage plays.
* Maintain puck control.
* Head on a swivel.
* Rebound control for goaltenders.

## Recommended Progressions

* None.

# 3 v 2 Back to Back Nets

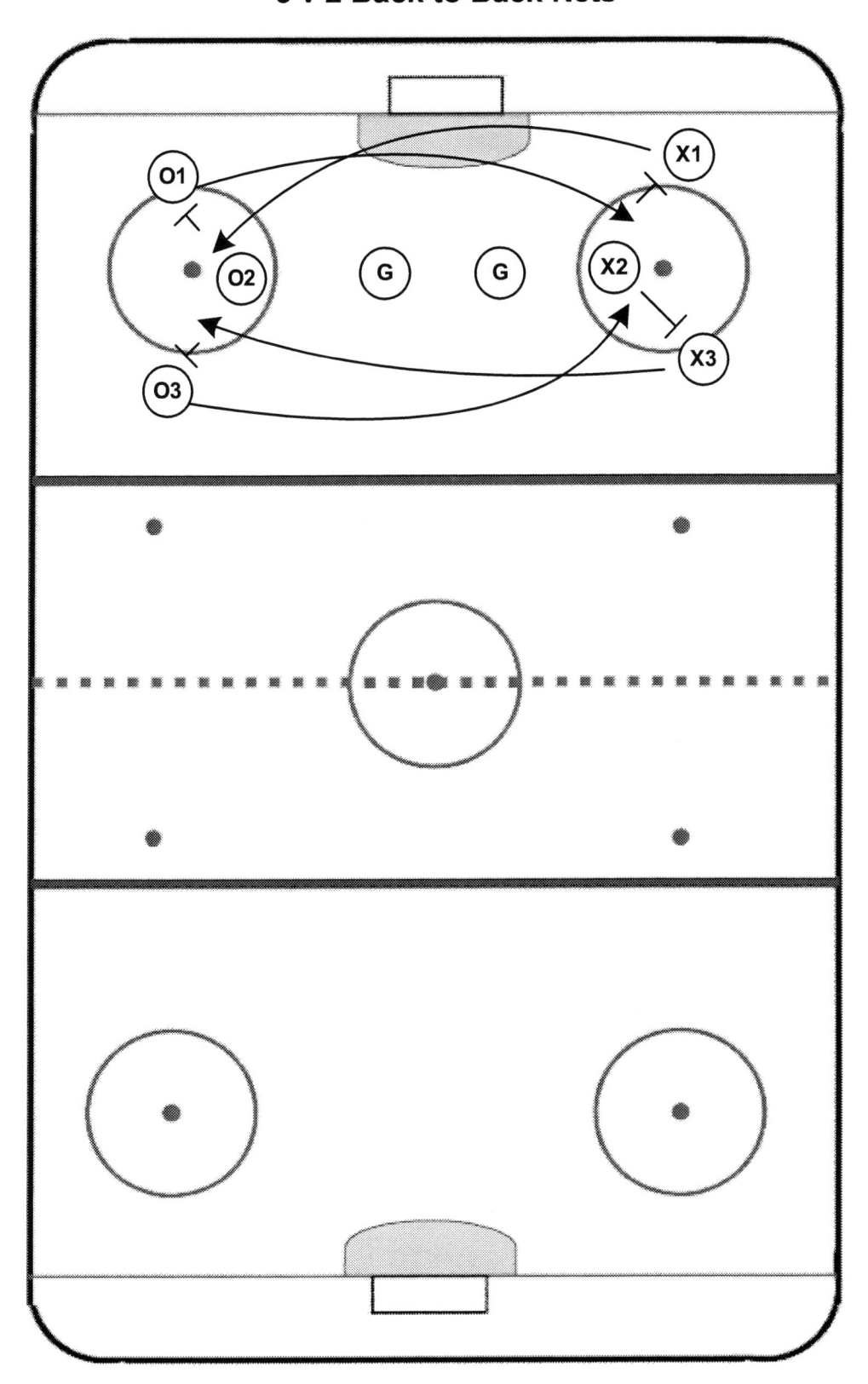

# 148     3 v 3 Full Ice with Offensive Support

## Emphasis and Objective

Develop 3 v 3 skills varying conditions.

## Drill Set-Up

* Divide into 2 teams (Team A and Team B), players to benches.
* 3 players each from Team A and Team B on ice along with an additional player (X1 and X2) positioned on each side of the ice for offensive support.
* Game begins as a full ice 3 v 3 with X1 and X2 supporting puck.
* X1 and X 2 must stay on the boards and are always on offense creating a 5 v 3 situation.
* Once there is a change of possession, X1 and X2 join the other team and attack on offense 5 v 3.

## Key Teaching Points

* Great for conditioning.
* Stay on-side, X1 and X2 must stay up with the play.
* Move puck and see the entire ice.
* Create 2 v 1's in all zones.
* 45 second shifts, continuous.

## Recommended Progressions

* Move X's below goal-line for 4 v 3 situation.

# 3 v 3 Full Ice With Support

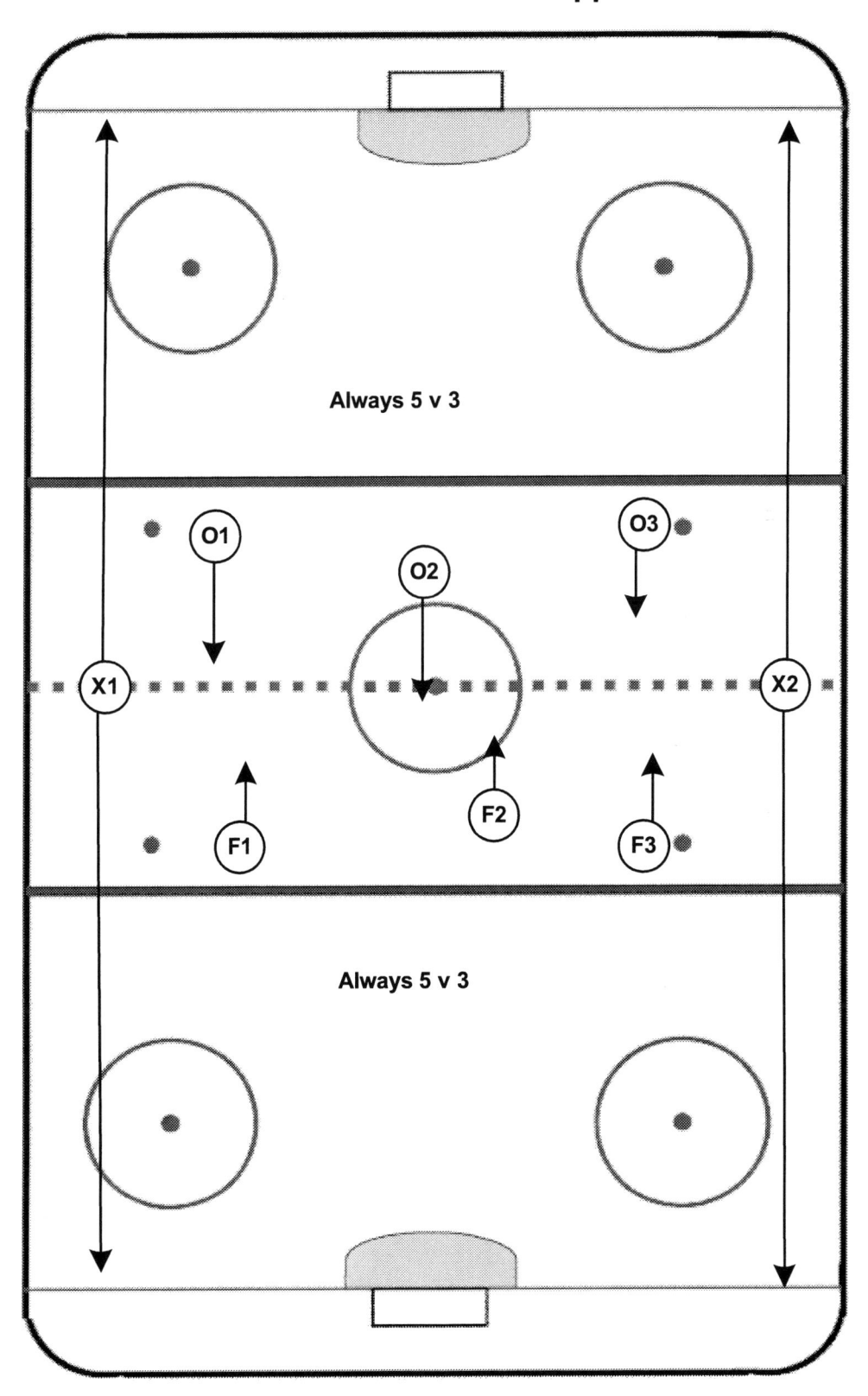

Always 5 v 3

Always 5 v 3

# 149     2 v 0 Showdown

## Emphasis and Objective
Game to develop scoring and defensive skills.

## Drill Set-Up
* Players form 2 groups at opposite blue-lines. Goalies move nets to center of each blue-line.
* 2 players in each line, each with a puck attempt to score on opposite goaltender.
* Player without the puck must decide to join his rush or defend his goal.
* When a goal is scored, scoring team digs puck out of goal, passes to the next 2 players in their line and proceeds to the end of their line.
* Team wins when each group of 2 has scored.

## Key Teaching Points
* Score goals.
* Read the situation.
* Make quick decisions.
* Compete and have fun.

## Recommended Progressions
* None.

# 2 v 0 Showdown

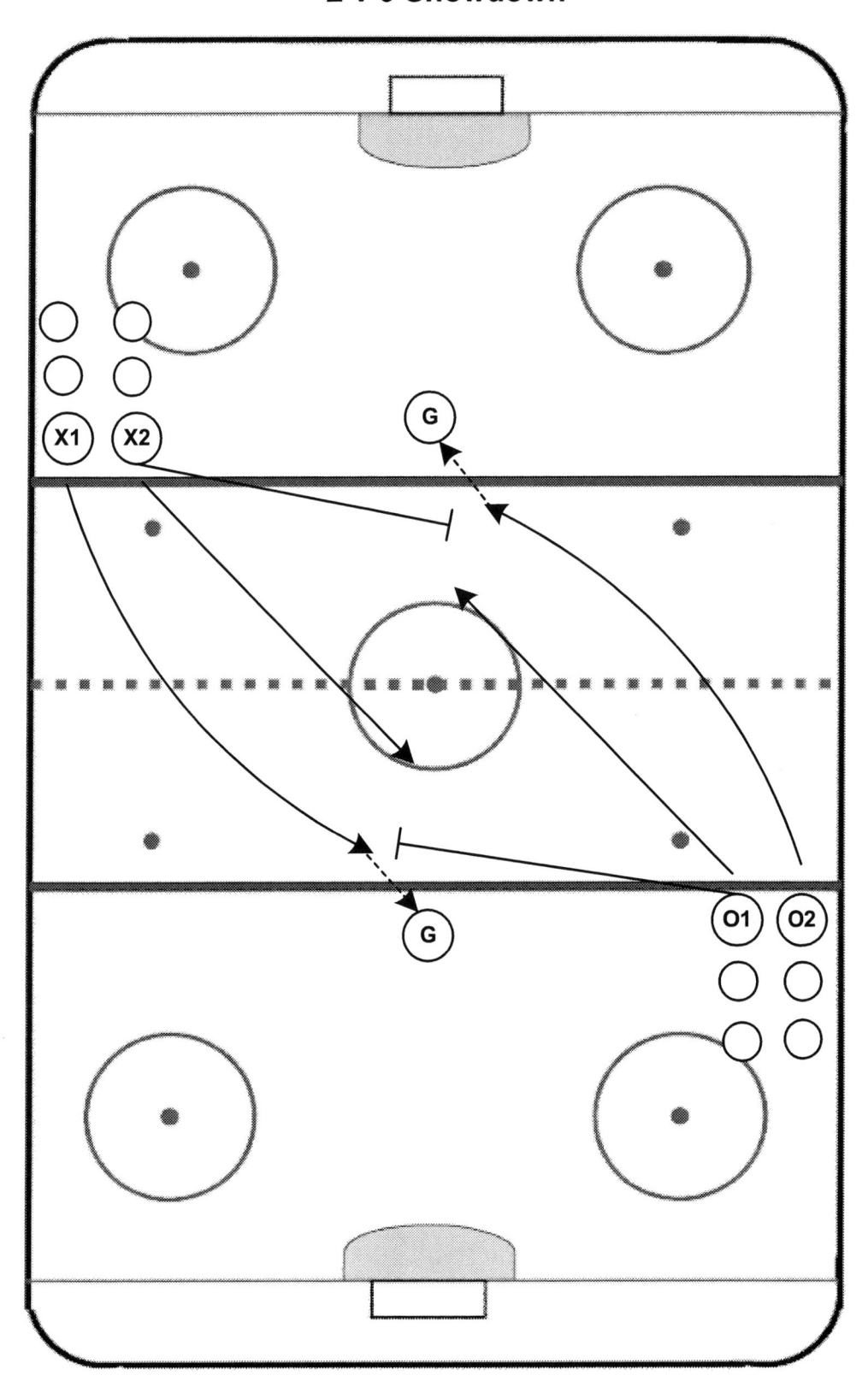

## 150     Japan 2 v 0 Challenge

### Emphasis and Objective
Fun drill for scoring.

### Drill Set-Up
* 2 lines of players on each red-line facing opposite directions.
* Each group of 2 must score 2 goals. 1 point awarded for each 2 goals scored.
* On the whistle, 1st 2 players in each line attack goal 2 v 0.
* After scoring the 1st goal, players receive a pass from the next group in line and attempt to score goal #2.
* Once team has scored 2 goals, they sprint to the red-line signaling the start for the next group.
* If goaltender freezes puck or it is deflected out of the zone, both must regroup outside the blue-line before attacking.

### Key Teaching Points
* Compete and have fun.
* Score goals under pressure.

### Recommended Progressions
* 1 v 1, 3 v 0.

# Japan 2 v 0 Challenge

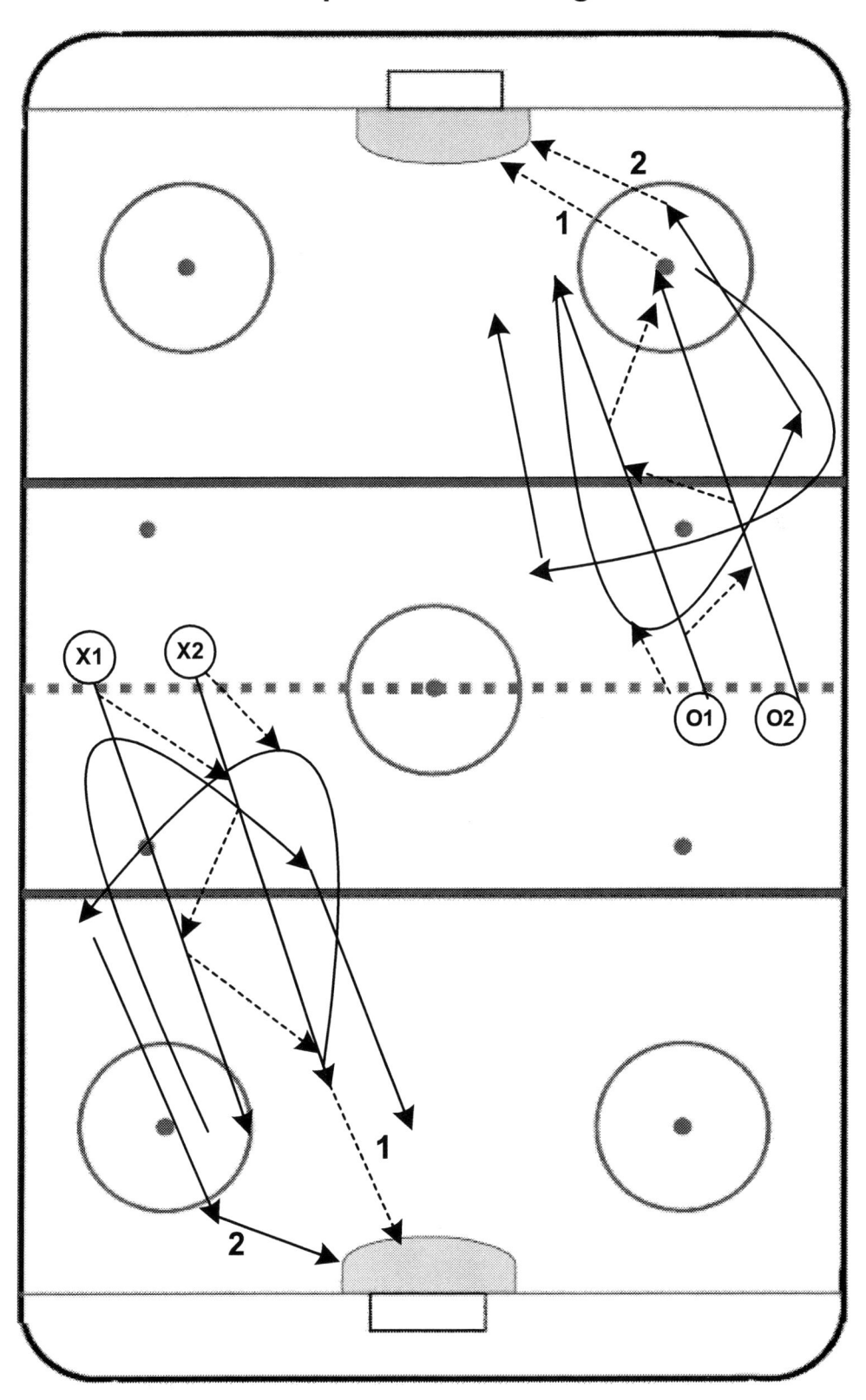

# 151     Quick 3, 3 v 0, 3 Goals

## Emphasis and Objective

Fun drill, scoring contest.

## Drill Set-Up

* Players divide up in teams of 3, half on each bench. Pucks in the center.
* 1st 2 teams on the red-line facing opposite directions.
* On the whistle, each team of 3 attacks their zone 3 v 0.
* Each player must touch the puck before scoring, after scoring, regroup onside and attack again.
* 1st team to score 3 goals wins.
* Play until there is a winning team.

## Key Teaching Points

* Move the puck.
* Good goal scoring habits.
* Teamwork.

## Recommended Progressions

* None.

# Quick 3

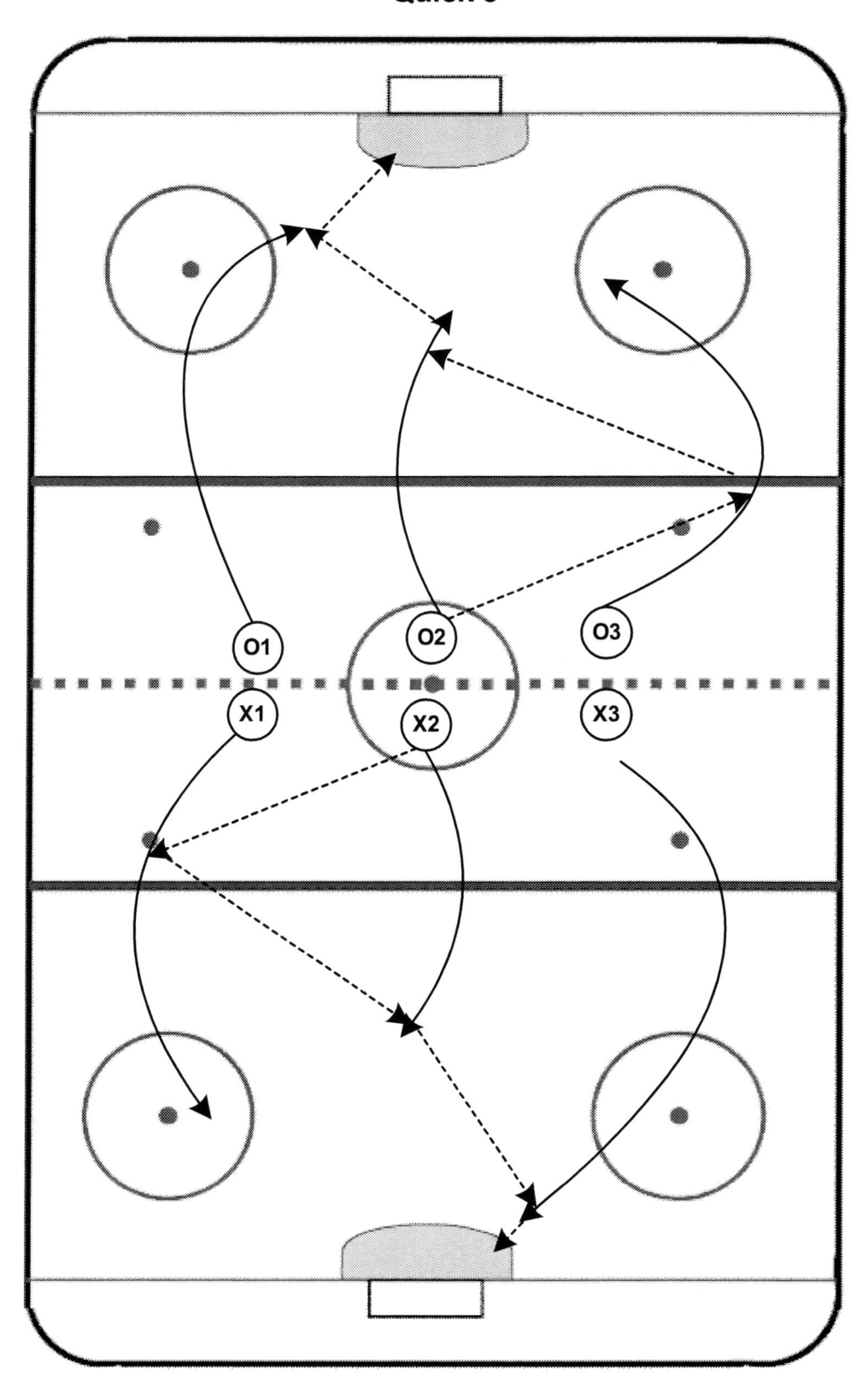

## Coaches Choice

### Emphasis and Objective
Fun drill in a variety of situations.

### Drill Set-Up
* Players in 2 lines at either side of the red-line, C in between lines with pucks.
* C fires puck across the ice and calls out a number of players to create a variety of situations: 1 v 1, 2 v 2, 3 v 3, 2 v 1, 3 v 1 etc.
* Players play full ice until a goal is scored.
* After a goal, sprint to the back of the line.
* There can be several games going on at the same time.

### Key Teaching Points
* Compete.
* Read the situation.
* Great for conditioning.
* Keep head up.

### Recommended Progressions
* None.

**Coaches Choice**

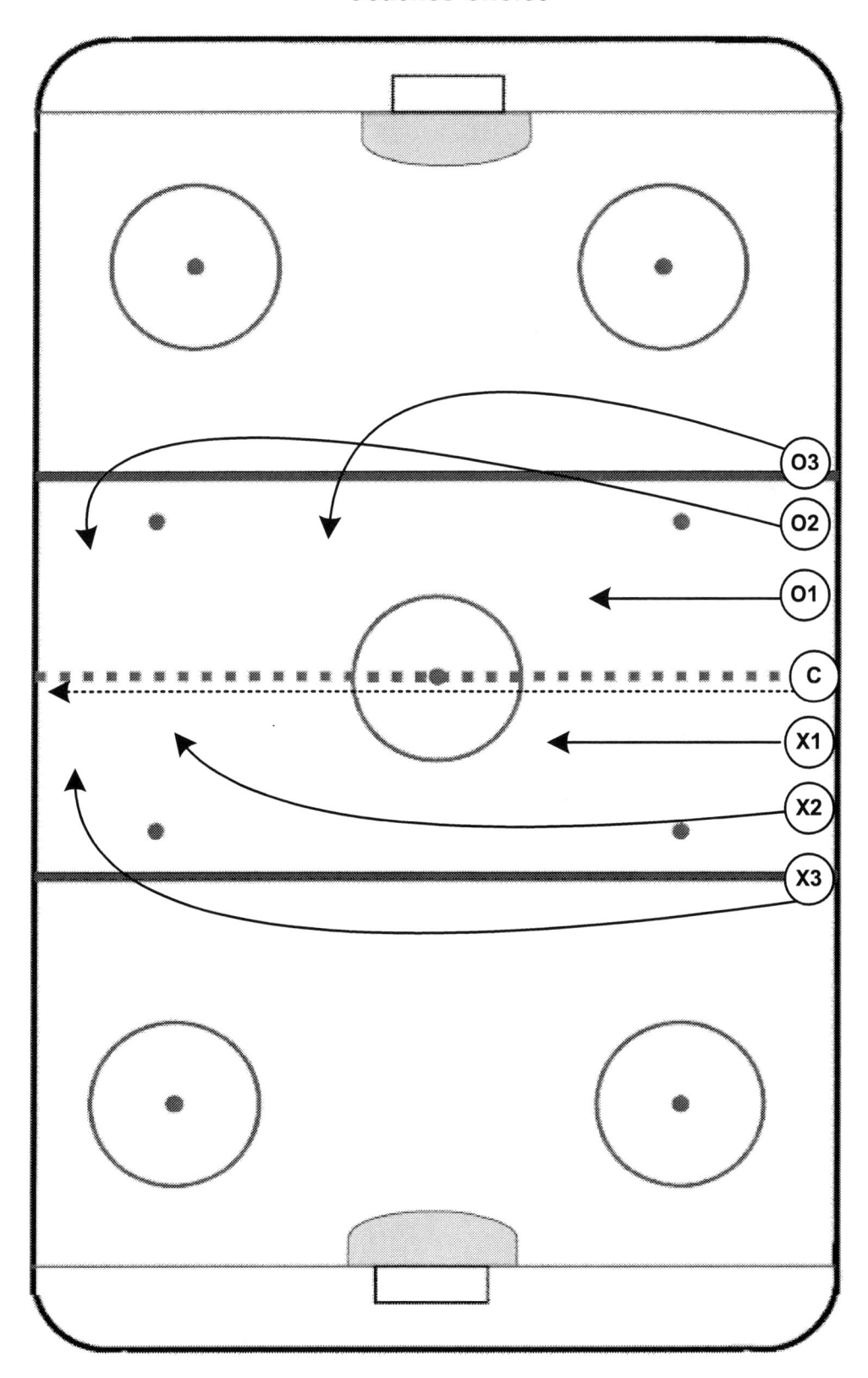

# 153 King of the Mountain

## Emphasis and Objective
Conditioning drill with competition.

## Drill Set-Up
- Players divided up equally in the 5 circles without sticks.
- 2 players in each circle preparing for a 1 v 1 challenge.
- On the whistle, the players try to remove one another from the circle.
- The winner stays in the circle for the next challenger.
- The champion is King of the Mountain.

## Key Teaching Points
- Compete.
- Persistence.
- Conditioning.

## Recommended Progressions
- None.

# King of the Mountain

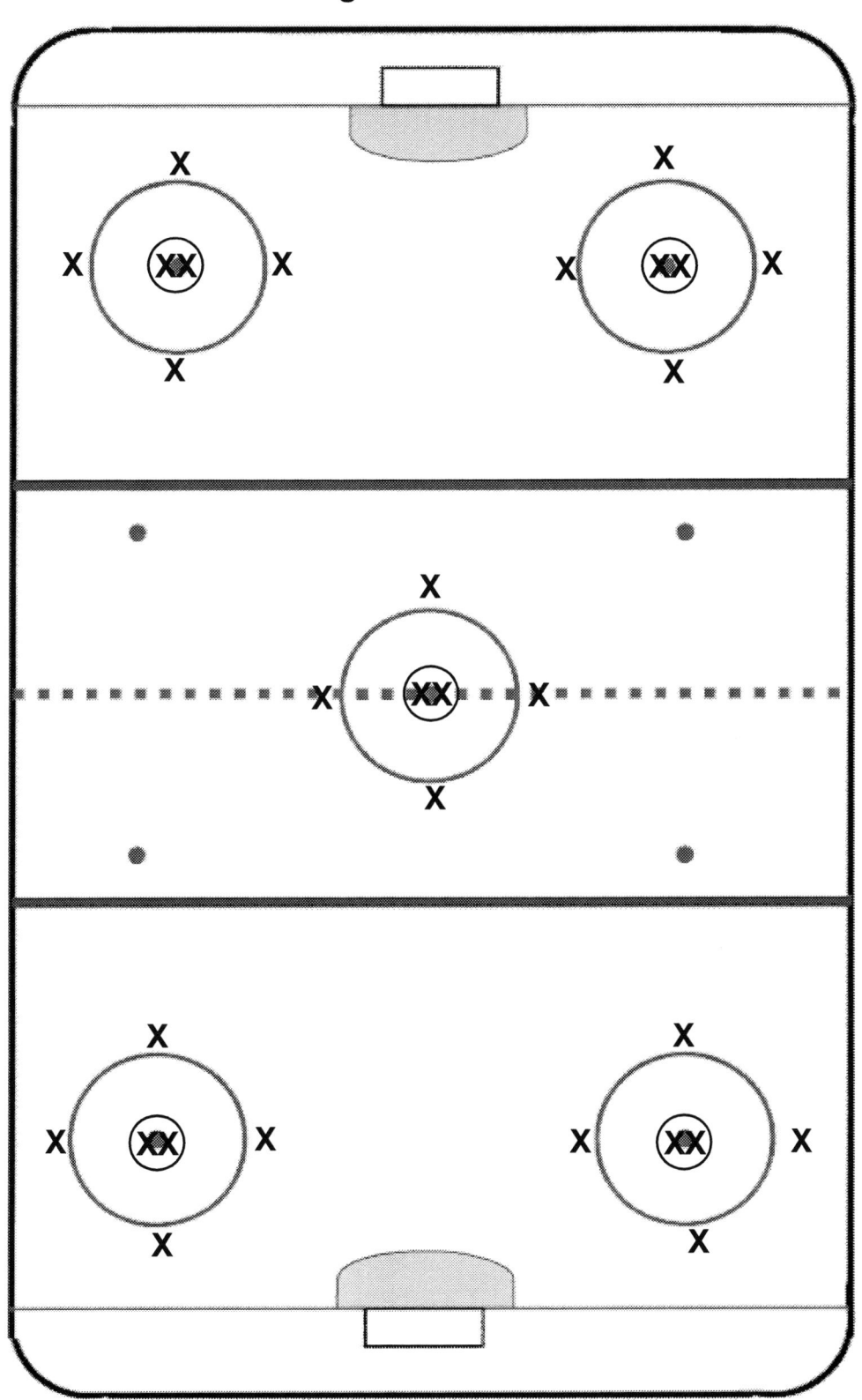

# 154     Split Second Scrimmage

## Emphasis and Objective

Make quick decisions in a scrimmage situation.

## Drill Set-Up

- Divide into 2 teams, one at each bench.
- 1 line and 2 D from each team on the ice.
- From a face-off, full scrimmage.
- Players may handle the puck in the defensive and neutral zones for no more than 3 seconds. Unlimited time in the offensive zone.
- On a 3 second violation, possession changes, offending team must do 10 push-ups and leave the ice.
- 30-45 second shifts.

## Key Teaching Points

- Puck support all over the ice.
- Puck movement.
- Team work.
- Competition.

## Recommended Progressions

- 4 v 4, 3 v 3.

# Split Second Scrimmage

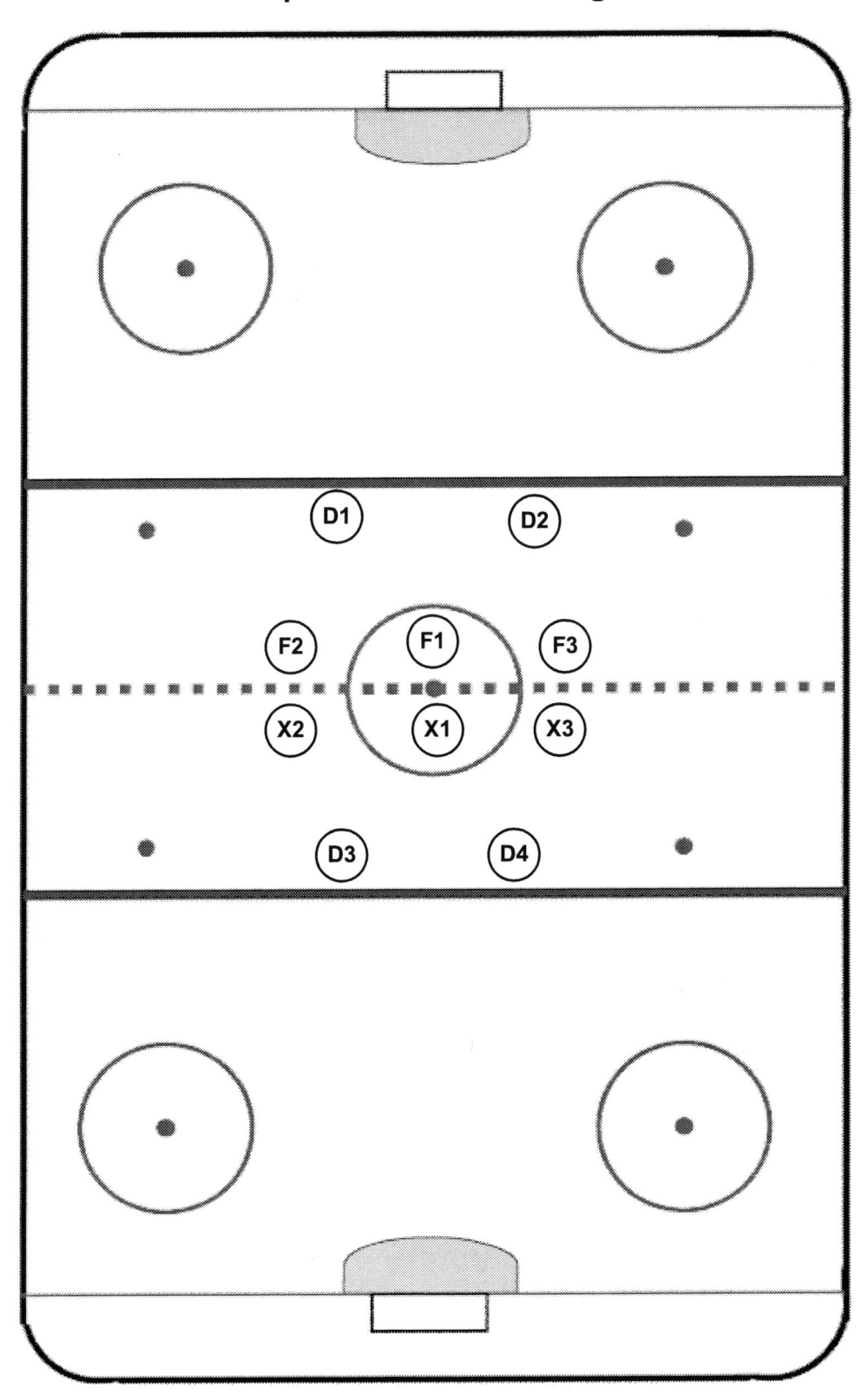

# 155     Defense Join the Rush, 4 v 3

## Emphasis and Objective

Competitive situational game with defense joining the offensive rush. Improve recognition skills and play reading.

## Drill Set-Up

- 4 D in the neutral zone (D1, D2, D3, D4), Four groups of 3 F's (F's, X's), two on each side of the red-line.
- On the whistle, F1, F2 and F3 attack X1, X2 and X's 3 v 3, with D1 or D2 joining the rush making it a 4 v 3.
- When the puck turns over, X's must pass the puck to the D3 or D4 in the neutral zone where they regroup and X4, X 5 and X6 prepare to attack with D3 or D4 joining the rush.

## Key Teaching Points

- Read the play.
- Use the whole offensive zone.
- Communication.
- Puck movement.
- Cycling.

## Recommended Progressions

- None.

# Defense Join the Rush, 4 v 3

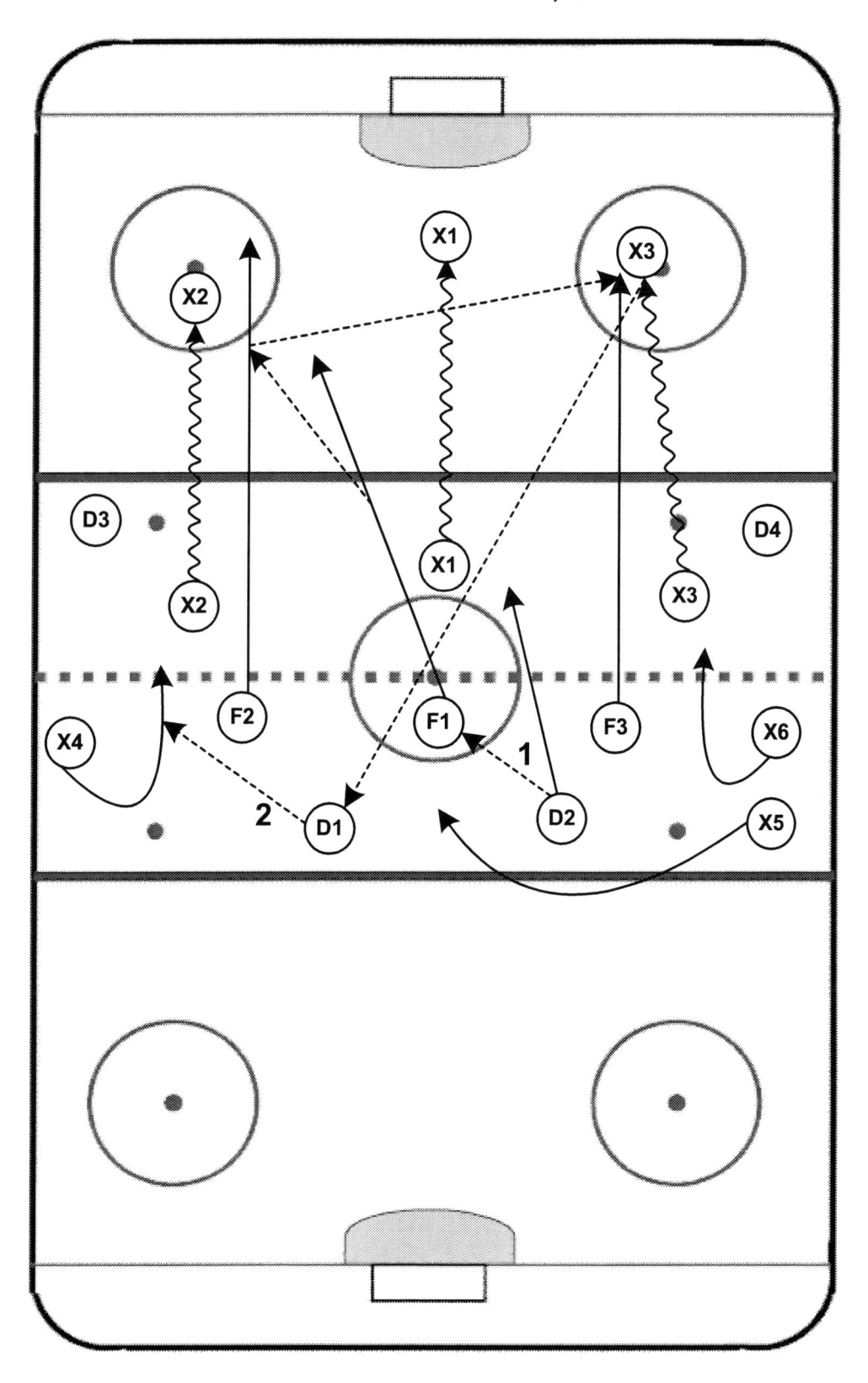

# 156 Keep Away Challenge

## Emphasis and Objective
Game to improve puck protection skills.

## Drill Set-Up
* Players divide in pairs around the ice.
* X with pucks, on the wall, with no sticks, Y with sticks.
* On the whistle, X protects puck with body.
* 30-45 second shifts.

## Key Teaching Points
* Body position.
* Competition.

## Recommended Progressions
* None.

# Keep Away Challenge

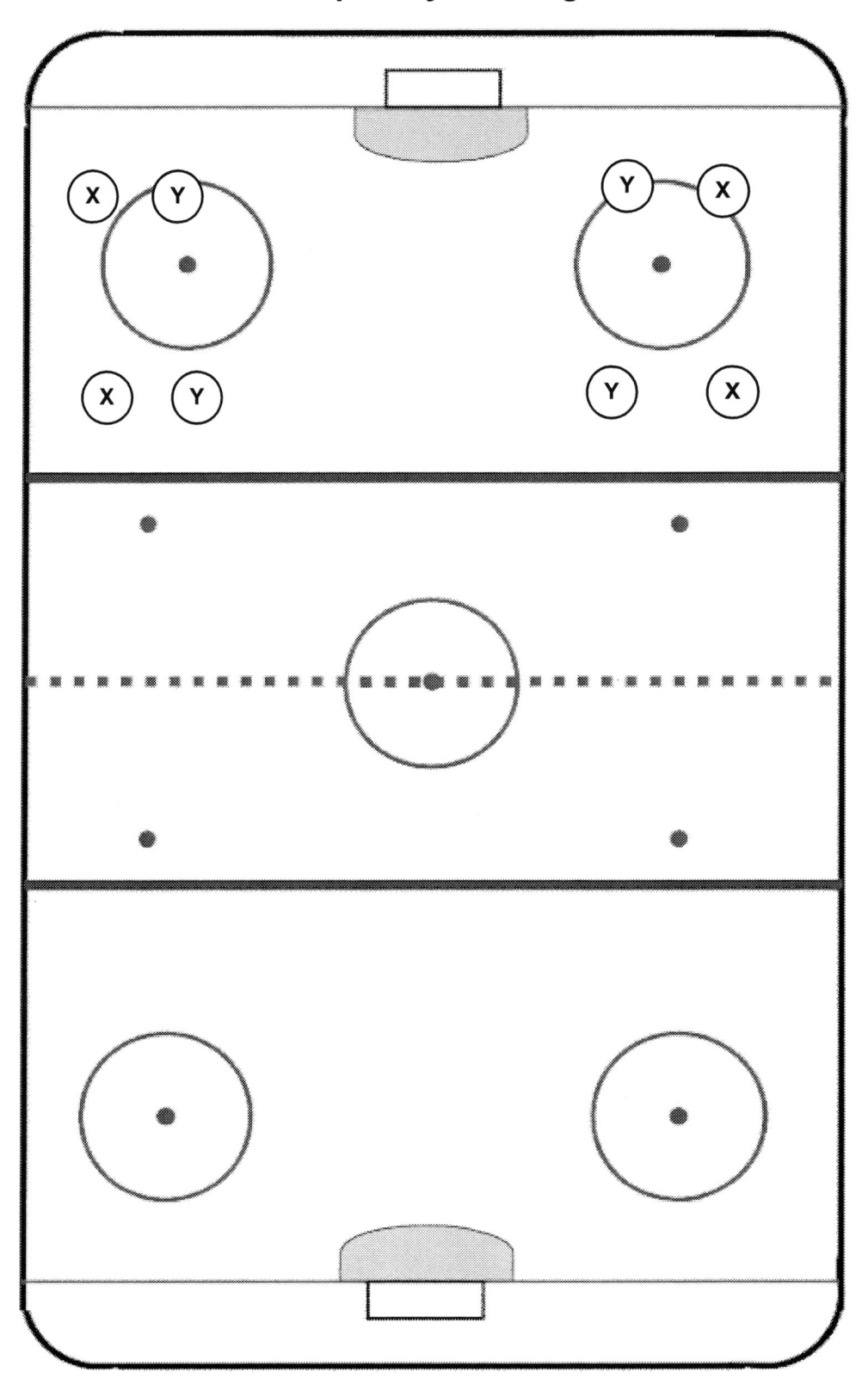

# 157 — 1 v 1 Keep Away

## Emphasis and Objective
Game to improve stick handling and puck protection skills.

## Drill Set-Up
- Players divide in pairs throughout the ice.
- On the whistle, X1 stick handles and keeps the puck from X2.
- If X2 gains control, X1 is now on defense.
- 30-45 second shifts.

## Key Teaching Points
- Stick handling skills.
- Competition.

## Recommended Progressions
- None.

# 1 v 1 Keep Away

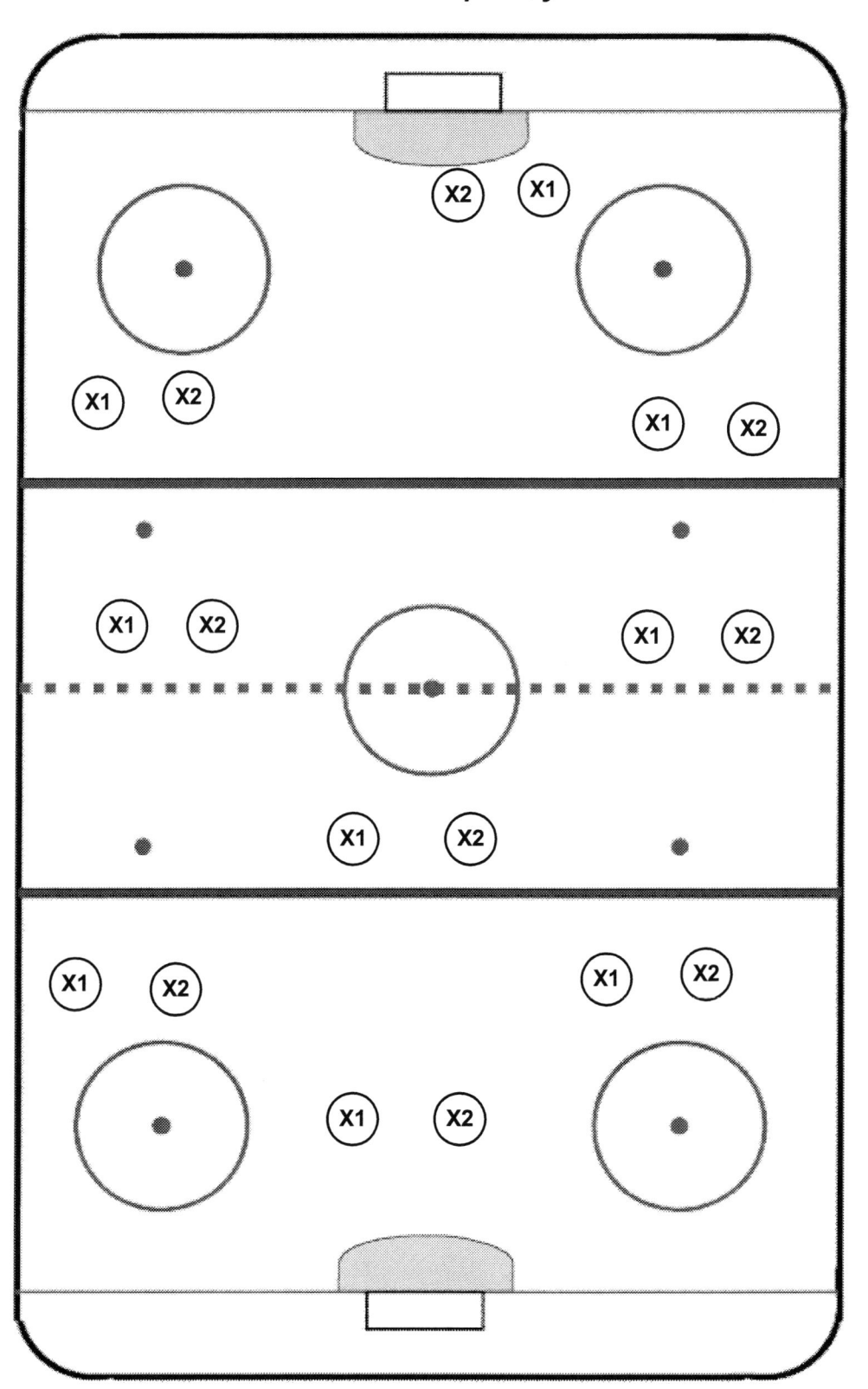

# 158 Cherish the Puck

## Emphasis and Objective
Improve stick handling skills in a confined area.

## Drill Set-Up
* All players including G in one zone with pucks.
* On the whistle, players begin stick handling inside the zone.
* While stick handling, players attempt to knock other pucks out of the zone.
* If puck is lost, player must steal another puck.
* Alternate fast and slow on 30-45 second intervals.
* Play to a champion.

## Key Teaching Points
* Head up.
* Stick handling skills.
* Compete.

## Recommended Progressions
* None.

# Cherish the Puck

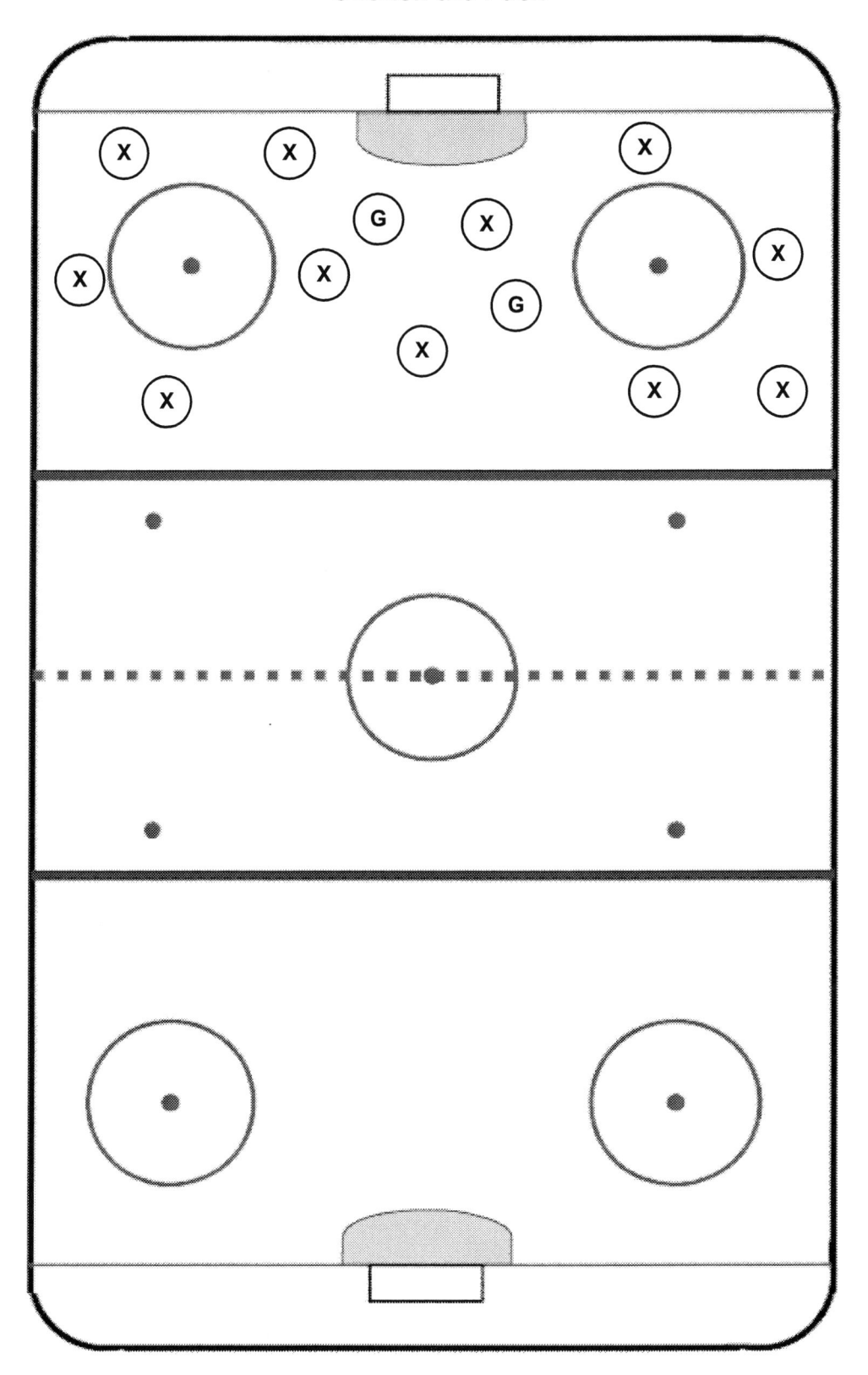

# 159. Pom, Pom, Last One Standing Wins!

## Emphasis and Objective
Fun skating drill.

## Drill Set-Up
- All players without sticks, on the goal-line.
- One player in the neutral zone.
- On the whistle, the players on the goal-line attempt to reach the far end without being tagged.
- If tagged, join in the middle and become a chaser.
- Play to a champion.

## Key Teaching Points
- Skating skills.
- Competition.

## Recommended Progressions
- None.

# Pom, Pom, Last One Standing Wins

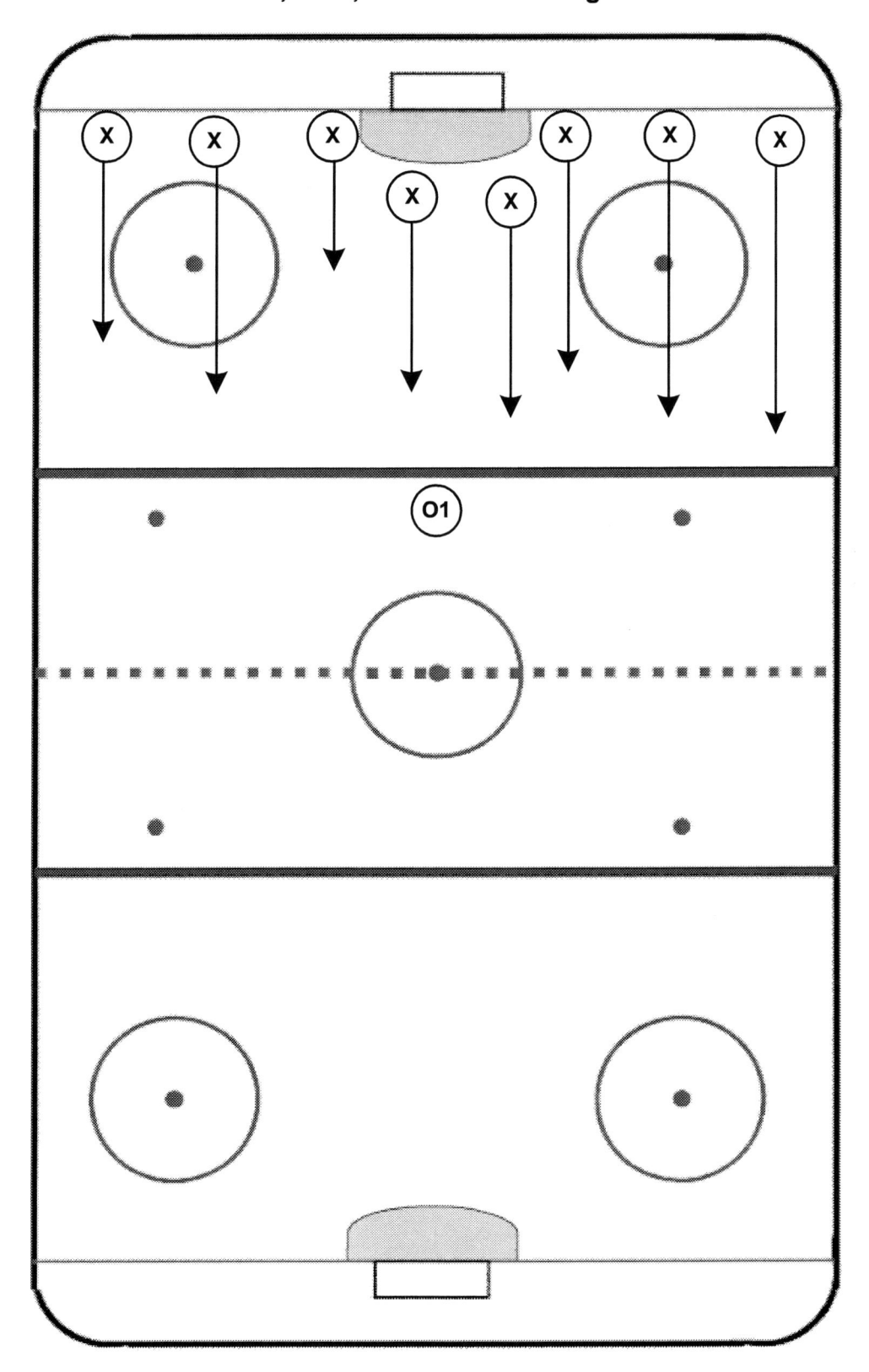

Photo credit Tim Connolly and Gustavus Adolphus College

# 10

## Sample Practices

To serve as a guide for planning practice sessions, the following are examples of types of sample practices that can be used to help plan your practice sessions. Included are sample sessions using the traditional 1 hour full ice format, half ice practices, learning station format and position specific practices.

Maximizing your ice time and designing practices that challenge your participants is the ideal goal. Each session should take careful planning and should accomplish a pre-determined set of goals. Enthusiastically well planned practices are the most valuable and produce the greatest results.

Always use off ice and pre practice time for stretching and practice preparation. Vary the types of drills used in everyday sessions, keep your approach fresh and include physical conditioning throughout practice.

The following is the suggested content of each practice that will not only enhance individual skill development but will improve the overall performance of your team. Regardless of the length of your practice sessions, the time of the season or the age of your participants, it is important to always incorporate the following concepts in each session:

1. A complete Warm-up for all players including goaltenders.
2. Fundamental skill development drills(skating, passing, shooting, angling etc.).
3. Odd numbered attacks. The name of the game is the ability to convert and make plays in out numbered rushes. Practice this concept **EVERYDAY**!!
4. Team drills and concepts concentrating on any number of team related concepts of choice (forechecking, backchecking breakouts, neutral zone, play, special teams etc.).
5. Ending the session on a positive note and frame of mind.

## Sample Practice 1

| Time | Drill | Name |
|---|---|---|
| :08 | Drill 11 | The Snake |
| :07 | Drill 8 | Bump it Back |
| :10 | Drill 63 | Split Second 2 v 2 |
| :10 | Drill 71 | Hornet 2 v 1 |
| :10 | Drill 29 | Czech Breakout and Regroup, 5 v 4 to a 5 v 5 |
| :10 | Drill 151 | Quick 3, 3 v 0 3 Goals |
| :05 | | Cool Down/Stretch |

-----

## Sample Practice #2

| Time | Drill | Name |
|---|---|---|
| :08 | Drill 3 | Round the Horn 2 v 0 |
| :10 | Drill 53 | 1 v 1 Oriole Gap |
| :10 | Drill 82 | Both Ways From Center, 2 v 1 |
| :12 | Drill 34 | Defensive Challenge |

**DIVIDE TEAM IN TWO GROUPS. 1 IN EACH END, SWITCH GROUPS AT 7.5 MINUTES**

| Time | Drill | Name |
|---|---|---|
| :15 | Drill 49 | Forechecking Skill Development |
|  | Drill 114 | Quick Tip and Cover |
| :05 | | Cool Down/Stretch |

## Sample Practice #3

| Time | Drill | Name |
|---|---|---|
| :08 | Drill 6 | 1 v 0, 2 v 0, 3 v 0, 3 Shot Warm-up |
| :08 | Drill 21 | Continuous Breakouts |
| :10 | Drill 83 | The Snap |
| :10 | Drill 65 | 3 v 3 Chaser |
| :12 | Drill 43 | Defensive Coverage |
| :10 | Drill 146 | 3 v 3 Across Ice |
| :02 | | Cool Down/Stretch |

---

## Sample Practice #4

| Time | Drill | Name |
|---|---|---|
| :05 | Drill 10 | 3 v 0 Return |
| :05 | Drill 14 | Laker Delay |
| :10 | Drill 80 | Half Ice Attack, 2 v 1 |
| :10 | Drill 85 | Free Flow, 3 v 0 to a 3 v 2 |
| :12 | **SPLIT SQUAD** | |
| | Drill 115 | Shin-hi Shooting |
| | Drill 108 | 3 v 0 Cycle Behind the Net |
| :15 | Drill 93 | Continuous Power Play |
| :03 | | Cool Down/Stretch |

## Half Ice Sample Practice #1

| Time | Drill | Name |
|---|---|---|
| :08 | Drill 113 | Two Shot, Double Circle |
| :08 | Drill 89 | Tri-Angle Attack |
| :10 | Drill 63 | Split Second 2 v 2 |
| :10 | Drill 59 | 2 v 2 Confined Areas |
| :10 | Drill 48 | 5 v 5, 1/2 Ice Forecheck |
| :10 | Drill 145 | 3 v 3, 2 Pass Minimum |
| :04 | | Cool Down/Stretch |

---

## Half Ice Sample Practice #2

| Time | Drill | Name |
|---|---|---|
| :05 | Drill 13 | Cross and Drop |
| :10 | Drill 71 | Hornet 2 v 1 |
| :10 | Drill 44 | The Chipper, 1/2 Ice Zone Attack |
| :10 | Drill 41 | Funnel Defensive Play |
| :10 | Drill 42 | Russian D Coverage, 3 v 3 to 5 v 5 |
| :10 | Drill 147 | 3 v 2 Back to Back Nets |
| :05 | | Cool Down/Stretch |

## Learning Station Format

| Time | Drill | Name |
|---|---|---|
| :08 | Drill 12 | 4 Spot Shuttle |
| :08 | Drill 1 | Chaos |

**THREE STATIONS, ONE IN EACH ZONE**
**10 Minutes Each Station**

| | | |
|---|---|---|
| Station 1 | Drill 106 | 1 Time Quick Shot |
| Station 2 | Drill 66 | 3 v 3 Down Low Coverage |
| Station 3 | Drill 156 | Keep Away Challenge |
| :10 | Drill | Pom, Pom Last one Standing Wins! |
| :04 | | Cool Down/Stretch |

---

## Position Specific Format

| Time | Drill | Name |
|---|---|---|
| :08 | Drill 16 | Golden Bear: 4 Circle Stickhandling |
| :08 | Drill 7 | The Rocket, D Support to 5 Shots |

**TWO GROUPS: FORWARDS, DEFENSE GOALIES IN BOTH ENDS**

<u>Forwards/Goalie</u>
| | | |
|---|---|---|
| :30 | Drill 130 | Goal-line Drive |
| | Drill 135 | Attack the Goal-line, 2 Shots |
| | Drill 129 | Behind the Net, Pass and React |

<u>Defense/Goalie</u>
| | | |
|---|---|---|
| | Drill 128 | Spartan 3, 1 v 1 |
| | Drill 124 | Pivot and Shoot |
| | Drill 126 | D Agility Skate and Shoot |
| :10 | Drill 154 | Split second Scrimmage |
| :04 | | Cool Down/Stretch |

Photo courtesy of Mike Thill

# Drill Locator

This section is designed to be used a a guide as many of the drills in *Hockey's Greatest Drills for Great Practices* test and challenge many of he games' concepts. The Drill Locator section is a great tool when looking to practice that special situation or looking introduce fresh ideas and concepts.

## A                  Drill Number

Angling        24, 28, 30, 34, 39, 40, 41, 42, 43, 49, 52, 56, 58, 59, 66, 117, 119, 128

Attacks

1 v 1        51, 52, 53, 54, 55, 56, 64, 126

2 v 1        32, 44, 69, 70, 71, 72, 73, 74, 75, 76, 77, 78, 79, 80, 81

2 v 2        40, 58, 89, 60, 61, 62, 63, 64

3 v 1        82

3 v 2        23, 44, 83, 84, 85, 86, 87

3 v 3        64, 65, 66, 67, 68, 69, 86

## B

Backchecking        34, 36, 37, 38, 39, 40, 41, 42, 65, 85, 86

Breakout skills        21, 25, 27, 29, 32, 33, 34, 35, 46, 55, 72, 83, 84, 118

## C

Cycling        34, 45, 106, 107

## D

Defensemen Drills     22, 30, 47, 51, 56, 75, 78, 80, 87, 112, 113, 114, 115, 116, 117, 118, 119, 120, 121, 122, 123, 124, 125, 126

Defensive Coverage     31, 34, 35, 41, 42, 43, 48, 59, 66, 103, 120

## F

Forechecking Drills     33, 34, 43, 48, 49, 67

Forward Drills     98, 99, 100, 101, 102, 103, 104, 105, 106, 107, 108, 109, 110, 111

Fun and Games     12, 142, 143, 144, 145, 146, 147, 148, 149, 150, 151, 152, 153, 154, 156, 157

## G

Game Situations     21, 25, 29, 32, 34, 35, 38, 46, 109, 121, 151

Goaltender Drills     127, 128, 129, 130, 131, 132, 133, 134, 135, 136, 137, 138, 139, 140, 141

Goalie Out     See: *Pulling the Goaltender*

## N

Neutral Zone     12, 23, 24, 25, 27, 28, 30, 32, 44, 50, 62, 67, 82, 84

## P

Passing Skills     3, 4, 5, 6, 7, 8, 9, 10, 11, 12, 13, 14, 15, 17, 18, 19, 20, 21, 22, 74, 77

Pulling the Goaltender     92, 93, 96, 97, 148, 154

# R
Regroups                    *See Transition and regroups*

# S
Scoring                     26, 45, 46, 47,54, 71, 86, 88, 99, 100,
                            101, 12, 104,105, 108, 110, 111, 112

Special Teams               91, 92, 93, 94, 95, 96, 97

Stickhandling               1,16, 17

# T
Timing                      2, 5, 6, 14, 15, 19, 20, 22, 23, 78, 136

Transition/Regroups         12, 22, 23, 24, 25, 26, 27, 29, 32, 38,
                            46, 50, 52, 80

# W
Warm-up Drills              1, 2, 3, 4, 5, 6, 7, 8, 9,10, 11, 12, 13,
                            14 15, 16, 18, 19, 47

# About the Author

## Tom Carroll

Tom Carroll is an accomplished coach that has dedicated over 17 years to instructing, developing and coaching players at all levels. He has spent countless hours at the practice rink working with top athletes of all ages and abilities throughout the United States and Canada. **Hockey's Greatest Drills for Great Practices** is a compilation of drills used in NHL, NCAA Division 1, US Select Team, Junior, Prep School and youth practices. These proven drills and sample practice sessions are designed to challenge your athletes and allow them the freedom to develop to their fullest potential.

With a Bachelor's Degree from University of Wisconsin and a Master's Degree from the University of Notre Dame, Tom Carroll's coaching career includes stops at the Prep School level, the USHL and NCAA Division 1 level at the University of Notre Dame. Also included in his coaching experiences are all-star selections, international select all-star competition, US National Select Team Camps of all ages and instructing at several hockey camps throughout the United States. **Hockey's Greatest Drills for Great Practices** combines these experiences and presents them in one complete and ultimate collection.

Tom Carroll's playing career is highlighted by a number of championships including two Minnesota State High School Championships and two NCAA Division 1 National Championships at the University of Wisconsin as well as participation in International competition. Throughout his career, Tom Carroll has been fortunate to work with and draw upon the experiences of several of hockey's legendary coaches and includes those experience and countless others in **Hockey's Greatest Drills for Great Practices**.

# ORDER YOUR ADDITIONAL COPIES TODAY!!

**HOCKEY'S GREATEST DRILLS FOR GREAT PRACTICES**

Tom Carroll

For more information on how you can receive additional copies of **Hockey's Greatest Drills for Great Practices**, contact:

Tom Carroll
Ash Creek Station
PO Box 3501
Des Moines, IA 50322
or
Call or FAX 515-987-8527